P9-DYD-848

AMGEN

Amgen Inc.
One Amgen Center Drive
Thousand Oaks, CA 91320-1799
805.447.1000
www.Amgen.com

Dear Doctor:

Amgen Inc., manufacturer of NEUPOGEN® (Filgrastim), is pleased to present you with this complimentary copy of *Marketing Your Clinical Practice* by Neil Baum, MD.

This book is designed to assist you in practicing in today's challenging oncology market. Baum offers strategies that focus on:

- Exceeding the expectations of patients and their families
- Motivating staff to improve quality of patient care
- Developing extraordinary communication skills with patients and colleagues

Amgen is committed to you, the oncology practitioner, and shares your quest to improve and extend the lives of all cancer patients.

For more information on Amgen's products or the numerous educational programs we offer, please contact your local Amgen Professional Sales Representative.

Sincerely,

Rick Mafrica
Director
Oncology Sales

Ken Keller
Associate Director
Oncology Marketing

Marketing Your Clinical Practice

Ethically, Effectively, Economically

Neil Baum, MD
Clinical Associate Professor of Urology
Louisiana State University
New Orleans, Louisiana

Gretchen Henkel
Professional Writer
Los Osos, California

AN ASPEN PUBLICATION®
Aspen Publishers, Inc.
Gaithersburg, Maryland
2000

This publication is designed to provide accurate and authoritative information in regard to the Subject Matter covered. It is sold with the understanding that the publisher is not engaged in rendering legal, accounting, or other professional service. If legal advice or other expert assistance is required, the service of a competent professional person should be sought. (From a Declaration of Principles jointly adopted by a Committee of the American Bar Association and a Committee of Publishers and Associations.)

Library of Congress Cataloging-in-Publication Data

Baum, Neil, 1943-
Marketing your clinical practice: ethically, effectively, economically / Neil Baum, and Gretchen Henkel—2nd ed.
p.; cm.
Includes bibliographical references and index.
ISBN 0-8342-1745-7
1. Medicine—Practice. 2. Medical care—Marketing. I. Henkel, Gretchen. II. Title.
[DNLM: 1. Practice Management, Medical, 2. Marketing of Health Services.
3. Physician–Patient Relations. W 80 B347m 2000]
R728 .B36 2000
610'.68'8—dc21
99-059817

Orders: (800) 638-8437
Customer Service: (800) 234-1660

About Aspen Publishers • For more than 40 years, Aspen has been a leading professional publisher in a variety of disciplines. Aspen's vast information resources are available in both print and electronic formats. We are committed to providing the highest quality information available in the most appropriate format for our customers. Visit Aspen's Internet site for more information resources, directories, articles, and a searchable version of Aspen's full catalog, including the most recent publications: **www.aspenpublishers.com**
Aspen Publishers, Inc. • The hallmark of quality in publishing
Member of the worldwide Wolters Kluwer group.

Editorial Services: Ruth Bloom
Library of Congress Catalog Card Number: 99-059817
ISBN: 0-8342-1745-7

Printed in the United States of America

2 3 4 5

I dedicate this book to my best friend, my wife, **Linda**.

Thank you for your advice, support, and inspiration in writing this book.

But most importantly, thank you for all that you do to make us so proud of our children, *Alisa, Lauren*, and *Craig*.

—*Neil Baum, MD*

Dedicated to you, *the physicians*, and *the people who depend upon you every day*.

—*Gretchen Henkel*

Table of Contents

Contributors List

Patricia T. Aalseth, RRA, CCS, CPHQ
Documentation and Coding Consultant
University Physician Associates
Albuquerque, New Mexico

Roger G. Bonds, MBA, CMSR, FMSD
President
National Institute of Physician Career Development
Atlanta, Georgia

Michael J. Burke, BME, MBA
President
Dialog Medical, Inc.
Snellville, Georgia

John F. Demartini, DC
International Speaker, Author, and Consultant
The Concourse of Wisdom
School of Philosophy and Healing
Houston, Texas

Karen E. Davidson, Esquire
Attorney at Law
Mackarey & Davidson, PC
West Conshohocken, Pennsylvania

Cynthia D. Fry, MBA
Senior Manager and Functional Leader for Physician Business Services
PricewaterhouseCoopers LLP
Philadelphia, Pennsylvania

Foreword

There is no substitute for good medicine, for caring and for compassion for your patients. Today, those basics will not be enough to fill up your appointment book. It will take good, ethical marketing and it will take exceeding patients' expectations about their health care that make for a successful physician and practice.

Our clinic has attracted patients from all over the world, and we believe this is a result of fulfilling a need of helping patients stay healthy, providing useful and current educational materials, and offering outstanding, state-of-the-art services for our patients. In addition, our clinic uses the very same marketing techniques described by Dr. Baum in this book to make others aware of our services and our expertise.

Although our clinic already applies many of the marketing ideas suggested by Dr. Baum in this book, there are new concepts that we plan to implement in the near future. Regardless of your current commitment to marketing and practice promotion, I believe you will find additional ideas that you can easily, effectively, economically, and ethically implement into your practice.

Kenneth Cooper, MD, MPH
Cooper Clinic
Dallas, Texas

Introduction

If your name is C. Everett Koop, if you are the only physician in a community of 20,000, if you have discovered the cure for cancer, or if you're a pathologist and do not see live patients, then read no further.

But if your appointment book has holes in it that make the pages look like Swiss cheese, if you have a contracting population base, if you are seeing fewer patients this year than you were two years ago, or if managed care has moved your existing patients to another health care provider, then this book is for you. It can help you sculpt the kind of practice you want, target your patient population, and get more of a handle on your business. All these goals can be attained by learning how to market your practice effectively, efficiently, and economically.

But, you say, you do not have the extra capital to invest in a marketing program.

Effective marketing does not mean hiring a high-priced consultant and creating a five-color brochure with a snappy logo. Effective marketing means taking extraordinary care of the patients you already have. You can do that simply and economically.

After reading this book, you will have hundreds of marketing ideas that can be inexpensively implemented and that you can start using immediately. And when you do, you will find that you have happier patients, a more enthusiastic staff, and greater personal satisfaction.

GOING THE EXTRA MILE

Fifty years ago, physicians made house calls. Medicine was a high-touch profession, and there was a close bond between physicians and their patients. As physicians became more dependent on diagnostic technology, they lost some of the art of communicating with their patients.

But what do patient surveys now indicate? That patients want to be treated as human beings. They want their physicians to diagnose and treat their illnesses. But

xxi

they also want their doctors to give them comfort and reassurance. They do not want to wait 45 minutes in drab reception areas only to be greeted gruffly and then handled as a number, or a diagnosis, such as "the gall bladder in room 3."

Having a successful practice is not just a matter of putting your name on the door, installing a telephone, and sending out announcements. It requires doing something extra. It requires going the extra mile for your patients, for your referral sources, and for the managed care plans with which you contract. Marketing is finding out what patients want and fulfilling their needs and desires. It is also finding out what they do not want and designing your practice accordingly.

One of the best ways to assess your practice is to pretend you are one of your own patients.

Ask yourself questions like these:

- *Would you want to wait two hours for patient care?*
- *Would you want to have a diagnostic study and then wait 7 to 10 days for the results?*
- *Would you want your doctor to withhold information about complications or alternatives to a medication or surgical procedure?*

If you answer no to these questions, then you can be certain that your patients would answer the same way.

I think the most profound marketing strategy you can implement is to listen to your patients. Seek their opinions and the opinions and advice of your staff. Then take what you find out and put it to good use.

The ideas in this book did not come from a marketing seminar or a book on customer satisfaction. Nearly every idea in this book I have used in my practice, and I think that you can use them, too. This book is full of simple techniques that have been tested and that work.

You do not have to copy these ideas exactly. If you simply observe how other businesses serve their customers well, you will discover plenty of your own ideas. That is what I have done. I have taken examples from other businesses and industries and incorporated them into my practice.

As a doctor, I adhere to what I call the "extra-mile philosophy." This philosophy requires you to go the extra distance for your patients, to exceed their expectations, and to provide a little more than other doctors. And your patients will remember you for it. Many businesses, from office product suppliers to upscale department stores, have found that providing deluxe services to their customers ensures that those customers will keep coming back. Nordstrom department stores are well known for their aggressive attention to detail, which distinguishes them from their competitors. What Federal Express sells is really no different from its competitors' products. UPS, DHL, and even the U.S. Postal Service basically offer the same express mail options. But Federal Express has carried customer service to a level of excellence. Its efforts have paid off—Federal Express has been the recipient of the Malcolm Baldrige National Quality Award. Federal Express received this award not only because it delivers packages by 10:00 the next morning but also because it exceeds its customers' expectations.

A medical practice is no different from other businesses in this respect. And in today's health care market, it is difficult to compete on price. What you can do is make sure you are filling your appointment book. You do that by making your patients feel special, by taking the time to inquire about their families, and by returning their calls promptly. Offer your patients the kind of deluxe customer service you appreciate and they will keep coming back to your office. What's more, they will tell others about their happy experiences. Word-of-mouth marketing worked when I first started in practice and is still effective today.

When I first went into practice in Houston, Texas, I had the luxury of being associated with an older physician, Dr. Norborne Powell, who really knew the "art" of practicing medicine. He took me under his wing and showed me some of his techniques for endearing himself to referring physicians and patients. The philosophy of service I espouse incorporates techniques I learned from Dr. Powell and ideas I get every day from watching how other businesses serve their customers well. This philosophy, I believe, is the key to growth for all businesses—especially private medical practices.

Let me give an example of how this philosophy typically pays off. A woman came to my practice. I asked her how she was referred to me. She told me that she had heard about me while in the surgical waiting room at Touro Infirmary.

Whenever I operate on someone, I go out to the waiting room before the surgery starts. I introduce myself to the family. I tell them that they will get three messages: the first, when we begin the surgery; the second, when things are going well and are under control; and the third, when I am finishing up.

That woman had heard all my messages as they were delivered to a particular family. She asked them who their doctor was. Later she told me, "At that time I decided, based on your compassion for that family waiting out there, that if I ever needed a urologist, you would be the one I would choose."

Now, sending out messages during surgery is a simple thing. In fact, my nurse does not even wait any more for me to send the messages. When she sees how things are going, she just asks me if she should send out the appropriate message. A message provides reassurance to a family waiting to hear something, anything, about how the surgery is going. And that is what I believe marketing is all about—the little things you do that make a big difference.

I have expanded this concept to include my colleagues as well. Referrals from other physicians form a substantial part of my practice. As a physician, I realize that I am in a unique position to provide courtesies to my referring physicians.

When these courtesies are provided ethically, they will be remembered and appreciated—and rewarded through an increase in referrals.

Here is an example of a little touch that made a big difference with a potential referring group practice. There was a large obstetrics practice that consisted of about five doctors from whom I wanted to get infertility work. They knew I did semen analyses and infertility workups. But nothing I did seemed to get their attention. I sent them articles I wrote and notices of talks I was giving, but I got no response.

Finally I resolved I was going to make it easy for them to do business with me. I sent them sterile semen analysis cups. On these cups were printed instructions for obtaining semen specimens. Those cups meant I was saving these obstetricians time—time that they would have spent giving the instructions. After I sent the cups, consultations from that practice started to increase. As we tracked the business, my office staff and I figured out that a decrease in consultations meant it was time to send more cups! The point is that what I did made it easy for their practice to do business with me. I became user-friendly.

I have noticed that market-conscious primary care physicians use similar techniques when referring patients to me. For example, detection of microscopic blood in a patient's urine warrants sending that patient to a urologist. Now, the primary care physician can simply leave the transaction up to the patient. In this case, the patient shows up in my office and may or may not know there was blood in his or her urine. I have to spend time trying to track down the reason for the visit and possibly repeat a test. However, the primary care physician can simply write a one-sentence note to me and send it with the patient: "Neil, please see Mr. Smith for microhematuria." It takes only a minute, but it makes all the difference in the world. It makes my job easier and that physician more user-friendly. More than likely, the next time I need to send a patient to a primary care physician, that doctor's name will come to mind. So you see, just by taking the extra time, going that extra mile, you will make it easier to do business with you and your practice.

THE FIVE PILLARS OF SUCCESS

A successful practice has five components:

1. *the patients who are already in your practice*
2. *the capacity to attract new patients*
3. *a motivated staff to take care of those patients*
4. *good communication with referring physicians, other professionals, and managed care plans*
5. *the technological and consulting expertise that bolster your ability to persistently fine-tune your marketing efforts.*

These five components are just like the poles supporting a tent: Remove any one of them and the tent will collapse. For example, if you have patients but not a motivated staff, you can be sure you will not have an effective practice. If you have a motivated staff but no patients, you can be sure you will not be a happy camper.

This book discusses each of the five component pillars of a successful practice. It gives you examples from an existing private practice on how to attract new patients, how to develop the loyalty and bonding of patients already in your practice, and how to keep staff members motivated, organized, and dedicated to caring for your patients. The section on communicating with other physicians, professionals, and managed care plans gives you tangible strategies for becoming "user-friendly" with your colleagues as well. Finally, you'll learn about the extras that support your practice—from marketing consultants to attorneys conversant in compliance—in the fifth pillar.

If you implement just one or two of the ideas in this book, you will be making a valuable investment in your practice.

Do you want to create your ideal practice? Do you want to attract certain types of patients? Do you want to increase your income? If the answer to any of these questions is yes, then read on.

WHY MARKET YOUR PRACTICE?

Many physicians may feel uncomfortable with the concept of marketing their practices. After all, doesn't that place them in the crass world of slick newspaper ads and snappy radio and TV commercials? In a word, no!

Whether you realize it or not, you have been marketing your practice since you first opened your doors. When you put your name in the Yellow Pages under the heading "Physicians and Surgeons," you are marketing your practice. When you write a referral letter to a primary care physician, you are marketing to your colleague.

Simply put, marketing is making the public and your peers aware of your services and your areas of interest and expertise in a professional and ethical manner. In this book, I present hundreds of ideas on how to market your practice ethically and economically.

When I went into medicine, I did not have a clue that marketing was going to be a necessary ingredient of my practice. I thought that I would do what generations of physicians before me had done: I would hang up my shingle, I would practice good medicine, and patients would flock to my door.

Interestingly enough, that is exactly what happened when I went into practice in Houston. In 1976 it was the era of the oil boom. I opened my practice with an investment of $10,000. I had a typewriter, one exam table, gloves, a microscope, some stationery, and a sign for the door. Partly because of Dr. Powell's example and partly because of the booming economy, my entry into solo private practice in 1976 was virtually effortless.

But when I moved my practice to New Orleans in 1978, it was an entirely different story. There were 7 urologists in my building and 14 full-time urologists on the staff at Touro Infirmary, where I practiced. I had no patients. After six weeks in practice in New Orleans, the alphabetical dividers in my file cabinet outnumbered the patient charts. I used to tell my secretary, "Cynthia, please, close the file cabinet. We do not have very many patients, but if any of them saw the reality of what was behind that file cabinet, they wouldn't have a lot of confidence in this doctor."

Business was really slow. Several times I considered taking my family back to Houston. Then I remembered my training in male sexual dysfunction. I had completed my urology residency at Baylor College of Medicine, where Dr. F. Brantly Scott developed the inflatable penile prosthesis. I was aware that there were approximately 20 million American men suffering from impotence. Half of them had impotence on a chronic or permanent basis. Of those 10 million men, only 100,000 had received surgical treatment for their impotence. That was less than 1 percent of all those who had this problem.

These statistics indicated there was a need that was not being met. There was an opportunity in the marketplace. And because I was trained in this particular procedure, all I had to do was inform the public that help was available and that no longer did they need to "suffer the tragedy of the bedroom."

And that was how I got started. I found out I did not have to wait to be discovered. Through marketing, I could inform potential patients of what was available and make it a whole lot easier for them to decide to come to me.

There are many such opportunities for private practice physicians today. If you do not search for these opportunities, the number of patients in your practice could dwindle. But if you are able to identify relevant unmet needs and define your niche in the marketplace, your practice will grow and flourish.

Today, Americans are more health conscious than ever before. Consumers spend an enormous amount of money on health care services each year—more than they spend on automobiles or vacations.

Health maintenance and preferred provider organizations offer powerful incentives to employers who want to save on health care costs. But despite the increasing enrollment of these organizations, there is a sizable contingent of patients who prefer having their own physicians. And they are willing to pay more for health care providing they get not only quality care but also user-friendly care. This appears to be a trend with most American businesses. According to a recent poll conducted by the *Wall Street Journal*[1] and NBC News, customers are willing to pay more for a product if their service needs are met.

This is good news for private practice physicians. The days of unlimited patients are over in most metropolitan communities. Physicians who ignore the necessity of marketing could find themselves in a situation where there are not enough patients to maintain their practices. But physicians who incorporate solid marketing strategies into their business plans will likely see their practices grow and thrive.

After you read this book you will have the answers to the question, "why should someone choose me for their medical care?" You will be able to quantify and measure those reasons. You will also be able to relate those answers in a subtle fashion to your existing patients and communicate the answers clearly to potential new patients.

When speaking to a group of physicians, I often ask the following question: "How many of you have a quality practice?" I then ask those who can answer 'yes' to raise their hands and keep them raised. Nearly every hand in the room goes up. I then ask, "How many have objective evidence or have measured the quality of your practices?" Nearly every hand then goes down. Today, it will not be enough to *think* you provide outstanding services and quality medical care. You must take the time to measure quality, outcomes, and patient satisfaction. Only then will you have the answer to the question, "Why should patients use my medical practice?"

After reading this book, you will have all of the tools and resources that you will need to effectively, ethically, and economically market your practice. What you do with these tools is up to you. These tools are not rocket science, or magic. The tools are not intended to provide a quick fix for erosion of patients and loss of referrals to your practice. Nor are they mandates that you must incorporate into your practice. But they are guidelines that will teach you how to win the marketing game. The only purpose of the tools is to provide you with a road map to follow as you make an effort to provide outstanding services, to inform others about your areas of interest and expertise, to make your practice fun and exciting for your patients and staff, and ultimately to increase your own enjoyment from your profession.

Remember,
When a person or practice fails,
Some people call it fate.
More often it is bad marketing
Discovered far too late.

Neil Baum, MD
Gretchen Henkel

NOTE

1. Amanda Bennett, "Making the Grade with the Customer," *Wall Street Journal,* November 12, 1990, B2.

Acknowledgments

To my dear mother, *Sara Baum*, who has been my source of creativity and has put the magic in my life.

To my father, *Ralph Baum*, who always served as a source of encouragement for all my projects.

To my father in law, *Fred Gottesman*, who was my role model and who taught me the importance of the extra mile philosophy.

To my mother in law, *Charlotte Gottesman*, who has set the example by always going the extra mile, and then some, for me and my family. .

To *Jackie Aucoin and Sandra Aytona*, my wonderful staff members, without whose unyielding devotion this book would not have been possible. You have made it possible to implement many of the ideas mentioned in this book.

To *Dr. Christian Chaussy*, professor of urology at Harlaching Klinik, Munich, West Germany, a special friend who has the ability to remain clearly focused and persistent until the goal or objective of the moment is accomplished.

To *Rabbi Ed Cohn* of Temple Sinai in New Orleans, a dear friend and consultant on living who has provided me with insight on putting life's priorities in order.

To *Kelly Davis* from Medical Group Management Association, who has always responded so quickly with the answers to the most difficult requests and questions.

To *Dr. John Demartini, Roger Bonds, Pat Aalseth, Karen Davidson, Cynthia Fry, and Craig Yates*, who have served as contributors to the book and provided so much of the content for this new edition.

To *Jane Garwood, Suzanne Niemeyer, and Jack Bruggeman* of Aspen Publishers, Inc., who planted the seed of a revision of this book and who have been helpful in making our deadlines.

To *Dr. Ken Goldberg*, a colleague who has provided me the feedback on my marketing ideas and has also shared his ideas and allowed me to use them in my practice.

To *Shannie Goldstein*, a colleague and special friend who applies her sensitivity to all aspects of our practice.

To *Dr. Jim Gottesman and Mike Burke*, my colleagues at Dialog Medical, who have contributed ideas, chapters and encouragement for many of my projects

To *Gretchen Henkel*, my coauthor and editor, a wonderful woman who took my ideas and put them into easily readable prose.

To *Mary LeBlanc and Cathy Castellon*, my research assistants, who always go the extra mile and tied together all the loose ends to make this book possible.

To *Bob Katz*, my accountant, who pays attention to the numbers and the business side of my practice and allows me to focus on the patients.

To *Dr. Michael LeBoeuf*, author of "How to Win Customers and Keep Them for Life," a friend and invaluable guide to becoming an author and public speaker.

To *Stan Levenson* of Levenson Public Relations in Dallas, Texas, who has given me his time and invaluable advice, not only on this book, but also on many marketing concepts.

To *Drs. Richard Levine, Ronnie Swartz, Alfred Colfry, Jerry Rosenberg and Susan McSherry*, my urologic colleagues who have allowed me to test many of my marketing ideas and provided me the time to write this book.

To *Gary Mandleblatt*, a special friend who taught me that there's magic in everything you do.

To *Shelley McIntosh*, the bravest young lady I have ever met and who is an inspiration to us all.

To *Dr. David Mobley*, a fellow urologist who shares everything he has and takes my suggestions and makes them even better.

To *Bill Sheffield*, the hardware and software guru, who made it possible to have the working technology to write this book.

To *Dr. George Suarez*, my best pupil, who took what I had to teach and gave it back to me in a new improved version.

To *Nathan Zepell*, the ultimate survivor, who taught me about persistence.

And finally, *to all my wonderful patients*, who provide me the opportunity to practice the greatest profession in the world. Without them and their feedback this book would have never been possible.

Love the Ones You're With: Keeping the Patients You Already Have

If a doctor treats his patients well, they will provide him with advertising more effective than any he can buy.

Editor, *Private Practice*

Yes, it is nice to get new patients, but it is more important to keep the ones you have. In most professions and businesses, keeping a customer costs only one-fifth of what it costs to acquire a new one.[1] The medical practice is no exception to this rule. If you are not doing a good job with the patients you already have, then spending thousands of dollars on a marketing plan to bring in new patients is pointless. The patients you have right now are the backbone of your practice. They should be getting the proper care that they deserve.

But, you say, your patients have been with you for years. They are like family. That may be. But this book is about improving your practice for yourself and your patients. Even with a stable and loyal group of patients, there may be some areas of service that you are neglecting.

Like most areas in this country, your community has probably seen an increase in managed care patients. Perhaps there has been an economic downturn and patients are less able to pay for your services. Now is the time to focus on your existing patients and make certain that everyone in your practice has a positive experience each time he or she interacts with you and your staff.

Although one response to managed care, capitation, and a depressed economy is to increase the volume of patients you see, this is often the least attractive alternative. Increased volume means more staff and increased overhead, which translate to less profit. More important, though, increase in volume means decreased time spent with each patient, so the overall quality of your patient's experience in your office is diminished. Being attentive to the needs of your existing patients is one of the best ways to retain them and enhance your bottom line.

The chapters in this section of the book are designed to help you survey those patients' needs and then implement some ideas to serve them better. And you can bet that if you make these patients happier with the care they receive in your office, others will soon hear about it. That is what this part of marketing is all about—getting others to toot your horn.

NOTE

1. Patricia Sellers, "Getting Customers To Love You," *Fortune,* March 3, 1989: 38–39.

CHAPTER 1

Giving Your Practice a Checkup

Not only do your patients need an annual checkup, so does your practice.

Listen to your patients' impressions of your practice and you will improve the quality of care you give. In the introduction, I suggested that you look at your practice from your patients' perspective. An even better method is to ask your patients what they think.

In this chapter I introduce techniques for considering your practice from the point of view of your patients and other physicians. These will help you assess your current standing with your existing patients and referring physicians. A healthy practice always needs to attract new patients. However, to keep your practice vital, you also have to keep the patients you already have. Even practices that are full or closed need to evaluate their services periodically and listen to their patients. Changes always occur and the cup may not "runneth over" forever. Besides, if your patients and staff are satisfied, your work will be more enjoyable.

Today it is vital to know the needs and expectations of your patients and referring physicians. This information can be easily obtained by taking a survey of various aspects of your practice. This will also provide you with an update on its strengths and weaknesses. Patients are a valuable source of information and can help you improve the quality of care you provide.

Here are five effective techniques for determining how patients perceive your practice and for evaluating your performance and reputation:

1. conduct personal interviews
2. conduct patient surveys
3. create a focus group
4. use a suggestion box
5. commission a "mystery shopper" evaluation.

The first four techniques will be covered in this chapter. The mystery shopper technique will be addressed in Chapter 2.

Another key piece of your practice checkup is to survey your colleagues and peers. The last section in this chapter tells you how to do this.

PERSONAL INTERVIEWS

One way to obtain feedback about your practice is to ask your patients directly about their experiences with you and your office staff. This method is expensive, and it is the least popular technique for acquiring information. Most patients feel "put on the spot" and will not reveal their true feelings during a face-to-face inquiry.

However, informal conversations with your patients can reveal a great deal of information about your practice. Patients are more likely to respond honestly to specific rather than general questions. *You might ask a patient:*

- Do you think the wait in the reception area (not the "waiting room") was excessive?
- Would you like us to call or fax your prescription over to the pharmacy so it will be ready for you when you go to pick it up?
- Would you like us to have a website so that you could schedule your appointments with our office and receive reports and lab results without having to come in or call us?
- If we had a nutritionist available, would you make use of his or her services?

When you ask questions such as these, you show concern for your patients' time as well as their pocketbooks, and the answers will probably be quite helpful.

You could also conduct a survey that focuses on how promptly you see patients. This technique is described in Chapter 3, which outlines how to perform a time and motion study.

PATIENT SURVEYS

Written patient surveys are probably the most popular method for obtaining feedback from patients. You can give written surveys to patients at the time of their office visits or send the survey in the mail. The advantages of sending the survey are that it allows your patients to remain anonymous, and they can complete the survey at their leisure. The disadvantages are that this is more expensive, and people often do not return them. The response rate will tend to be higher if you provide a self-addressed, stamped return envelope.

What To Ask

The survey should be short and should require no more than three to five minutes to complete (see Exhibits 1–1 and 1–2). I suggest the survey be limited to both

Exhibit 1–1 New Mexico Heart Institute Patient Satisfaction Survey

At the New Mexico Heart Institute, we value your opinion and welcome your feedback. Our goal is to provide you with the very best medical care, as well as the most comfort and convenience as possible. Your comments will help us evaluate our operations to ensure that we are truly responsive to your needs. Thank you for your help.

Please be assured that while the staff and physicians will receive your feedback, your identity will be kept confidential. Please check the information below and make any necessary corrections:

Date of visit: _____ Physician seen at that visit: _____

Location of visit: _____ Are you a new or existing patient? _____

Study performed at last visit _____ (Echo, treadmill, nuclear, or none)

Please answer the following questions and return to the New Mexico Heart Institute in the envelope provided.

I. Using a scale of GOOD, FAIR, POOR, or DOES NOT APPLY, please rate the following aspects of your visit: *If you answer any of the questions with POOR, it would be helpful to us to know what the problem was.*

1. Ease of using our automated phone system   _____
2. Availability of appointment times   _____
3. Directions to the office   _____
4. Parking at the office   _____
5. Ease of check-in at the front desk   _____
6. Appearance of waiting room   _____
7. Comfort of exam room (where you saw the doctor)   _____
8. Appearance of procedure room (where your test
   or lab work was conducted)   _____

II. Using the scale of EXCELLENT, GOOD, FAIR, POOR, VERY POOR, or DOES NOT APPLY, please rate the personal manner (such as courtesy, respect, sensitivity, or friendliness) of the staff you interacted with at your last visit. *If you answer any of the questions with POOR or VERY POOR, it would be helpful to us to know what the problem was.*

1. The scheduling secretary that helped you make the appointment _____
2. The receptionist at front desk   _____

continues

Exhibit 1–1 continued

3. The Medical Technician that showed you to the exam room   _____
4. The Medical Technician that conducted any test or lab work   _____

III. This next set of questions asks about the physician you saw at your last visit. Please rate your satisfaction in these areas using a scale of 1 – 5, one being dissatisfied and five being most satisfied. *If you answer any of the questions with 1 or 2, it would be helpful to us to know what the problem was.* How satisfied were you with...

1. The amount of time the doctor spent with you   _____
2. The physician's answers to any questions you had   _____
3. The doctor's explanation of any new medications prescribed   _____
4. The personal or "bedside" manner of the physician   _____

Any other comments you'd like to make about the physician or staff you interacted with that day?

IV. The next set of questions deals with waiting times. Please let us know if the following were either BETTER THAN YOU EXPECTED, WHAT YOU EXPECTED, or TOO LONG

1. Time you waited to get an appointment   _____
   If you answered TOO LONG, please answer the following:
   What do you consider to be the longest time you should be expected to wait? _____
2. Time you waited in the reception area   _____
   If you answered TOO LONG, please answer the following:
   What do you consider to be the longest time you should be expected to wait? _____
3. Time you waited in the exam room to see the doctor   _____
   If you answered TOO LONG, please answer the following:
   What do you consider to be the longest time you should be expected to wait? _____   _____

V. Please answer the following with a YES, NO, or DOES NOT APPLY.

1. Did you receive an appointment reminder at least 24 hours before your scheduled appointment?   _____
2. Were you kept informed if your appointment time was delayed?   _____

continues

Exhibit 1–1 continued

3. Would you recommend the New Mexico Heart Institute to a friend that needed heart care?   _____

4. Did most of the staff you met that day smile or greet you by name?   _____

Only answer the next set of questions if you had an echo, nuclear, or treadmill study performed at your last visit. If you did not have any of these tests performed, continue on to the end of the survey.

VI. This next set of questions asks about any test or studies performed at your last visit. Please rate your satisfaction in these areas using a scale of 1–5, one being dissatisfied and five being most satisfied. *If you answer any of the questions with 1 or 2, it would be helpful to us to know what the problem was.*
How satisfied were you with...

1. The explanation of the procedure   _____
2. Your comfort during the procedure   _____
3. Your privacy throughout the procedure   _____
4. The physician's explanation of your test results   _____

Thank you for your help!! Please either turn in the completed survey at the front desk before you leave today or mail the completed survey to:

New Mexico Heart Institute
1001 Coal Ave. SE
Albuquerque, NM 87106

Questions? Please call us at 505-224-7092

OPTIONAL:

Name: _____

Phone: _____

_____ (yes or no) I would like to be personally contacted about my comments.

Please record any additional comments below or on the back of this page.

Courtesy of New Mexico Heart Institute, Albuquerque, NM.

Exhibit 1–2 Patient Satisfaction Survey

To provide you with the best possible care, we need your feedback.

1. How did you decide to come to this practice?

   ____ Recommended by another patient

   ____ Recommended by another doctor

   ____ Physician referral service

   ____ Yellow Pages

   ____ Office close to home

   ____ Recommended by family

   ____ Recommended by hospital

   ____ Local medical society

   ____ Office close to work

   Other:_____

2. When you telephone our office, is your call answered courteously?

   ____ Yes ____ No   Comments: _____

3. Are you able to obtain an appointment easily and timely?

   ____ Yes ____ No   Comments: _____

4. During your last visit to our office, how would you describe your treatment by our staff?

   ____ Warm/friendly   ____ Cool/unfriendly   ____ Courteous

   ____ Professional   ____ Unprofessional

   Other:_____

5. How interested do we seem to be in you as a person when you visit the office?

   ____ Genuinely interested and concerned

   ____ Usually interested and concerned

   ____ Sometimes disinterested and unconcerned

   ____ Usually disinterested and unconcerned

6. Do you find our waiting room warm and comfortable?

   ____ Yes ____ No Comments: _____

7. Are the waiting room materials to your taste? ____ Yes ____ No

   If "No," your preference:_____

continues

Exhibit 1–2 continued

8. When you arrive at our office, how long do you normally have to wait after your scheduled appointment time? _____ minutes. If you wait longer than 30 minutes, are you given an explanation for the delay? _____ Yes _____ No

9. How would you rate the overall quality of care you receive?
   _____ Outstanding _____ Good _____ Fair _____ Poor
   Comments: _____

10. How would you rate the doctor on patience, warmth, and interest in your problem? _____ Outstanding _____ Good _____ Fair _____ Poor

11. Does the doctor fully explain your illness and treatment to you?
    _____ Yes _____ No   Comments: _____

12. Are you comfortable recommending our services to your family and friends?
    _____ Yes _____ No   Comments: _____

13. What other services could we offer that you would like available for you or your family?
    _____

14. Have the financial policies of this practice been completely explained to you?
    _____ Yes _____ No   Comments: _____

15. During your last visit, were the charges explained to your satisfaction?
    _____ Yes _____ No   Comments: _____

16. Is our superbill helpful in filing with your insurance for reimbursement?
    _____ Yes _____ No   Comments: _____

17. Other: _____
    _____
    _____

Thank you for taking time to complete this information.
We value our patients' comments.

_____   _____
Date   Signature (optional)

Source: Reprinted from N. Baum, *Take Charge of Your Medical Practice*, pp. 273–274, © 1996, Aspen Publishers, Inc.

sides of a single 8½-by-11-inch piece of paper or two one-sided pages. Begin with an opening paragraph or cover letter (see Exhibit 1–3) that outlines the purpose of the survey (i.e., to evaluate the strengths and weaknesses of your practice and ultimately to provide better health care for your patients). Yes-no or multiple choice questions are the easiest to quantify.

Suggested questions include:

- Do I see you on time for your appointments?
- Is my office staff friendly and courteous?
- Are my office hours convenient?
- Is it easy to make an appointment?
- Do my staff and I return phone calls in a timely fashion?
- Would you like me to provide you with the opportunity to purchase your medications in the office if the prices were competitive with local pharmacies?

I do not suggest you ask any questions regarding your fees, because most patients consider medical fees to be too high. Finally, you may want to conclude with an open-ended question, such as, "What can I do to make your experience with me and my office more pleasant?"

Whom To Include

Choose a good cross section of patients, if you choose to mail your survey. Include some active and inactive patients, as well as patients who you know have left your practice.

Exhibit 1–3 Sample Cover Letter To Accompany Patient Survey

Dear Patient:

My staff and I want to provide you and your family with the highest quality health care possible. To help us evaluate our effectiveness, we would like your opinions of my practice.

Your answers and suggestions on the following questionnaire will help us continue to improve the health care we provide you. Please take a few minutes to give us this important information and return it to us in the enclosed stamped and self-addressed envelope.

Thank you,

Dr. Neil H. Baum and staff

Customizing the Survey

Exhibit 1–1 shows an example of a sample survey used by the New Mexico Heart Institute. However, the most effective survey will be one that has been customized for your particular practice. I have included my own patient satisfaction survey in Exhibit 1–2 for some additional ideas.

For best results, instruct patients to return the survey to your home or to a post office box address. If the survey is sent to your office, critical or negative comments regarding your office personnel may not reach your attention. Chances are that is not going to happen, but if patients perceive problems with your staff, then you want to be made aware of their problems and concerns.

Implementing the Survey

I recommend that an office survey be conducted at least once every two years. One good rule of thumb, according to the American Medical Association, is to survey at least 20 percent of your existing patients, or a minimum of 200, whichever is greater. It is also a good idea to survey your inactive patients, because you will often obtain very important information about your practice and why they are no longer patients. Include a self-addressed stamped envelope when you mail the survey, to encourage their participation. You, the physician, should personally review all the surveys. Keep an open mind as you do this, remembering that the purpose is to improve your practice. Even though you may get criticisms, most of the comments will probably be positive ones. But it's the criticisms that will help make improvements in your practice.[1]

Tabulating the Results

We keep our surveys simple. Most of them have yes or no answers. This makes tabulating the results of our surveys easy—we simply count the number of responses received and the number of yes or no answers for each question. I do not think it is necessary to use any method that is more complicated.

Using the Results

You have worked hard to devise a concise patient survey. A number of patients have mailed them in. Make sure you do not relegate these valuable letters to the "black hole" in your filing system. Those survey comments and answers are a gold mine. All you have to do is address the concerns and you will be a hit with those who took the time to answer, and with the rest of the patients already in your practice.

It is important to prioritize the comments. If your survey shows that an over-whelming percentage of patients feel they are not being seen on time, then that problem has to take high priority and should be addressed first. On the other hand, if only one or two people claim your office hours are inconvenient, that issue can

---

Exhibit 1–4 Letter To Establish Focus Group

Dear [Patient],

I hope this letter finds you well and enjoying your summer. I am writing to a select group of people in my practice whom I especially enjoy serving to ask a favor. At a recent staff meeting we were discussing how blessed we are to be serving so many people who truly appreciate us and from whom we receive so many positive compliments about the quality of our medical care. I want you to know how much I appreciate you, but I do not feel I have resourced you as much as I possibly should.

As you know, I and my staff strive to stay up with the latest advances and to upgrade the level of medical care continually. For a practice to be truly excellent, the technical care, skill, and judgment must conform to the very highest standards, but that alone is not enough.

There are numerous other factors that come into play in order to make your experience truly excellent, and this is where I need your help.

I would like you to be a part of a small group of people selected to provide specific feedback on how I and my staff are doing. I would appreciate about an hour and a quarter of your time on Tuesday, August 2, from 7:30 to 8:45 in the evening at my office. Refreshments and light snacks will be served. I would like to discuss the following questions:

1. What do you feel are the strengths of my practice?
2. What do you feel are the weaknesses of my practice?
3. Do you think weekend appointments would be helpful?
4. Do you have any problems making an appointment?
5. Are there any services that you feel I should add that would make my practice more attractive?
6. Are you satisfied with the referrals I make to other physicians?
7. Are there any other suggestions you have to improve the quality of your experience with me or my office?

I will be calling you in a few days to confirm your participation. Thank you once again for your friendship and support.

Sincerely,

Neil Baum, MD

be lower on the list.

The best time and place to address the survey results is in a staff meeting. For instance, after one patient survey, we found that we were getting lots of complaints about delays in the office. We then started brainstorming possible solutions for the problem. One of the things we did was to invite a dentist and his staff to a "lunch and learn" program. This dentist had a reputation for being absolutely on time for patient visits. When he and his staff arrived, we asked them for information on how to improve the timing in our office. We asked them if they could explain to us how they did it, and we got several good ideas from that meeting.

FOCUS GROUPS

With a focus group, the most important step is the selection of participants. An effective focus group consists of a cross section of diverse, opinionated, and vocal individuals who are asked to assess your practice. When selecting participants for my focus groups, I choose patients who are keen observers and patients who are also complainers. Avoid "yes" men and women. The purpose of the focus group is not to hear how wonderful you are. It is really to troubleshoot your practice, and that is why you want vocal, articulate complainers as your participants.

Milton Seifert, MD, from Excelsior, Minnesota, meets regularly with a 60-member patient advisory council for guidance on everything from billing to aesthetics.[2] Dr. Seifert asserts this council is important to nearly every nonmedical decision made in his practice. Input from this group has paid off in positive patient satisfaction surveys.

Dr. Seifert has also used the council as cheerleaders when he had to renegotiate his managed care contracts. When several managed care organizations demanded deeper discounts, his dedicated patients on the council called a local hospital to write letters to the managed care organizations to reverse their demands. They were ultimately successful in this lobbying effort. His patient advisors have also suggested structural improvements to his office that included railings in the restroom and wheelchair ramps at the entrance—and this was long before the Americans with Disabilities Act of 1990 required such changes.

Invitations and Reminders

Once I have selected my participants for the focus group, I try to call each person myself and personally invite him or her to assist me in evaluating my practice. I then send a cover letter that includes the purpose of the focus group and an agenda that I would like them to think about before the meeting (see the sample cover letter in Exhibit 1–4). The day before the focus group meets I have my office staff call and remind the participants of the meeting.

The meeting is held in my reception room and is limited to one and a half hours. I provide coffee, soft drinks, and dessert. I pay parking fees or, in the case of participants who prefer not to drive at night, taxi fare. I ask permission to tape-record the meeting so I am not distracted by having to take notes.

Running the Meeting

After introductions, briefly reiterate your reasons for inviting your participants to your office. Ask provoking questions. Solicit examples from them of excellent customer service. Request ideas for improvement based on their experiences at other medical offices and other businesses.

At one of my focus groups, I learned that several patients were interested in evening and weekend office hours. Because I am in solo practice, this was not practical for my office. But we found a solution: I agreed to have Saturday morning hours on the one weekend a month that I am on call. The other urologists in my call group agreed to do the same. Consequently, on any weekend, one urologist will be able to see patients in his or her office.

We also learned that patients did not like paying to park under our building. The focus group participants claimed that most other hospitals and doctors' offices in our area did not charge, so we added validated parking to our services.

Another focus group finding was that patients did not know where to go to pay their bills and schedule their next appointments. This feedback made us realize that we had a signage problem. It was easily corrected by providing signs at the business office and wherever the exit signs appeared in the office.

Follow-Up

It is important to let each person know you appreciate his or her input. I send each participant an immediate thank-you note. Later, whenever we institute a change that came out of the focus group, I send a follow-up note discussing the changes.

SUGGESTION BOX

In our office, we have a suggestion box in the reception area. It has a sign on it stating, "Please let us know what we can do to improve our service to you." On top are pencils and 3-by-5 index cards. The patients have the option of signing their names. The most important regular task is to check the suggestion box daily.

Providing a suggestion box is a legitimate method of identifying and solving problems. Therefore, do not treat the suggestion box as window dressing. Take it seriously and make it a functional part of your ongoing practice survey techniques.

We clean up our reception area twice a day, at noon and at the end of the day. Checking the suggestion box twice is a part of that routine.

When patients sign their names, we call them, thank them for their suggestions,

---

Exhibit 1–5 Information Sheet Kept on Each Referring Physician

What's Important Now

Name _____ Date of Birth _____

Telephone (W)_____
    (H)_____

Address (W) _____
    (H) _____

Education
 College _____
 Medical School _____
 Postgraduate _____

Special Areas of Interest
_____
_____
_____

Hobbies and Recreational Activities _____
_____
_____

Marital Status _____ Spouse _____
Children _____
_____

Conversational Interests
_____
_____
_____

Dining Preferences
_____

Additional Notes
_____
_____
_____

and respond to them right away. We let them know what our follow-up on their suggestions has been, especially if we implement one of their ideas.

PHYSICIAN SURVEYS

Finally, you want to evaluate or survey your referring physicians. This can be done by using either a written or a verbal survey. I think holding an informal meeting is probably the easiest and most comfortable method. The meeting can be casual and can be held at a restaurant or in one of your offices at the beginning or end of the day.

For this method to be successful, the feedback has to go both ways—in addition to soliciting critiques of your practice, you must provide your colleagues with constructive comments regarding their practices. I think most physicians will be pleasantly surprised how useful this type of candid conversation with peers can be.

For example, I wanted to field-test my computerized referral letter with my colleagues. I received unanimous approval of the concept. As a matter of fact, a few of them adopted the letter for their practices. The group also generated the idea of using the fax machine to give same-day service.

How To Survey Your Peers

A survey of colleagues does not have to be as formalized as a written patient survey. You can select physicians with whom you feel comfortable. Ask them to meet you for lunch or just for coffee.

When I wanted to survey my colleagues, I tried to obtain a cross section: some older physicians, some contemporaries, and a few younger physicians. When I met with each of them, I asked them whether they were getting good feedback from the patients they sent to me. I asked whether my reports were getting to them in a timely fashion. I asked whether there was anything I could do to make my practice more user-friendly.

In response to these direct questions came some informative answers. One physician told me that one of his pet peeves was that my office would call him and then put him on hold for 15 seconds while my staff got me on the line. "Look," he said, "this is just one of my quirks. I can't explain it, I know it isn't necessarily right, but it just galls me. But just know that that's one of my idiosyncrasies. Please respect it and be on the phone when your office calls me." And so I am. I would not have known that detail had I not brought up the subject with him. This information—that he does not like to hold on the telephone—was then recorded on that physician's Rolodex card. We also record this information on each physician's WIN sheet (WIN is short for What's Important Now, which I adapted from Harvey Mackay's 66-question customer profile).[3] (See Exhibit 1–5.) That way, whoever places the call to him will see that note and make sure that I am immediately available to take the call.

I have another example. The normal routine is for the admitting physician to do the discharge summary. One of my colleagues, during my survey of fellow physicians, asked if I would do the discharge summary, because I was receiving a bigger fee from doing the surgery and providing the postoperative care. I told him, "Fine, I'm happy to do it." I would not have known that physician's thoughts had I not surveyed him.

These discussions with your peers can be quite informal. What I tell my referring physicians is, "Look, we send patients back and forth. I want to get better, and the only way I can do that is if you give me some feedback on how I'm doing. If there's anything I can do to improve the practice and give you better service, can you let me know?"

I usually have a list of written questions:

- If you need a consult right away, is your patient seen in a timely manner?
- Is my office friendly to your patients?
- Do I get my notes back to you on time?
- Do you feel that we are user-friendly?
- Are there any problems that you are having that I need to know about?

I also carry a notepad to write down answers, which lets my colleagues know that I am serious and not just casually using their time. I also make sure to send a follow-up thank-you note to those physicians who agree to meet with me and provide me with feedback.

This is a process that I repeat every 6 to 12 months to keep on top of what my referring physicians are thinking about my practice. I believe it is a good idea for any physician in private practice.

Whether it is one of your patients or your colleagues, you need to ask what Dr. Michael Le Boeuf calls "the platinum questions": "How am I doing? How can I get better?"[4]

The Bottom Line   *When you solicit honest feedback from your patients and referring physicians, you may get some surprises. But if you listen and learn from their responses, and implement their suggestions, you will improve the quality of the care you give, and the quality of your bottom line!*

NOTES

1. Patient Survey Questionnaire, *Practice Development Resources*, American Medical Association, Chicago, IL, 1990.

2. *Family Practice News,* September 1, 1998.

3. Harvey Mackay, *Swim with the Sharks without Being Eaten Alive* (New York: Ballantine Books, 1988), 25–34.

4. Michael Le Boeuf, *How To Win Customers and Keep Them for Life* (New York: Berkley Books, 1989), 65–66.

CHAPTER 2

Mystery Shop 'Til You Drop

It is better to ask some of the questions than know all the answers.

James Thurber

The best questions you can ask your patients are: "How am I doing?" and "How can I better serve your health care needs?" Only by asking these questions can you discover how to improve your practice for yourself and your patients.

Everybody, including physicians, sees him- or herself as wonderful. And why not? If you are not getting any feedback, it is easy to assume you are doing a great job. Sometimes the only critical feedback you get is when a patient leaves the practice, when a patient starts complaining, or when an attorney asks for a copy of a patient's records. But then you usually think it is the patient's fault. So you never really get a chance to assess your practice objectively.

If you want to make improvements, you have to be willing to look at yourself and your practice—warts and all, to hear some things you do not want to hear, and to examine the fine details of your practice under a microscope. In the preceding chapter, I outlined the most commonly used patient survey techniques. One of the best ways to critique your practice is to have someone pose as a patient and visit your practice.

Now, you cannot ask your staff, your spouse, or your office manager to do it. They have so much bias that they could not possibly be objective. Also, if they walk in the door trying to impersonate a patient, it would not be a mystery! But you can invite a mystery shopper to your practice. It is an excellent opportunity to look objectively at your practice through the eyes of a sophisticated surrogate patient. A mystery shopper is a marketing professional who has been trained to survey and evaluate the ways in which businesses serve their customers. Typically, they are hired through marketing or public relations firms.

This technique has been used by businesses for years. In the past 10 years, hospitals have used mystery shoppers to evaluate the user-friendliness of their facilities. According to a 1997 article in the *New York Times,* mystery shopping consultants are also gaining favor as an increasing number of health maintenance organizations and doctors offices try to attract more patients.[1] A search on the Internet yields scores of companies devoted to mystery shopper research.

A mystery shopper gives you an opportunity to identify those "moments of truth" when the patient interacts with you and your staff. If you can manage those moments of truth effectively, patients will feel good about you and your practice. They will not only remain as loyal patients but they will also tell others about their positive experiences with your office.

When you decide to hire a mystery shopper, be prepared to move out of your "comfort zone." Resolve not to be defensive about the results. The only way to get better at what you do is to be willing to hear objective criticism and to make the necessary changes.

Here is how I arranged for the mystery shopper to come to my office. I asked my hospital's public relations department to locate a professional mystery shopper to evaluate my practice. I refrained from telling my staff that the mystery shopper would be coming, and I suggest that you do the same. I did not want my staff to be on their "good behavior" only for the evaluation. In addition, I was not told when the mystery shopper would be visiting. I wanted to be critiqued according to the same standards as my staff.

Once you arrange for a mystery shopper, there are several things you should do. You should ask to see the questionnaire that will be used to evaluate your practice. Most mystery shoppers work from ready-made questionnaires (such as the one presented in Exhibit 2–1), but you may be able to add some items regarding the observations you would like to have included.

The idea behind the mystery shopper is to get as authentic an impression of your office as possible. You should make sure the shopper intends to include the following suggestions.

The mystery shopper should call for a routine appointment, but then ask to be seen earlier than the date given. For example, after making the appointment the mystery shopper can call back and state that he or she needs to see the doctor sooner. This allows the shopper to observe how your staff handles this typical situation.

The mystery shopper should also ask for directions to the office to verify that the staff can provide adequate instructions over the phone. He or she should record whether the appointment scheduler discusses fees and the method of payment on the initial visit.

The mystery shopper might also ask about your credentials (for example, whether you are board certified). This is an important point—you need to know if your staff can describe your qualifications accurately to prospective patients.

Exhibit 2–1 Mystery Shopper Checklist

Call the doctor's office to make an appointment. Your ailment is a urinary tract infection. Tell the office that you are new in town and will be bringing your records with you to the visit.

1. *Ask for directions to the office from a specific neighborhood.*
2. *Ask what insurance they take, the cost of an initial visit, and if they take VISA or Mastercard.*
3. *Ask the office hours.*
4. *When you make this call, also check:*
   - promptness of staff in picking up the phone
   - courtesy in greeting
   - tone of voice
   - willingness to give information to you
   - willingness to work the appointment into your schedule
   - promptness in scheduling the appointment
   - any preinstructions, preparations, etc.
   - knowledge of directions, office information, hours, insurance, etc.

The next day, call the office and cancel the appointment. Wait a day and call back to reschedule. Check the above factors again.

The day you go to the office, fill out the application with bogus information.

Check the following:

- general appearance of office
- promptness of greeting upon walking up to window
- manner in which you are greeted (eye contact, smile, pleasant voice, etc.)
- amount of time you wait before being seen
- general comments of patients around you in the office (you might ask a few patients what the doctor is like, explaining that you are new in town and this is your first visit)
- noise factor in office
- any other items or factors you notice

Source: Data from Cynthia Quant, formerly of Touro Physician Services, New Orleans, LA.

The mystery shopper arrives 15 to 30 minutes before the scheduled appointment. This allows the shopper ample time to register and then sit in the reception area and listen to the conversations of the patients and their families. Often these conversations will provide insight and valuable information about how your patients perceive you and your staff. During this time the mystery shopper takes note of general reception area decor, reading materials, pamphlets, and brochures, as well as other items you may have provided to occupy patients while they are waiting for the doctor.

If your practice has a significant percentage of senior citizens, it will be important for your mystery shopper to evaluate your practice from their perspective. Ask the mystery shopper to consider the lighting, the legibility of your print material, the comfort of your chairs in the reception area, the ability to accommodate wheelchairs and other patient aids, and the extraneous sounds that make listening to the doctor difficult. In Chapter 20 you will learn other techniques to make your practice attractive to seniors and matures.

The mystery shopper records the time he or she enters the office, the scheduled appointment time, the time he or she is escorted to the examining room, and how long it takes you to arrive in the examining room.

The mystery shopper should note whether your staff members are courteous. Do staff members smile? Do they introduce themselves and use their titles? Do they use the patient's name? Do they appear interested in the patient? Do they appear to enjoy their work?

When you arrive in the examination room, the mystery shopper should observe your manner and your style of history-taking. Do you immediately start asking about the shopper's medical problem or do you ask about his or her family, work, and hobbies? Depending on the background and skills of the mystery shopper, he or she can pretend to have a medical problem. This is important for evaluating how you take a history.

Mystery shoppers can identify themselves at this stage and avoid the physical examination. This was the case with my mystery shopper, whom I did not suspect until, at the conclusion of taking her history, I told her that I was going to step out of the room and tell the nurse to come in so that I could examine her. At this point, she said, "Wait, wait, that won't be necessary. I'm your mystery shopper!"

While mystery shoppers will want to avoid the physical exam, they usually still go through the checkout process and either pay by check or cash, which should be refunded immediately. Another possibility is to allow the mystery shopper to say, "I forgot my checkbook at home" to observe your staff's diplomacy in handling this typical situation.

Finally, the mystery shopper should provide a written summary of his or her experience in your office. It is only through close scrutiny of yourself and your staff that you can identify those "moments of truth" when you and the staff members have the opportunity to make a good impression. When you do make a good impression, you can be sure that you have fostered loyalty in a patient. That person will not only return to your practice but will also tell others about his or her positive experience with you and your office staff.

By the way, our report card from the mystery shopper was a good one. Otherwise, I would not be writing this book!

The Bottom Line   *Taking the extra step of hiring a mystery shopper will help you unravel the hidden secrets to practice success.*

NOTE

1. David J. Morrow, "To Rate Hospitals, She Dons a Wig and Practices Her Cough," *New York Times,* March 30, 1997: Section 3, p. 9.

CHAPTER 3

Don't Be Late
for a Very Important Date

Timeliness is next to godliness.

Hospital Health Network, August 1996

What do you do when you see a police officer in your rearview mirror? Like most drivers, you automatically take your foot off the accelerator. Whenever my appointment secretary thinks I am slowing down during office hours, she places a time-and-motion sheet (Exhibit 3–1) on the patient charts. It serves a similar purpose as seeing a police officer on the highway. It is my signal that I should get into gear, because I am being watched by my staff. The only difference is that when I know I am being watched, I go faster, not slower.

My attention to time management had its genesis in what Tom Peters, a nationally renowned author of *In Search of Excellence* and consultant to Fortune 500 companies, has called the two keys to success in business: first, find out what the customer (patient) wants and give him or her more of it; second, find out what the customer (patient) does not want and be sure to avoid it. Ask any patient what he or she dislikes about the health care experience, and you will find that nearly everyone will mention "waiting for the doctor." Spending time in waiting rooms probably accounts for more patient dissatisfaction than any other aspect of medical care. One patient put it this way: "Physicians consistently double-book, stacking us up in the waiting room like planes on a runway. At least with the airlines you get a free drink."[1]

While not many of us can make significant changes in health care legislation, all of us can be more sensitive to patients' number-one complaint about their physicians: that doctors do not respect patients' time. We can all make a greater effort to see our patients in a timely fashion. In this chapter I will show you how to be an

Exhibit 3–1 Sample Time-and-Motion Sheet

Patient Name _____ Date _____ _____ Scheduled appointment _____ Patient arrival time _____ Time patient was brought into exam room _____ Time physician spent with patient (mins.) _____ Time patient left office

on-time physician by managing the time in the office more effectively. At the end of the chapter, 12 "time-busters" are provided for you to try in your practice.

Today there are more time demands on physicians than ever before. We have more paperwork, dictation, and other nonpatient obligations that take away from our primary patient care responsibilities and result in less time for our personal and family lives. The result is burnout and dissatisfaction with our work.[2] Managing time is not only the key to a successful practice, but it's also the key to an enjoyable one.

Do you want to evaluate the efficiency of your practice? Do a time-and-motion study and then empower your staff to implement it. This is one of the techniques I use to help myself and my staff be more conscious of time.

DO NOT KEEP PATIENTS WAITING

In today's fast-paced, consumer-oriented society, patients expect to be seen and treated promptly. Waiting for the doctor for 30 to 60 minutes or more may have been tolerated years ago, but it is no longer acceptable to most patients today.

Not long ago, a Florida ophthalmologist found himself in small claims court defending himself against a lawsuit brought by a patient made to wait for two hours. The patient was an engineer and valued his time at $50 an hour, so he sent the doctor a bill for keeping him waiting. When the doctor failed to respond to the $100 invoice, the patient took him to small claims court, won the suit, and was awarded $101 for "breach of contract." The patient gave the money to charity, but the story didn't end there. He was invited to tell his story on "The Tonight Show" and nearly ruined the doctor's practice.[3] Of course, this is an extreme example. And I prefer to think about the advantages I gain from being on time. One of the best ways to build a practice is to see patients on time. Conversely, you can lose patients by failing to demonstrate that you value their time.

Patients understand and appreciate good customer service. And a big part of good service is no waiting. Patients are exposed to both good and bad examples of customer service at restaurants, hotels, banks, and department stores. Keeping patients waiting for excessive periods without explanation sends a signal that the doctor's time is more valuable than theirs. Patients interpret this abuse of their time as discourteous and disrespectful. You want to avoid this impression of your practice at all costs. So, how do you start?

Declare to yourself and your staff that managing time will be a priority. Make sure you and your staff understand the value of time and its importance in marketing your practice. Think about the positive results of being on time and how it will make a favorable impact on your practice. Also recognize that being on time will reduce stress in your professional life.

IDENTIFY PROBLEM AREAS

I suggest that you begin by surveying your existing patients regarding their perceptions of how time is handled in your office. In Chapter 1, I explained how to conduct a written patient survey. One of the questions on that survey can be, "Are you seen on time when you schedule an appointment with the doctor?" You can poll patients at the time they are seen in your office or by mailing surveys to patients selected at random. Make the form simple and direct and keep it short. You can provide blanks for extra comments at the bottom of the sheet.

Next I suggest conducting a time-and-motion study for several weeks. This will give you hard facts about how you manage time in your practice. To conduct the study, simply attach a time-and-motion sheet (Exhibit 3–1) to the front of each patient's chart. Record the time the patient arrives, the time of the scheduled appointment, the time the patient was seen, and the time the patient left the office. This technique will identify problem areas and offer potential solutions to such problems.

After you have surveyed your patients and conducted a time-and-motion study, examine your office scheduling procedures. Do your staff members "double book" in an effort to finish the day early? Do they fail to triage patients adequately and allow nonemergency situations to create excessive waits for patients who have scheduled appointments? These questions should be reviewed at staff meetings to identify the problems.

Look for specific examples of scheduling problems and discuss them with your staff. For example, if you find that most days have two to three emergencies that disrupt the scheduled visits in the appointment book, then schedule in a few open slots for such emergencies.

Finally, schedule specific times for callbacks to patients and tell patients approximately when to expect your return call. That way they will not be waiting anxiously by the telephone, and you have informed them that you respect their time, too. Notifying patients of the approximate time you will be calling encourages them to be available and to keep the telephone lines open. This avoids an unfriendly game of telephone tag. (In Chapter 43, "Let Technology Simplify Your Life," I will show you how to win the game of phone tag.)

MANAGE INTERRUPTIONS

I recommend making every effort to avoid interruptions when you are with patients. While many physicians may feel that they get more accomplished by handling several things at once (a human version of computer "multitasking"), you may do your practice more harm than good with this habit.

I will never forget the time I was interrupted for "emergencies" three times while trying to care for the same patient. When I returned to the exam room after the third time, the patient politely asked for his records, saying, "Dr. Baum, I like you and I like your office staff. You enjoy a very nice reputation in this community. However, I am not receiving your undivided attention." How could I argue with him? His comment was absolutely correct, and there was nothing I could say that would make him change his mind.

As a result of this fiasco, I decided to define "emergencies" and educate my staff as to the specific indications for interrupting me while I am in the room with a patient. I now accept an interruption if there is a call from the emergency room, the operating room, the recovery room, or the intensive care unit. Other patients, personal friends, and cold-calling stockbrokers are told that I will return calls at 4:30 PM and are asked to leave their number.

When a colleague calls and asks to speak to me, he or she is told the following: "Dr. Baum is with a patient. If it is an emergency, I can ask him to come to the phone right now. If not, I will have him call in just a few minutes when he comes out of the room." It has been my experience that most of my colleagues are sensitive to the fact that I do not want to be interrupted and will accept my returning the call in a few minutes.

Now, in order to make this philosophy work with colleagues, I have to behave in the same manner toward them. When I call a colleague, I ask if he or she is between patients or when I might call back. If the office tells me that the physician will call me back, I tell my receptionist that I am expecting a call and that I can be interrupted. I then tell the next patient, "I am expecting a call from a colleague. Can I begin our visit and will it be okay if I am interrupted?" I have never had a patient who refused to accept that approach.

DO NOT IGNORE DELAYS

The worst thing you can do if you are delayed is to ignore the situation. This only escalates the tension. If you see that you will be late to the office, notify your staff as soon as possible.

Encourage your staff to obtain a daytime telephone number for each patient. This is helpful when you need to alert patients about a delay or to contact them if cancellation times become available.

Routine appointments can be scheduled several weeks in advance. Make sure you explain to patients that your staff does this to keep time open for emergencies and urgent visits. The patients need to be told that you follow this procedure to avoid excessive delays in the office. When you explain your procedure to your patients, they are nearly always understanding and accept your scheduling policies.

If you are delayed and patients are already in the office, have your staff personally walk into the reception area, explain the delay to those waiting, and give an estimate of how long patients can expect to wait. Leaving the patients in the reception area without an explanation is a sure way to promote "contagious hostility" among the patients.

To show patients that you place a premium on their time, a sign can be placed in the office stating: "If you have been waiting more than 20 minutes, please notify the receptionist." This sign will also catch the occasional patient who forgets to sign in or notify the receptionist and "gets lost" in the reception area.

Providing pleasant distractions in your reception area helps decrease the anxiety associated with delays. (For more suggestions, see Chapter 6.) Some practices located in shopping centers provide patients with beepers and contact the patients when they can be seen. In my practice, we give patients beepers and coupons for coffee at a nearby coffee shop. We offer them a free cup of "designer" coffee and then beep them when there is an opening in the schedule.

Another nice gesture is to provide patients with refreshments, such as decaffeinated coffee or bottled water. This shows concern for their health and also makes it easier for patients to provide urine specimens.

If you are late, you should remember to use the magic words, "I'm sorry." It is important to acknowledge your delay and apologize for it. Most patients will not get upset over a legitimate delay. An apology signals to your patients that you are sensitive and that you value their time.

If there has been an excessive delay, you may detect hostility on the part of a patient (the body language is hard to miss: distended jugular veins, clenched fists, the patient leaning forward in a pounce position). In this type of situation, you might consider a small but significant discount on your fee. I have done this on several occasions and watched patients change their attitude immediately. I have even empowered my staff to write off the patient's bill if they see or hear that the patient is very upset about the delay in the office. This write-off occurs about once every three months, and I have been amazed at the response from patients and people who have heard about the write-off policy. The write-off of the office visit is worth more to your reputation than the $50 to $75 of income.

You can also reinforce your sensitivity to excessive delays by sending an apology letter (see Chapter 13, "Leave a Paper Trail…That Leads to the Bottom Line"). Remember, your patients' goodwill and their positive image of you and your practice should be your foremost concern.

Finally, encourage your staff to develop an "on-time mentality." Empower your staff to move you along if patients are waiting or appear to be anxious. What works for me is seeing the time-and-motion sheet on a patient's chart. There may be other signals that help you move along, such as a certain piece of music (like Ravel's "Bolero") or another audible cue that you and your staff previously have agreed upon. My staff has created humorous cards imprinted with "Hustle Your Bustle" and "Let's Move It" that are flashed in front of me when I begin running behind schedule.

Today, being on time is vital to retaining patients. You can also encourage new patients to enter your practice if you develop a reputation in the community of being an "on-time doctor."

With more to do and less time to do it in, your practice effectiveness and success, as well as your happiness, are dependent on your ability to manage time. Each one of us has only 24 hours in the day. How that precious commodity is used is what differentiates a doctor who enjoys his or her practice from a doctor who is a slave to it.

TWELVE TIME-BUSTERS

The following suggestions will help you manage your time more efficiently.

1. ***Do not allow telephone interruptions while you are seeing patients.*** Leaving a patient to answer a phone call does not make the patient feel important or that he or she has your undivided attention. However, my staff has a system of using certain numbers on the beeper, such as 911 if there is a call from the emergency room, 411 if another physician is calling, and 000 if

my wife or family must speak to me. In addition, make it a policy to return all routine calls at a specific time, such as 11:45 AM or after 4:30 PM. If your patients and colleagues know your telephone policy, they will respect it and interrupt you for emergencies only.

2. **Handle paperwork and mail only one time.**[4] Read your mail and reports at a time of day when you can take action and delegate tasks to your employees. Make use of Post-its™ to alert you to special details that need attention from you or your staff.

3. **Dictate in real time.** Do not wait until the end of the day or week to dictate letters or discharge summaries. Dictate in front of the patient when the facts are fresh in your mind. This adds to the accuracy of your history and allows your patients to make corrections or additions during your dictation. Dictating in real time reassures your patient that you are communicating with his or her referring physician. Dictate discharge summaries when the history and hospital course are easily remembered.

4. **Learn effective scheduling.** Leave a half-hour open during morning or afternoon office hours to accommodate add-ons and emergencies. Do not fill that half-hour until the office opens in the morning. Do not worry about this open time. That half-hour almost always gets used—if not with seeing patients, then with catching up on your dictation and paperwork.[5]

5. **Estimate the length of a patient visit and schedule accordingly.** A new patient with a chronic problem may take 25 minutes of your time, while a returning patient with a recurrent urinary tract infection, for instance, may only require 5 minutes. However, a patient with a newly diagnosed cancer may require 35 to 40 minutes and should be scheduled at the end of the day when you have time to answer all of his or her questions. A patient to whom you are disclosing a diagnosis of cancer or revealing a significant life-threatening diagnosis such as diabetes, lupus, or renal failure deserves your undivided attention.

6. **Create a to-do list for the day and week.** There are a number of paper and electronic systems on the market to aid you in keeping track of your schedule. You may want to use a Day-Timer calendar, Sharp's Wizard, 3COM's Palm Organizers, or Compaq's Aero Palm Size PCs.[6] Prioritize your to-do list with 1s, 2s, 3s, and 4s: 1s are must-dos, 2s are important but not imperative, and 3s and 4s are "sliders"—you can move these to another list. Check off completed tasks. It gives you a feeling of accomplishment to see a list with check marks beside the 1s and 2s.

7. **Use office videos for patient education.** By using office videos to explain common procedures, I have been able to enhance my office efficiency by 20–30 percent. See Chapter 15 to find out how to create your own videos.

8. **Learn to delegate to and empower your staff.** Allow your staff to make nonmedical decisions about office procedures and equipment. Give them the responsibility to solve problems on their own. Hire and train employees who are self-starters and can take the initiative to solve problems effectively and efficiently. (In Chapter 34, I will teach you how to hire and train that self-starting employee.)

9. **Do not spend time between surgical cases drinking coffee and reading the paper.** Make phone calls, invite medical records personnel to the doctor's lounge so you can sign charts, or outline an article you want to write for the local newspaper (or, better yet, outline that book you have been meaning to write).

10. **Educate yourself with audiotapes.** Driving to and from work and hospitals can be a great time to stay current with your continuing medical education credits. Tapes are available for nearly every specialty. Also, consider obtaining tapes on nonmedical subjects, such as business, or taped novels or foreign language instruction (Berlitz distributes an excellent series). Your local bookstore is a good source for such tapes.[7]

11. **Form a networking journal club.** You cannot possibly read all the medical literature all the time. As outlined in Chapters 18 and 35, you can exchange articles with colleagues from other specialties.

12. **Finally, exercise regularly, even if it is only walking up and down the stairs in the hospital or your office building.** You will feel better and you will allow the pressures of your practice to defuse in a healthy fashion.

The Bottom Line   *In many ways, effective time management boils down to plain good manners and practice of the Golden Rule:*
   If you treat patients the way you would like to be treated, the chances are good that they will continue to be loyal to you and your practice.

NOTES

1. *USA Today,* August 15, 1991.
2. Ann McGee-Cooper, *You Don't Have To Go Home from Work Exhausted* (Dallas: Bowen and Rogers, 1985).
3. C. Richard Coben, "I Caught the Wrath of a Patient Made To Wait," *Medical Economics,* February 20, 1989: 215, 218.
4. Michael Le Boeuf, *Working Smart: How To Accomplish More in Half the Time* (New York: Warner Books, 1979).
5. Michael Goitein, "Waiting Patiently," *New England Journal of Medicine,* 323, no. 9 (1990): 604–608.

6. To order a product catalogue from Day-Timers, Inc., call 800-255-5005; or use their website address: *www.daytimer.com*. The Electronic Wizard is manufactured by Sharp, and models are priced from $30 to $149—the latter comes with e-mail options. 3COM's Palm Organizers range from about $250 to $500, and offer e-mail and other program options. Other manufacturers such as Casio and Philips have comparable pocket-sized computer/organizers as well, and all are available at most office supply superstores.

7. Nightingale-Conant has a catalogue of "best-listening" tapes on success, motivation, and time management. Call (800) 323-5552; *www.nightingale.com*.

CHAPTER 4

Identifying
Moments of Truth

When the moments of truth go unmanaged, the quality of service regresses to mediocrity.

Karl Albrecht and Ron Zemke, *Service America*

As physicians, we all want to be judged on the quality of the care we offer. The fact is, patients' opinions of us are strongly influenced by such variables as courtesy, attention to detail, and reliability. That is why "moments of truth"—those brief interactions that have relatively little to do with medicine but a lot to do with satisfying patients—are so important. During those moments patients form positive, negative, or neutral impressions about a physician or practice. Once made, those impressions are difficult to change.

CREATE A PATIENT CYCLE

You can identify moments of truth for your practice by doing a "contact analysis" of each interaction between a patient and the practice.

In my practice we created a patient service cycle (see Figure 4–1). We tracked a typical patient from the moment the person called to make an appointment through paying the bill and leaving the office. The cycle does not end there. It begins again when the patient reenters the cycle or, better yet, tells a friend or family member, who then enters the cycle.

We assigned each staff member one segment of this cycle, such as the telephone, the reception area, the examination room, or the business office. Each staff member then identified all positive and negative interactions that occurred in his or her segment.

33

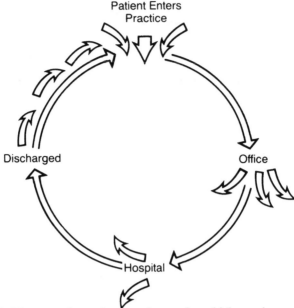

Figure 4–1 Diagram of a patient service cycle, which can be used to identify moments of truth. *Source:* Adapted from *Service America* by K. Albrecht and R. Zemke, © Karl Albrecht, 1985.

WHAT TO WATCH FOR

Several situations warrant careful attention. Phone contact with your practice is one of the most critical areas. All day, new and returning patients call your office to make appointments. How does your receptionist or appointment secretary handle this moment of truth, which is often the patient's first contact with your practice? Is he or she abrupt or impolite? Does he or she put the patient on hold for several minutes? Any discourtesy can create a negative impression of your practice. If the patient's perception is negative, that moment of truth may make the patient hesitant about visiting your office. The result may be a needlessly anxious patient.

Picture the opposite scenario: The receptionist answers the phone and enthusiastically identifies him- or herself. The receptionist uses the caller's name and is pleasant and enthusiastic throughout the conversation. This creates a positive moment of truth. Most likely, the patient will approach the office visit very positively. And certainly the patient's anxiety level will be reduced. More ways to enhance telephone etiquette in your office are discussed in Chapters 32 and 43.

Moments of truth are not restricted to making appointments and telephone calls. For instance, you need to examine how staff members settle patients' bills. Do you need to reduce the time it takes to complete patient information forms? At my practice, my staff and I decided that refilling prescriptions was a moment of truth that we were not managing successfully. So, we streamlined our procedures by recording the telephone number of the patient's pharmacy in his or her chart (see Chapter 5), thus reducing the time it takes to contact the pharmacy. We also thanked patients who refilled their prescriptions during the week rather than the weekend. This was a positive reinforcement of our request that they refill prescriptions during office hours.

Patients will have a positive experience even before they come to your practice if your staff members send a "Welcome to the Practice" package prior to their first visit. This package might contain the practice brochure, a newsletter, a map, as well as patient education material about the patient's stated medical problem or complaint. (In Chapter 43, I discuss effective use of computerized patient education material.)

Another moment of truth is the bottleneck that can develop when patients have to fill out forms and questionnaires in the reception area. You can avoid this by sending the forms to the patient ahead of time so that the form can be completed at home.

Obtaining authorizations for patients to be seen by the physician can also create delays. Most of us have had patients kept waiting an inordinate amount of time while someone in the office contacts an insurance company or primary care physician to obtain an authorization. This should be the patient's responsibility and that fact should be clearly explained in the "Welcome to the Practice" package (see sample letter in Chapter 13). When contacting patients prior to their visits, your appointment secretary or receptionist can remind patients of the necessity of obtaining the authorization prior to their visit.

The authorization issue has developed because of the incursions of managed care. In this environment, you will want your patients to report their positive experience to both their managed care plans and their employers, who are paying the bill. Managed care plans often survey members, asking about their experiences with the providers and their staffs. Practices that do not provide easy access, that keep patients waiting, that treat authorizations as a "burden," and whose staffs are unfriendly risk being dropped from the plan. This can mean the loss of hundreds and sometimes thousands of patients who will not be allowed to use your services.

DON'T FORGET THE HOSPITAL AND OUTSIDE TESTING FACILITIES

Examine the moments of truth that occur when your patients have to deal with the hospital (see Figure 4–2). At my practice, patients told us that when they are sent for x-rays or to the lab, they found no reading materials to help them pass time. We solved this by sending them out our door with reading materials, making sure that the materials were appropriate to their medical conditions.

When you send patients for testing or scans, a list of "tips" about the procedure would be most welcome, especially if they have not undergone such testing before. For example, until all hospitals and imaging centers have the newer "open" machines, the following might be helpful to patients about to undergo a CT or MRI scan:

Be prepared to lie on a table that slides into a large cylinder. If you have trouble with claustrophobia, let the imaging center know this before-

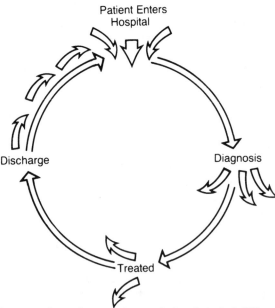

Figure 4–2 Diagram of a patient service cycle in a hospital. When the patient is referred to the hospital for tests or procedures, a negative moment of truth can adversely affect your practice's image. This cycle can identify those moments and help you correct them. *Source:* Adapted from *Service America* by K. Albrecht and R. Zemke, © Karl Albrecht, 1985.

hand. They can usually prescribe a mild sedative to help you relax. Another way to deal with close quarters is to have a washcloth or towel on hand and put that over your eyes. Keeping your eyes closed will also help you relax. Remember that you will not be able to wear any jewelry or metal during this test, so it is best to leave these items at home.

Your hospital may help you with the task of defining the moments of truth outside your practice, and it will most likely be interested in your findings. (In Chapter 40 we will provide you with additional examples of how to help make your hospital your marketing ally and how to work with hospital staff and administrators to manage the moments of truth for your patients.)

OTHER METHODS OF DISCOVERY

Other methods of identifying moments of truth include patient surveys that can be either mailed to the patients or filled out while the patients are in the office (see Chapter 1). A suggestion box placed in the reception area often will uncover areas that need improvement.

As mentioned in Chapter 2, hospitals and other health care providers have begun to use mystery shoppers, who record their moment-of-truth experiences and help define service cycles (see Chapter 2). I have used this method quite successfully in my practice. You can also ask family and friends how they are treated when they call your office or what their impressions are when visiting the practice.

TURN NEGATIVES INTO POSITIVES

Once we identified our moments of truth, the entire staff reviewed them at the staff meetings. We first looked at the negative moments of truth and prioritized them, stressing the ones we felt needed immediate attention.

We then listed all the possible solutions to each problem and selected the approach that we would implement. We also tried to identify a way of measuring the results of the intended solution. Finally, we set a deadline for implementation.

Here is how we used this method of identifying the moments of truth to resolve the "Case of the Missing Papers." I frequently operate on patients at outpatient surgery centers. Our routine was to give patients their orders and consent forms in the office. We told them to bring their paperwork with them to the hospital on the morning of the procedure.

Over time, it became clear that some patients were forgetting to bring their paperwork. This delayed the procedure for 30 to 60 minutes. As a result, patients and their families experienced additional anxiety. It also caused delays in the operating room schedule and in my office scheduling. We identified this as a negative moment of truth that urgently needed a solution. We decided the best way to resolve this problem was to have my nurse collect the patients' papers and take them to the outpatient facility once a week. This way, we could guarantee that the paperwork would not be lost or forgotten. Each patient was then simply contacted the day before and reminded of the time and place of the outpatient procedure.

A moment-of-truth analysis can be an invaluable method of learning about your practice. You can identify those contact points where patients feel positive about you and your practice. Once you identify your moments of truth, you can begin to manage them. In the realm of quality of service, you will be a cut above the rest.

The Bottom Line   *Patients do not care how much you know until you first show how much you care. You can show them how much you care by managing the moments of truth.*

CHAPTER 5

If Domino's Delivers, So Can We

He who gives great service gets great returns.

Elbert Hubbard, nineteenth-century American writer

Patients are no different from other people—they recognize good service when they see it. To find ways of going the extra mile for your patients, you have only to observe your own nonmedical experiences. In your daily life you are probably surrounded by excellent examples of outstanding customer service. You know when you have received good service from a hotel, a restaurant, your attorney, or your pharmaceutical representative. You can take many of these instances of good service and translate them to your medical practice.

LEARNING FROM DOMINO'S

Let me give you an example of finding an application of customer service that I incorporated into my office procedure. One evening I called the local Domino's to order a pizza. The woman who answered the phone at Domino's asked my name. I said, "Neil Baum." She then asked, "Are you Dr. Baum?" I thought perhaps that she was one of my patients and that she might reward me with a few extra mushrooms or pepperonis! Her next question was, "Do you still live at 123 State Street?" This question was followed by, "Last Sunday you ordered a 16-inch pizza with extra cheese and sausage. Will you be ordering the same thing or may I interest you in our special of the week?"

At this point I became very attentive to our conversation. I wondered how she could possibly know so much about me and my prior experience with Domino's. The answer, of course, was the store's computer system. She had access to all the company's transactions, which were stored in a databank. In the ensuing 10 years since that exchange, that technology has become commonplace. We have all become accustomed to being included in the databases of our service providers—from our car mechanic to the grocery stores. However, the concept is still not universally applied when it comes to medicine. People should be able to expect the same degree of attentiveness from their health care providers. The more we know about our patients' likes, dislikes, hobbies, families, work, and leisure, the more likely they are to feel that they are special and that we see them as complete people, not just as organ systems, diseases, or diagnoses.

Back then, I was so impressed by the "Domino's Method" that I tried to think of a way to use this technique in my practice. My office was computerized, but we did not have the hardware or the staff to duplicate their method. So, I devised a noncomputerized system to achieve the same effect. I created a half-page form to be placed in the front of each patient's chart under the demographic information (see Exhibit 5–1). *This form contains the following information:*

1. patient's name
2. patient's birth date
3. medical diagnoses
4. names of the patient's other physicians
5. patient's medications
6. date the prescriptions were last filled
7. name and telephone number of the patient's pharmacy
8. personal information
9. e-mail address

My staff and I fill in the appropriate information as it is obtained.

Using our "vital statistics" system, a conversation between my office nurse and Mrs. Smith, who wants her Feldene prescription refilled, might go like this: "Mrs. Smith, your last prescription was filled one month ago. Are you still using Walgreen's Pharmacy on Main Street? I know their number. I will check with Dr. Baum and call the prescription in for you.... Isn't next week your birthday? I hope you have a nice day.... How's your new granddaughter? Please call us if there is anything else we can do for you, Mrs. Smith. Good-bye."

Since my office has been using this system, the response from our patients has been excellent. The staff is also very positive about this project—they enjoy the feedback they get from the patients.

HOW PERSONAL INFORMATION NOTES ARE USED

There is no better way to let your patients know that you care about their total well-being than to keep and use personal information notes.

Exhibit 5–1 Vital Statistics Form

Name _____

Date of Birth _____

Physicians _____

_____

_____

_____

Pharmacy # _____

Allergies _____

_____

_____

_____

Diagnosis_____

_____

_____

Medications _____ Date: _____

_____ Date: _____

_____ Date: _____

_____ Date: _____

_____ Date: _____

Other Health Care Providers _____

_____

Personal Information _____

_____

_____

_____

You cannot treat patients as if they were machines or just organs, cardiovascular systems, or GI tracts and expect them to come back to your practice. And yet, sometimes, when I am in a hurry and launch immediately into a patient's medical problem, I find myself feeling almost like an auto mechanic who asks, "What's wrong with your car?" When I do that, I shortchange the patient. In addition, I miss out on much of the enjoyment of being a physician. And let's face it, that enjoyment is part of the reason we became physicians in the first place. Contrary to our bad press, we do not do what we do just for the money. Doctors could work the same amount of hours as financial analysts, stockbrokers, or insurance salespeople and earn just as much money. There are other attractions to practicing medicine—the satisfaction, the gratification, what I call the "warm fuzzies" that let you know you are doing a good job.

Many patients will share feelings and inner thoughts with their physicians that they would not share with friends or even their spouses. To hurry into a patient's complaints before showing that you are interested in the patient is to miss out on one of medicine's greatest experiences.

And, if you do not engage them in conversation, your patients may feel that you perceive them as sets of symptoms and not whole people. One of the best ways to lay the groundwork and make your patients feel comfortable is to develop the habit of discussing nonmedical topics in the first 30 to 60 seconds of each patient visit. My rule of thumb for new patients is to spend at least two minutes talking about nonmedical topics before launching into a discussion of their chief complaint. The best way to make patients feel comfortable is to show an interest in them beyond your interest in their medical problems or symptoms.

I happen to be an extrovert and I am curious about people, so asking questions comes naturally to me. If you are not a born conversationalist, there are still lots of ways for you to engage your patients in conversation and thus glean interesting facts about them. Then you can find some common ground. Patients will feel more rapport with you if they can find common areas of interest. That puts you and the patients on an equal footing and makes them feel comfortable in your presence.

If you are interested in honing your conversational skills, I recommend the book *How To Work a Room*.[1]

I use a variety of ice breakers to begin a conversation. I start with the handshake. If a person has a strong handshake or appears trim, I make a comment such as, "Wow, you have a really firm grip. Do you lift weights?" "Are you a jogger?"

I might ask about the patient's hobbies. If I know someone who shares one of the hobbies the patient lists, I will mention that fact. If the patient is a child, I might ask if he or she saw the recent *Star Wars* episode or other current children's movie releases.

I look at the patient's address on the chart. Perhaps I know someone in his or her neighborhood. I look at the patient's occupation. In the case of patients who are retired, I ask how they are enjoying their retirement or what they are doing in their spare time. I ask about their previous occupation or about their grandchildren. (You can never go wrong inquiring about grandchildren!)

You cannot possibly remember all the details you gather about your patients' lives unless they are friends or have been patients for many years. Make sure that you and your staff write these details down in the personal information notes portion of the vital statistics form. Do not leave anything out, no matter how trivial it seems. During or after the visit, I record notes about my patients' families, hobbies, work, vacations, and, of course, their children.

We keep these notes in each patient's chart, and I quickly review the information before I walk into the examining room. I ask the patient a few questions based on what I have read on the vital statistics sheet. Interestingly enough, I have never had a patient notice that my questions are derived from these notes! Even if they did, I cannot imagine anyone objecting that I show enough interest in their non-medical history to write it down.

I also refer to the personal information notes when I speak to a patient on the phone, and I ask my staff to do the same. For example, we use the notes when making appointments for patients or refilling prescriptions.

My patients really appreciate my interest in them. I have also found the ice-breaker approach useful when I see new patients, who are frequently anxious or nervous about their first visit. When I ask about a patient's work or family, I can feel the patient relax. I frequently hear a sigh of relief, which is a signal that I can proceed with the medical history.

My staff and I have learned to value the personal information notes. They provide a wonderful way to let our patients know that we care more about them than their diagnoses, medications, and internal organs. And because our patients know we care, they pass the word along.

LESSONS LEARNED FROM THE CONTAINER STORE

Examples of excellent customer service are everywhere and you can apply what you see to your own practice. For example, I visited the Container Store in Austin, Texas. I was looking for computer cable covers for my daughter's computer. I asked a clerk who was stocking the shelves where I might find the cable covers. The clerk asked, "May I show you where they are located?" She took me to the section where I found the tubes and then she walked me to each area of the store to locate the remainder of the items on my "to do" list. This was a WOW experience for me. It is no wonder that this is one of America's most successful retail chains, because it has employees who delight in helping customers solve problems and who are given the freedom and confidence to do so.

At my office, we decided to learn from the Container Store and provide every employee the freedom and confidence to do whatever is right and in the best interest of the patients. Now when a patient or a visitor asks a staff member, "How do I find Dr. Halsted's office?" the employee will often walk the person to that office. This is just one way of spreading the news that our practice is user-friendly and service-oriented.

The Bottom Line   *If Domino's makes the most of delivering pizzas, then certainly we in the medical profession can maximize service by delivering the highest* *quality health care. Pinpoint the techniques that work in other businesses and translate them to your practice. The results will almost certainly be a pleasant surprise.*

NOTE

1. Susan Roane, *How To Work a Room* (New York: Warner Books, 1988).

ADDITIONAL RESOURCES

- Leonard L. Berry, *Discovering the Soul of Service* (New York: Free Press, 1998).
- Kevin Frieberg and Jackie Frieberg, *NUTS! Southwest Airlines' Crazy Recipe for Business and Personal Success* (Austin, Texas: Bard Press, 1996).
- Robert Spector and Patrick D. McCarthy, *The Nordstrom Way* (New York: Wiley, 1995).

CHAPTER 6

Your Reception Area Is Your Opportunity To Create a Good First Impression

Perfection is not attainable. But if we chase perfection, we can catch excellence.

Vince Lombardi, Coach, Green Bay Packers

When your patients hear the words *waiting room,* what do they picture? Do they think of long delays, of being bored or anxious in a haphazardly arranged room? Do they think of losing valuable work time or money?

Put yourself in your patients' shoes. While waiting to see your physician, you most likely feel worried about something—otherwise you probably would not have made the appointment. You may be in pain and you are probably fearing the worst about your symptoms.

How you organize your office reception area can do a lot to allay your patients' doubts and fears. Your aim should be to make your patients feel relaxed and comfortable. After the initial telephone call, your reception area is a patient's first contact with you and your practice.

Patients often form judgments about the physician and the entire practice the moment they walk through the front door. By understanding that your reception area is an important part of the image you present, you can use it to give patients a warm, positive feeling. Remember, you do not get a second chance to make a first impression.

Wouldn't it be nice if your reception area made a positive first impression? In this chapter, I provide 25 suggestions that you can implement easily and inexpensively to improve your reception area and the image that you present.

At the end of this chapter, I have listed resources that can be helpful in redesigning your office space. Exhibit 6–1 contains a checklist you can use to evaluate your present reception area. The best way to begin your survey is to walk into your

45

Exhibit 6–1 Reception Area Evaluation Checklist

You can photocopy this checklist or bring along a clipboard for making notes as you do your survey.

1. Enter your office as a patient would.
Is the suite number prominently displayed? Yes _____ No _____
Is the door easy to open? Yes _____ No _____
Is the path to the reception desk apparent? Yes _____ No _____
Is the office wheelchair-accessible? Yes _____ No _____

2. Still pretending you are a patient, walk up to the reception desk to notify the staff of your presence.
Is it clear how patients should sign in? Yes _____ No _____

3. Once you have signed in, turn around and look at the reception area itself.
Does the room appear cluttered? Yes _____ No _____
Comfortable? Yes _____ No _____
Is it easy to find a seat? Yes _____ No _____

4. Imagine the receptionist has told you the wait will be about 15 minutes.
Are the available magazines current and nicely displayed?
Yes _____ No _____

5. As you sit down to read, notice whether music or video soundtracks are playing.
Is the volume acceptable? Yes _____ No _____

6. Notice the temperature in the room.
Is it too cool? Yes _____ No _____ Too warm? Yes _____ No _____

7. Are pleasant distractions offered? Yes _____ No _____

own reception area and ask yourself, "If the doctor were delayed, would I be comfortable waiting here for 30 to 45 minutes?" If the answer is no or even maybe, try implementing a few of the following suggestions.

AVOID NEGATIVE PERCEPTIONS

Do not call your reception area the "waiting room." To most patients, "waiting room" suggests the location where they cool their heels waiting for the doctor to get around to seeing them. It is no wonder, then, that most patients see waiting rooms as uncomfortable places. You can avoid any negative perception by using "reception room" or "reception area." The word *reception* conveys a whole different feeling than the word *waiting*. It is much more inviting. When you designate a room as the reception area, you are saying, "This is where we receive our patients. We provide them with pleasant distractions where they can relax and perhaps even enjoy themselves as we make every effort to see them in a timely fashion." A reception area is a place where patients can be comfortable, learn about your services, and be educated about their health. You would be surprised at the difference that using "reception area" instead of "waiting room" can make.

If you are currently designating the reception area as a waiting room, the name will need to be changed. This will require some effort from you and your staff. To help your staff remember, you can post a sign on the door leading from the inner office to the reception room. That way, staff members will see it when they open the door to get the next patient. Also, staff members should gently correct each other whenever the old name is used. Remember that people need ample time to change a habit. One study demonstrated this fascinating quirk of human nature.[1] A group of researchers took wastebaskets that had been on the left side of work desks and placed them on the right side. They found that most people continued to throw their wastepaper to the left for as long as three weeks thereafter. So do not expect everyone to be able to substitute the new name in a single day.

RECONFIGURE YOUR RECEPTION AREA

A list of resources to help you redesign your reception and office areas is provided at the end of the chapter. Short of hiring an interior designer, you can put the following suggestions into practice immediately.

Make your reception room into a living room. It should have the relaxed appearance of your living room at home. If space permits, try arranging the chairs (or couches) randomly rather than placing them along the perimeter of the room as in a bus or train station. Figures 6–1 and 6–2 should give you an idea of the difference between inviting and noninviting furniture arrangements.

Pay attention to lighting. The room will have a softer appearance if you light it with table lamps instead of overhead fluorescent light fixtures.

Provide attractive objects in the reception area. A patient's senses will be stimulated positively when there are attractive objects in the room. Many physicians have appreciated that an aquarium is a pleasant distraction for patients of all ages. People seem to relax when they sit and watch fish swimming in an aquarium. Keep in mind, though, that an aquarium and potted plants require a significant amount of maintenance. The old dictum still holds true: Never go to a doctor who has dead plants or dead fish!

Display an arrangement of cut flowers. Fresh-cut flowers placed on a table in the reception area are not only pleasing, but they are also a low-maintenance dis-

Figure 6–1 An example of an inappropriate arrangement of furniture in a reception area.

traction. Most florists have delivery services and will provide a nice arrangement every Monday that will usually last until the end of the week. However, make sure one staff person is responsible for checking the arrangement and discarding yel-

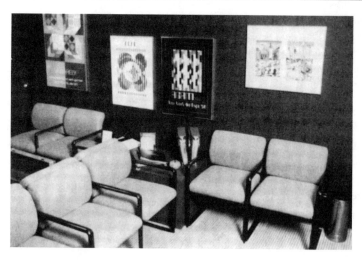

Figure 6–2 An example of a pleasing arrangement of furniture in a reception area.

lowing or brown flowers. The florist can also provide attractive floral settings keyed to the colors and plants associated with various holidays, such as Valentine's Day, the Fourth of July, Thanksgiving, Hanukkah, and Christmas.

Get rid of the "doctor's office smell." Many offices have those familiar and unpleasant medicinal smells. An attractive bowl of potpourri provides a pleasant aroma. The smell creates a nice atmosphere and avoids the negative effect of unpleasant odors. The potpourri aroma can be enhanced with special scented drops when the fragrance diminishes. Bowls of potpourri can also be used in the restrooms and the examination rooms for the same purpose.

PROVIDE DISTRACTIONS

Provide easy and entertaining puzzles. Your patients will feel more relaxed if they have something to look at or do in the reception area. I provide games and puzzles in varying degrees of difficulty, from finger puzzles to Rubic's cubes.

Bring in examples of your collections. If you are comfortable with the idea, why not display memorabilia or artifacts from your hobbies or recreational activities? This shows your patients that you have other interests. For example, you might mount your stamp collection in picture frames and hang the frames along the wall. If you are an ophthalmologist, you might consider a wall arrangement containing antique eyeglasses.

Of course, you need to be conscious of your patient base when deciding which collections to display. If you are a pediatrician, small items in glass cases would not be appropriate. You also need to take some care in choosing the displays and their location. Be mindful of the traffic patterns that such displays would create.

One San Francisco dentist, Tom Kuhn, DDS, who is a yo-yo champion and designer of custom yo-yos, displays antique and uniquely painted yo-yos in a glass case along the side wall of his office reception area, located in a remodeled Victorian house. This makes for a great conversation piece, and if Dr. Kuhn has time between patients, he has been known to delight people with a demonstration!

Play soothing music. Pleasant auditory distraction is easy to accomplish with one of the "easy listening" or "smooth jazz" stations that are popular in most metropolitan areas. You can also purchase a compact disk player that accepts five or six disks and plays them in a random or prerecorded fashion. Record companies such as Windham Hill Records distribute especially pleasing albums of guitar and piano jazz, as well as composite sound tracks of forest or rainfall sounds. Windham Hill Records can be reached toll-free at 1-888-64-WHILL and maintains a website at *www.windham.com.*

If you have teenagers among your patients, you can provide them with portable radios or cassette players (with headphones, of course, so they do not distract others in the reception area).

Consider using the reception area as a screening room. The TV can be used to promote you and your practice. If you have been on TV or have had a seminar videotaped, you can play the tape periodically on the TV in the reception room. There are companies that will install a television with a video CD player so that patients can watch short programs—interspersed with advertisements—about nutrition, parenting, exercise, heart disease, and stress management. Sponsored by pharmaceutical companies, these programs are produced by Cable News Network (CNN) and are free to physician offices.

Probably the most popular is AccentHealth. Produced by CNN's Emmy Award-winning health unit, AccentHealth programs focus on healthy lifestyles. Your patients will be exposed to a variety of topics, such as nutrition, coping with colds and flu, and preparing healthy snacks for kids. Health trivia questions keep them enlightened and entertained. AccentHealth can be reached toll-free at 1-800-791-8756 and maintains a website at *www.cnn.com/accenthealth.*

The fully integrated system using tapes on a loop requires no set-up time by you or your staff. AccentHealth supplies the video CD player, the television monitor, complete installation of the system, plus maintenance and service. A new program containing the latest developments in health and medicine is installed each month and the system turns on and off automatically according to your office hours. AccentHealth is available to primary care physicians, pediatricians, and obstetrician-gynecologists. In order to qualify for the program, you must have a practice with two or more full-time physicians and see a minimum of 250 patients per week. The average patient wait time must be less than 60 minutes, and patient visits must occur infrequently throughout the month, so that they do not see the same program more than once.

Results from a national survey of patients who watch AccentHealth programming revealed that 96 percent reported that having such a system in the reception area made the time go more quickly. Nearly 100 percent said that the programming provided useful, health-related information. This kind of program clearly demonstrates that your reception area shows that you are concerned about your patients' overall health and satisfaction. It provides value-added health information that patients genuinely appreciate.

I have some words of caution about using a television in your reception area. If you are not careful about volume levels, the television can actually become an irritant to some patients. I think it is best to place the TV in a corner of the room (or an alcove or separate room, if you have one) so that no one is forced to look at or listen to it.

PROVIDE A VARIETY OF READING MATERIALS

Subscribe to health-related magazines. Most medical offices provide magazines such as *Time, Newsweek, Reader's Digest, People,* and *National Geographic.* Today's patients are very interested in their health and more knowledgeable about health and wellness than ever before. You can encourage this trend by providing them with health-related magazines and periodicals. Since I started providing health-related reading material in the reception area, most of my patients prefer reading the health magazines to the conventional publications. The following is a suggested list of national health magazines, including subscription information:

- *Health,* a bimonthly magazine published by Times Publishing Ventures of San Francisco, CA, deals with health and medical issues, with special departments on food, family, sports, drugs, and the mind. Call 1-800-274-2522 for subscription information. E-mail: *editors@health.com.*
- *Men's Health* carries articles with a "male" slant about physical and emotional health issues. It is published quarterly by Rodale Press and is worth subscribing to if you have a large number of male patients. Call 1-800-666-2303 for subscription information; they also maintain a website at *www.menshealth.com.*
- *Shape,* published by Weider Publishing, is a monthly magazine about women's health and fitness issues. Call 1-815-734-6309 for subscription information; they also maintain a website at *www.shapemag.com.*
- *Fit,* published by the Goodman Media Group, offers fitness tips and inspirational stories; call 1-800-877-5366 for subscription information.
- *Natural Health, The Guide to Well-Being,* is published bimonthly by Weider Publishing, the publishers of *Shape*; call 1-800-526-8440 for subscription information.
- *Psychology Today,* published by Sussex Publishers, can also make for engrossing reading; call 1-800-234-8361 for subscription information.
- *Parents,* published by USA Publishing, offers readable and helpful articles for families with children; 1-800-727-3682.

Provide a few health or medical newsletters. Newsletters are designed to be read quickly and easily. Providing these kinds of reading materials also reinforces your concern for your patients' health. One of the best-known and best-written newsletters is the *Mayo Clinic Health Letter* (1-800-333-9038; *www.mayohealth. org*). It contains timely articles about advances in disease treatment, diagnostic technology, and general issues in medicine. A more radical approach to food safety and nutritional guidelines is presented in *Nutrition Action,* a health letter published by the Center for Science in the Public Interest in Washington, DC (1-202-667-7483). Another newsletter that is appreciated by patients interested in nutrition and wellness is *Dr. Andrew Weil's Self Healing—Creating Natural Health for Your Body and Mind* (1-800-523-3296; *www.drweil.com*).

Assemble your own medical notebook. You may want to inform your patients of a particular area of interest in your practice or within your specialty by providing reading material on this subject in the reception room. For example, I am interested in infertility, impotence, and incontinence. Those in orthopaedics often have an interest in sports, while pediatricians are necessarily concerned with parenting issues. You can clip newspaper and magazine articles relating to these interests and place them in a notebook in plastic protective covers with the subject matter clearly written on the outside of the notebook. To avoid patients taking these sheets, we place a note on the binder offering to make copies of articles for the patients. Since I started collecting these articles, I have noticed that not only are my staff on the lookout for these articles but patients also will bring or send in pertinent articles on these specific subjects.

Assemble a notebook containing general medical information. Subjects such as wellness, nutrition, sports medicine, sexually transmitted diseases, cancer prevention, and smoking cessation are of interest to nearly all patients. You can provide another notebook with general medical information. Almost all magazines and newspapers now contain several health-related articles.

Do not forget to supply daily newspapers. In addition to the regular reading material, you can provide your patients with a copy of the daily local newspaper. Depending on the demographics and socioeconomics of patients in your practice, you might consider other daily newspapers such as *USA Today* or the *Wall Street Journal*.

Find unusual reading material. For instance, try adding reproductions of the old Sears and Roebuck catalogue to your library of reading material, especially if you have elderly patients. It is amazing how many of my patients enjoy looking at these. The 1908 version of the catalogue is available in reprint (see "Additional Resources" at the end of this chapter). This is just one example of unusual yet interesting reading material. You or your staff may discover others.

GUIDE YOUR PATIENTS TO INTERNET SITES

Steer patients through the Internet. The number of patients with Internet access continues to climb, and patients are increasingly seeking health and medical information on the Internet. You can help your patients read valid and appropriate medical information by making copies of useful and accurate articles found on the Internet. I download material that I think is accurate as well as useful and then place these pages in plastic cover sheets and insert them into topic-specific notebooks. I also place a note in the front of each book indicating that patients can get copies of any of the pages by asking the receptionist or nurse. In addition, if the website address is clearly displayed, this will encourage patients to visit that site as one that has been recommended by your office as having good content and useful information.

MORE ABOUT YOU AND YOUR STAFF

Put the spotlight on yourself. It is nice to display your diplomas on the wall so your patients can see your medical background. However, most offices do not provide a single area where you can display your credentials for all of your patients to see. That is why I suggest you provide a current curriculum vitae (CV) in the reception room. I also recommend that, in the notebook containing your CV, you list your continuing medical education courses. The patients not only want to know where you were yesterday but what you are doing today to stay current with the fast-paced changes that are occurring in medicine. It is also important that your staff be thoroughly familiar with your CV and continuing education courses so that they can answer patients' questions.

Introduce your staff. All new patients are interested in knowing about the doctor and his or her staff. I suggest that you provide a captioned picture of each staff member. The caption might include a description of the staff member's job and training as well as interesting nonmedical information about his or her family and hobbies. This information can be placed in a notebook in the reception area. These notebooks can help new patients identify you and your staff and feel more comfortable about you before the first meeting.

Put up a bulletin board. A reception room bulletin board can be an effective way to market your practice. On this bulletin board you can inform the patients of any talks, programs, or support groups that you are going to participate in or recently have participated in. It is also a means of informing your patients of your community or nonmedical involvement. The bulletin board can also tell about your staff and their accomplishments, hobbies, or interests. I also provide a joke for the day or a quotation on health, wellness, success, or motivation. Jokes and quotations are available in calendar form at most bookstores. Another suggestion is to place healthy and nutritious recipes on the bulletin board and offer to provide copies. These can be obtained from most women's magazines or from the dietitian in your hospital. This is also a good place to post your website and e-mail address.

Show patients your byline. Patients are impressed by articles written in local magazines and newspapers by or about their physician. Many patients enjoy seeing their physician's name in print, even if articles that appear in medical journals may be too technical for most readers. Such publications make patients feel that they are in the hands of an expert. If the articles appear in lay magazines or newspapers, then it is nice to provide copies of these articles for the patients.

Make use of your accolades—advertise the thank-yous. Almost all physicians receive glowing or complimentary letters from their patients. These are often discarded or placed in the patients' charts. Thank-you notes, placed in a nice scrapbook, can add favorably to the patients' perception of the physician and the office. According to local, state, and national medical societies (including the American Medical Association) that I have contacted, there is no problem with violating patient confidentiality if you are sure to obtain the patients' permission for placing letters or notes in your reception area scrapbook.

These "fan" letters can be especially helpful as a pre-introduction for new patients, who may be feeling rather anxious about being examined by a new doctor. If they happen to peruse your notebook containing glowing and complimentary notes from your previous satisfied patients, this could reduce the anxiety they might be feeling. They might say to themselves, "Wow, I am seeing an expert. If I have to go to the hospital, he'll take good care of me and he'll even come to see me on his day off. I am glad I chose this doctor." This book of thank-yous, which I title *The Warm Fuzzy Book,* is the most-read book in my reception area. Patients have asked me, "What do I have to do to get into that book?" My response is always the same: "All you have to do is write me a letter!" *The Warm Fuzzy Book* actually perpetuates itself.

OTHER TOUCHES

Always notify patients if there is a delay. If you are delayed, for whatever reason, it is a nice gesture for your office staff to tell waiting patients of the delay and give them an estimate of when you will be returning to the office. Patients should be given an opportunity to reschedule their appointments or to leave and come back when you are expected. If a patient elects to stay, ask your office staff to offer the patient and his or her family coffee, tea, or soft drinks. If you have a VCR in the office and there are children in the reception room, your staff should play an appropriate video for them until you return to the office. (See Chapter 3 for more tips on handling delays.)

Let patients make necessary phone calls. I think it is nice to provide your patients with a courtesy phone in the reception area. Ideally this should be a separate line from your business phones. You can block patients from making long distance calls by simply calling your telephone company and requesting this service, which usually comes with a small monthly charge (in my area BellSouth charges $4.50 a month).

Display your office mission statement. Many businesses and medical offices express their goals and purpose in a mission statement or pledge. Our office pledge was created by the staff. It states, "This office is committed to: (1) excellence, (2) the best health care for our patients, and (3) the persistent attention to little details because we think they make a big difference." This pledge is displayed in the reception room, the office, and in the employee lounge. I think a mission statement or pledge is important for the patients to see as soon as they enter the office. It informs the patients of what they can expect from the doctor and his or her staff, and it sets the tone for a productive relationship.

Provide a suggestion box. If you follow this recommendation, make sure you check the box daily and answer all comments, positive or negative, immediately. If you implement any of your patients' suggestions, be sure to let them know with a written thank-you note. You will be amazed at how some of your existing patients can improve the service that you deliver to all of your patients.

The Bottom Line   *Remember, the reception area is what your patients will see first when they enter your office. When you make the reception area a relaxed and comfortable place, you set the stage for a more pleasant doctor–patient relationship.*

NOTE

1. Maxwell Maliz, *Psychocybernetics* (Englewood Cliffs, N.J.: Prentice-Hall, 1960), 152–153.

ADDITIONAL RESOURCES

- The *1908 Sears Roebuck Catalogue* is still available through Lakeside Products, Chicago, Illinois, for $9.00 plus $1.99 for shipping and handling; call 1-800-777-4404.
- For information regarding the following sourcebooks, originally published by Medical Economics Books—*Designing and Building Your Professional Office*, 2d ed., and *Remodeling Your Professional Office*—call the current distributor at 1-800-MED-SHOP (1-800-633-7467) or contact them via their website at *www.medicalbookstore.com*.
- Another valuable sourcebook is Cynthia Leibrock with Susan Behar, *Beautiful Barrier-Free—A Visual Guide to Accessibility* (New York: Van Nostrand Reinhold, 1994).

CHAPTER 7

Improve Patient Compliance— Provide Medication Information

Every doctor has encountered the following scenario. You write a prescription for a patient. After taking one or two tablets, the patient develops an allergy or a serious side effect and has to discontinue the medication. The patient has spent $40 or more for that medication, but the pharmacy will not take it back or give a refund. So you write another prescription, and the patient has to pay more money. Just underneath the surface, or maybe right out front, that patient is seething, angry at you and the pharmaceutical industry.

The consequence of this series of events is terrible: The patient gets a negative impression of the pharmaceutical industry and the medical profession. Read this chapter and I guarantee this situation will not arise again.

Like most physicians, I have a cabinet full of samples from pharmaceutical representatives (drug reps). In the past I have used the samples for indigent patients, giving them a full two-week course of antibiotics if they cannot afford the medication.

I have developed a simple system for all patients that effectively uses sample medications and avoids the situation described above. First, I give all patients receiving a new prescription a two- to three-day supply of samples in addition to their prescription. I instruct my patients to use the samples first. If they have no unusual or allergic reactions, they should then fill the prescription. I also find it useful, when obtaining a culture and determining sensitivity, to provide samples until the sensitivity pattern has been revealed. This avoids the situation in which a patient buys a full prescription only to learn that the medication is not the best drug for the infection.

Next, patients are provided with instructions for taking the medications (see one example in Exhibit 7–1). The instructions inform the patients of the common, the less common, and even the rare side effects associated with the medications. Also included in this information sheet are precautions, such as avoiding alcohol and

Exhibit 7–1 Instructions for Taking Nitrofurantoin

Nitrofurantoin
(nye troe fyoor an' toyn)

BRAND NAMES: Furadantin, Macrobid, Macrodantin

WHY is this medicine prescribed?

Nitrofurantoin, an antibiotic, eliminates bacteria that cause urinary tract infections. Antibiotics will not work for colds, flu, or other viral infections.

This medication is sometimes prescribed for other uses; ask your doctor or pharmacist for more information.

HOW should this medicine be used?

Nitrofurantoin comes as a capsule and liquid to take by mouth. Nitrofurantoin usually is taken two or four times a day for at least 7 days. Shake the oral liquid well before each use to mix the medication evenly. Take it with a full glass of water and with meals. Follow the directions on your prescription label carefully, and ask your doctor or pharmacist to explain any part you do not understand. Take nitrofurantoin exactly as directed. Do not take more or less of it or take it more often than prescribed by your doctor.

What SPECIAL PRECAUTIONS should I follow?

Before taking nitrofurantoin,

- tell your doctor and pharmacist if you are allergic to nitrofurantoin or any other drugs.
- tell your doctor and pharmacist what prescription and nonprescription medications you are taking, especially antacids, antibiotics, benztropine (Cogentin), diphenhydramine (Benadryl), probenecid (Benemid), trihexyphenidyl (Artane), and vitamins.
- tell your doctor if you have anemia, kidney disease, lung disease, nerve damage, or glucose-6-phosphate dehydrogenase (G-6-PD) deficiency (an inherited blood disease).
- tell your doctor if you are pregnant, plan to become pregnant, or are breast-feeding. If you become pregnant while taking nitrofurantoin, call your doctor. Nitrofurantoin should not be taken by women in the last month of pregnancy.
- you should know that this drug may make you drowsy. Do not drive a car or operate machinery until you know how this drug affects you.

- remember that alcohol can add to the drowsiness caused by this drug.
- plan to avoid unnecessary or prolonged exposure to sunlight and to wear protective clothing, sunglasses, and sunscreen. Nitrofurantoin may make your skin sensitive to sunlight.

What should I do IF I FORGET to take a dose?

Take the missed dose as soon as you remember it. However, if it is almost time for the next dose, skip the missed dose and take any remaining doses for that day at evenly spaced intervals. Do not take a double dose to make up for a missed one.

What SIDE EFFECTS can this medicine cause?

Although side effects from nitrofurantoin are not common, they can occur. You urine may turn dark yellow or brown; this effect is harmless. Tell your doctor if any of these symptoms are severe or do not go away:

- upset stomach
- vomiting
- loss of appetite

If you experience any of the following symptoms, call your doctor immediately:

- difficulty breathing
- fever or chills
- chest pain
- persistent cough
- numbness, tingling, or pinprick sensation in the fingers and toes
- muscle weakness
- swelling of the lips or tongue
- skin rash

What STORAGE CONDITIONS are needed for this medicine?

Keep this medication in the container it came in, tightly closed, and out of reach of children. Store it at room temperature and away from excess heat and moisture (not in the bathroom). Throw away any medication that is outdated or no longer needed. Talk to your pharmacist about the proper disposal of your medication.

continues

Exhibit 7–1 continued

What OTHER INFORMATION should I know?

Keep all appointments with your doctor and the laboratory. Your doctor will order certain lab tests to check your response to nitrofurantoin.

If you have diabetes, use Clinistix or Tes-Tape instead of Clinitest to test your urine for sugar. Nitrofurantoin can cause Clinitest to show false results.

Do not let anyone else take your medication. Your prescription is probably not refillable.

If you still have symptoms of infection after you finish the nitrofurantoin, call your doctor.

This leaflet does not contain all the possible information about this drug. Your doctor or pharmacist can give you additional information to answer any questions you may have.

Adapted with permission from American Society of Health System Pharmacists (ASHP). *Medication Teaching Manual: The Guide to Patient Drug Information,* seventh edition. Bethesda, MD: ASHP; 1998, pages 651–2.

warnings about drug and food interactions. In addition to this sheet, we also fill out the form "A Dozen Questions To Help You Understand Your Medicines" (see Exhibit 7–2).

Since most physicians commonly prescribe from a group of perhaps 15 to 30 drugs the majority of the time, you can provide your patients with information on the most commonly asked questions about these medications by preparing a sheet on the most commonly prescribed drugs that you use or refer them to *The Pill Book* (see Additional Resources), which lists the precautions associated with hundreds of drugs.

When I write a prescription, I attach it to the front of the chart and hand it to my nurse. She then gives the patient the appropriate drug information sheet. While the patient is reading the drug interaction information, my nurse retrieves the samples from the sample closet. The nurse asks the patient if he or she has any questions about the medications and then writes in the chart that the patient received samples and the drug information form.

Let me give you an example of just how useful it is to have patients read such information before they leave the office. It is not possible for me to cover every side effect or drug interaction with each patient—there just isn't time. On one occasion I prescribed a quinolone antibiotic. The patient read the drug information that the nurse gave her, which mentions theophilline-containing medications as one of the contraindications of using quinolones. As it happened, this patient was using a theophilline inhaler for her chronic obstructive pulmonary disease. She mentioned this to the nurse, who told me, and I changed the prescription to another medication. This drug information prevented a patient leaving with a prescription that could have resulted in lethal levels of theophilline. By the way, I now ask every patient about theophilline before prescribing a quinolone!

Exhibit 7–2 A Dozen Questions To Help You Understand Your Medicines

1. What are the brand and generic names of the medicine?

Brand _____

Generic _____

*2. What is the medicine supposed to do?*_____

_____

3. How should I use the medicine?

by mouth?_____

in the eye or ear?_____

on the skin?_____ other?_____

how much?_____

how often?_____

for how long?_____

with meals? _____

4. What should I do if I miss a dose? _____

_____

5. When should I expect the medicine to begin to work?

_____

6. How will I know if the medicine is working?

_____

7. What should I do if the medicine doesn't seem to work?

_____

_____

*8. What side effects should I watch for?*_____

_____

_____

continues

Exhibit 7–2 continued

How long will they last? _____

_____

_____

What should I do if they occur? _____

How can I lessen the side effects? _____

_____

9. While using this medicine, should I avoid:

driving? ___ Yes ___ No

drinking alcohol? ___ Yes ___ No

eating certain foods? ___ Yes ___ No

taking certain medicines? ___ Yes ___ No

Are there any other precautions? _____

10. How should I store the medicine? _____

11. Can I get a refill? ___ Yes ___ No

When? _____

12. Are there special instructions about how to use the medicine?

_____

_____

We also give our patients a cost-comparison sheet of the drug prices at four or five pharmacies in the area. We circle the prescribed medications with a yellow highlighter pen. This allows patients to select a pharmacy close to the office or their residence where they can purchase the medications inexpensively. Often the drug companies will provide cost information regarding their particular medications at the various pharmacies. Table 7–1 is a sample cost comparison sheet of the type we give to our patients. We update this cost-comparison sheet annually.

You can also alert your patients to the Internet sources for ordering drug products, if they do not already know about them. Several are listed in the Internet Sources section at the end of this chapter. Your patients will appreciate the fact that you are searching out sources of the best bargains for them.

Table 7–1 Sample Cost Comparison Sheet

Drug	#	Castellon	C & G's	Winn Dixie	Rite Aid
Macrobid	30	39.20	42.06	47.06	57.98
Ditropan XL 5mg	30	53.00	55.55	70.56	90.69
Pyridium 200mg	30	31.15	34.36	32.84	42.98
Vibratabs 100mg	28	90.90	96.48	121.73	123.98
Cinobac 500mg	28	54.15	62.86	75.67	78.69
Cipro 250mg	28	85.30	90.15	104.07	117.69
Floxin 200mg	14	45.95	49.95	55.39	63.98
Floxin 400mg	14	57.00	56.45	69.08	77.69
Trovan 100mg	14	68.35	71.35	87.33	100.98
Trovan 200mg	14	83.80	83.25	105.36	121.98
Viagra 50mg	10	74.50	75.85	85.71	91.69
Bactrim DS	28	25.45	36.15	40.49	61.69
Noroxin 400mg	28	71.25	82.34	101.21	114.69

Finally, when I recommend a procedure or medication that requires self-injections or sterile technique or that is likely to produce significant side effects, I will contact the patient by telephone. I ask if the patient has had any problems or has any questions. I think this reassures the patient, and it allows me to troubleshoot any potential problems. (For details on calling patients at home, see Chapter 8.)

Another step to make prescribing easier is to have color-coded prescription pads printed. Medications in the same drug class can be printed on the same pad with a different color for each group. Then all you have to do is circle the medication and specify the number of tablets or pills and dosing instructions. You save time and reduce the number of prescription pads floating around your office. (Exhibit 7–3 is a sample of the prescription pad.)

Exhibit 7–3 Prescription Pad

NEIL H. BAUM, M.D.
SUIT 614
3525 PRYTANIA
NEW ORLEANS, LA 70115
(504) 891-8454

DEA # AB 8981703

NAME _____ AGE _____

ADDRESS _____ DATE _____

Rx

	DISP.:
CARDURA 1/2/4	Q.D.
HYTRIN 5mg	
DITROPAN XL 5/10	SIG. T
CASODEX 50mg	Q.D.
FLUTAMIDE 125mg	B.I.D.
PROSCAR 5mg	T.I.D.
FLOMAX .4mg	Q.I.D.
	P.R.N.
	H.S.

Refill _____ times PRN NR

_____ M.D.   _____ M.D.
Product Selection Permitted   Dispense As Written

Many offices now fax prescriptions to pharmacies, so that the prescription is ready when the patient arrives to pick it up. Pharmacies do not like this because patients spend less time in the store (and thus are less likely to buy other items), but your patients will certainly appreciate it.

Without exception, my patients appreciate my approach to using sample medications. If each step is recorded in the patient charts, this approach also provides medical-legal protection in case your patient experiences an adverse reaction to the medication.

In addition, if you use this approach, you will save your patients money. This method of using sample medications lets your patients know that you are aware of the spiraling cost of health care and that you are doing your part to keep down their expenses. Now that is a "spoonful of sugar" to help the medicine go down.

The Bottom Line *Your patients are likely to be knowledgeable about their diagnosis, evaluation, and medications. If you can provide them with additional information about their medications, as well as pricing, your services to your patients will be greatly appreciated.*

ADDITIONAL RESOURCES

- Leonard L. Berry, *Discovering the Soul of Service* (New York: Free Press, 1998).
- Lawrence Chilnick, *The Pill Book: The Illustrated Guide to the Most Prescribed Drugs in the United States*, 5th ed. (New York: Bantam Books, 1992).
- Sidney M. Wolfe, MD, ed., *Worst Pills, Best Pills: A Consumer's Guide to Avoiding Drug-Induced Death or Illness*) (Washington, DC: Public Citizen's Health Research Group, 1993).

INTERNET SOURCES

www.drugstore.com—This website allows on-line price comparisons of most major medications and lets customers order and have prescriptions mailed to them. Additional services include newsletters and patient advice, Rite-Aid refills on-line, and pharmacists who will answer your questions about your medications.

www.pharmacy.com—Although at press time the "pharmacy" was not open, the ability to order drugs on-line should be available by publication date. Additional services: creating your own web page and free e-mail.

www.planetrx.com—This website is a full-service on-line pharmacy devoted to health and wellness needs of patients.

www.rxlist.com—This is also a reliable site for good, accurate drug information.

CHAPTER 8

Marketing on 10 Minutes a Day

This is the first time a member of your profession has taken the time to call me at home and check on my condition. Undoubtedly it will foster a better relationship between you and me.

A letter from a patient after I had called him at home.

As I travel throughout the country, I frequently am asked about the best way to begin marketing a medical practice. If I had to pick one marketing idea that is the most effective, easiest to accomplish, and least expensive, it would be the practice of calling your key patients. By incorporating this technique into your daily routine, you actually can save time and endear yourself to your patients.

This chapter will help you identify the key patients in your practice, decide who should call the key patients and when, and discover the advantages of contacting them. There are few disadvantages to this technique, but I also present some dos and don'ts to help you sidestep possible pitfalls.

WHO ARE YOUR KEY PATIENTS?

Your lawyer, your accountant, or your wife's best friend are not among your key patients. Your key patients are the patients for whom you need to go that extra mile.

Key patients often need extra reassurance or follow-up. It has been a while since doctors admitted patients to the hospital for diagnostic studies. The practice used to be for those same doctors to visit patients the night before the procedures. They also did a history and a physical examination. They then did rounds after the procedures and saw the patients the next morning before discharge. Patients who remember those days still expect to see and hear from their physicians before and after certain procedures. Because you cannot always visit them in person, it is a nice gesture to call your patients before and after they have outpatient procedures.

There are several types of patients who should be treated as key patients. Key patients typically have questions about their health care and need extra reassurance. They require more time and attention than you are able to give during a routine office visit. Frequently they have questions about impending outpatient procedures that were not covered in the office. Also, because these procedures are scheduled weeks, even months, in advance, occasionally patients forget about them. Telephoning them prevents "no-shows."

Who Comprises This Group of Key Patients?

Here are some examples of key patients I have identified in my practice:

- *Patients you have seen for outpatient procedures.* For example, if I do an outpatient IVP and cystoscopy requiring sedation, I call the patient at home after the sedation has worn off. Calling patients at this time significantly improves their understanding of the findings and recommendations.
- *Patients recently discharged from the hospital.* These patients usually have questions regarding medications, allowed activities, and follow-up appointments. Even the most careful discharge planning by hospital nurses will not answer all their questions.
- *Patients sent for diagnostic studies (for example, a CT scan to differentiate cyst from tumor).* I don't think these patients want to wait until their next appointment for the results. Certainly, if the tests are positive or suggest a hospital admission or surgery, you may want to discuss these results with the patient in person.
- *Patients who previously would have been admitted to the hospital but today are being managed as outpatients.* They always appreciate your calling them at home and feel reassured that you are concerned about their health and well-being.
- *Patients who are starting medications, such as insulin, which may have significant side effects if used improperly.* Calling these patients can both allay their apprehensions and allow you to gauge how the treatments are going.
- *Someone with high blood pressure whom you are monitoring.* You can call this patient and make sure that his or her blood pressure is being taken at home regularly. You will also be able to ask the patient about the medications and find out if there are any adverse side effects.
- *Someone new to your practice.* You can simply call this person and say, "I just wanted you to know it was really nice to meet you in the office. I want to make sure that I've answered all your questions."

- *Someone whose claim has been denied, perhaps due to improper coding.* (See Chapter 12, "Clean Up Your Claims and Create 'Practice Appeal.' ")

Based on the particular makeup of your practice and your specialty, you will be able to immediately add to this list. The most important step is to identify these patients and then act on the list by instituting a contact system.

WHO SHOULD CALL THE KEY PATIENTS?

Ideally, you should be the one to call the key patients, but this is not always possible. If you are unable to contact a key patient, have your nurse make the call. The nurse can triage the patient's questions and inform you if the patient has any he or she cannot answer. By having the nurse make the initial contacts, you will need to make fewer calls each evening.

WHAT TIME SHOULD YOU CALL KEY PATIENTS?

The evening is the best time to call. Most people are at home, and you are no longer pressured by your office schedule. You can avoid having to make repeated attempts to reach patients by having your staff inform the patients approximately what time you will be calling. The callback list (see Exhibit 8–1) prepared by my office staff takes, at most, 10 to 15 minutes each night to complete.

Exhibit 8–1 Callback Sheet for Key Patients

Date _____

	Patient	Phone #	Reason for Call	Notes
1.				
2.				
3.				
4.				
5.				
6.				
7.				

WHAT ARE THE ADVANTAGES?

When I first started calling my key patients, they were so astounded that they told their friends. Strangers would recognize my name and say, "Oh, you're Dr. Baum—the one who calls his patients at home!" Isn't that a nice image to have? The first advantage to this technique is the response of your patients. Few things you do will be as appreciated as your calls to patients at home. You can almost hear the patient saying, "I can't believe my doctor is taking the time to call me at home." When I mention this technique in my talks on marketing and ask other physicians about their experiences, they report that this practice always produces a positive response.

Second, calling your patients at home allows you to anticipate (1) problems that may require an office visit before the next scheduled appointment or (2) admission to the hospital if they are not doing as well as expected.

Finally, when you call your patients at home, you reduce the number of calls that you receive from your patients. If they know that you are going to be calling them, patients are less likely to interrupt you with their calls. Thus, if you spend just a few minutes each night calling your patients, you ultimately will have more time with your family and friends.

POSSIBLE DISADVANTAGES

Occasionally you will find yourself talking to a patient who does not want to end the conversation and who expects an entire 20-minute consultation on the telephone. In that situation, you need to cut the conversation short. With a little diplomacy, you can manage to extricate yourself. If this happens to you, it is helpful to say, "I know you need some more time. I'm going to ask you to make an appointment and come in to see me, because it sounds like there are some other issues we need to go over." This preserves the purpose of calling your key patients, which is to troubleshoot problems, not to give telephone consultations.

You may experience another possible pitfall if you are not careful about your choice of words over the telephone. Something in your greeting or tone of voice may cause the patient to wonder, "Is there something wrong? Why is my doctor calling me if it isn't to break some really bad news?"

You can easily avoid this problem by doing two things: (1) keeping your tone of voice lighter and (2) asking specific questions. Do not open the conversation with a general question, such as "Are there any problems?" Instead, keep your queries specific. For example, after I perform a vasectomy, I call the patient at home and might say something like this: "I'm calling to see how you are doing. Is the pain under control? Have you passed your water? Is the bleeding the size of a quarter?" Exhibit 8–2 provides a checklist for instituting this system.

Exhibit 8–2 Key Patient Checklist

When preparing to call your key patients, keep the following points in mind:

1. Identify the key patients using the criteria listed in this chapter.
2. Have your nurse triage the patients first and make a list of the ones you need to contact at home.
3. Keep your voice pleasant.
4. Ask specific questions, such as "Is the pain under control?" Avoid general questions, such as "Are you having any problems?"
5. Keep the conversation brief. If a patient seems to need more time, suggest scheduling an office visit for an extended consultation.

I do not think anything I do gives me more instant feedback and gratification than the responses I receive from calling my patients at home. Calling key patients gives you one of the best returns on your investment of marketing time. It is one of the most valuable methods of developing loyalty among your patients. The 10 minutes you spend calling are the 10 best minutes you can spend to market your practice. This simple but direct method will be appreciated by your patients and create a positive image of you and your practice.

The Bottom Line   *There is no better way to promote your practice than to contact your key patients at home. Give it a try. You will not be disappointed. Calling your key patients could be the key to unlocking your marketing success.*

CHAPTER 9

Different Strokes for Different Folks: Dealing with Demanding Patients

Those who enter to buy support me.
Those who come to flatter please me.
Those who complain teach me how I may please others so that more will come.
Only those hurt me who are displeased but do not complain.
They refuse me permission to correct my errors so that I may improve my service.

Marshall Field

I have a patient who had seen seven urologists before she came to our practice. She went to all those doctors not because her medical problem is so complicated but because her personality was too difficult for most physicians and their staffs to handle. This woman will call me or the nurse once, sometimes twice, a day. But she has been with our practice for five years now. Why? Because we have elected her the most important patient in our practice. We believe that if we can manage her—and she is tough—then we can take care of anyone.

I have told my staff, "If that woman ever leaves this practice, we are a failure." They are instructed to always return her calls, to treat her affectionately, and to make her feel important. I have done this for a purpose. If I can take care of the patients who are demanding and difficult, who take time and often take advantage, then I can take care of the rest. And it has paid off, in surprising ways.

The patient I am talking about is elderly and lives in a hotel. One day she called to say she needed her catheter changed. Her maid had the day off, so she could not easily come in to my office. I told my nurse to go to the woman's hotel and change the catheter, which she did. The patient was so impressed that she donated $1,000 in my honor to the local hospital!

69

A complaining patient is actually your practice's best friend, because he or she offers you an opportunity to provide better service. This chapter will give you some techniques for turning the negatives into positives.

MARKETING AND DIFFICULT PATIENTS

Most physicians who have been in private practice for a number of years can probably claim to have treated thousands of patients. Most patients are very pleased with the health care services that are provided. Yet there are usually a few patients who make life difficult. And those patients can continue to cause trouble even after they have left the practice: Statistics show that satisfied patients will tell three people of their experiences, whereas a dissatisfied patient will tell 20.[1]

I will never forget one of my female patients who had a neurogenic bladder. She was using disposable catheters for self-intermittent catheterization and called our office to obtain a box of disposable catheters. My nurse told her that we had the catheters and that she would bring the box of them out to the patient's car if she would call from her cell phone when she was in front of the building. The nurse also mentioned the cost of the catheters, according to our office policy to charge for durable medical goods. My nurse met the woman at her car and everything went as planned until my nurse asked for the payment. The patient said she had forgotten her checkbook, according to my nurse, so the nurse did not give her the catheters. The woman drove off in a huff, went home, and immediately called the office to ask that her records be transferred to another physician in the community. An apology from me and my nurse and even letters and a plant sent to her home as potential peace offerings did not deter her from leaving my practice.

But that is not the end of the story. The patient told her beautician about her horrible experience with my practice and how "greedy and avaricious" Dr. Baum was. The beautician told dozens of her clients—one of whom was my wife—about the usurious Dr. Baum. Talk about trouble and embarrassment! Here was a situation in which I had won the battle but clearly lost the war. If I had it to do over again, I would have given that patient free catheters for a lifetime if it would have prevented her telling so many people about her bad experience with my practice.

Needless to say, at the next staff meeting we discussed the fiasco and changed our policy for such situations. Now patients are still informed about paying for durable medical supplies, and we request the payment. But if they are unable to pay right at that moment, patients still receive the product. We simply bill them at a later date.

You may sometimes be tempted to avoid your difficult or complaining patients. Resist that urge. Give those patients your undivided attention and you will see tangible results.

Dealing with difficult patients is often as much a challenge as making a difficult diagnosis or performing delicate surgery. However, patients who complain but are then offered satisfactory solutions to their problems become steadfastly loyal. Difficult patients whose problems are successfully resolved will publicize their respect for you, your staff, and your hospital.

There are lots of techniques for dealing with difficult patients. I have found the following 12 steps useful.

1. *The first rule in dealing with a difficult patient is not to box yourself in.* Select a time when you are in a frame of mind to be a good listener. Make sure you will not be distracted when you speak to the patient. Do not try to tackle the patient's problems when you are tired or preoccupied. You cannot be an effective problem solver when you have other patient responsibilities. Dealing effectively with a difficult patient requires your undivided attention.

2. *When you talk with a difficult patient, do not try to downplay the seriousness of the complaints.* It is important that you allow the patient to vent his or her problems or complaints. The patient has probably spent 20 minutes or more thinking up a speech. You must allow the patient to get it all out, even if you know that the patient is wrong. Above all, once the patient has started talking, do not interrupt.

3. *After you have heard the story, apologize sincerely.* Right or wrong, the patient feels hurt. Now, it could be that the patient has misinterpreted the facts. However, an apology is invariably needed before the patient can move forward.

4. *Next, make an empathetic statement, such as "I'm sorry to hear you had this problem."* Let the patient know you understand the problem. For example, you might say, "I know you must be very disappointed with your care or service at my office." This kind of a response, coupled with your apology, tells the patient that you understand the problem and are sympathetic, and it allows the patient to become less defensive. Often this kind of response is all that the patient is seeking.

5. *The first step in resolving a difficulty is to establish rapport with the patient.* Make the jump from the facts involved in the situation to the human or emotional level. Let the patient know you are on the same side of the fence. Tell the patient that your only priority is to solve the problem. Explain that the patient's goodwill is important to you and that you will make every effort to solve the problem personally.

6. *Above all, do not be defensive.* Let the patient know that you are not in a confrontational stance. Remember, you are working with, not against, your patient. If you both work together, it is a win-win situation.

7. *Now you must take control of the situation.* You have listened to all that your patient had to say and you have apologized. Now assemble the facts and move toward a solution. Your solution must be based on facts and accurate information. Ask the patient additional questions. By doing this, you will be sending the message that you are interested in finding a solution.

8. *To develop a plan of action, start by asking the patient: "What would you like to see done?" "What could I do to solve the problem?" or "What do you think would be a fair or appropriate solution?"* For example, a patient was once upset when he received a bill for an assistant's fee for a surgical procedure. When I explained the necessity of having an assistant, he accepted my explanation and paid the bill. (I also learned from this experience to have my office manager explain to patients before surgery that they will receive such a bill—no surprises means fewer problems.) When both you and the patient work out a solution together, you can reach an effective conclusion much more easily and quickly.

9. *Many complaints involve money.* To maintain your patient's goodwill, you need to have a plan or philosophy to deal with these complaints. For example, when a patient complains about the bill for a visit that involved more than one medical problem, I usually offer to discount my fee for diagnosis of the second problem. Also, as I point out in Chapter 13, prior notice of your billing policies will go a long way toward avoiding billing disputes.

10. *Once you and the patient have accepted the plan of action, sell that plan.* Explain how your course of action will solve the problem. Speak only in positives. Do not say, "I can't get that lab report until Friday." Instead say, "I can assure you that I'll have that report on Friday."

11. *Depending on the magnitude of the problem, you or your staff should check to ensure that the plan has been carried out and the results are acceptable to the patient.* For example, if you requested that a colleague call the patient, contact the patient and check that this action was completed to the patient's satisfaction. Timely follow-up is vital. This indicates to the patient that you and your staff are sincerely concerned and have placed a high priority on finding a solution to the problem.

12. *Finally, document your interaction with the problem patient.* Do this on a separate piece of paper—one that does not necessarily have to become part

of the patient's records. These notes will be helpful if you cannot resolve the patient's problem successfully.

In today's competitive market, it is important to make every effort to encourage constructive criticism from patients. Complaining patients offer the greatest challenges and also the most rewarding opportunities. If you respond in a positive fashion and present discontented patients with acceptable solutions, you will convert your complainers into satisfied customers.

The Bottom Line   *When you elevate patient satisfaction that incorporates the most difficult patient, you have raised the bar, and all subsequent patients who are less demanding will be easier to please.*

NOTE

1. T. L. Aagaard, *Doctor to Doctor Workbook To Enhance Your Practice* (Kansas City, MO.: Midwest Medical Books, 1986), 4.

ADDITIONAL RESOURCES

- Bob Richards and Jeanan Yasiri, "Putting the Patient First," Englewood, CO: Medical Group Management Association, 1997.
- Jacob Weisberg, "Does Anybody Listen? Does Anybody Care?" Englewood, CO: Medical Group Management Association, 1994.

CHAPTER 10

Track Your Oldies and They Will Become Goodies

It is always great to attract new patients, but do not forget the additional sources of revenue that are sitting dormant in your practice right now. Develop an efficient patient recall system and the patients you already have whom you have not seen in a while will add new vigor to your practice. And that new vitality can ultimately stimulate the bottom line.

Patients are almost always given appointment cards to remind them about their scheduled checkups. Unfortunately, many patients forget about their checkups or lose the card and "fall through the cracks" of your practice. This chapter provides several methods to fill those cracks and catch the lost revenue.

Why have a recall system? First, it lets your existing patients know you are concerned about their health. A note, letter, or phone call not only serves as an effective reminder but also shows you care about your patients' continued well-being. Second, when you remind patients to return for follow-up or annual examinations, you retrieve an excellent source of income that otherwise would have been lost. Finally, a recall system is a medically and legally sound practice. We all are aware of the consequences when a patient with cancer is not contacted to return for a follow-up examination. Documented recall protects against such disasters.

Using a computer is probably the easiest method of generating a list of patients who require follow-up notification (see Chapter 43, "Let Technology Simplify Your Life," and the additional resources listed at the end of this chapter).

Before I had a computer, my office staff kept a list of patients who needed routine follow-up examinations. Typically, these were patients with cancer or progressive renal disease or patients on a regimen of chronic testosterone injections who required semiannual prostate examinations. We reviewed the list every three months. We checked the charts and identified the patients who needed a follow-up appointment. My staff then notified patients with a letter reminding them it was time to come in. We placed a copy of the letter in the patient's chart. If a patient did not respond to the letter, we contacted the patient by phone and documented the phone call in the chart. This "no frills" patient tracking system was functional but very time-consuming for my staff.

Another technique is to ask your hospital to provide a list of your patients with certain diagnoses or treatments. Its extensive database should make this request easy to fill. For example, you can request that your hospital supply you with all of the names of your patients admitted in the past five years with the diagnosis of diabetes. You can check the patients' office charts to be sure that they have had a referral to an ophthalmologist within the past year, or that they have had an office appointment to check their glycosalated hemoglobin level to ensure good control of their diabetes.

If your office is not fully computerized, or the computers are dedicated to other tasks, I suggest an inexpensive patient recall system that I call my "poor man's tickler file" system. Patients are asked to fill out postcards (see Exhibit 10–1) addressed to themselves. Each card is then filed in a box under the month and year the patient must return for an appointment. At the beginning of each month, the appropriate cards are mailed to remind the patients of their appointments. A list of the cards sent out is kept at the receptionist's desk, and all patients who call back for an appointment are checked off the list. Patients who do not call back are contacted by the receptionist. I have selected a unique design for our cards that fits my practice. Often dentists' cards have cartoons about teeth and cavities on them. Many other designs are available. You may want to key your recall postcards to your specialty or to something about your personality or hobby.

We now use a computerized patient tracking system created by American Medical Systems (see "Patient Tracker" under Additional Resources). This program allows for easy tracking of patients by date, diagnosis, medications, or any other field or topic that you select. For example, patients who were using injections or urethral suppositories of prostaglandin for the treatment of erectile dysfunction wanted to be notified when the new oral medication, sildenafil (Viagra), was approved by the Food and Drug Administration and available in the pharmacies. We used the tracking system and identified all those patients receiving injections or suppositories of prostaglandin, and sent them a personalized computer-generated letter informing them of the new drug and the necessity of making an appointment in order to obtain a prescription. This resulted in several hundred office visits from existing patients. Not a bad return on the investment for a few key strokes on the computer.

Having a recall system in place has proved invaluable in another way. It has allowed my staff and me to catch mistakes we might not have found. For example, one patient had an abnormal chest X-ray, but his report was inadvertently filed before someone called him back. We did not realize our mistake until his

Exhibit 10–1 Reminder Postcard Sent to Patients

Neil Baum, M.D.
Urology
3525 Prytania, Suite 614
New Orleans, LA 70115
Telephone (504) 891-8454

It's time again . . .
for your regular examination!
Please call today and we will
arrange an appointment for
you at your convenience.

postcard for a return visit came up in the tickler file. When we looked in his chart, we found the misfiled X-ray report, and called him immediately. Thank goodness for the recall system!

The Bottom Line   *Tracking is not only good marketing. It also makes for good medicine.*

ADDITIONAL RESOURCES:

- Postcards for patient recall can be ordered from Semantodonics/SmartPractice, 3400 E. McDowell Street, Phoenix, Arizona 85008; (800) 522-0800; *www.smartpractice.com.*
- Patient Tracker is available from American Medical Systems, 11001 Bren Road East, Minnetonka, Minnesota 55343; (800) 328-3881.

CHAPTER 11

Resurrecting Records: A Transfer Request Does Not Mean Good-Bye

Most physicians dislike receiving a form letter requesting that a patient's records be sent to another doctor. I am no different. Those requests usually remained on my desk for weeks waiting for me to dictate a summary and to photostat the pertinent lab, operative, pathology, and X-ray reports. But not any longer. After this happened several times, I decided to turn this negative event into a positive one by following these four steps.

1. *I contact the patient myself and ask why he or she is having the records transferred.* I have conducted several office surveys, but some of the best information I have obtained is from patients who intend to leave my practice. I have found them to be honest, sincere, and forthright in their responses when I call them directly. This is because I make it clear that I really want to know why they are leaving the practice.

   I would certainly want to know if a patient was leaving because of a rude employee or because he or she considered my fees too high. I want to be apprised of any lack of attention to detail on my part or on the part of my staff. I am also interested in my patients' opinions of the hospital I work with and its services.

   Not all reasons for leaving should be viewed as negatives. In many situations, patients request a transfer of records because they are moving to other areas of town or to other cities. Most commonly, patients are joining other health plans and need to have their records for their new doctors.

2. *Once I have discovered the patient's reasons for leaving, I send the records to the patient.* I learned this technique serendipitously. I do a lot of male infertility evaluations. Sometimes I have to tell a man his situation is hopeless for fathering a child and that he needs to consider either artificial insemination using donor sperm or adoption. Before consenting to these

two alternatives, most men want another opinion. I used to send the patient's records to the other urologist, and when that doctor told him the same news, the patient frequently would request yet another expert opinion. He would thus ask for his records to be sent to a third urologist. I learned I could cut my office staff's photocopying time considerably by sending the records directly to the patient.

Sending the records directly to the patient accomplishes two goals. First, it informs the patient that I have complied with the request. The patient can now make an appointment with the new doctor, who will have access to the records. Second, if the patient seeks additional opinions, he or she has the records and does not need my staff to spend time making additional copies.

3. *In addition to sending the records to the patient, I enclose a personal letter.* (See Exhibit 11–1.) This letter, which reinforces my phone call, explains that the patient is a valued client, that my staff and I harbor no ill will, and that the patient is welcome back in my practice at any time in the future if there should be a change of mind.

4. *Finally, I contact the patient by phone in a few weeks and inquire about his or her health.* This phone call, when the patient has sought another opinion, serves as a check on my medical judgment. It is always reassuring when the experts agree with you. And if the experts do not agree, you need to know that too. I believe this follow-up call is critical because it demonstrates that you have concern and compassion when the patient knows there could be no ulterior motive. I think this is the image of caring that we as physicians want the public to have of our profession.

Exhibit 11–1 Letter To Accompany Transfer of Patient's Records

---

Date

Dear [Patient],

At your request. I am sending you a copy of your complete medical records. It has been a pleasure to serve your medical needs over the past months, and I as well as my office staff will miss you. I wish you continued good health, and if I or my staff may ever again be of service to you, please do not hesitate to call.

Thank you for the confidence you have placed in my medical care.

Sincerely,

Neil Baum, MD

I have used this simple and effective strategy for several years. Taking a personal approach to an uncomfortable or potentially negative situation is helpful. I have also found that a significant number of patients have returned to my practice. I attribute this "return business" to my use of this strategy. I suggest you give it a try.

The Bottom Line   *Let patients know that you do not take it personally when they request a transfer of records. Foster an attitude that you can "still be friends" and you will be amazed at how many patients will return to your practice.*

CHAPTER 12

Clean Up Your Claims and Create "Practice Appeal"

Patricia T. Aalseth

Do your patients frequently call your office with questions about their insurance? Do your patients ever receive an explanation of benefits form from their insurance carrier indicating that your services were not "medically necessary"? Do your patients have questions about co-payments and co-insurance? If you answered "yes" to one or all of these questions, the information in this chapter will help make your practice "claims friendly."

More importantly, there will be no loss of rapport between you and your patients and you will be reimbursed more quickly. This chapter outlines steps you can take to ensure that you submit "clean claims" and detail how to tell your patients they can receive help with any insurance problems.

CODE IT RIGHT THE FIRST TIME

Coding is based on documentation in the patient's record, period. In today's regulatory environment your practice must make no exceptions to this rule. Dictating in real time, as mentioned in Chapter 3, will help ensure that you have accurately recorded the patient's condition and the services provided. Consider the use of dictation "reminders" or outlines that will jog your memory about key terms to include. (An outline for consultations is shown in Exhibit 12–1.) Insurance company reviewers will be able to read and interpret your reports more easily if the terminology you use matches that in the code book.

To help with correct coding, make sure that your pertinent office forms are in order. Have your staff complete an annual review of the forms used in your office.

Patricia T. Aalseth, RRA, CCS, CPHQ, is a medical practice specialist with University Physician Associates, 1650 University, NE, Suite 115, Albuquerque, NM 87102; (505) 272-3644.

Exhibit 12–1 Dictation Outline for Consultations

"This consultation was requested by: _____

(doctor's name and address)

for the following reason(s): _____."

History:

Chief complaint
History of present illness
Review of systems
Past / family / social history

Physical Exam:

General multisystem exam OR complete single-system exam
Multisystem exam:
Head/face
Eyes
Ears / nose/ mouth / throat
Neck
Cardiovascular
Chest / breasts / axilla
Respiratory
Gastrointestinal / abdomen
Genitourinary
Musculoskeletal / back
Extremities
Neurologic
Psychiatric
Hematologic / lymphatic / immunologic

Medical Decision-Making

Differential diagnoses
Management options
Data reviewed
Risks associated with diagnoses and/or management options

Counseling/Coordination of Care

"I spent __% of the ___-minute consultation discussing with the patient the

following: _____"

continues

Exhibit 12–1 continued

"My opinion / advice regarding this patient is: _____ "

"I have initiated the following: _____ "

"I have communicated with Dr. _____ about the patient via (check one below)."

Consultation results communicated via:

_____ Phone call with Dr._____ _____ (date)

_____ Fax sent to Dr._____ _____ (date)

_____ E-mail sent to Dr. _____ _____ (date)

_____ Letter sent to Dr. _____ _____ (date)

Focus on eliminating duplicate information, using current coding terminology, and presenting a professional appearance. Forms that have been photocopied over and over until they are lopsided and fuzzy look sloppy and prompt patients' thoughts about other areas where you might also be cutting corners in their health care. If you ask patients to complete forms, such as a personal history or review of systems, make sure the print is large enough for all age groups, and that adequate space is provided for thorough answers.

Nothing will prompt a claims rejection faster than the use of outdated diagnosis or procedure codes. The purchase of new editions of the *International Classification of Diseases* and *Current Procedural Terminology* each year is a must. See the "Additional Resources" list at the end of this chapter for more information on obtaining code books.

When you provide educational opportunities for your staff at staff meetings and through continuing education, as described in Chapters 30 and 31, make sure that coding and claims processing are included. See Chapter 45 for specific information about coding.

BEAT THE CLOCK

A late claim is a denied claim; some payers now have claims filing limits as short as 30 days. If you do not meet the payer's limit, you can be sure the claim will be denied and you will likely have no recourse for collecting your fee, which may make your patient responsible for the entire bill. Ask your staff to contact the major payers for patients in your practice and determine their filing limits. A wall

Exhibit 12–2 Sample of a Wall Chart for Claims Filing Limits

Payer	Filing Limit
Medicare	End of calendar year following year service is provided
Blue Cross/Blue Shield	90 days
HMO New York	60 days

Note: This is just an example. Payer claims limits vary from locale to locale, so have your staff fill in the appropriate filing date limits for your area.

chart listing this information is a good reminder for the office area where claims are prepared (see, for example, Exhibit 12–2).

THE RIGHT STUFF

"Clean" claims are not only submitted in a timely manner, they also contain all the "right stuff." This includes:

1. patient demographics: name, address, date of birth, gender
2. insurance information: group and plan numbers, insured's name and number, relationship of patient to the insured
3. occurrence information: if visit due to accident, pregnancy, previous illness
4. correctly coded diagnoses, procedures, and supplies
5. prior authorization numbers
6. provider ID, PIN number, etc.

GET PERMISSION, NOT FORGIVENESS

Prior authorization for many services is crucial to obtaining payment from managed care companies. Make sure your staff is familiar with which procedures need authorization from which payers. Set up a notebook or computerized listing containing a page for each payer and noting the procedures for which they require prior approval. If your practice includes surgery or patient visits at a hospital or surgical center, make sure your staff understands that prior approval must be obtained for services for which you provide and bill, regardless of the site of service.

Establish a standard procedure for handling prior authorizations, including:

1. making periodic contact with all major payers to obtain updated prior approval requirements

2. screening by the office person scheduling the visit or surgery to determine the need for prior approval
3. assigning responsibility for obtaining prior approvals to an office employee who has enough clinical knowledge to speak competently with the payer about the justification for the proposed service
4. instituting a prior approval form or stamp (see Exhibit 12–3) for patient record documentation
5. adding a field for this number to the office superbill or charge document
6. referring the case to you for further action if it is not approved

THE ERRORS OF OUR WAYS

Despite the best efforts of your staff, some claims will be denied. The first challenge is figuring out why! The remittance advice you receive from the payer will be filled with denial acronyms or alpha/numeric codes instead of plain English. In many cases, the explanations sent to the patient may be just as cryptic, so your staff and the patient will both be trying to figure out why reimbursement was denied.

Keeping a notebook with denial codes of the larger payers in your practice will enable your staff to converse knowledgeably with patients about what the problems are and how the staff will assist with an appeal, if appropriate. The provider manuals or monthly newsletters you receive from payers may contain lists of denial codes; for additional assistance, contact the payer's provider relations staff.

Exhibit 12–3 Stamp or Note for Documentation of Prior Authorization in Patient's Chart

[Date]

Contacted _____ [name of insurance company]
for prior authorization for _____ [name
of proposed procedure or service] for _____ [name of
insured patient].

Spoke with _____ [name of person
spoken to] who authorized_____[service
or alternate service, as appropriate] for_____
[proposed date or time period]. The authorization number is _____.

_____
[signature of staff]

Denials usually fall into a few major groups:

1. *Noneligible patient:* Make sure your staff keeps a photocopy of the patient's insurance ID card so they do not need to bother the patient with a phone call to verify insured or plan numbers. In some cases, this type of denial is due to computer glitches by the payer, so it is worthwhile calling to verify.

2. *Invalid diagnosis or procedure code:* Get those code books out and make sure you are using codes that were valid on the date of service, and coded to the greatest number of digits. (See Chapter 45 for more instructions.)

3. *Conflict between the procedure code and the site of service:* Make sure your inpatient services are coded using Evaluation and Management codes meant for inpatients, not outpatients.

4. *"Not medically necessary" service:* These denials are potentially the most destructive to the relationship you have carefully cultivated with your patients, because they may cause the patient to question your medical judgment. Educating patients ahead of time is your best defense in cases like this!

The following is a sample of a conversation your staff might have with a patient.

Patient: "Does your office bill the insurance company?"

Staff: "Yes, we do. Our experience with 'X' carrier is that sometimes we may have trouble with the first submission of a claim."

Patient: "What? I thought your office was an approved provider for 'X.'

Staff: "We definitely are, and Joyce, in our office, deals with their office all the time. If you receive any notice of claims denial, please call us right away, because we will be more than happy to deal with the insurance company for you."

Conversations such as this serve as an alert to patients that processing of claims may require additional time and that adversarial letters may appear. However, the conversation does reassure the patient that someone in the practice will serve as an advocate for the patient with the insurance company.

THE TRUTH AND NOTHING BUT THE TRUTH

Most patients still do not understand that insurance does not cover all services. You will be doing your patients a favor if you provide educational materials making this absolutely clear. Your office brochure (Chapter 16) outlines your payment and insurance policies, but additional printed information may be invaluable (Exhibit 12–4) to help your staff explain the following common insurance terms.

Deductible

- What is a deductible?
- How much is the deductible for this patient? (Use a fill-in blank.)
- What does this mean to the patient (that is, will he or she have to pay this amount out of his or her own pocket every year before the insurance starts paying)?

Co-Pay

- How much is the co-pay for this patient? (Use a fill-in blank.)
- When is the co-pay due?

Noncovered Services

- What services are almost always noncovered? (This is particularly important if your practice provides cosmetic or other elective services.)
- How does noncovered service affect payment?
- When is payment for noncovered services due?

"Not Medically Necessary" Services

- This does not mean the patient did not need the service, it means they did not fit the arbitrary criteria drawn up by the insurance company.

Patients appreciate receiving advance information, in terms they can understand, explaining how insurance works and why some claims are not paid. You will find they are more willing to pay their share if they understand why, rather than just being told "insurance does not pay for that." Practices that make the effort to inform their patients often receive comments such as "nobody ever took the time to explain that to me before" or "now I understand why I am paying this amount." Patient education of this type is part of the "extra mile" that will help you get new patients and keep the ones you have.

SQUEEZING THE TURNIP

Some of your patients will require additional assistance with their insurance claims. In particular, claims that have been denied as "not medically necessary" may be paid if you and your staff are willing to appeal them. This is a service your patients will truly appreciate because it shows that you believe in your work and are willing to stand up for it (and for them).

Exhibit 12–4 Patient Financial Education Form

Dear Patients:

Many of you have health insurance coverage. We would like to take this opportunity to provide you with information about what your policy includes and to explain some of the common terms used by insurers.

Deductible: The amount you must pay out of your own pocket each calendar year before the insurance starts paying its portion. Some policies have individual deductibles and/or family deductibles.

Example: If your policy has a $250 deductible, you must pay the first $250 worth of charges in the calendar year before the insurance starts paying.

Co-pay: The fixed amount your policy requires that you pay for various services, such as office visits, prescriptions, etc. The co-pays for some services are higher to prevent inappropriate utilization of services.

Example: If, instead of contacting your regular physician, you go to the emergency room (ER) for a sore throat, the ER co-pay will usually be much higher than it would have been for an office visit.

Coinsurance: The percentage of a covered charge that is your responsibility to pay after the insurance has paid its part.

Example: If your insurance pays 80 percent of a $100 office visit, you are responsible for the other 20 percent, or $20.00.

Medically necessary services: Most insurers have drawn up criteria to judge whether they think a service is "medically necessary" or not. This often means that each type of service is linked with a list of diagnoses for which that service has been deemed appropriate. If your diagnosis is not on the list, your claim for payment may be rejected. This does not mean that the service was inappropriate or unnecessary. In some cases, the claim may be approved once additional information has been provided to the insurer. Our staff will be glad to assist you should you receive denials of this type.

Noncovered services: Some services are never covered by your policy. When purchasing coverage, review the limitations of the policy to see what is missing. Most often, noncovered services include cosmetic procedures, custodial care (nursing home), dental procedures, and services or treatments deemed to be "experimental" or not yet accepted as a standard of care for certain conditions. Some policies do not cover services provided without a patient complaint, such as a routine physical exam on a healthy patient. Some services may be covered at a rate less than others, such as mental health at 50 percent instead of 80 percent.

Most of the legwork can be done by your staff: determining the reason for the denial; pulling the patient's record and making sure it was coded correctly; and providing you with a copy of the claim form and the relevant documentation, along with the patient's chart. A standard appeal letter format can be used, with spaces for: (1) a description of the denied service, (2) the reasons you feel it was necessary for the patient's well-being, and (3) references to the literature in terms of the service being generally accepted by the medical community for the condition being treated (see Exhibit 12–5).

Exhibit 12–5 Letter to Payer Appealing Noncoverage Determination

[Date]

Dr. [Name of Medical Director], Medical Director
[Name of Insurance Company]
[Address]
[Address]
re: [Patient name]
[Patient insurance ID #]
[Claim number and date of service]

Dear Dr. [Surname of Medical Director]:

I am writing on behalf of [patient name] to provide additional information regarding the treatment I provided on [date of service], for which your company did not approve payment.

This patient has [describe patient's condition and any extenuating circumstances which made the treatment necessary; include information about previous methods of treatment that have not been successful and the reasons you felt this method would be better].

I am enclosing articles from the [specialty] literature that describe the efficacy of [treatment] and recommend its use. I appreciate your taking the time to review these materials. I am sure you have, as I do, the patient's well-being as your first concern. We are hopeful you will authorize payment for this necessary treatment. I would be glad to discuss this case with you at your convenience should you have questions.

Sincerely,

[Your name, title]
[Specialty]
[Address]
[Address]
[phone / fax / e-mail]

Your appeal should be communicated to the medical director or medical advisor of the payer. Physician-to-physician communication is often effective in obtaining payment, as long as you make it clear why you did what you did.

DIALING FOR DOLLARS

When your office is notified by a payer that a claim is rejected, chances are the patient has heard about it first. You may want to include in your group of "key patients" (Chapter 8) those with rejected claims over a specified dollar amount. These patients need telephone follow-up for their financial health, just like other key patients who need concern about their physical health. I recommend that one staff member in your office receive extra training on insurance matters and that person make the initial calls to patients with rejected claims. Patients will be astonished that your staff is willing to help them make sense of the insurance nightmare. Should the appeal process result in a continued denial, the patient will at least feel that your office made an extra effort to help him or her obtain coverage.

Successful marketing means that patients have a positive experience with your practice even when it comes to paying for your services. You can be an outstanding physician, provide great medical services with a stellar staff, yet have a dissatisfied patient because an insurance company balks at paying your fees. You can increase patient satisfaction, reduce patient anxiety about your fees, and improve your bottom line if you make every effort to communicate with your patients about their payments and responsibilities.

The Bottom Line *Becoming a "claims-friendly" office when it comes to your patients' insurance claims will decrease patient stress, increase patient loyalty, and build excellent word of mouth for your practice.*

ADDITIONAL RESOURCES

Both CPT and ICD code books are available from the following sources:
- **American Medical Association (AMA)**
  1-800-621-8335 or *www.ama-assn.org/catalog*
- **Medicode/St. Anthony's**
  1-800-999-4600 or *www.medicode.com*
- **Channel Publishing**
  1-800-248-2882 or *www.channelpublishing.com*

CHAPTER 13

Leave a Paper Trail...
That Leads to
the Bottom Line

There's power in the pen, the pencil...and even the word processor.

A new patient calls your office for an appointment. The receptionist sets up the appointment and gets his or her telephone number. If your practice is like most practices, that is the only contact the new patient will have with your office until the confirmation call 24 hours before the appointment. But if the appointment secretary obtains the patient's address, then you can send a "welcome to the practice" letter. And if you do that, you will be starting the first appointment on the right foot.

Letters can be a gracious way to create and maintain good relations with your patients and colleagues. In my office we send letters all the time. We send letters to current patients thanking them for prompt payment, for referring a relative to the practice, or just to wish them happy birthday. We send letters to referring physicians thanking them for referrals and letting them know what treatment was given to their patients.

There are ways to make even a computerized form letter more personal. Several examples are provided in this chapter. By using effective letters and memos, you have the opportunity to create a good impression with your patients and referring physicians.

WELCOME TO THE PRACTICE

The welcome letter can be from the appointment secretary, the office manager, or even you. The letter should be warm, friendly, and informative. Do not mention payment in the letter because the patient is likely to assume that is the purpose of

90

the letter. (The payment policy should always be mentioned during the initial phone conversation with the new patient.)

You can include the office brochure, a copy of the recent newsletter (if you have one), and a map or directions to the office. You can also mention any instructions you want the patient to follow prior to the visit. For example, in my office we always request a urine specimen on the first visit. In our welcome letter, we suggest the patient drink fluids right before the appointment to make it easier to obtain a urine specimen. This avoids hearing the excuse, "I just voided," and the resultant longer office visit. Exhibit 13–1 is a sample welcome letter.

Exhibit 13–1 Sample Welcome Letter

September 13, 1999

Play Account
140 Gould Street
Harvey, LA 70058

Dear PLAY ACCOUNT:

We would like to take this opportunity to thank you for choosing our office for your urologic care and to welcome you to our office. We are pleased that you have chosen us to provide you with your medical services.

Enclosed is an information booklet to help answer any questions you may have regarding our office. We want you to know about our office procedures and what to expect at the time of your first visit. Please complete the enclosed patient forms and bring them with you on your appointment date along with your insurance cards, referral (if applicable), and co-payments and/or deductibles. We will be collecting a urine specimen, so we suggest you drink fluids right before your appointment to make it easier to obtain the specimen.

This letter will confirm your appointment on _____ at _____. If you are unable to keep this appointment, please call us as soon as possible and we will reschedule a more convenient time for you.

We look forward to seeing you and if you have any questions, please feel free to call the office.

Sincerely,

Receptionist
Enclosure

THANK YOU FOR CONSULTING US

This letter should come from you and not your staff (see Exhibit 13–2). Send it to follow up after a patient's first visit to your office. Let the patient know that you welcome any questions regarding medical problems and that you or your staff will be happy to offer assistance at any time.

THANK YOU FOR YOUR PROMPT PAYMENT

If you have a patient who has paid a bill prior to the insurance payment, send this letter (Exhibit 13–3) along with the refund check. Too often doctors send patients refund checks without an explanation or with just a copy of the bill with the zero balance. If we want to encourage patients to pay before their insurance companies do, we have to let them know that we appreciate their doing so.

THANK YOU FOR THE REFERRAL

I receive from referring physicians lots of tasteful cards printed on quality, expensive paper with the names of the patients I referred written in the blanks. Although the gesture is appreciated, this type of notification is not very helpful to me. Such a card only indicates that the patient arrived in the physician's office and

---

Exhibit 13–2 "Thank You for Consulting Us" Letter

This letter is sent to every patient after the first visit.

[Date]

Dear [Patient],

Thank you for visiting our office and for giving us the opportunity to offer you assistance and health care.

I trust your initial contact with us established the personal, courteous medical relationship we strive to provide for you. We are constantly trying to improve our patient care. Please let us know if you have any suggestions or comments regarding our service.

Please give us a call if you have further questions. Thank you again for consulting with us. The office staff and I welcome you to our practice.

Sincerely,

Neil Baum, MD

Exhibit 13–3 Letter To Accompany Refund Check Reimbursing Payment on Services Covered by Insurance

---

Play Account
140 Gould Street
Harvey, LA 70058

DEAR PLAY ACCOUNT:

Enclosed you will find a refund in the amount of $_____, which represents an overpayment on your account. An overpayment was caused by patient or insurance payments. We appreciate the conscientious manner in which your account balance has been handled.

If you should have any questions, please don't hesitate to call this office.

Sincerely,

Sandra Lee Aytona
Business Manager
Enclosure

---

was seen. It does not give me a clue about the diagnosis, the medications prescribed, or the plan of treatment.

Whenever I see a patient from another practice, I send the "computerized referral letter" or "lazy person's referral letter" (see Exhibit 35–1).

When patients refer a friend or family member to you, I suggest sending a personal letter (see Exhibit 13–4), handwritten if possible. Make sure you mention in

---

Exhibit 13–4 Thank-You Letter for Referrals

September 13, 1999

Arnold Lupin
3715 Prytania Street
New Orleans, LA 70115

Dear Arnold Lupin,

Thank you for your kind referral of Play Account to this office. We are appreciative of your gesture and consider it a compliment that you have sent Play Account to our office.

Sincerely,

---

the letter that you appreciate the referral and consider it a compliment when a satisfied patient sends a friend or family member.

HERE'S A NEW PATIENT

Whenever you make a referral to a colleague, send the physician a note, either through the mail or with the patient. *This should be a one-sentence note that indicates the purpose of the referral. It accomplishes two purposes:*

1. It saves the referring doctor time in trying to determine the reason for the referral. It is not unusual for a patient to be uninformed about the necessity for the referral.
2. Some patients forget who referred them. Sending the "here's a new patient" note ensures that you get credit for the referral.

YOUR BALANCE IS $0.00

There are occasions when a patient has an outstanding balance and you have made a decision to adjust the balance to $0.00. Whenever you adjust a patient's bill to $0.00, send the patient a letter indicating that the balance due has been written off. This is a nice way to let the patient know that you are compassionate and understanding. Exhibit 13–5 is the computer-generated letter we send to patients. It has worked to bring several patients back to the practice who were staying away because they were embarrassed about owing money.

Exhibit 13–5 Letter Notifying Patient That Balance Due Has Been Written Off

[Date]

Dear [Patient],

I am happy to tell you that your balance of [amount] has been written off. You no longer have a balance with us.

If you require further medical attention, please let us know. If it is a regular visit, you can pay us by cash at the time of treatment. If you have an emergency, we will help you establish a way to pay for your care.

We wish you good health and all the best.

Sincerely,

Neil Baum, MD

Exhibit 13–6 Card Acknowledging Mention in Local Newspaper

SAW YOU IN THE NEWS

Whenever one of your patients or fellow physicians appears in a local newspaper or magazine, it is nice to acknowledge this by sending them the article with an accompanying note (see Exhibit 13–6). If you see one of your colleagues on TV, send a note with a comment about the show or interview. By the way, your staff can be helpful in locating these articles for you. Ask them to be on the lookout.

SORRY ABOUT THE DELAY

It happens to the best of us. Sometimes we are detained by an emergency and get far behind on our appointment schedules. As mentioned in Chapter 3, your staff should be trained to handle any delays as graciously as possible. Whenever you are excessively delayed, however, you can show your patients that you are truly sorry by sending a computerized letter (see Exhibit 13–7) apologizing for the delay and assuring them that it will not happen again.

BIRTHDAY CARDS

Everyone likes to be remembered on his or her birthday. This is true for your patients and referring physicians alike. With your office computer, you can easily generate a monthly list of your patients' birthdays. The cards are written a month in advance, sorted into weekly packets, and mailed at the beginning of the appropriate week. That way each card arrives either a day or two before or after the birthday. I try to sign all the birthday cards and to mention something personal. For instance, to a patient who has had kidney stones, I might write, "Happy Birthday, and don't forget to drink lots of water!" It takes a little more time, but it is worth the effort of putting in that extra touch.

WELCOME TO THE AREA

Every July and August you will receive several announcements from new physicians setting up practice in your community. Rather than throwing those an-

---

Exhibit 13–7 Apology for Delay Letter

[Date]

Dear [Patient],

I am sorry about the delay that occurred today in the office. We make every effort to see our patients in a timely fashion and we promise to do better next time. Today we had several emergencies and my schedule was thrown off considerably. I hope you will accept my sincere apology. I promise you it will not happen again.

Sincerely,

Neil Baum, MD

Exhibit 13–8 Fax Authorization for Office Visit

Today's Date:

FROM: Neil Baum, M.D.
TO:
Plan physician:

....

RE:
Patient's Name _____
Identification Number _____

....

The patient listed above is scheduled to be seen tomorrow in the office. Please provide approval for the following tests or procedures. Call if there are questions or concerns.

Procedure(s) Planned:

[ ] Office Visit	[ ] Catheterization	[ ] Sono/Bx prostate
[ ] Urinalysis	[ ] Cystoscopy	[ ] Sono Residual urine
[ ] Culture/Sensitivity	[ ] Cysto/Dilation	[ ] Sono Scrotum
[ ] PSA	[ ] Cysto/Remove Stent	[ ] Bladder Ca Treatment
[ ] Cytology	[ ] Cysto/Bladder Washing	[ ] Rx Condylomata
[ ] Bladder tumor antigen	[ ] Intracavernosal injection	[ ] CMG
[ ] Other _____	[ ] Other _____	

PLEASE FAX BACK THE APPROVAL AS SOON AS POSSIBLE

Authorizing Agent Signature _____ Date _____

Authorizing Agent Name _____

---

nouncements away or scribbling "congratulations" on them and returning them to the senders, write a letter welcoming each new physician to the community. Follow up with a visit to the office and an invitation to your office. You can be sure new physicians will remember these gestures—especially if you refer patients to them early in their careers.

THANKS FOR THE COMPLIMENT

Nearly all physicians receive glowing letters of appreciation from their patients. You should send copies of these letters to referring physicians to let them know what good experiences the patients had with you and your practice. After all, your effective treatment of a referred patient is a reflection on the referring physician.

And do not forget to acknowledge the letters or cards—let patients know how much you appreciate their notes.

SUGGESTION BOX REPLIES

Your reception area should contain a suggestion box (see Chapter 1). Check this box daily and immediately answer any comments, whether positive or negative. If you implement any of your patients' suggestions, be sure to let them know. For example, one patient suggested that the hook for clothes behind the door in the examination rooms needed hangers. We sent him a note that we had tried hangers

---

Exhibit 13–9 Referral Form

To: Dr._____
Address_____
City_____   Telephone _____
From:
This will introduce my patient,_____
Patient's Primary Physician is _____
Reason for Referral:
[ ] Evaluation/Treatment of _____
[ ] Second Opinion for _____
[ ] Clear for SurgerySurg. _____   Date _____
[ ] Take over Primary Care
[ ] Other _____
Remarks: _____
_____
Please:
[ ] Send Report to [ ] me [ ] other _____
[ ] Call me after seeing patient
[ ] Other

Exhibit 13–10 Request for Consultation

To: Dr._____   **DATE:** _____

Regarding Patient: _____

Patient's Primary Physician is _____

Reason for Request:

[ ] Evaluation/Management of _____

[ ] Second Opinion for _____

[ ] Clear for Surgery   Surgery: _____

                          Date Scheduled: _____

[ ] Take over Primary Care

[ ] Other _____

Remarks: _____

_____

Please:

[ ] Send Report to [ ] me [ ] _____

[ ] Call me after seeing patient

THANK YOU FOR YOUR ASSISTANCE,

Neil

---

but found they made too much noise when the door was opened and closed. The patient solved the problem by buying padded hangers for us!

AUTHORIZATIONS, CONSULTATIONS, AND MORE

Now that managed care is the rule of the day, obtaining authorizations for specialist visits has become commonplace. We have generated a fax authorization for office visits (see Exhibit 13–8) that makes this process as painless as possible. Patients and plan physicians alike seem to appreciate this streamlined way of doing business.

Some examples of other "paper trails" include our referral form (Exhibit 13–9), request for consultation (Exhibit 13–10), and the quick "stat" operative note (Ex-

Exhibit 13–11 Quick "Stat" Operative Note

Date:

Dear _____

Your patient _____ had the

following procedure: _____

The pertinent findings included:

_____

_____

I recommended _____

You will be receiving the dictated operative note. Please call me if you have any questions.

Sincerely,

Dr. Neil Baum

Exhibit 13–12 Letter To Generate Immediate Action

Dear Beauregard,

Mr. Ichabod Krane was seen for a problem of BPH and an elevated PSA. The physical examination reveals a moderately enlarged and benign prostate gland.

The urinalysis is normal. The PSA is 11.0 ng/ml.

I am recommending a transrectal ultrasound of the prostate gland and a prostate biopsy.

Since Mr. Krane is currently taking aspirin, I would like him to stop the aspirin for 10 days and repeat the bleeding time before the biopsy.

Sincerely,

Dr. Strangelove

__ Yes, you can stop the aspirin and restart it after the biopsy.

__ No, do not stop the aspirin.

---

hibit 13–11). In addition, I have also devised a letter to generate immediate action (Exhibit 13–12). This kind of communication allows your colleague to respond by simply checking off one of the options that you have provided. This makes it very easy for two colleagues to reach a decision regarding a patient's care with minimal time commitment. Also, both practices have a hard copy that can be added to the chart for medical-legal protection.

The Bottom Line *Because so many of our transactions these days are electronic and verbal, sending a written letter or memo conveys a level of attention to detail that is hard to beat. A letter adds a touch of class to your practice and lets your patients and referring physicians know that you do not neglect the fine print. This increases the positive experiences that patients and referring physicians have with you and your practice.*

CHAPTER 14

Stuffers Soften
the Bite of the Bill

Do you want to guarantee that your monthly statements get opened first? I have 12 sure-fire ideas that can put your statements on the top of the stack of mail to be opened instead of the bottom. "Bill stuffers" are the reason monthly statements from our office are never ignored.

Several examples of the bill stuffers we send out are shown in this chapter (see Exhibits 14–1 through 14–12). You can see that bill stuffers become an additional marketing opportunity. You can use them to include notices to your patients about new programs, support groups you are conducting, talks you have given or will be giving, or articles that you have written for local magazines or newspapers. If your office produces a monthly or even a quarterly newsletter, you can include that with the bill.

Today most practices generate their bills electronically. This does not preclude adding materials to educate your patients. Most software billing programs will allow you to customize a few sentences on the statement itself. For example, during Prostate Cancer Awareness Month (September of each year), we add the following reminder:

> Men, don't forget that September is Prostate Cancer Awareness Month. All men over age fifty should have an annual PSA blood test and rectal examination. If you would like to receive information about a free examination and blood test, please call the office and our staff will direct you to one of the free prostate screening sites in the community.

Another example of a customized add-on statement was an announcement of my lecture on biofeedback for treatment of urinary incontinence that was free and open to the public: "If you suffer from an overactive bladder and would like to learn of a new, nonsurgical, nondrug alternative, come to Bravo Italian Restaurant

Exhibit 14–1 Sample January Bill Stuffer

Dr. Baum's Collected Quotes on Success, Motivation, and Determination

Happy New Year! Here are a few quotes to supply some inspiration for all those New Year's resolutions that you have made!

Do not be a problem-oriented person. *Strive to become a solution-oriented person.*	Dr. Neil Baum
In order to gain, you have to give, not take.	Dr. Neil Baum
Go the extra mile . . . then go a little more.	Dr. Neil Baum
I do not accept failure, only setbacks.	Dr. Neil Baum
Let us not find fault, but let us find a solution.	Dr. Neil Baum
Success comes to those who are committed to the persistent and consistent attention to little details, because they make a big difference.	Dr. Neil Baum
Little things don't mean a lot. They mean everything.	Dr. Neil Baum
There is no goal or objective that you cannot accomplish or achieve if you are willing to prepare yourself in advance and if you are committed to working long enough and hard enough.	Dr. Neil Baum
You are only as successful as the number of available options and alternatives you have.	Dr. Neil Baum
Luck occurs when preparation meets persistence.	Dr. Neil Baum
Five years from now you will be the same as you are today, except for the books you have read, the people you meet, and the tapes that you listen to.	Dr. Neil Baum

---

on June 16, 1999, at 12 noon. You can reserve a seat by calling our office at (504) 891-XXXX."

CHOOSING YOUR TOPICS

I have chosen topics related to wellness, nutrition, humor, and seasonal events. For example, in February I send information on heart disease and routine examinations (Exhibit 14–2). Since April is National Cancer Month, our monthly bill stuffer (Exhibit 14–4) contains information about colorectal cancer and the impor-

Exhibit 14–2 Sample February Bill Stuffer

Because February is Heart Disease Month, it makes sense to include materials from the American Heart Association. Contact your local chapter for noncopyrighted materials.

Help Your Heart

American Heart Association

Women, Smoking and Heart Disease

At the turn of the century, cigarette smoking was considered risque for American women. By the 1950s it was fashionable. But today women are faced with the reality that what was once a "fashion statement" is now killing them.

Nearly 22 million American women still smoke. And the American Heart Association urges those women to consider some alarming facts:

• Smoking is the greatest single preventable cause of death in the United States.

• Heart attack is the No. 1 killer of American women.

• For women, smoking is the most significant risk factor for heart attack.

The solution: If you smoke, quit. Studies have shown that women who smoke are two to six times more likely to have a heart attack as non-smoking women. In fact, *any* smoker who has a heart attack is more likely than a non-smoker to die from it and is two to four times more likely to die suddenly.

In addition, women who both smoke and use oral contraceptives are in greater danger. Recent studies show that women smokers who use oral contraceptives are up to 39 times more likely to have a heart attack and up to 22 times more likely to have a stroke than women who neither smoke nor use birth control pills. More studies are needed to understand the influence of birth control pills on heart attack and stroke risk. However, it may be because they tend to cause slight to moderate elevations in blood cholesterol and blood pressure.

Studies show that if a woman starts to smoke, she is less likely to quit than a man. However, if she stops smoking, no matter how long or how much she smoked, her risk of heart disease rapidly declines.

In short, the days of "fashionable" smoking are over.

To get more information on the dangers of smoking and how to quit, contact your nearest American Heart Association.

Source: Reproduced with permission of American Heart Association.

---

tance of getting an annual rectal examination. In September I send the "Football Couch Potato" stuffer (Exhibit 14–9). During the remainder of the year or whenever there are no seasonal tie-ins, I use noncopyrighted reprints from various sources, or even quotes from my patients and friends.

Exhibit 14–3 Sample Bill Stuffer

𝕭ill of 𝕽esponsibilities

Preamble. Freedom and responsibility are mutual and inseparable; we can ensure enjoyment of the one only by exercising the other. Freedom for all of us depends on responsibility by each of us. To secure and expand our liberties, therefore, we accept these responsibilities as individual members of a free society:

To be fully responsible for our own actions and for the consequences of those actions. Freedom to choose carries with it the responsibility for our choices.

To respect the rights and beliefs of others. In a free society, diversity flourishes. Courtesy and consideration toward others are measures of a civilized society.

To give sympathy, understanding and help to others. As we hope others will help us when we are in need, we should help others when they are in need.

To do our best to meet our own and our families' needs. There is no personal freedom without economic freedom. By helping ourselves and those closest to us to become productive members of society, we contribute to the strength of the nation.

To respect and obey the laws. Laws are mutually accepted rules by which, together, we maintain a free society. Liberty itself is built on a foundation of law. That foundation provides an orderly process for changing laws. It also depends on our obeying laws once they have been freely adopted.

To respect the property of others, both private and public. No one has a right to what is not his or hers. The right to enjoy what is ours depends on our respecting the right of others to enjoy what is theirs.

To share with others our appreciation of the benefits and obligations of freedom. Freedom shared is freedom strengthened.

To participate constructively in the nation's political life. Democracy depends on an active citizenry. It depends equally on an informed citizenry.

To help freedom survive by assuming personal responsibility for its defense. Our nation cannot survive unless we defend it. Its security rests on the individual determination of each of us to help preserve it.

To respect the rights and to meet the responsibilities on which our liberty rests and our democracy depends. This is the essence of freedom. Maintaining it requires our common effort, all together and each individually.

Source: Developed and distributed by Freedoms Foundation at Valley Forge. © 1985 by Freedoms Foundation at Valley Forge. For additional copies of the Bill of Responsibilities or further information about Freedoms Foundation at Valley Forge, you may write Freedoms Foundation, Office of Public Affairs, Route 23, Valley Forge, PA 19481 or call (215) 933-8825.

Exhibit 14–4 Sample April Bill Stuffer

April is National Cancer Month, so our office sends out reminders to have a regular rectal exam to protect against colorectal cancer.

What You Need To Know about Cancer of the Colon and Rectum

Risk Factors

Certain risk factors are known to increase a person's chances of developing colon or rectal cancer:

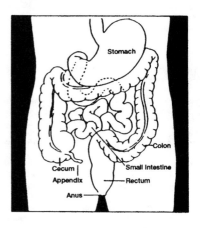

- *Age*—This type of cancer is seen more often in people who are over 40.
- *Family History*—A person with familial polyposis or close relatives with this inherited condition has a much greater chance of developing colon cancer. People with this condition develop many polyps in the intestine, which in time become cancerous.
- *Lifestyle*—For reasons that are not clearly understood, people who live in urban, industrialized areas seem to have more colon and rectal cancer.
- *Diet*—The foods people eat may have a strong effect on their chance of getting colon and rectal cancer. Diets high in fat have been linked to colon cancer. On the other hand, diets high in fiber appear to protect against colorectal cancer.

What is the colon?

The colon and rectum comprise the final segment of the digestive tract or the large intestine. It is the lower 4 to 5 feet of the intestine which travels around the borders of your abdominal area. The rectum is the last 4 to 5 inches at the end of the colon.

How does the colon work?

The principal function of the entire gastrointestinal tract is to provide the body with essential nutrients, fluids and electrolytes. A secondary function is to dispose of the waste residues from the digestive process. As waste products travel through the colon fluids are reabsorbed into the body and the semisolid waste material is moved through the colon until it exits through the rectum.

What are the facts about colorectal cancer?

Cancer of the colon and rectum is the second leading cancer killer affecting both men and women equally. An estimated 160,000 new cases per year will occur in the United States.

continues

Exhibit 14–4 continued

Fortunately, cancer of the colon and rectum is potentially one of the most curable cancers if detected and treated early.

Possible Warning Signs

When an illness affects the colon or rectum, a number of symptoms may appear. The ones listed below are warning signs of a possible problem:

- diarrhea or constipation
- blood in or on the stool (either bright red or very dark in color)
- stools that are narrower than usual
- general stomach discomfort (bloating, fullness, cramps)
- frequent gas pains
- a feeling that bowel doesn't empty completely
- loss of weight with no known reason
- constant tiredness

These symptoms can be caused by a number of problems such as the flu, ulcers, an inflamed colon or cancer. It is important to see a doctor if any of these symptoms lasts as long as 2 weeks. Any illness should be diagnosed and treated as soon as possible, and this is especially true for cancer of the colon and rectum.

Early Detection

Colorectal cancer usually shows no obvious symptoms in the early stages. One of the earliest signs of colorectal cancer is often occult (hidden) bleeding in the stool. Stool blood tests are designed as a screening procedure in the early detection of colorectal cancer as well as other gastrointestinal disorders.

The American Cancer Society recommends three tests as valuable aids in detecting colon and rectum cancer early in people without symptoms:

- The digital rectal exam should be performed by a physician during an office visit every year after age 40.
- The stool blood test is recommended every year after age 50.
- After a person reaches 50, a "procto" exam (proctosigmoidoscopy) is recommended to examine the rectum and lower colon. This exam should be done every 3 to 5 years after age 50.

For additional information on colorectal cancer, diet and nutrition and related information, contact:

**THE CANCER ASSOCIATION
800-624-2039**

Source: Reprinted from the National Cancer Institute, Bethesda, Maryland.

Here is an example of how bill stuffers can market your practice. The May 14, 1998, issue of the *New England Journal of Medicine* contained the results of a study by a group of urologists at the University of Southern California on the use of transurethral alprostadil for the treatment of erectile dysfunction.[1] This treatment (alprostadil in pellet form) provided an alternative to patients currently performing self-injections of the medicine directly into the corporal body of the pe-

Exhibit 14–5 Sample Bill Stuffer for Spring Months

In preparation for summer, we send this humorous bill stuffer.

Dr. Baum's Guaranteed Weight Loss Diet

Breakfast
poached robin egg, scraped crumbs from burnt toast, weak tea

Lunch
seaweed salad with a dozen poppy seeds
belly button of a navel orange

Snack
fuzz from two cling peaches

Dinner
one baked pigeon wing, five grains brown rice
two cherry tomatoes on lettuce bed, dehydrated water

Snack
one-ounce glass of steam

nis. Copies of an article from the lay press that summarized this new treatment were included with the bills in January and February, generating nearly one hundred requests from existing patients for appointments to discuss the medication. It also generated several new referrals when women who received the bill made appointments for their husbands and significant others. Several patients who did not respond to the urethral pellets later received penile implants. That is not a bad return from two months' worth of a single bill stuffer!

Use your discretion when choosing subject matter for your bill stuffers. Avoid controversy whenever possible. Do not try to use bill stuffers as vehicles to promote your favorite political causes, for instance. The goal is to find material that your patients will find enjoyable, possibly enlightening, and that will soften the bite of the bill.

Many of my patients have told me that they enjoy receiving their monthly statements. Now *that* is effective marketing.

OPPORTUNITY TO EDUCATE

By contacting the major disease and health advocacy organizations, you can obtain permission to reprint patient education material. You can choose to include

Exhibit 14–6 Sample Bill Stuffer

30,000 MEN WILL DIE THIS YEAR !

Be Part Of The Solution...
And There Won't Be A Problem.

● This is an opportunity to do something profoundly worthwhile and make a lasting difference.....in your own life and the lives of family and friends.

● Prostate Cancer is the most common cancer in U.S. men and more than 50% of these cases are diagnosed after the disease has already spread.

● Education and research are critical to promote early detection and elimination of this silent killer. Yet, Prostate Cancer receives less than 1% of all cancer funding.

Your Help Can Make The Difference!

Support the Robert J. Mathews Foundation in its efforts to raise money to eliminate Prostate Cancer through research, education and early detection.

Yes, I wish to join your effort to eliminate prostate cancer.
Yes, I am pleased to help by making a contribution.
Yes, please send additional information.

Please return this card to:
Robert J. Mathews Foundation
3435 American River Drive
Sacramento, California 95864
(916) 972-7055

Name _____
Address _____
Phone _____

Enclosed please find my check for $ ___
made payable to the Robert J. Mathews Foundation.
Or charge my ☐ VISA or ☐ MasterCard

Signature: _____ Expiration Date: ___

Thank you for helping us do something great for mankind!
All donations are tax deductible.

Exhibit 14–7 Sample Bill Stuffer

That's Not My Job

This is a story about four people named Everybody, Somebody, Anybody, and Nobody. There was an important job to be done and Everybody was sure that Somebody would do it. Anybody could have done it, but Nobody did it. Somebody got angry about that, because it was Everybody's job. Everybody thought Anybody could do it, but Nobody realized that Everybody wouldn't do it. It ended up that Everybody blamed Somebody when Nobody did what Anybody could have.

Exhibit 14–8 Sample Bill Stuffer

Just the good news, please doctor!

Andy Rooney

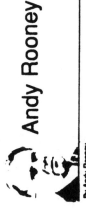

By Andy Rooney

In the middle of last Wednesday night, I was lying awake thinking all those terrible thoughts that come to your mind in the middle of the night. I'd had an itch in one spot on my back for several months which I decided, lying there, was skin cancer. Not only that, a flashing in the corner of my left eye when I looked out of the side of it occasionally, got me thinking I must have a brain tumor.

The following morning, I couldn't remember what was wrong with me, but I recall being worried so I made a doctor's appointment.

I have just returned from being inspected from head to toe and all the places in between and am pleased to report that I don't have any of the things I was sure I had in my nocturnal depression.

I like my doctor. After the examination we sat in his office and talked while he asked me a few perfunctory questions and made notes.

"Any trouble swallowing?"

"No. I'd be better off if I had a little trouble."

"Yeah. You could lose a few pounds ... but you knew that when you came here."

"How do you do all the paperwork?" I asked, nodding toward stacks of report forms behind him.

He shrugged, hopelessly. "Maybe we ought to go to the Canadian system," he said. "Canadian doctors are paid a salary and they don't have to do the paperwork."

"Doctors wouldn't like that," I said.

"Look," he said, "the number of Canadian doctors leaving Canada to come here has slowed to a trickle. A lot of them used to come. That says

something about whether they like their system or not. Any trouble breathing?"

"No. Not unless I'm trying to run uphill."

"Unusual number of respiratory problems, colds, flu?" he asked, his pencil poised, in a voice that suggested he knew the answer was no.

"No," I said. "I used to. There are only three people in my office now. That helps.

"Airplanes," he said. "They're the problem. I have a theory. These strange respiratory bugs result from the air travel that people are doing. Someone gets on a plane in Bangkok with one strain of a bug and the plane stops in London and picks up passengers with another strain of bug. People on the plane all breathing the same air. You want a flu shot? Probably a good idea. Some people think they cause the flu but they don't."

I didn't answer but I didn't want one.

"All these viruses change. The AIDS virus is

changing," he said. "Wait until it changes so it can be transmitted when someone coughs. Any chest pain at all when you exercise?"

"None. Wouldn't I get a warning if I was going to have a heart attack?"

"Not necessarily. About one in four don't. It accounts for the jogger they find by the side of the road. It's been five years since you had a colonoscopy. We better do that soon."

"O, Jeez," I said. "I thought I read something bad about that. Just this week."

"Where'd you read that?" he said quickly and defensively.

"I don't know," I said. "The Times."

"Hasn't been in The Times. The first thing I do every morning is read the paper. I wouldn't come in here without reading the paper. Patients come in, they've read about some new treatment and they want to know how come I don't know about it. I don't move before I read the medical news in the paper."

"You're talking to a reporter, you know. I may make a column out of this."

"You want a story?" he asked. "When my first wife died, she wanted to be cremated and have her ashes cast over Long Island Sound. The children and I went out on the Sound and I scattered the ashes and then I got thinking ... she had a lot of gold fillings. There was no gold in those ashes. Where does all the gold go ... you want a story."

I left, my worry about skin cancer and brain tumor gone. Now I have other things to worry about when I wake up in the middle of the night.

Source: Courtesy of Tribune Media Services, Orlando, FL.

Exhibit 14–9 Sample Bill Stuffer for Fall Months

```
○○○○○○○○○○○○○○○○○○○○○○○○○○○○○○○○○○○○○○○○○○○
○                                                          ○
○   DR. NEIL BAUM'S MONDAY NIGHT FOOTBALL   ○
○       COUCH POTATO EXERCISES              ○
○                                                          ○
○○○○○○○○○○○○○○○○○○○○○○○○○○○○○○○○○○○○○○○○○○○
```

So, you're watching another game . . . and you think, "How can I stay in shape?" Did you know that your couch can be your very own health club? Here's how—do these simple exercises during every game!

Hamhock Stretch
Prop your feet on the coffee table. Reach for your toes. Keep your knees straight! Hold for one commercial.

Popcorn Reach
Place popcorn bowl on the floor next to the couch. Reach for your kernels one at a time.

Pretzel Reach
Place pretzels in the middle of the coffee table. Reach for your pretzels one at a time.

10 + 12 oz. Curls
Do you need instructions?

continues

Exhibit 14–9 continued

Can Crush
Give it a good squeeze! Alternate hands.

Field Goal Attempt
Place your trash can at least 3 yards away. Toss your crushed can. . . . If it goes in, give yourself 3 points. If not, repeat exercises 4 to 6 times.

2-Minute Warning Bathroom Run
Go for it. . . . Fast! At the end of each run, check your pulse.

Halftime Kicks
Kick one knee straight at a time. Alternate. Try to keep time with the band.

Marching
March in place—you may sit or stand.

Couch Push-ups
Sit in front of the couch. Put your hands on the couch and push! Repeat 10 times.

Isometrics
Squeeze your cheeks. Hold for one replay. Repeat throughout the game.

Exhibit 14–10 Sample Bill Stuffer for Older Patients

For All Those Born Prior to 1940!

We are Survivors!!!!! Consider the changes we have witnessed:

We were born before television, before penicillin, before polio shots, frozen foods, Xerox, contact lenses, Frisbees, and the Pill.

We were born before radar, credit cards, split atoms, laser beams, and ball-point pens; before pantyhose, dishwashers, clothes dryers, electric blankets, air conditioners, drip-dry clothes, and before man walked on the moon.

We got married first and then lived together. How quaint can you be?

In our time, closets were for clothes, not for "coming out of." Bunnies were small rabbits and rabbits were not Volkswagens. Designer Jeans were scheming girls named Jean or Jeanne, and having a meaningful relationship meant getting along well with our cousins.

We thought fast food was what you ate during Lent, and Outer Space was the back of the Trivoli Theatre.

We were born before house-husbands, gay rights, computer dating, dual careers, and commuter marriages. We were born before day-care centers, group therapy, and nursing homes. We never heard of FM radio, tape decks, electric typewriters, artificial hearts, word processors, yoga, and guys wearing earrings. For us time-sharing meant togetherness, not computers or condominiums; a "chip" meant a piece of wood; hardware meant hardware; and software wasn't even a word!

In 1940, "made in Japan" meant junk and the term "making out" referred to how you did on an exam. Pizzas, McDonalds, and instant coffee were unheard of.

We hit the scene when there were 5 and 10 cent stores where you bought things for five and ten cents. For one nickel you could ride a streetcar, make a phone call, buy a Pepsi, or buy enough stamps to mail one letter and two postcards. You could buy a new Chevy Coupe for $600 but who could afford one; a pity, too, because gas was only 11 cents a gallon!

In our day, cigarette smoking was fashionable. GRASS was mowed, COKE was a cold drink, and POT was something you cooked in. ROCK MUSIC was a Grandma's lullaby.

BUT WE SURVIVED!!!!! AND THERE IS NO BETTER REASON TO CELEBRATE!!!

Source: Courtesy of Dr. Saul Schneider, New Orleans, LA.

Exhibit 14–11 Sample November Bill Stuffer

[Date]

Dear [Patient],

This has been a busy and fulfilling year for all of us. As we enter the beautiful holiday season, we are reminded of many of the things for which we are thankful. At the top of our list are special patients like you.

It has been a pleasure to provide you with the best care possible. As the holidays approach, we pledge to continue to serve you, your family, and your friends. We welcome any suggestions so that we can continue the quality service you deserve.

Thank you for your friendship and patronage. These are the best compliments we can receive from our patients.

Have a very Happy Thanksgiving.

Sincerely,

Neil Baum, M.D., and staff

Exhibit 14–12 Sample Bill Stuffer

Success

"To laugh often and much; to win the respect of intelligent people and affection of children; to earn the appreciation of honest critics and endure the betrayal of false friends; to appreciate beauty, to find the best in others; to leave the world a bit better, whether by a healthy child, a garden patch or a redeemed social condition; to know even one life has breathed easier because you have lived. This is to have succeeded.

Ralph Waldo Emerson

this information whenever there is a national awareness month (for instance, May is National Arthritis Month). Key the patient education material to your patient base. If you are a pediatrician, you may want to include materials from the Juvenile Diabetes Foundation. Here are a few major website addresses to help generate ideas for your bill stuffers.

- American Cancer Society—*www.cancer.org*
- American Heart Association—*www.americanheart.org*
- Arthritis Foundation—*www.arthritis.org*
- Juvenile Diabetes Foundation—*www.jdfcure.org*

The Bottom Line   *Try inserting some creative, educational, and fun "stuff" along with your monthly statements. When you use bill stuffers, you give your patients something useful, something uplifting, or something comical when they open their bills. In return, those bill stuffers will give back one hundred-fold in increased referrals, calls, and goodwill for your practice.*

NOTE

1. I. Goldstein, T.F. Lue, H. Padma-Nathan, R.C. Rosen, W.D. Steers, and P.A. Wicker, "Oral Sildenafil in the Treatment of Erectile Dysfunction," *New England Journal of Medicine,* 338, no. 20 (1998): 1397–1404.

CHAPTER 15

A Picture Is Worth a Thousand Words: Creating Office Videos

We are living in an electronic and video age. Everything from aerobic exercise to home remodeling has been videotaped for easier communication. Many physicians have found that office videos help them educate their patients. You do not have to be Steven Spielberg to make a videotape that will be useful to your practice. Creating a video is easy and inexpensive, and an office video can serve as a great marketing tool.

WHAT ARE THE ADVANTAGES?

First, an office video makes your office more efficient. While one patient is viewing a videotape of an operation, procedure, or medical problem, you can be seeing other patients. An effective video can act as a surrogate assistant, addressing and answering the most frequently asked questions about a particular procedure or treatment. Because it relies on visuals, a videotape also helps patients understand complex subjects, such as anatomy and physiology.

Second, the video serves as medicolegal documentation that you have explained a procedure and its potential complications. To make the medicolegal protection stronger, have your patients sign the chart or a consent form that has additional lines to confirm that the video has been viewed (for example, see Exhibit 15–1).

Finally, a video can serve as a nice "loaner" to your patients, their families, or their friends. For example, if I perform a vasectomy, my patient may mention a friend who is interested in some information. I might loan the videotape to the patient so that his friend has an opportunity to learn about the procedure. And if that friend decides to have a vasectomy and he does not have a urologist, and I am listed with his managed care plan, he is most likely to call my office.

Exhibit 15–1 Example of Consent Form Patients Sign When They View a Video of an Operation or Procedure

---

CONSENT TO VASECTOMY

DATE: _____

    I, [Name of Patient], hereby freely and voluntarily request and authorize Dr. Neil Baum, M.D., to perform on me the operation known as bilateral vasectomy. In making this request, I am acting under my own free will, my actions are not the result of duress or compulsion from anyone, and I am competent and of legal age (eighteen years of age or older) to make this request.

    I understand that bilateral vasectomy means the removal or division of a segment of each vas deferens, each of which conducts sperm. Moreover, the purpose of this operation is to cause me to be sterile, that is, unable to produce children by causing pregnancy in a female partner. Furthermore, by undergoing this operation, I am knowingly expressing my preference for surgical sterilization as a means of contraception over any other known conventional method.

    I agree that I will present specimens of my semen as requested by Dr. Baum following the operation so that the absence of sperm in the semen can be determined. I understand that contraception should not be abandoned until I am advised by Dr. Baum or one of his assistants. The operation is intended to be irreversible; however, it may not have this effect, that is, the result of sterility is not guaranteed, and I may not be sterile as a result of the operation. I hereby forever release and agree to hold harmless Dr. Baum from any and all claims arising out of or connected with the performance of this operation.

    I have seen the video presentation on vasectomy that describes the procedure, complications, and postoperative suggestions.

WITNESS: _____

WITNESS: _____

_____
Signature of Patient

CONSENT OF SPOUSE

DATE: _____

    I, wife of the above-named patient, hereby stipulate that I have read and understood the above "consent to vasectomy" executed by my husband, and I hereby agree to such consent and all the particulars. I also forever release and agree to hold harmless Dr. Baum from any and all claims arising out of or connected with the performance of the bilateral vasectomy operation to be performed on my husband.

WITNESS: _____

WITNESS: _____

_____
Signature of Spouse

POTENTIAL SUBJECTS FOR OFFICE VIDEOS

Are there procedures or problems that you explain several times each day, or operations that you do more than two or three times a week? These are good subjects to consider for an office video. For example, in my urology practice I have created videos on the following subjects: evaluation of hematuria, prostatitis, and recurrent urinary tract infections; evaluation and treatment of impotence; vasectomy; evaluation and treatment of urinary incontinence; and IVP and cystoscopy.

If you are a primary care physician, you might want to create videos on managing hypertension, the importance and timing of annual physical exams, good nutrition, cancer screening and early warning signs of cancer, and the like. Orthopaedists might want to offer videos on low back pain, preventing foot injuries, prevention and treatment of carpal tunnel syndrome, neck pain, and rehabilitation after injury.

If your field is obstetrics and gynecology, your patients can benefit from videos on vaginal versus Caesarean section deliveries; basics for first-time mothers; the advantages and disadvantages of breastfeeding; a survey of available birth control methods; and, for middle-aged patients, a video on managing menopause. Pediatricians could make use of videos on immunization schedules, otitis media and tonsillitis, treating fevers, the "BRAT" diet and other treatments for managing diarrhea, the common cold, teething, the "fussy" baby, Sudden Infant Death Syndrome prevention, and toilet training. The possibilities are endless!

A staff video is a wonderful way to introduce the members of your office. I have a video introducing me and my staff. (See Exhibit 15–2 for the outline of this video script.) I use this staff video as a marketing tool with managed care plans, sending it along with my application. This creates the opportunity for the managed care plan administrators to "meet" the doctor—you become more than just an application, a curriculum vitae, and a record of malpractice insurance. I doubt that every managed care director views my video. However, the feedback has been positive from the ones who have watched it. (See Exhibit 15–3 for an example of a letter I received in response to my staff "video brochure.")

HOW TO CREATE A VIDEO

The first step is to prepare a script or story. This does not mean a professional screenplay. It is simply a narration that will accompany the visuals in the videotape. In the preparation stages, I record a discussion with a patient on the topic I am considering for a video. I have the discussion transcribed and use it as a guide for an outline to prepare the video script (see Exhibit 15–4).

I suggest looking at videos that are created by actors and actresses. These can be purchased or rented from companies that specialize in videos on medical topics.[1] I

Exhibit 15–2 Outline of Office Staff Videotape Script

Welcome to our practice

What is a urologist?

What does a urologist do?

Education of physicians and personal life

Introduction of staff

Narrated video tour of office

"The doctor will be in the room shortly to take your history and to perform a physical examination."

Summary

---

would not suggest substituting a commercial video for a personalized video of you and your practice. The commercial videos are generic and do not exactly tell your story. Also, a video of you makes your patient feel that you are giving him or her a personalized message.

You should also review patient pamphlets on the subject published by drug companies, medical manufacturers, and professional organizations. This review will provide you with ideas for your script and a format for the video.

Exhibit 15–3 Letter from Managed Care Plan Administrator Who Watched Office Video

---

Dr. Baum,

Your video brochure is such a nice introduction to you and your practice. It is apparent that your patients receive state-of-the-art medical care from a caring staff. And I can see that they sometimes even have a little bit of fun.

Kimberly McIntire
Director of Network Marketing
Tenet Healthcare
New Orleans, LA

Exhibit 15–4 Script for Vasectomy Video

Introduction:

Hello, my name is Dr. Baum and I would like to take a few minutes to talk to you about vasectomy. A vasectomy is the most common method of male contraception performed in the United States. It is safe, can be performed with minimal discomfort to you as an outpatient, and is relatively inexpensive compared with other forms of contraception. For all practical purposes, a vasectomy is irreversible. That is, although it can often be reversed, you should consider the operation only if you have completed your family. In the next few minutes I will discuss the following three areas: the procedure, the postoperative precautions, and the complications that can occur with vasectomy.

The Procedure:

Points to emphasize:

Can be done as an outpatient procedure.

Can be performed with local anesthesia similar to that in a dental office.

Takes fifteen to twenty minutes to perform.

Demonstration with rubber band and hemoclips.

Postoperative Precautions:

Points to emphasize:

You are not sterile immediately after the procedure. Twenty ejaculations or three months are required to empty the vas of sperm. Repeat semen analysis.

Use scrotal support for two to three days.

Apply ice bag over incision for four to six hours after the procedure.

Must lie flat for the remainder of the day.

Minimal activity for first twenty-four hours. No exercise, swimming, or yard work.

Moderate activity on second postoperative day. Walking, driving, bathing.

Resume all activities on third postoperative day. Work, exercise, sexual activity.

No aspirin or aspirin products for three days. Use Extra Strength Tylenol for pain.

Complications:

Pain.

Bleeding (demonstrate showing veins in hand in dependent position).

Infection <3%.

Failure <1 in 5,000 cases.

Will not effect potency or sexual activity.

Conclusion:

I know you may have some questions regarding the vasectomy procedure. If you open the door at the end of the video, I will know that you have completed your viewing and I will return to the room to answer your questions. I will also provide you with a handout that summarizes the entire video. Thank you.

In the case of most videos, the script contains:

1. a definition of the procedure or test
2. a description of how the procedure or test is performed
3. a detailing of the necessary preparation
4. what the patient can expect after the procedure is performed
5. the complications and their relative frequency

If you carefully plan the sequence of presentation when you write the script, you will save time in the editing stage.

I conclude each video with this statement: "I know you may have some questions regarding [name of the procedure]. If you open the door to let me know that you have completed viewing the film, I will return to the room and answer any questions that you may have."

After you have made a few tapes of just yourself, you might try to include one of your patients. Allow the patient to describe his or her experience with the procedure or operation.

After the script is ready, write the highlights on 8-by-10″ sheets, which can be used in place of a teleprompter. At this point, you are ready to shoot the video. This can be easily accomplished with a home video camera. The quality of these cameras has increased, while the prices have decreased. I recommend using the high-quality 8 mm camcorders for taping because the videotape will be sharper and have better resolution than what is produced by either the VHS or VHSC format cameras. You will also need a tripod and video lights. Most hospital audiovisual departments own all this equipment and frequently will loan it to you or provide you with assistance in creating the video. Videotape in a quiet room, with the camera mounted on the tripod. Make sure you are not interrupted. If you use a room in your office, remove any distracting objects from the background and hold all phone calls during the videotaping process. First do a test sequence and play it back. I suggest shooting the video three times all the way through from three different angles. That way you can edit these versions together to create more visual interest. As far as dressing the part, see Chapter 28 for the most effective on-camera color combinations.

After shooting the film, editing is the most important step. Professionals use a special videotape editing machine, but you can easily edit your video on your own computer with the consumer-friendly video editing programs now available. If making videotapes is something you intend to do, investing in such a program is a good idea. (See Additional Resource at the end of this chapter for information on one excellent program and the PC/Mac requirements to support the program.) These programs allow you to create titles and type on screen, an especially helpful feature for repeating important points from your presentation.

You can also edit using two videocassette recorders (VCRs), although this will result in a more "choppy" look between scenes in your final copy. Most electronic stores can explain the hookup necessary to copy from one VCR to another. Keep the edited length to between 7 and 10 minutes. Few videos should be longer than 15 minutes. Remember, CNN can give you its entire newscast in 18 minutes!

Creating your first video will usually take several hours of shooting and several hours of editing. Once you get the hang of it, you can turn out a video in a fraction of that time.

Once you complete a few videos with the above technique, you can add more sophistication to your presentation by using computer-generated graphics and slides. The additional equipment needed is often available in hospital audiovisual departments. You may not want to invest the time to learn the videotape editing programs yourself (although I can guarantee that once you experience the ability to manipulate your scenes, adding titles and music with the click of the mouse, you may be "hooked"). In that case, if you contact the computer, photography, or film departments of local high schools or colleges, you will be able to find students who are interested in video photography. They can be of valuable assistance to you and will probably find your project exciting and interesting. Most students will work for a nominal fee if you provide the materials or reimburse them for the supplies.

WHERE TO SHOW THE VIDEOS

I began with a single VCR and monitor in one of the exam rooms. After I created several videos, I realized that I could show more than one video at the same time, using different exam rooms. Now I have monitors in every room. I also provide patients with written summaries of each video after they have seen the tape.

You can also get more mileage out of your videos by sending a sample or two of the health-content tapes to the managed care plans that include you in their directories. Often they will distribute your videos to the plan members.

For example, I gave a noontime talk on the prostate gland to a large local oil company that had several thousand employees. The health nurse who had set up the program told me how much she enjoyed it and wanted handouts for those who could not attend. I told her I had the talk on videotape and would be happy to send two copies to her. She made additional copies of the tape and handouts and sent them to all of the company's oil rigs in the Gulf of Mexico. The employees watched the video (there's not a whole lot to do on an oil rig in your "off" hours!) and several men later called my office and became patients.

The Bottom Line *Office videos can educate your patients, introduce you to managed care plans, and add value to your practice. So do not just shoot from the hip—let the medium relay the message!*

NOTE

1. For patient education videos, contact Milner-Fenwick, Inc., 2125 Green Spring Drive, Timonium, MD 21093; 1-800-638-8652.

ADDITIONAL RESOURCE

• **AVID Cinema** is an excellent, low-cost, easy-to-learn videotape editing program specifically designed for people with no prior editing experience. For more information, go to *www.avidcinema.com.* The program comes installed in the new Imac computers and is also available for PCs with Windows for around $200. To run the program you will need a video capture card, a processor with a speed of 200 MHz or higher, and at least 3 GB of additional hard drive space. The 8 mm cameras can be cabled directly into your computer, but if you are using VHS or VHSC format tape, you will need to use your VCR and cable that into the computer. The program allows you to import your original shots and then edit them, shortening, adding titles and interesting scene fades, and adding music from a CD. The program also automatically furnishes you with your exact running time.

CHAPTER 16

Need More Patients? Brochures Are the Cure

Your patients are not mind readers. If you don't tell them what you do, how will they know?

I learned this lesson the hard way. A longtime patient of mine came in for his annual checkup. During the examination, I discovered that he had had a penile implant.

"Where did you get this?" I asked him.

"Well, I went to Dr. Jeckel, across town."

"Why didn't you come to me for that? I also do implants."

"Really? I didn't know that."

It was hard for me to believe that one of my own patients had gone to another doctor for treatment of impotence! I vowed that never again would a patient of mine not know about the full range of services I offer. That is why I now have a practice brochure. It has all the requisite information—appointment scheduling, insurance billing, office hours, and so on—but it also contains explanations of the most common procedures I perform and it tells patients what my areas of specialization and interest are.

I think every doctor should create a paper trail. Never let your patients go out the office door without something in their hands with your name on it. And in the new millennium, it should be more than just a prescription.

A practice brochure creates all kinds of marketing opportunities. It can inform your current as well as your potential patients of your services, your office policies, and your practice philosophy. It can save your staff time by cutting down on the repetitive questions they are asked, such as, "How can I bill my insurance company?" or "Do you accept credit cards for payment?"

Most practice brochures are pretty standard. I describe my own below to indicate some of the elements I think are most important.

WHAT TO INCLUDE

Whether you are creating a brochure for the first time or revamping an existing one, it helps to collect samples of brochures that you like from other practices or businesses. You can start out by simply photocopying your brochure. However, a printed version will look more professional. A typical office brochure usually has six to eight panels (or pages) of information.

Your first step will be to write the copy for the brochure. As you write, keep in mind that the brochure should clarify your office procedures. Use language that is clear, concise, and easy to read, as if you were talking to your patients. Try to use words like *we, you, us,* and *our.* Avoid medical terms unless they are commonly used or unless you define them in the brochure. If you are not experienced in writing for the lay reader, you can write a rough draft and then ask someone to help you edit the copy.

Introduction

Your brochure introduces you and your practice to the reader. In one paragraph, briefly note your education, your board certification, any professional organizations to which you belong, and any special training you may have completed. Next, describe or define your specialty and any areas of interest within that specialty. If you are active within the community, you should include your participation in community service.

It is a good idea to include a picture of yourself. If you have a small group practice, include pictures of all the doctors. New patients, in particular, appreciate having a picture of the doctor in the brochure. Patients are usually anxious about meeting their doctor. You can decrease this anxiety by letting them know who you are and what you look like. For your brochure photo, choose a clinical backdrop. Wear your white lab coat rather than the formal dress used for pictures in local county medical directories.

Most patients do not know which organ systems a urologist treats. They usually do not know whether urologists treat women and children. Many patients may not be able to differentiate between, for instance, a neurologist and a neurosurgeon. Therefore, spell out what your specialty is. If your practice has an unusual history or you have a unique background, mention this in the introductory remarks.

State the philosophy of your practice early in the brochure. A copy of our practice philosophy appears in the reception area of the office and also on the first page of our brochure (see Exhibit 16–1).

Exhibit 16–1 Sample Introductory Page of a Practice Brochure

Neil Baum, M.D.
Urology, Board Certified

We are committed to:

- Excellence

- The best health care for our patients

- The persistent attention to little details because we think they make a big difference.

Specializing in Innovative Treatment for Impotence, Male Infertility, Urinary Incontinence, and Problems of the Bladder and Prostate.

Office Policies

It is a good idea to have a separate heading for each of your office policies. Do not try to jam all the information about appointments, phone calls, and billing into the same paragraph. Separate the information into bite-size paragraphs. Patients will be more likely to read the information and remember it.

Your appointment policy should be described in detail, including how you handle walk-in appointments and emergencies. You need to state your cancellation policy. If you charge for missed appointments, mention it here. This is the last thing with which to surprise a patient. You should also mention how far in advance to call for an appointment.

There are probably several matters that you are willing to discuss over the phone. Let your patients know what these are. For example, will you give laboratory results over the phone? Do you refill prescriptions over the phone? If you do not routinely refill prescriptions, you may want to state your reasons for this. Describe what types of requests can and cannot be handled by the nurse. In addition, you can inform patients that routine prescriptions are refilled from 9 AM to 4 PM.

Monday through Friday. This simple sentence will avoid patients calling you in the evening or on weekends.

Mention what time you routinely return calls to patients. Then your patients will not have to wait all day for your return calls. Establishing a policy of routine callbacks can reduce the frequency of calls from patients to your office. Also, this policy is a nice way to let your patients know that you value their time. They will certainly appreciate the consideration and courtesy you give them.

If you provide any amenities or additional services, such as free parking, house calls, or transportation for elderly or visually impaired patients, mention them in the brochure.

State your policy on emergencies and after-hour calls. Reassure your patients that whenever you are not on call, another physician will be covering for you. You may want to include the physician's name and number. On rare occasions, the office secretary may not check out or activate call forwarding on the office line and your patients will have trouble reaching you by calling the office number. For this reason, I include my answering service number in the brochure.

Include information regarding your office's policies on payments, managed care plans, and insurance guidelines. If you expect payment at the time of service, mention it. You may want to explain that this keeps costs down by avoiding increases in billing and secretarial costs. State your policy on Medicare assignment and explain what assignment means to your patients. If you accept credit cards, list which ones. Discuss your policy on late or delinquent payments, especially if you add a monthly service charge. Include your office manager's name in case your patients have questions regarding their bills (this keeps them from asking to speak to you about their statements). State your policy regarding insurance forms, especially if you process the forms without a charge. This is a nice extra service that promotes prompt filing of insurance forms. It also puts your office in charge of the processing procedure and ensures accurate completion of the forms.

Directions

If you have patients who do not live nearby, include an easy-to-read map that shows the location of your office. Your hospital might be able to provide a camera-ready map that you can incorporate into your brochure. Insert the map on the last page of the brochure or, if the brochure is a self-mailer, place the map on the back flap.

"Extras"

To make your practice brochure even more useful, you can include helpful information. For instance, my practice brochure contains a list of commonly performed diagnostic procedures and a short definition of what is involved for each. Pediatricians might want to include an immunization schedule for children from infancy to age ten. Your brochure should also contain your website and e-mail address so patients can access your site and communicate with you via the Internet.

Finally, you may want to include a brief statement about your family, if this is appropriate. I also mention that I am available for talks on urologic subjects. I have received several public-speaking invitations as a result of including this information in my brochure.

PRODUCTION, DESIGN, AND PRINTING

After you have completed writing the brochure copy, ask someone to edit it for you. Your hospital's marketing and public relations departments often have staff members who do medical and lay writing and can be of assistance to you.

Now that you have created your brochure, how do you get it printed? The least expensive way is to type it out and photocopy it. A more professional look can be created by having the brochure typeset by a compositor, or typesetter, using a computerized desktop publishing system. You can add a logo and graphics, including a photograph of yourself and other physicians in your practice. For a fee, a graphic arts studio or freelance artist can design the layout of your brochure and provide line drawings or illustrations. It is a good idea to work with someone who has experience in medical graphics. Be sure to ask for examples of work and references before contracting anyone.

A less expensive method of getting graphic material is to contact an art student at a local art school or college. Although art work and graphics are a nice addition to your brochure, excellent brochures can be created without them.

Many desktop publishing programs are now available and can be used by you or your office staff to create the layout right on your own computer. (See "Additional Resource" at the end of the chapter.) One caveat, however: learning a desktop publishing system does not automatically make you a computer graphics designer. Those trained as graphic designers are better suited to create pleasing, readable designs. You may want to have your original design formatted on computer by a designer and saved to diskette so that minor corrections (changes of address, phone numbers) could be made without additional costs.

The key to buying real estate is "location, location, and location." During production of any print work, the key is to proof, proof, and proof. Working with your designer, you approve the design and layout samples. Next, your copy is run through a pagination system and the computer generates the first set of pages. If the design is complex, the compositor may opt to paste up the copy on cardboard sheets, commonly called "boards" or "mechanicals." Make sure that you and another person carefully check the draft pages for any remaining typographical errors and make all necessary changes. After you have released the brochure for printing, you will get one last chance to check the material when "bluelines" (photographic reproductions in blue ink showing how the final product will look) are generated right before the final printing.

Often very simple errors (like the omission of an important name or subtitle) will be missed in the early stages of proofreading only to be caught when the brochure has already been printed. Most printers will ask that you "sign off" on the work before it goes to press, stipulating that any further errors are your responsibility. So make sure you proofread everything carefully and have someone with a fresh eye read the copy as well.

DISTRIBUTING THE BROCHURE

After your brochure is printed, what do you do with it? Leaving a stack of brochures sitting on the counter is not the most effective use. I suggest you send a brochure and an accompanying introductory letter to all new patients. Send a brochure to all your established patients as well. Give a brochure to all patients you see in the hospital on a consultation basis. Offer brochures to referring physicians who frequently send patients to your office. If you do public speaking, have the brochure available to give to members of the audience if they ask for more information about you or your practice. Your brochure is a much nicer giveaway than your calling card.

If you participate in health fairs or screening clinics, take along lots of copies of the brochure. You can also leave copies in the emergency room to be given to new patients referred by the emergency room doctors. I take a few brochures to the emergency room prior to the month that I am on call. This ensures that the brochures will be distributed when they are needed. Finally, if you are a primary care physician, a pediatrician, or an obstetrician/gynecologist, you might consider obtaining lists of new residents in your community and sending them each a copy of the brochure with an accompanying welcome letter.

Remember that brochures need not always be in print form. As discussed in Chapter 15 on creating office videos, your brochure can also be in the form of a videotape. You can also get extra mileage out of your brochure by using the same content on your web page—see Chapters 24 and 25 for details.

The Bottom Line   *A brochure describing one's practice is no longer considered a luxury. It is a necessary ingredient of a practice's overall marketing strategy. Create one that is informative and helpful, and this giveaway will keep on giving back to you.*

ADDITIONAL RESOURCE

- According to *PC Magazine,* **PrintArtist** is an ideal product for those who love creating cards, banners, and posters but also have a need for creating professional-quality newsletters, brochures, reports, and web pages. PrintArtist is available from Sierra, P.O. Box 3404, Salinas, CA 92912; *www.sierra.com.*

External Marketing: Attracting New Patients to Your Practice

External marketing is nothing more than letting your professional colleagues and the public know what you do, how you do it, and where to find you. It is this component of any marketing program that makes some physicians uncomfortable. These physicians often think that "marketing" is synonymous with "advertising."

You can make the public aware of your services and expertise in an ethical and professional fashion. According to the shopping cart analogy (see Figure II–1), external marketing is encouraging individuals in the community to become your patients.

You do not have to spend a lot of money to do this. Physicians can market their practices effectively without spending any money or purchasing Yellow Pages advertising.

The essence of external marketing is writing and speaking. This section of the book will review simple, inexpensive techniques to increase your visibility among your peers and in your community. These techniques do not require additional staff or anything more than minimal assistance from your hospital public relations and marketing departments. They are worth literally thousands of dollars in new patient billings.

By reading the chapters in Part II, you will learn

- how to attract and maintain physician referrals
- how to encourage satisfied patients to do your marketing for you
- how to write articles for local magazines and newspapers
- how to prepare a speech for a lay audience
- how to contact the media and land personal appearances on radio and TV

External marketing need not be expensive, but it does take time and organization. Your budget can be as small as the amount required for buying stationery,

131

stamps, and an extra telephone line. If you implement just one or two of the suggestions from this section of the book, you can anticipate receiving thousands of dollars of publicity and promotion. In fact, your first marketing projects should be simple. You do not necessarily need to start marketing your practice with a

Figure II–1 Cartoon showing analogy between shopping and external marketing. You want to coax those new patients and physician referrals "off the shelf." *Source:* Courtesy of Mitsue Lejeune, Touro Infirmary, New Orleans, LA.

four-color brochure, a logo, or an expensive, full-page, two-color ad in the Yellow Pages.

This type of external marketing is within the guidelines of local, state, and national medical societies. Ethical external marketing does not violate the Hippocratic oath.

The keys to external marketing for your practice are to identify what it is about your practice that would be of interest to the public and to identify what is unique about you and your practice. You need to answer the question, "Why would someone want to become a patient in my practice?" In most instances, it is not the special medicines a doctor prescribes or the speed of his or her surgery that determines the success of the practice. It is usually the little things—your attention to detail and your image in the community—that patients and colleagues remember.

Since the 1980s, health care itself has been considered newsworthy—witness the regular features on most news broadcasts, the wave of Internet sites, and the regular health columns in major and local newspapers. The result of this is that assignment editors have space (or time) to fill. Do you have an unusual success story about a patient or a family, an article or interview about a new procedure, or information the public needs to know about a symptom or a disease? Any of these can result in free media exposure worth hundreds and even thousands of dollars to your practice. If you provide a reporter with basic information about you and your practice, the reporter can create an interesting story that will place you in a favorable light with the listening, viewing, or reading public.

One of the benefits of external marketing is that appearing on TV or being the subject of a local newspaper article highlights your expertise. Your appearance in the print or electronic media says to the public that the writer or producer thought that your information was newsworthy and important to the public. An endorsement from a media representative whom the public trusts is far more valuable than a paid ad in the newspaper or a TV commercial.

This section of the book contains several chapters on how to deal with the media, both print and electronic. If working with the media is not for you, there are lots of other ways to do external marketing, such as starting a support group or putting together a newsletter. These may better suit your personal style.

Remember, external marketing is basically writing and speaking. If you want to market outside your practice, you need to think about putting your writing and speaking skills into action. But starting small, by starting a network or support group, can also enhance your image. These next chapters provide one way to "ease into" the public sphere.

The amount of time it takes to attract new patients by depending on word of mouth can seem like an eternity. If you put the following ideas to work, I can assure you that you will no longer need to wait the two to three years it takes to attract new patients by word of mouth.

CHAPTER 17

Your Net Worth Is Related to Your Network

network *n.* **1.** a fabric or structure of cords or wires that cross at regular intervals and are knotted or secured at the crossings **2.** a system of lines or channels resembling a network **3.** an interconnected or interrelated chain, group, or system.

Webster's New Collegiate Dictionary

Networking has been a buzzword of business and industry professionals for years. When you hear the word *network,* you may picture a group of people standing around at a cocktail party or "doing lunch" at some famous watering hole. The idea is that if you get to know enough people, you extend your channels for getting new business.

The kind of networking I am talking about involves setting up systematic lines of communication to expand your marketing potential. When you incorporate networking into your marketing strategy, you have a powerful tool for disseminating information. You can create a network of patients who will spread the good word about your practice, or you can establish a network of fellow physicians who meet on a regular basis to discuss marketing ideas.

In this chapter, I review several examples of networking that can be applied to medical marketing.

NETWORKING SHARED EXPERIENCES

A patient network is similar to a support group, although it is not as formal. This kind of network is especially appropriate for patients considering whether to undergo a surgical procedure or treatment. For years the medical profession has used patients to discuss their experiences with other patients. Patients develop a great

135

deal of confidence and security when they hear firsthand from someone who has "been there." Perhaps the most well-known example is the ostomy patient who talks with other patients who have been told they need a cystectomy or colectomy or the Ready for Recovery network for breast cancer survivors who have had mastectomies.

It has been my experience that patients who have devastating problems like impotence, infertility, or urinary incontinence and who have been helped are frequently willing to discuss their positive experiences with others who suffer from similar conditions.

When you connect people with similar problems, you accomplish several goals:

- You help the patients considering the procedures to allay their fears and to arrive at a decision with confidence.
- You allow the patients who have completed treatment to give something back.
- You allow the patients who have completed treatment to help you with your marketing.

An example of how a patient network markets your practice is to allow a patient considering a procedure or treatment to call another patient who has undergone a similar procedure. For instance, if a woman is considering a surgical procedure for correcting incontinence, I arrange for her to speak with another woman who has already had the surgery and has had a good result.

It is fairly simple to set up this exchange. Here is how it is handled in my office. I keep a list of patients who have agreed to talk with other patients. I try to match the two women (the one who completed the procedure and the one who is considering it) with regard to age, diagnosis, and socioeconomic background. Someone in my office contacts the chosen patient from the list. He or she asks the patient what would be the most convenient time for a prospective patient to call.

The patient considering surgery is then given only the telephone number and the time to call. No names are ever exchanged, so neither patient's privacy is invaded. The patient considering surgery is given a sheet of instructions (see Exhibit 17–1) and a script to follow to make the call meaningful to her. We tell the patient considering surgery to write out a few questions before her call. We also tell her that, when she calls, she should identify herself as a patient of Dr. Baum's and ask for the lady of the house.

We have found that our patients respond really well to this technique. It is not unusual for a patient who has been undecided or ambivalent about a procedure to call the office and schedule the surgery immediately after talking with a patient who has had the procedure.

Exhibit 17–1 Phone Calling Instructions for Patient Networking

---

Mr. [Name]

- Call _____ and identify yourself as a patient of Dr. Baum's and ask for the man of the house. He does not have your name and it is not necessary to give him yours.

- You may ask him any questions you want regarding the procedure.

- I suggest that you write down any questions that you would like to have answered before you call.

On one occasion, a man called a patient who had a penile implant and asked if his wife could speak to the implanted patient's wife. The implanted patient's wife agreed to answer questions and helped reassure the other woman about the procedure. I have always realized that taking care of a man with impotence also involves his significant other. By asking partners of treated men if they would participate in the networking process, I found that these women could relieve the apprehension and anxiety of partners whose husbands were considering having a penile prosthesis. Interestingly, I discovered that many women were happy to answer questions. I believe this is due to the fact that their lives have been so positively affected by this surgery.

ALTERNATIVES TO PHONE CALLS

Some patients feel uncomfortable calling a stranger. In these cases, you can accomplish the same result by creating an audio- or videotape library of "testimonial" tapes. If you have a patient who is particularly articulate and open about a procedure, ask if you could interview him or her. You can then offer these audio- or videotapes to prospective patients when the need arises. That way, they can listen to or watch the tape in the privacy of their homes. To record such interviews is fairly simple, especially if you keep the following rules in mind.

Write down the interview questions beforehand. Arrange them in a logical progression (for example, first ask the interviewee when he or she first learned of the diagnosis and its proposed treatment, then ask what his or her reaction had been). Proceed to questions about the procedure itself (for example, the preparation, type of sedation, side effects, and time for recovery). Finally, have one or two questions designed to elicit examples of the patient's improved quality of life since the procedure.

Tape the interview in a quiet room. Do a test recording to make sure there is no hidden background noise. If making an audiotape, use a microphone, because the quality of the tape will be better. If videotaping, use a tripod for mounting the camera. This will keep the camera stable and eliminate focusing problems. Review the tape afterwards. Let the subject also review it. If portions need to be edited out, you may want to record the tape onto another master. Refer to Chapter 15 for tips on editing your videotape.

NETWORKING FOR FEEDBACK

Years ago in the investment community, the acronym OPM (other people's money) became popular. OPM meant that you leveraged your investments with other people's money to increase your wealth. Today we can use networking principles to develop a philosophy of OPE (other people's experience).

There just is not enough time to devise a marketing strategy by applying the method of trial and error. A better method is to get together with a group of other physicians to discuss new ideas in medicine and brainstorm the application of new and used marketing techniques.

This type of networking allows you to communicate with like-minded physicians and share your experiences regarding patient care, office management, and marketing. My physicians' networking group was started informally in the doctor's lounge at the hospital. When I discovered there were several physicians interested in the same marketing concepts, we began meeting every three or four months for breakfast at a nearby hotel coffee shop. There are five physicians in the group, all of them specialists.

At each of our meetings, we discuss issues such as quality patient care and marketing strategies. We each review marketing concepts we have tried and discuss our successes and failures. Then we get feedback from the group as a whole.

Everyone benefits from this process. When I mentioned that I used treated patients to network with new patients, one of my plastic surgeon colleagues picked up on the idea. He decided to ask one of his nurses who had had a breast reconstruction if she would mind discussing her surgery with other potential patients. This nurse now makes presentations to patients about to have mastectomies who are referred to her by general surgeons. She is also available for postoperative consults on the oncology unit. She receives requests to see women receiving chemotherapy who have questions about breast reconstruction. According to the plastic surgeon, this nurse has been invaluable in allaying the apprehensions of women concerned about their self-image and femininity after a mastectomy. By adapting this method, the plastic surgeon has made use of double networking—networking within our physicians' group and with his prospective patients.

Another of my colleagues had a retired senior citizen who was doing some part-time work in his office. This gave me the idea to ask a senior citizen who was a patient to become a patient educator. It was a natural hookup. The senior citizen was available, so whenever we had patients who needed to be informed about procedures, he ran the flipcharts and did the patient education for us.

Developing a network of like-minded physicians is like having a board of directors for your private practice. By participating in a physician's network, I get invaluable advice. Often my colleagues' suggestions have shown me ways to modify my plans or to turn a "lemon into lemonade." In the process of developing my practice logo, I took several different designs to my physicians' network group. I asked for the opinions of my colleagues before making my final decision. I also discussed the concept of the computerized referral letter with the group long before I began incorporating it into my practice. I always solicit my colleagues' opinions on the ethical and professional ramifications of ideas that I would like to try.

The marketing ideas presented in the group are frequently quite creative. One colleague who is an orthopaedist was interested in building referrals to his practice to do more hand surgery. He told the group about making presentations to manicurists and now keeps us posted with regular reports on how this marketing technique is working. Ideas such as these open up our thinking about the opportunities for referrals outside the traditional doctor-to-doctor referral patterns.

You can also apply the concept of networking on a national level. Assembling a group of physicians who share interests from different areas of the country can be a valuable resource.

I have been a member of a national group and it has been an enriching experience for all the members. Ten urologists with an interest in marketing meet twice a year at vacation spots throughout the United States. This group is sponsored in part by a medical manufacturing company. The company creates an agenda, and each urologist is given a topic to discuss for 20 to 30 minutes. The presentations are followed by an open discussion in an informal atmosphere. Many of the doctors bring materials and Power Point™ slides that they use in their seminars and support groups. Diskettes of the Power Point™ files are distributed to all the members of the group. The exchange of marketing materials and slides has been invaluable to all members of the group.

The concept for this group was the brainchild of Dr. Ken Goldberg, a urologist from Dallas, Texas. He suggested to a medical manufacturing company that several physicians get together in an informal atmosphere after a national urology meeting to discuss surgical procedures, the company's product, and techniques to inform the public about the product. The first meeting was such a success that the group was expanded to 10 urologists. An informal newsletter that summarizes the meetings is prepared by the manufacturing company.

Most of the urologists communicate with each other between meetings on a regular basis and share professional articles, research, and projects. This allows us to enroll more patients and collect more data than any of us could accumulate alone. For example, three of us from different areas of the country collaborated recently on a project using a new penile prosthesis. By combining our results, we were able to report on more than 500 patients in an article we submitted to one of the urology journals.[1] It would have taken much longer for any one of us to have enrolled this many patients in the study.

This concept is used in clinical trials conducted by regional and national collaborative oncology groups, but I think the concept of a national network such as ours could be attractive to physicians in other specialties and medical manufacturing companies alike. Physicians interested in forming a national network should arrange to get together with other physicians before or after a national meeting at which medical manufacturing or pharmaceutical companies exhibit their products. Invite a few of the executives from pharmaceutical or medical device companies to your meeting. At the meeting, discuss the companies' products and how they might be improved or how their distribution to your colleagues might be increased. When the company executives recognize that your group is functioning like a focus group and that you can serve as consumer consultants, they can tune into what their customers need, not just what their companies happen to be selling at the time. Once you demonstrate your value to these companies, they will be happy to participate in your network or even sponsor it by underwriting some of the costs. In addition, the Internet and chat rooms can be used to conduct regular "conversations" with your entire network.

Networking can also be accomplished by an informational exchange program with physicians in your medical community who see patients who overlap two or more specialties. For example, many older men with prostate problems also have peripheral vascular diseases and ophthalmologic problems. I have set up a notebook exchange with a peripheral vascular surgeon and an ophthalmologist in my community. In their reception areas, they have a book prepared by my office that discusses prostate problems in the elderly and the importance of regular prostate examinations. Accordingly, I also display their information in a notebook in my reception area. The opening page of this notebook contains a letter to my patients about peripheral vascular disease (see Exhibit 17–2). The next few pages are articles written by the other physicians on the signs and symptoms of both peripheral vascular disease and eye problems of the elderly. The articles describe what can be done to diagnose and treat these problems. At the end of the notebook a few of my colleagues' office brochures are displayed. This helps patients understand the interrelationship of the specialties and gives all the physicians in the notebook exchange program additional exposure.

Exhibit 17–2 Informational Letter about Peripheral Vascular Disease

---

[Date]

Dear [Patient],

   As you may know, vascular disease afflicts thousands of Americans every year. In most cases, it causes disabling pain that cheats men and women in their prime years of an active life. In too many cases, it results in the catastrophic consequences of amputation, stroke, and even death.

   Yet, when it is diagnosed early, most vascular disease can be treated without surgery, using new noninvasive techniques to measure blood flow and identify arterial blockages. The problems in diagnosis result from the ambiguity of its symptoms, which in early stages can mimic other disorders of advancing age, such as arthritis and loss of muscle tone.

   There are many people who suffer from vascular disease and do not even know it. These people often attribute the aches and pains they experience while walking to natural aging processes, such as arthritis or degenerative joint disease. However, many times these aches and pains can be early warning signs of vascular disease. Early detection is important because 6 percent of the population with vascular disease who go untreated will have to undergo limb amputation, which can drastically alter their lifestyle. If vascular disease is detected early, two-thirds of the patients can be treated with exercise only. To help in early detection, we have compiled the ten warning signs you saw at the front of this booklet.

   You may contact Dr. Ira Markowitz and obtain a free consultation from him. His cards are located at the back of this book. Please take one or ask my secretary to make the appointment for you. If you have any additional questions, please do not hesitate to ask me.

Sincerely,
Neil Baum, MD

COMMUNITY NETWORKING

   Finally, do not forget that networking in local civic organizations enhances your visibility and your good image within the community. Most civic, school, and special interest organizations are eager for physicians to become active members or to give presentations and speeches. For example, if your target market is young mothers, you would want to seek out PTAs and the Junior League. If you are interested in attracting older patients, get involved with the local chapter of the American Association of Retired Persons. (Chapter 20 will provide you with more examples on marketing to senior citizens.) Middle-aged business people can be reached by participating in local civic groups like Rotary or Kiwanis clubs (public speaking is discussed in Chapter 26).

Networking is not new but it has a number of excellent applications to most medical practices. It provides an opportunity to educate and help current patients and to attract new patients.

The Bottom Line   *Networking is the "contact sport" for the next millennium. Find like-minded soul mates and network with them on a regular basis. It really will make a difference in your net worth.*

NOTE

1. I. Goldstein et al., "Safety and Efficacy Outcome of Mentor Alpha-1 Inflatable Penile Prosthesis Implantation for Impotence Treatment," *Journal of Urology,* 157 (1997): 833–839.

There's Strength in Numbers When You Start a Support Group

You can get whatever you want in this world if you'll just help enough other people get what they want.

Zig Ziglar

You need not depend on physician referrals for new patients. You can take your message straight to the public. People are eager for good information on health and medicine. If you choose appealing, timely subjects, you can bring in new business by holding support group meetings. One of the pluses of this marketing technique is the use of patient "testimonials," which, as the last chapter pointed out, can be very effective.

One of my areas of interest is erectile dysfunction, and I regularly hold support group meetings at hospitals. I publicize these groups about a month in advance. For this subject, I make sure that I get the word out to senior citizen groups in the area.

At one of my support groups, a 65-year-old patient got up to speak. This man was a happy camper. He had recently received a penile implant, and he told the audience that following his implant surgery he felt like he was 18 years old again. His enthusiasm was so infectious that the responses from that support group were double the usual number.

Public speaking and support group programs can work for you, too. Using these programs, you can target audiences according to specific diseases, diagnoses, and treatments and even specific demographic groups, such as senior citizens or adolescents. Potential patients get to know who you are, what you do, and where to find you.

TOPICS, DATES, AND PLACES

Think about the kinds of patients you want to attract to your practice. Are they senior citizens? Then they are probably interested in nutrition, cancer prevention, diabetes, and heart disease. Are you targeting young professional couples? Then you may want to talk about health, exercise, preventive health maintenance, parenting, infertility, and annual checkups. The topics of wellness, nutrition, and cancer prevention are almost universally appealing. Otherwise, choose a topic that interests you.

After selecting the topic, choose a date for your meeting. Keep the following in mind:

1. Select a date two to three months in the future.
2. Decide on several possible alternative dates as well.
3. Do not choose a date close to a major holiday. Because I practice in New Orleans, for example, I would never pick a date either a week before or after Mardi Gras.
4. Tuesday or Wednesday evenings are the best nights of the week. Most people do not schedule social engagements during the middle of the week.
5. If your target audience members are senior citizens, they may not be able to attend or drive at night. A Saturday morning or weekday afternoon meeting might be better for them.

Your hospital often has meeting rooms available free of charge. To avoid any problems, I suggest getting a written confirmation of the date and time for which you have reserved a room. Try to have the meeting at the same time each month. That way, the public and your hospital become familiar with your program.

CHOOSING SPEAKERS

Alcoholics Anonymous and cancer support groups are excellent examples of people sharing common experiences in a supportive group environment. These organizations have been successful because newcomers are given inspiration and gain confidence from hearing about others who have gone through the same cure or treatment. For this reason, I ask my successfully treated patients to participate in my support groups.

Initially I thought it would be difficult for patients to share their experiences in front of strangers at a public meeting. Yet, when asked, most have agreed to participate. When you carefully select the right people, they can be very reassuring and comforting to prospective patients.

Even though patients are usually happy to relate their experiences one on one, some may be uncomfortable with the thought of standing up and speaking to strangers.
Here are some suggestions to help relieve their anxieties:

- Rehearse with the patients.
- Provide the patients with suggestions or topics to cover. For example, what treatments did they have before? How had their problem affected their quality of life? What was the hospital experience like? What was the immediate post-operative recovery like? How did they feel several months later? Would they recommend the procedure to family members or friends with the same problem? Would they do it again?
- Show a video of a support group meeting or invite the patients to attend a meeting without speaking. In this way, the meeting format will be more familiar to them.
- Protect the patients by disallowing questions that are too embarrassing or too technical to answer.
- Send the patients thank-you notes to let them know how much you appreciate their participation in the support group program.

GETTING PEOPLE TO THE MEETING

Publicizing your support group or talk is probably the most important step. Many times this can be done without any expense to you or your hospital. If your topic falls under the heading of public or community service, the media will announce the meeting free of charge.

You can submit a press release to the radio, television, and print media. Send the press release to the attention of the health editor about four to six weeks before the meeting. Hospital public relations departments can help you prepare a press release and advise you about its placement. In communities where support groups are a new concept, the local newspapers are sometimes willing to give you free publicity by writing a column about your meetings. The newspapers are also interested if you have something newsworthy, such as the first, the newest, or a unique approach to medical problems.

Nonprofit organizations (churches or senior citizen groups, such as the American Association of Retired Persons) are also a good source of free publicity. They will often include your meeting announcements in their publications. For example, a funeral home sends a quarterly newsletter to several thousand families in New Orleans; the newsletter announces the meetings of my impotence support group. Just make sure that you are aware of the deadlines and send in your press releases in plenty of time.

If you are attempting to attract the yuppie crowd, contact the local health clubs and ask to have your support group announced on their bulletin boards or in their newsletters.

Ask your hospital to include the announcements in their mailings. Place the support group announcements on hospital bulletin boards as well as in reception areas and elevators.

Finally, place announcements in your own office—the only place you do not have to ask permission and where you have a ready-made receptive audience.

On the day of the meeting, plan to put up proper signage or directions to the meeting room. I suggest putting up large arrows pointing in the direction of the room at the major entrances of the building. They should be in place about 30 to 45 minutes before the meeting begins.

SETTING UP THE MEETING

Remember who your audience is and provide appropriate refreshments. If you are speaking to diabetics, have sugar substitutes for the coffee and low-sugar snacks. I think it is a nice idea to provide a pleasant distraction before the meeting, such as a video related to your topic. For example, I usually show a copy of a national talk show dealing with impotence. This sets the tone for the meeting, gives people who arrive early something to do, and brings them closer to the front of the room.

I also recommend you provide a sign-in sheet to record the names and addresses of all those who attend. Then you can use this list to contact attendees later through a newsletter or other office mailers.

Most hospitals have meeting rooms with different seating arrangements. It has been my experience that a circular arrangement is best if you are not using slides or other audiovisual aids. If you use slides or overhead transparencies, then the standard classroom arrangement is best. Make sure you arrive early and encourage audience members to move to the front to allow space for the latecomers in the back. If you are using slides, arrange for an extra projector, or at least an extra bulb, in case of a breakdown (Murphy's Law applies especially to audiovisual equipment).

CONDUCTING THE SUPPORT GROUP MEETING

Make sure you start on time. The entire meeting should last about 60 to 90 minutes. At the end of the presentation, open the floor for questions from the audience. I usually give each of several members of the audience a 3-by-5 card with a question on it before the meeting starts. I ask each person if he or she would mind asking the question on the card or one of his or her own. This seeds the audience and gets the question-and-answer session off to a good start.

You can also hand out blank 3-by-5 cards and ask members to write their questions on them. I usually include in the stack of question cards some of my own. This stimulates the audience to ask more questions. It also ensures that among the questions are some I want to answer.

This portion of your program will run more smoothly if you try to anticipate every conceivable question and objection in advance. It is a good idea to raise some of the objections yourself. This will show that you are fair-minded.

Offer to answer questions privately after the presentation has been completed. Be prepared to stay around afterwards. Many people will want to ask specific questions but may be too uncomfortable during the formal presentation.

Distribute brochures or handouts with your name, address, and telephone number at the end of the presentation so the audience is not distracted during the talk. Handouts are important for several reasons. They allow people to review the content of the presentation in the privacy of their own homes so they can focus on questions they may have about their particular problems. Handouts also give them the opportunity to contact you in your office at a later date.

FOLLOWING UP

Within one week of the support group presentation, you can send a follow-up letter and appropriate additional information to those on your sign-in sheet. The letter should thank them for attending and let them know you are available for answering any questions. You can then use their names to add to your database and periodically contact them when new treatments or diagnostic techniques are available.

How often should your support group meet? There are many factors that might influence your decision, but remember that frequent and consistent repetition is the key to any successful marketing technique. Image building not only depends on the subject matter but also on the frequency of exposure.

Try to track or record the results of your support group. You will want to know how many people attended, how many became patients in your practice, and what income was derived from these patients. With this information you can accurately determine the cost and energy per patient of running your support group. This information will indicate how useful the support group really is.

It requires lots of energy and effort to run a successful support group, and you can shorten the learning curve by sharing experiences with your colleagues. Consider developing a focus group for your support group. The focus group will help you identify techniques that work and techniques that tend to be less successful. Sharing successes and failures with your friends can make your program more successful. You do not want to have to learn how to run a support group by trial and error.

Instituting and maintaining support groups can be an excellent method of increasing the specific types of patients you want for your practice. However, there are two drawbacks: (1) support groups take time, and (2) the benefits or results are often not realized for months afterwards. Most audience members in my support groups wait 6 to 12 months after attending a support group meeting before they call for an appointment. I remember one man who came to see me for impotence. He carried my handout in his wallet for 18 months before he gained the courage to come in.

The Bottom Line   *Take your message directly to the people. By starting a support group, you build trust and loyalty among patients, who then take it upon themselves to "get the word out" about you and your practice. Remember, if you help enough people get what they want (find a solution to their medical problems), they will help you get what you want: a successful and enjoyable practice.*

ADDITIONAL RESOURCES

- James C. Humes, *Standing Ovation—How To Be an Effective Speaker and Communicator* (New York: Harper and Row, 1988).
- Malcolm Kushner, *Successful Presentation for Dummies* (Foster City, CA: IDG Books Worldwide, Inc., 1996).

CHAPTER 19

Marketing to Ethnic Communities

The United States has traditionally been perceived as a melting pot of various nationalities. Whereas the major tide of immigrants in the early twentieth century largely was composed of Caucasians of European descent, the latest wave of immigrants—from about the mid-1970s until today—has been more widely multicultural and multiracial. Although African Americans remain the country's largest minority group (12.7 percent, according to the 1998 update of the 1990 census), Hispanics now make up more than 11 percent of the total population. While the southwestern and eastern states are experiencing the largest influx of immigrants, the trend toward larger Hispanic and Asian American populations seems to be evident nationwide. In the Southwest and West, the surge in Hispanics has been evident for decades. But even states like Arkansas, Georgia, Nevada, and North Carolina have seen a doubling of their Hispanic residents since 1990. Asian and Pacific Islander groups, although constituting a smaller percentage of our population, are also increasing in numbers, growing from 3 percent of the total population in the early 1990s to almost 4 percent by the end of 1998.[1] Serving the health care needs of these patients can present a challenge, as well as many unique marketing opportunities, to the enlightened physician.

In this chapter, I review some of the techniques to keep in mind when you market your practice to ethnic and foreign-born patients. Whether you decide to target these groups specifically depends largely on the demographics of your community. If you do, in fact, want to reach them, you must be sensitive to and respectful of cultural differences.

DO YOUR HOMEWORK

Hispanic (sometimes used interchangeably with *Latino*) and *Asian* are very broad terms and are used to describe people who are from the same general geographic zone but have different cultural traditions. You cannot assume that placing a "Se Habla Español" sign on the door and having a bilingual receptionist are all that is necessary to attract Spanish-speaking patients. Hispanics move to the United States from every country in the southern hemisphere, and there are people of Hispanic descent from the northern hemisphere as well. You cannot assume that a patient from Mexico has the same interests, attitudes toward health care, cultural idiosyncrasies, and religious beliefs as someone from Argentina, for example.

Similarly, the Asian American population includes Chinese, Japanese, Koreans, Filipinos, Vietnamese, and Pacific Islanders, among others, and their political and cultural histories are widely divergent. If you want to let these ethnic groups know that you are interested in providing health care for them, you must acknowledge and respect their differences so that they will feel comfortable coming to you. You also need to recognize that native-born and foreign-born members of these communities will have different health care needs as well as different attitudes toward our health care system.

As a health care provider, you need to understand the dietary backgrounds of the ethnic population you wish to attract. This becomes important for medical history taking as well as for recommending diets if your ethnic patients have to be admitted to your hospital. As their physician, you should know the types of food that your patients usually eat. For instance, many immigrant Asian Pacific Americans dislike dairy products, and a good percentage may have genetic lactose intolerance.[2] Many people from India are vegetarians, although you should not assume that someone who looks Indian and speaks with an Indian accent originated from that country. Many Indians migrated as merchants and adopted the foods and dishes of their "second" countries. In addition, you should educate yourself about the varieties of vegetarians: the ovo-vegetarians (diet includes eggs), the lacto-vegetarians (diet includes milk and vegetables), and the total vegetarians, or vegans (diet does not include dairy or seafood products). The nutritionist at your local hospital is a good source of information about vegetarianism.

A practice serving ethnic and foreign-born patients will often be faced with special medical problems that are not commonly seen in a medical practice that chiefly serves native-born Americans. For example, infectious and parasitic diseases can be more common in some new immigrants. Southeast Asian immigrants and refugees have a higher percentage of parasitism and tuberculosis than the general population.[3] As a result, physicians who treat recent immigrants know that they often have to screen for diseases that have been virtually eradicated from the United States. Patient education may often be necessary to advise families of vaccination programs. In addition, physicians treating Asian immigrants may be required to distinguish between the telltale lesions left after moxibustion (performed by heating tiny glass cups and placing them on the skin to draw out toxins as part of acupuncture treatments) and cigarette burns, which would otherwise trigger a report of child abuse to authorities.[4]

Many minority populations are prone to specific genetic disorders: African Americans have a higher incidence of sickle cell anemia, and Jewish people are at greater risk for Tay-Sachs. Recent immigrants from Southeast Asia have a higher incidence of alpha and beta thalassemia and hemoglobin E carrier state.[5] Japanese immigrants have a higher incidence of stomach cancer than Anglo Americans or even second-generation Japanese-Americans.[6]

Many immigrants, especially those from small rural communities, still depend on or are influenced by the practice of folk medicines. If you wish to attract patients accustomed to relying on folk remedies, you must find ways to incorporate these traditional practices (providing they are not harmful) into your treatment plans.

If you do not know it already, you will be encountering distinct belief systems that must be understood and respected. During my residency at Baylor University, for example, I treated patients from Mexico who, upon admittance to the hospital, began to remove the plants from the rooms at night. They believed that the plants would consume oxygen at night and thus deprive the patients of the oxygen they needed.

Physicians who provide obstetrical care should be especially sensitive to the reluctance of many immigrants to give birth in hospitals. With the effective use of translators, the concerns of patients and their families can be addressed in a caring way.[7] If you have taken the time to inform yourself about your patients, their customs, and their beliefs, situations like these that arise can be easily dealt with, and you will be able to make your patients feel at ease and still give them the care that they need.

TECHNIQUES TO ATTRACT ETHNIC GROUPS

Investigate the demographics of your community. This is crucial if you want to select an ethnic group with whom you would like to work. As in the case of most marketing, it is best to select a single group and target your marketing at that group. It is nearly impossible to be successful at marketing to several ethnic groups at the same time.

Learn to speak the language of the ethnic group you mainly serve. You will have an advantage in attracting foreign-born immigrants if you can speak their language. However, you can also serve their needs if you have someone on staff who can translate. It is a good idea, though, for you to learn some basic vocabulary, such as greetings, farewells, and the names of body parts. This will not only make diagnosis more efficient, but it will also make your patients feel welcomed.

Provide translations of educational materials for your patients. If these are not already available from pharmaceutical or medical manufacturing companies, have the most frequently used ones translated into their language. The nearest university or college might be a good resource. Often the language departments can refer you to people who do freelance translating. If you are located near a medical university, inquire at outpatient clinics to see whether they have translators on staff who sometimes "moonlight." You can hire these people on an hourly or per-project basis for your translating needs. Another possibility is to ask the medical manufacturing and pharmaceutical companies with whom you deal to translate their educational materials for you.

Depending on the makeup of the ethnic community, there may be some members who are illiterate. An office video narrated in the patients' language is an excellent means of communication. Depending on their experience, certain individuals may be willing to participate in a video in their own language.

Work with the local healers. Many immigrants who do not speak English will rely on folk healers for their health care. Many folk healers will prescribe herbal medicines or other traditional healing methods, such as acupuncture, and are often powerful figures in their local communities. Called shamans or curanderos, they are held in high esteem as the guardians of the physical as well as the psychic health of their communities. Folk healers also serve as culture brokers between the members of the ethnic groups and the outside world, including the health care system. Contrary to widely held assumptions that they operate totally outside the system, curanderos often make medical referrals and will help patients make medical decisions. As you get to know the ethnic community you are targeting, have someone introduce you to the curandero. Do some homework ahead of time. If you are flexible about combining modern technology with traditional medicine, the healer will often make referrals to you.

Participate in the ethnic community's civic organizations, churches, and schools. Offer to write medical articles in the community newspapers. Often the newspaper staff will help with the translation. If you have a pediatric practice, offer to set up a free immunization day at one of the community elementary schools. Make sure you bring bilingual brochures and plenty of handouts. In this way, you will become a visible force in the community.

Do not forget to place your name and telephone number in the ethnic community's Yellow Pages. The community might have special holiday books in which holiday wishes can be inexpensively purchased.

Offer evening and weekend office hours. This will endear you to most of your working patients but particularly to new immigrants who have new jobs and are anxious about leaving work to obtain health care during the day.

Include family members. Most immigrants have strong family attachments. For both social and economic reasons, extended families tend to live together and

Exhibit 19–1 Sample Expressions in Vietnamese and Greek

Greek Expressions	Vietnamese Expressions
Thank you: Efharisto	LÀM O'N (Please)
Hello: Yiasou	CÁM O'N (Thank you)
Goodbye: He're	*Hello or goodbye (same word):*
You're welcome: Parakalo	
How are you? Pos e'se	CHÀO CÔ (to a young woman same age as you)
	CHÀO EM (to a girl younger than you)
	CHÀO CHỊ (to a woman older than you)
	CHÀO BÀ (to a lady)
	CHÀO ANH (to a man younger than you)
	CHÀO ÔNG (to an older man)
	CHÀO BÁC (to a close old man or woman)
	CHÀO CỤ (to an old man or woman)

therefore tend to play a vital part in the selection and follow-up of health care. Relatives and family friends will often be present in the exam room and at the hospital bedside to provide emotional support. This can be frustrating to the physicians and hospitals and can result in delays in medical treatment. Accepting the value of the extended family is one of the best ways to endear yourself to foreign-born patients.

Most ethnic groups have an effective word-of-mouth network. If you are accepted by a few members of the ethnic group, word will travel fast and you can expect to become a lifelong provider of health care to their community. This also applies to certain religious groups. For example, Jehovah's Witnesses, who do not accept blood transfusions, will tell their friends and fellow sectarians about doctors who will treat them and agree to honor the proscription against blood transfusions and transfusion of blood products.

One of the benefits of marketing to ethnic groups is that grateful patients will often refer sick family members from their native countries to the United States for their health care needs.

Because of our changing demographics, there is an excellent opportunity to market your medical services to ethnic populations. For example, I have several referring physicians from Vietnam in my community and they have a large number of fellow countrymen as patients. I have been asked to write articles for a Vietnamese medical and dental journal and also to speak at Vietnamese medical and dental association quarterly meetings. I have found that my acceptance by both the doctors and their patients has escalated considerably by my learning a few words of Vietnamese to use in my talks and with their patients. Being able to say "hello," "thank you," and "good-bye," in another language is not that difficult and helps you connect on a human level with your local ethnic community. As illustrated in Exhibit 19–1, a short Vietnamese and Greek vocabulary list, even simple terms can be difficult in some languages, so ask for coaching!

The Bottom Line   *By understanding and respecting the unique health care needs of immigrant and ethnic populations, you can attract large numbers of new patients and their families to your practice.*

NOTES

1. Associated Press, "Census Reflects Growing Diversity," *San Luis Obispo County Tribune*, September 15, 1999.
2. Jane S. Lin-Fu, "Population Characteristics and Health Care Needs of Asian Pacific Americans," *Public Health Reports,* 103, no. 1 (1988): 18.
3. Ibid., 24.
4. Ibid.
5. Ibid., 25.
6. Ibid., 23.
7. Ibid., 24.

CHAPTER 20

Closing the Generation Gaps: Marketing to Boomers and Seniors

I don't skate where the puck is, but where the puck will be.

Wayne Gretsky

As mentioned in the previous chapter, "Marketing to Ethnic Communities," you will increase your patient base if you pay attention to the demographics of your area and key your marketing efforts accordingly.

If you are looking for opportunities to stay competitive and flourish in the next millennium, you will be wise to take into consideration current population trends—specifically, the two largest population groups in America today: the boomers and the seniors. After reading this chapter, you will have a better idea of each group's defining characteristics and lots of ideas about addressing their unique needs. If you can demonstrate that you are sensitive to their needs, each group will show their appreciation by continuing to use your services.

If you make decisions to attract a certain group or segment of the population, you can focus on their perceptions of the marketplace. If you understand boomer and senior lifestyles and social values, you can influence their purchasing decisions rather than trying to understand more commonly selected demographic factors like income, education, and gender.

WHO ARE THEY?

Although it is difficult—and sometimes unfair—to group people according to their generation, for the purposes of this chapter we will be talking about the general traits of these large groups of patients. People's world views are often molded by the economic, social, and cultural environment in which they spend their youth and young adult years.

155

Consumers can be divided into three broad generations—the "matures," the "boomers," and the "Xers." The matures, or seniors, were born between 1909 and 1945 and came of age under the shadows of the Great Depression and World War II, as well as the Korean War. Matures grew up in tough times and their core values are what we refer to as traditional values. As a rule, they tend to value discipline, self-denial, hard work, obedience to authority, and are often financially and socially conservative.

Born between 1946 and 1964, baby boomers (boomers for short) are the most populous and influential generation in America. They were born to prosperity during America's booming postwar economic expansion. They enjoyed unprecedented employment and educational opportunities.

Xers were born after 1964. They have experienced tumultuous political and economic changes. They are a savvy generation, enthusiastically ready, willing, and able to take on the challenges they face. For now, though, we will focus first on the boomers and then the seniors.

PROMOTING YOUR PRACTICE TO BABY BOOMERS

The value system of the boomers, often called the "me generation," was built on the sense of entitlement created by their presumption of continued economic growth.

Profile

Baby boomers represent nearly 80 million Americans with a median household income of $43,000. They own their own homes and most are employed, including the women, who were the first generation to benefit from increased opportunities open to females. Most boomers grew up under the watchful eyes of doting mothers who did not work and who read Dr. Benjamin Spock for parenting advice. The older boomers are now reaching their peak earning years. Most boomers are fixated on self-improvement and individual accomplishment.

Because of their experiences, boomers as a group share certain commonalities, such as:

- *Boomers are big spenders*, since during their youth they were freed from worry about basic survival. Many boomers have taken spending to the extreme, going into large amounts of debt because they were confident that there was plenty more where it came from.
- *Boomers expect success and prosperity.* During their formative years there was a strong sense of entitlement and expectation that fueled this mentality of what they felt they deserved or was coming to them.

- *Boomers desire to be in control, are very competitive, and always want to win.* They want to show off their accomplishments and their trappings of success. The philosophy of many "yuppie" (young, upwardly mobile) boomers is, "He who dies with the most toys wins." Business analysts believe that boomers will keep spending whether they need to or not, or whether they can afford to or not. And this spending applies to health care services as well.
- *Boomers expect 100 percent customer satisfaction* and they will carry their displeasure with even small mistakes all the way to the courts.
- *Boomers have experienced more stress than any other generation in history.* The major cause of boomer stress is too many things to do, too many responsibilities to manage, too many decisions to make—and too little time. Boomers are searching for less stress through simplification. This is a major hot button for boomers and any practice that can identify ways to reduce stress for the patients will be very attractive to boomers.
- *Boomers are interested in technology and how it will simplify their lives.* Boomers are hungry for information that tells them that the service or procedure they are about to have is the best for them. They also want to participate in the decision-making process, especially when it comes to their own health care. While the matures from the preceding generation are still likely to accept a prescription, a pat on the back by the doctor, and a smile from the nurse suggesting they look forward to their next visit, you will not be able to get away with that approach when talking to boomers. They want to know the risks and benefits of, as well as alternatives to, whatever treatment you propose. They are also increasingly interested in what complementary medicine has to offer.
- *Although boomers are big spenders, they are also price sensitive.* They do not want any surprises. Unexpected fees will erode the rapport between boomers and their doctors, so do not be afraid to frankly discuss costs with them.

Meeting the Needs of Boomers

The two major value trends that are attractive to boomers are: (1) the need for simplification and (2) the need for control. Although managed care simplifies medical decision making, it often does so by wresting control from doctors as well as patients. Boomers are interested in selecting their own physicians. They do not want to be told which physician they must see for which medical problem they happen to have. They want to have control of this decision-making process.

Boomers are not going to retire in the same way that matures retired. They plan to retread instead of retire. This will be a plus for the medical profession, as boomers will be seeking new devices and treatments that will allow them to go back to work and stay active.

Boomers will contribute to the expanding definition of health care in America. Many of them are prepared to spend a much bigger chunk of their discretionary income on health care, if it helps them feel better, look better, and live longer than their parents. Rather than put up with deteriorating vision, people are flocking to have corrective laser surgery and intraocular implants. Weekend warriors are willing to undergo procedures such as ligament reconstruction if that means they can be back out on the ski slopes and on the tennis courts.

With all these factors in mind, it makes good economic sense to attract boomers to your practice.

Here are 10 tips to help you do just that:

Tip 1. Boomers want to be seen on time. There is probably no other aspect, including your fees, that disturbs boomers more than having to wait for the doctor. Most boomers remain employed and will not tolerate waiting for the doctor. In today's fast-paced, consumer-oriented society, boomers expect to be seen and treated promptly. Boomers understand and appreciate good customer service, and a big part of good service is no waiting. Chapter 3, "Don't Be Late for a Very Important Date," supplies lots of ideas on how to get a handle on your patient scheduling (conduct a time-and-motion study); deal with scheduling difficulties; and eliminate long waits.

Tip 2. Before launching into his or her medical history and physical examination, develop rapport with the boomer patient. The best way to do this is to use personal information notes, described in detail in Chapter 5, "If Domino's Delivers, So Can We." Essentially, the technique involves keeping sheets in patients' charts that allow you to add notes about their personal lives. Your staff can be encouraged to add to these notes whenever they have a telephone or in-person encounter with patients. Then you simply read over the notes before you step into the exam room.

Tip 3. Use the patient's name whenever possible. Everyone likes the sound of his or her own name. Make every effort to use the boomer's name each time you or your staff encounter the patient. For example, encourage your receptionist to use the caller's name at least twice during every phone conversation. You might conclude the phone call, "It's nice to talk with you, Mrs. Boomer. We look forward to seeing you next Thursday at 4:00." This personalizes the call and is appreciated by your boomer patients.

Tip 4. Provide educational material. Boomers are interested in information on their medical conditions. Provide them with a list of websites that you believe are useful and that provide reliable, accurate information. As an extra touch, you can ask your scheduling nurse or receptionist to identify patients' medical problems before they come to the office and send them educational material in their welcome to the practice letters. This makes for well-informed boomers who now can participate in any decision making regarding their medical condition. In Chapters 6 and 7, we provide you with several excellent websites that offer reliable health information for your patients.

Tip 5. Treat your boomer patients as key patients and call them at home. Chapter 8, "Marketing on Ten Minutes a Day," outlines the process for identifying key patients and the protocol for calling. This simple technique will go a long way toward endearing boomer patients to you and your practice.

Tip 6. Provide boomers with easy access to the practice. Boomers with a medical problem do not want to wait to get an appointment with the doctor. They are not impressed if the doctor has a three- to four-week waiting period in order to be seen. I suggest that you keep open one or two time slots each day to add urgencies and emergencies. You will find they almost always get filled and this is very appreciated by your boomer patients. Also, boomers appreciate very early morning, late afternoon, and weekend appointments so they do not have to miss work to come to the doctor's office.

Tip 7. Demonstrate that you are on the cutting edge of technology. Boomers want to know that their doctor is savvy about new technology. Place copies of your curriculum vitae and certification of attending continuing education courses where your patients will see them, perhaps in a notebook in the reception area or in the exam rooms. If you have a website, be sure to tell your boomer patients that they can log on and receive educational materials from your website and even make appointments with your office through the Internet. (Chapter 25 has more information on setting up a program for patients to have their own web page for medical information.)

Tip 8. Provide boomers with one-stop shopping for their medical care. Busy boomers will probably consider it inconvenient to visit the doctor, then go to the lab for blood work, and then to the hospital for their diagnostic studies. You can make your practice attractive to boomers by offering all or almost all these services in your office or your building.

Tip 9. Make the reception area comfortable for your boomer patients. First, you must refer to the area where patients enter the office as the reception area and not the waiting room. (See Chapter 6 for the philosophy behind the reception area and ideas on how to make it an appealing place to be.)

The reception area should be comfortable with pleasing sights to see, nice sounds or music to hear, and pleasant smells, such as fresh cut flowers or potpourri. Pay attention to the boomers' tastes in reading material. Consider subscribing to financial magazines, travel magazines, and upscale publications such as *Southern Living, Architectural Digest, Veranda,* and *House Beautiful.*

Tip 10. Exceed their expectations. Boomers are looking for value. Let them know that you will not only meet their expectations regarding their health care but will make every effort to exceed them. For example, you can call or fax their prescriptions to the pharmacy so that their medications are ready when they arrive at the pharmacy. Consider paying for their parking. You can also give them information about their medication, which includes the purpose of the drug, the side effects, and contraindications to the use of the medication. Anything you can do to make their visit to you and your office a positive health care experience will endear yourself and your practice to this population.

Keep reading for tips on how to reach the people at the other end of the generation gap: the seniors.

PROMOTING YOUR PRACTICE TO THE MATURE MARKET

Many physicians and hospitals believe that marketing to senior citizens begins and ends with providing large-print magazines in the reception area and helping with transportation. Making your practice senior-friendly means that you must take into consideration many more factors and accommodations than those magazines. This marketing approach involves addressing both physical and psychological needs to make your older patients feel more comfortable.

Physiological Changes of the Matures

Changes that have implications for marketing or patient comfort generally occur after age 60. Aging entails significant physiologic alterations, including sensory changes, decreased manual dexterity, and other impairments. Practices that want to be attractive to senior citizens need to take these predictable changes into account and help their older patients adapt to them.

There isn't a physician who cannot describe the physiologic changes in the senses that occur in the elderly. But few have considered these physiologic changes from the perspective of a patient visiting their practices.

Allowing for sight and hearing impairments is important for health care providers. Failure to hear and see information can lead to anxiety, depression, and even paranoia. Common visual changes that need to be considered in making an office senior-friendly include problems with glare, slower response to changes in illumination, decreased depth perception, and failure to discriminate subtle gradations of color. At age 60, the angle and amount of light can determine a person's ability to see and read. In the past, marketers have paid little attention to light because they concentrated predominately on consumers in their forties and younger.

Hearing deficits also need to be considered. For example, music that is piped into the exam rooms and reception area may make it difficult for senior patients to hear the doctor. This can decrease patients' level of comprehension when talking with the doctor about their care.

Other health issues must be kept in mind in catering to older patients. Starting at age 40, most people experience a noticeable decrease in muscle strength. This usually does not become a problem until age 60, when decreasing muscle strength becomes a health care concern. Dexterity and fine motor movements also become impaired in seniors. Such reduced ability has implications for office design and access.

At the same time, attention span and memory can be fading. Therefore, it is important to provide instructions to caregivers and significant others if you feel that your patients are not comprehending your advice. Seniors often require lengthy explanations that must be spoken slowly and clearly to be understood. Whenever possible, provide written information handouts in large print (greater than 14 pt type). But even this approach requires extra sensitivity. You may want to wait until a patient requests instructions in a louder voice before you assume that there is a hearing deficit. Changes in attention span can also prompt some seniors to become anxious with excessive waits in the reception room. Also, older patients may not tolerate temperature changes as well as younger people do. For example, an older patient may become chilled when undressed in the exam room. Take care to regulate the temperature and have light covers or sheets available.

Other changes occur, too. Aging and sexuality are strongly interconnected. For example, every urologist is aware that male patients have age-related decreases in erections. Impotence affects 10 percent of men at age 50 and nearly 60 percent to 70 percent of men at age 70. Yet in many cases the libido or sex drive in the older man remains intact. Many older patients, both men and women, experience sexual dysfunctions but are uncomfortable broaching the subject with their physicians. A sensitive physician will tactfully ask a patient, "Do you have any problems with intimacy with your partner?" This question signals that you are comfortable discussing the subject, even if the patient prefers to discuss it later.

A Lesson in Empathy

By making yourself and your staff sensitive to the physical and physiological changes in older patients, you can create empathy for the seniors in your practice. At my practice, this lesson involved having a staff member walk in the shoes of a senior patient—quite literally.

As is described in Chapter 31, "Add Sparkle to Your Staff Meetings," one of the staff members was temporarily converted to a senior citizen so she could experience firsthand what our patients were experiencing when they entered our office. We created cataracts and reduced vision by placing a patch over one eye and applying a viscous soap over her glasses. Her hearing was decreased by placing ear plugs in each ear. She was provided with a walker and gloved hands to simulate arthritis. A knee was braced and bandaged to reduce her mobility.

With her new attire, this instant "senior" went to the bank in the office building lobby, made a transaction, and then approached our office as a patient. She went through the entire office following a patient's typical routine.

Following this role playing, she described to the rest of the staff her feelings as well as the physical barriers she encountered. The exercise made the entire staff more sensitive to the problems affecting many of the senior patients visiting our practice.

Furthermore, it brought some concrete changes. We removed some chairs that were difficult to get in and out of. We added a writing desk where seniors can now fill out a patient history sheet, instead of sitting in a chair and using an unstable clipboard.

From Patient Needs to Practice Changes

Once you take into account the physiological constraints that your senior patients face, it is possible to plan and accommodate these and make your practice senior-friendly.

Many of the following suggestions can be put into place with little or no cost:

Tip 1. Transportation is often a concern for seniors. Getting to and from the doctor's office should not impose difficulty. Some practices, particularly ophthalmologic practices, offer transportation. Another possibility is establishing an arrangement with taxi companies for discounted fares for senior patients. It is also important to have the telephone numbers of public transportation readily available for your senior patients.

Tip 2. Make your office easy to find. Check the signage and building. Can it be seen easily from a car, both in early morning and late afternoon, when the angle of the sun can impair visibility? If your office is in a building with an elevator, be certain that floor numbers are easy to read. If you provide patients with a brochure, include a photograph of your building and send it to your new patients before their first visit.

Tip 3. The parking lot should have sufficient parking for patients with physical impairments. It is important to enable drivers to bring senior citizens near the building entrance. Also, the doors to the building and your office should easily accommodate wheelchairs.

Tip 4. Provide adequate light and color breaks to denote changes in elevation. If patients need to go up or down stairs to get to your practice, keep in mind that depth perception decreases with age. Be sure that handrails are easy to grab. Check that there is space between the rail and the wall so that patients do not scrape their hands.

Tip 5. Provide safety rails in the restroom to assist patients getting on and off the toilet. Levers are easier to open than knobs for patients with arthritis or limited hand mobility. Better yet, automatic doors eliminate all door-opening problems.

Tip 6. Design your office interior with the senior or low-vision patient in mind. Subtle gradations in color, like pastels, will be lost on most aging eyes. Bright contrasting colors are senior-friendly. Signs should be in large type with contrasting colors.

Tip 7. Your reception area deserves attention. Are chairs firm and with armrests? Is the furniture arranged to avoid obstacles? Hallways need to be carpeted since slick tiles are an invitation to spills. Is there good lighting? Do you have an array of reading materials in large print?

Tip 8. Keep an afghan or portable heater for patients who need extra warmth, if your office is chilly.

Tip 9. All printed materials should be designed with the aging eye in mind. Keep type large and in short lines, and use contrasting colors. Matte or non-shiny paper is best to avoid glare. If you use photographs in your brochures, be sure they depict older patients as vibrant, active individuals.

Tip 10. Your staff must be keyed to the needs of the seniors. The staff member who reviews new patient insurance forms should offer to assist with paperwork.

The practices that really want to cater to the mature market will need to recognize the importance of the Internet as more and more senior citizens come online. We have provided our senior citizens with useful websites that we believe will be of interest to them. Here is a partial list:

- *www.senioralternatives.com* (a virtual tour of selected retirement communities around the country)
- *www.elderweb.com* (lots of links to specific subjects including a useful housing guide)
- *www.ec-online.net* (comprehensive information about Alzheimer's disease)
- *www.aarp.org/indexes/health* (This site, maintained by the American Association of Retired Persons, includes pages about health, wellness, and caregiving. The latter provides discussions on how seniors can care for themselves and for those around them.)

Person-to-Person Interactions

It is interesting that when seniors are queried about their age, they report that they feel 75 percent of their chronological age. A sensitive doctor will interact with seniors at that psychological age rather than their chronological age.

Here are a few dos and don'ts:

- *Avoid labels that make too much of the age of your senior patients*, like "fifty-plus," "elderly," or "grays." Instead, the preferred or accepted terms are "mature," "senior adult," or "senior citizen."

- *Seniors do not like to be reminded of their infirmities or handicaps any more than they like to be reminded of their age.* Older people have the remarkable capacity to deny or ignore what might be troublesome to a younger person. If an impairment isn't relevant to the reason for the patient's current visit, don't make a big deal of it.
- *One of the primary psychological needs of the aging and elderly is their need for feeling independent and useful.* We can make our health care service attractive to this age group by providing products and services that preserve their independence.
- *Provide written instructions regarding the safe use of medications.* Older patients are at a high risk for complications associated with medications. Senior citizens often have multiple medical problems and frequently take several medications. Also provide them with information on the side effects and what to do should the side effects occur.
- *Take into account the limited fine-motor capabilities of your patients.* Often "childproof" containers are not senior-friendly for patients with arthritis, Parkinson's, or hemiparesis. (In households or situations where children might be present, childproof containers are still the rule.)
- *Many older patients are creatures of habit.* Try to provide consistency for them. If a senior citizen finds it convenient to have an appointment in the early morning, do not schedule follow-up visits in the late afternoon. Accommodate their schedules and habits whenever possible.
- *The attitude of everyone at a practice is critical.* Train your staff to treat older patients with courtesy, respect, and consideration.
- *Older people can be rude, insensitive, and angry—just like younger people.* This chapter has looked at common problems, but do not prejudge or routinely categorize your older patients.
- *Older patients, especially those living alone, often seek socialization and interaction with the staff during their visit to health care providers.* Staff members who are friendly and comment on a patient's new hairdo or new outfit are a plus to your senior patients. When seniors show negative behavior, your staff should be prepared not to respond to it in a negative or defensive fashion—it is counterproductive.

To keep it light: in our practice, we like to make jokes a lot. See Exhibit 20–1 for an example of a senior friendly bill stuffer that our older patients often enjoy. (Actually, your boomer patients may also get a laugh, since many of the items are from their past, too.)

Nearly every physician will be encountering older patients. In many practices, they will make up the majority of patients. Developing sensitivity to these older patients is not only good marketing but good medicine as well.

Exhibit 20–1 How Many of These Do You Remember?

1. Blackjack chewing gum
2. Wax Coke-shaped bottles with colored sugar water
3. Candy cigarettes
4. Soda pop machines that dispensed bottles
5. Coffee shops with tableside jukeboxes
6. Home milk delivery in glass bottles with cardboard stoppers
7. Party lines
8. Newsreels before the movie
9. P. F. Flyers
10. Butch wax
11. Telephone numbers with a word prefix (Olive–6933)
12. Peashooters
13. Howdy Doody
14. 45 rpm records
15. S&H Green Stamps
16. Hi-fi's
17. Metal ice trays with levers
18. Mimeograph paper
19. Blue flashbulbs
20. Beanie and Cecil
21. Roller skate keys
22. Cork popguns
23. Drive-ins
24. Studebakers
25. Wash tub wringers

       If you remembered   0–5 = You are still young
       If you remembered   6–10 = You are getting older
       If you remembered 11–15 = Don't tell your age
       If you remembered 16–25 = You're older than dirt!

The Bottom Line *If you understand the values that motivate the buying decisions of both your boomer and senior patients, you will stand a much better chance of spotting trends way ahead of the competition. Aim to please your boomers and seniors and you will be reaching patients first in profitable new ways.*

CHAPTER 21

Write That Masterpiece— and Send It to the Lay Press

"Publish or perish" applies to medical practices and medical marketing.

How many referral or new patients do you get from the articles you have written for professional journals? There is a good chance that your answer will be "none." My curriculum vitae (CV) lists nearly 100 articles I have published in peer-reviewed professional journals. I have not seen a single referral or a new patient as a result of these articles. However, I have written several hundred articles for local newspapers and magazines that have generated hundreds of new patient visits to my practice.

Anyone who has published in professional journals knows that an article may require hundreds of hours of time and energy. Although these efforts add to your prestige within the medical community, the return on your investment, money-wise and marketing-wise, is very low. Writing an article for a local magazine or newspaper takes only a fraction of the time required for a peer-reviewed article and can generate dozens of new patients. For example, I wrote an article called "The Prostate—A Gland of Pain and Pleasure" that appeared in a senior citizen bulletin and generated nearly 50 office visits, five transurethral resections of the prostate, one radical prostatectomy, and one penile prosthesis surgery.

By writing articles for local newspapers and magazines, you can effectively promote your practice and your areas of interest and expertise. In this chapter, I discuss the advantages of publishing in the lay print media and the techniques of this style of writing.

WHY WRITE FOR THE LAY PRESS?

Published bylined articles in the lay press increase your visibility, your credibility, and, ultimately, your profitability. People are more likely to believe what you say if you have written it down first.

By writing articles for the local press, you can easily become a media resource. Reporters and editors will notice your pieces. Often they will contact you for articles or ask you for quotations to be included in articles they are writing. And, if you are responsive, they will keep you in their databases as a content person to call on whenever your specialty is in the news. You can promote this transition yourself. For example, when Joe Torre, manager of the New York Yankees, had surgery for prostate cancer, I contacted the local paper, the *Times-Picayune,* and offered to provide information about prostate surgery. Several years earlier, when Ronald Reagan had his colon polyp removed, the newspaper had contacted me for information for a story on the operation. Because this was not my area of medical expertise, I contacted a colleague who was happy to be quoted as the local expert on the subject.

HOW TO SELECT A TOPIC

Topics of interest to lay readers in your community undoubtedly include wellness; nutrition; cancer prevention; sexually transmitted diseases, such as AIDS; and sports medicine. You can create an interesting article about new procedures, new treatments, a unique case with an excellent result, or the use of new technologies, such as lasers to correct vision problems.

Do some research before you select your topic. Note what medical stories receive local and national attention on television. When a public figure, such as an athlete, entertainer, or politician, has a medical problem that is making national news, you might contact the local print media and offer to serve as a local expert on the subject. In most instances, newspapers will prefer to print an article with a local twist rather than use wire service articles. Give some thought to the demographics of your surrounding area. If, for instance, there is a substantial population of aging baby boomers in your area, you can be sure that topics related to menopause, bone health, heart disease prevention, and joint preservation will be of interest. If, on the other hand, there are lots of young families in your community, any topic related to pediatric medicine or parenting will get their attention.

Study the health news section of your local newspaper. Read national women's magazines, such as *Redbook, Family Circle, Allure, Self,* and *Vogue,* which often have excellent coverage of health issues. The print media is interested in personality profiles of health care professionals and of exceptional people coping with disability, illness, or the unique circumstances surrounding an illness.

Ideally, you should try to select a topic that is familiar to you and is identified with your practice. Then either find a new angle that will excite the readers in your community or tie the subject matter to a current event. The purpose of any article is to inform, entertain, or persuade the readers. The best articles will do all three.

Characteristically, physicians are capable of writing to inform the reader. Your challenge will be to arrive at a style and content that elevate the information above the level of simple explanation. If your article contains appropriate anecdotes and humorous stories, it will be more likely to attract and hold the reader's attention.

One caution in selecting a topic: Avoid subjects that are controversial, such as abortion and euthanasia, unless you are willing to take the heat.

MAKING A PITCH TO THE EDITOR

If you have met the health editor of a newspaper or magazine, you can contact him or her with your suggestion for a story. Otherwise, the standard approach is to send a query letter (see Exhibit 21–1). This is a short letter that describes the subject of your article, indicates the angle you will take, and includes some information about yourself. The query letter is the equivalent of a sales pitch. You will need to spend some time "up front" studying the publication to which you submit your query. Is your article appropriate? Are you targeting the right audience for your article?

Once you have written a query letter, you must ensure it gets to the appropriate editor. If necessary, you can call the editorial desk and ask for the name and title of the correct editor for the section you think is appropriate for your article, or where you have seen other related articles appear. Take that one extra minute to ask for the correct spelling of that editor's name and title—nothing is more indicative of amateurism in a writer than misspelled words, names, or titles. Whether your community is a small city or a large metropolitan area, keep in mind that the editor is a very busy person. Your query letter should be written to make an immediate impression on the editor, who probably receives dozens every day.

Your query letter should really be a condensed version of your proposed article, with a beginning (or lead), a middle, and an end. The editor will be looking for a "hook" or unique opening to attract the reader. After all, if your query letter is dry and uninteresting, how can the editor expect the story to be any different? Start the letter with the most interesting aspect of what you want to write about. Start with an eye-opening statistic, such as the number of people in the community affected with the health problem that you are going to discuss. The next paragraph might describe the benefits of the article to the reader. The third paragraph mentions your qualifications to write the article. (In most cases, having "M.D." after your name will qualify you as a reliable source.) The last paragraph offers additional information, including how and when to reach you. Limit the query letter to one page.

One of the best hooks I ever read was in a query letter by an executive from Chemwaste Corporation, a recycling company that was concerned with environmental issues. The letter began: "It takes 75,000 trees to provide the paper for a single edition of the Sunday *New York Times*. Perhaps we should take a picture of

Exhibit 21–1 Sample Query Letter

January 25, 2000

Mr. Michael Lafavore
Executive Editor
Men's Health
Box 114
Emmaus, PA 18099-0114

Dear Mr. Lafavore,

Did you know that even after the introduction of the "miracle drug" Viagra, some men are still suffering the tragedy of the bedroom?

I see these men by the scores every week. I am a urologist in private practice in New Orleans, Louisiana, and one of my areas of interest and expertise is the diagnosis and treatment of impotence.

I have written a number of articles on this subject in both the professional and lay literature. I have coauthored with Dr. Steve Wilson a book for men entitled, *Ecnetopmi: (Impotence) It's Reversible.*

Dr. Wilson and I would like to suggest an 800- to 1,000-word article for your publication, *Men's Health.* We are suggesting an article that is positive, upbeat, and reassures men that help is available for nearly all men who suffer from this problem. Our message is that in the year 2000 "no one needs to suffer the tragedy of the bedroom."

I am enclosing my curriculum vitae, several articles that I have written, and our book.

I look forward to hearing from you.

Sincerely,

Neil Baum, MD

---

the forests so our children can see what they look like. Better yet, if we recycle, we can preserve the trees and our children can even climb one."[1] That beginning captured my attention and motivated me to read the rest of the letter.

Once you have sent the query letter, you must be prepared to track it. Unless you have a scientifically proven cure for cancer, or a better drug to treat impotence than Viagra, a follow-up call is a necessary part of the getting-published game. In many cases your query letter will not be looked at for weeks, so find out if the editor received the letter and had a chance to read it. Some writers send a self-addressed, stamped envelope with the query letter to make it easier for the editor to reply. One writer I know includes with her query a stamped, self-addressed postcard with boxes next to the following statements:

- Received your query and will reply in _____ weeks.
- Received your query but we are not interested at this time.
- Received your query and want to talk to you right away.

If, when you call the editor, he or she is "still thinking about it," offer to provide additional information. Make the call short and call back in a few weeks. If you do not get an answer within two months, politely let the editor know that you intend to pitch to another publication. Then do it.

The etiquette regarding e-mail is still evolving when it comes to contacting an editor whom you do not know personally. If the editorial desk will give you the editor's e-mail address, then by all means use it, but do not abuse it. Common sense should prevail in an e-mail conversation, as it does with phone conversations. Do not "bug" the person with frequent messages sent too soon after your query.

Remember, there are other places to publish besides the local newspaper. If you are targeting senior citizens, contact the local branch of the American Association of Retired Persons (AARP) and offer to write an article for its newsletter, or write a query letter to *Modern Maturity*, the national magazine of AARP (*www.aarp. org*; the editorial office is located at 601 E Street NW, Washington, DC 20049). If parents are your target audience, contact parenting and children's magazines. There are also many city and regional magazines that take articles written on health care issues. *The Writer's Market*, published every year by Writer's Digest Books, is an excellent resource for possible outlets for your writing. It is available at bookstores, at your local library's reference desk, or through the Internet at Amazon.com and other booksellers.

Finally, keep your eyes open for writing opportunities. For example, I was asked to give a talk on urinary tract infections at a health club. I went to the club and no one was there to hear my talk. As I was walking out, I noticed the club's newsletter. I asked the director if the club published articles by physicians. He said no one had ever asked him before. I suggested an article on the use of testicular examination to screen for the most common kind of cancer in men between the ages of 20 and 40. This article was published in the newsletter and went out to 5,000 health club members in that age range. It resulted in 10 office consultations and lots of phone calls from concerned young men.

DOING THE HARD WORK

Once an editor has asked you to submit your article, how should you go about writing it? I can only discuss what has worked for me. Each person will have a different way of writing, so once you find your style, you will know it.

I believe the easiest way to start is to tape-record an interview with a patient (with his or her permission, of course) in which you discuss the patient's illness or medical problem. Grateful patients are especially likely to agree to an interview. A three- to five-minute discussion can supply the basic material for an article for most newspapers and magazines.

Get the tape recording of the interview transcribed. Then ask the hospital marketing or public relations department to assist you in editing the article for the print media. Another possible resource is the local college. Teachers and students sometimes will provide editing assistance at a nominal fee.

Once the article is written, personally deliver it to the editor in order to establish a face-to-face relationship. This latter advice applies if the publication is a local one. If you do not hear from the editor within a few weeks, follow up with a telephone call. Always make sure you deliver your article on time and in the format requested (hard copy, diskette, e-mail). That is the most valuable commodity to a busy editor. If an editor accepts your masterpiece and has to badger you for the final copy, it is likely that you will never be asked to write again for that editor or publication.

CAPITALIZING ON YOUR CLIPS

You can get additional marketing mileage from your articles long after they have been published. For example, the articles can be framed and hung in your reception area or examination rooms. I can assure you that your patients would rather read articles written by you than see your diplomas on the wall. Copies of the articles can be sent to your referring physicians and to patients as bill stuffers along with their monthly statements.

If you have negotiated to keep all reprint rights, you can submit the articles to other publications for a second printing—and usually get paid a small fee for giving them the right to reprint your article.[2] Add the articles to your CV. The articles can be placed in a bound book in your reception area, and you can offer to provide photocopies to any patient who requests them. Finally, you can send copies to the local radio and TV stations and suggest that you be interviewed for a story on the subject. One of the advantages of writing articles is that they have a long shelf-life compared to radio and TV appearances, which only reach those who were listening or watching.

BE PREPARED FOR REJECTION

Do not expect to publish every article you write or to get a positive response on every query. Never forget that John Grisham, the lawyer turned best-selling novelist, sent his first book manuscript to dozens of publishers before it was accepted.

Everyone hates rejection. We physicians are programmed to get people well and to expect quick results from our interactions with our patients. As a consequence, many of us are reluctant to attempt to use the print media for the purpose of marketing our practices. However, you will find that getting published is not especially difficult once you learn to accept the rejections that come with the territory.

The Bottom Line   *Like medical skills, writing skills can be learned and polished. The more you do, the better you get. And the better you get, the more patients you will attract to your practice.*

NOTES

1. Roger Ailes, with Jon Kraushar, *You Are the Message (Secrets of the Master Communicators)* (Homewood, IL: Dow Jones-Irwin, 1988).
2. See the American Civil Liberties Union, *The Rights of Authors and Artists* (New York: Bantam Books, 1984) for information about copyright law. Also consider joining the Textbook Authors Association, P.O. Box 535, Orange Springs, FL 32182-0535, which offers services to authors and a variety of handbooks on publishing rights and contracts.

CHAPTER 22

Nothing Does It Better...
Than a Newsletter

Do you ever long for the "good old days," when the practice of medicine wasn't so encumbered by compliance regulation, the necessity to obtain authorization for a patient visit, and the need to apply to dozens of managed care plans in order to be able to see your patients? It is not unusual; many physicians, especially those in private practice, feel that way. Even those who have begun practice in the last 10 years and know only the current managed care model may wonder where the magic has gone. Buried under a deluge of gatekeepers, practice guidelines, and stringent referral policies, many physicians have started to experience "burnout."

For anyone who wants to put in a little creative effort, though, medicine still offers fantastic opportunities. Making use of marketing techniques not only increases your income, it lifts some of the burden from your shoulders. Various media offer you a chance to enhance your image and have some fun doing it. By producing a patient newsletter, for instance, you can generate excitement among both new and longtime patients.

As a marketing tool, a newsletter is similar to public speaking. By emphasizing your credibility and your concern for your patients' health, you simultaneously build the loyalty of your old patients and attract new patients to your practice.

Unlike public speaking, however, a newsletter does not deliver instant feedback. In this chapter, I review the essentials of creating your own newsletter. It can be an ambitious undertaking. You may want to develop a newsletter after some of your other marketing strategies are in place. It is certainly not the first project to consider when marketing your practice. Depending on the amount of time and money you want to invest, there are several alternatives, including subscribing to a newsletter service.

WHY WRITE A NEWSLETTER?

The last decade of the twentieth century has seen an explosion in health and medical information designed for public consumption. More than ever before, patients want to learn about health and fitness and the prevention, diagnosis, and treatment of disease. At the same time, patients often complain that their physicians do not communicate effectively. One of the most frequent reasons patients leave a practice is the doctor's failure to communicate.[1] The days of handing a patient a prescription and saying "Take one tablet a day and call me in two weeks" are over. Patients have a far greater desire to receive information from their health care providers. In fact, many are not waiting to query their physicians for information. With the affordability of personal computers and the explosion of the Internet, more and more patients are turning directly to that source for their health and medical information. In 1999 alone more than 22 million Americans used their computers to seek medical information. That number is expected to climb by 70 percent a year, says Scott Reents of the market research firm Cyber Dialogue, Inc.[2]

But while more and more patients seek information on the Internet, not all are well-equipped to evaluate that information, some of which is patently false and much of which has not been subjected to peer review. A study reported in *Cancer* found that more than one-third of websites listed under the disease Ewing's sarcoma did not contain any peer-reviewed information, and a full 6 percent had incorrect information regarding the survivability of those who had had it.[3]

A newsletter can address all these concerns. Patients are more likely to choose to stay with a physician who helps them learn how to take care of themselves and who communicates with them. A newsletter will also provide an instant forum for your ideas. You can headline new treatments and drug therapies, provide helpful hints for good health, and generally communicate more with your patients and the public. You can also provide listings of reputable medical website addresses in your newsletter, thus saving your patients from sifting endlessly through useless information. This increases your credibility as a health care provider who is interested in patients' desires for more information.

A newsletter keeps your patients current in other ways. For example, your patients on average might visit your practice a few times each year. A newsletter will increase your exposure to your patients by a factor of two to four, depending on how frequently it is printed.

Surveys of physician practices have demonstrated that there is a positive correlation between practice gross and the use of newsletters. According to Cheryl Farr, an effective newsletter can increase the number of new patients who enter a practice.[4] It can also reactivate existing patients who have not been seen for several years. Publishing a newsletter is one of the best methods to capture a current or prospective patient's undivided attention. Newsletters have one advantage over other forms of media—there are no advertisements to distract the reader.

Use a newsletter to inform your patients of the latest available technologies. You can also feature articles on new procedures or services that you are incorporating into your practice. For example, in my urology practice I wanted to spread the word about intracorporeal injections of prostaglandin for the treatment of certain patients with erectile dysfunction. I included an excerpt of an article I had written on this subject in the quarterly newsletter. We then used the newsletter as a bill stuffer for the next month, targeting our male patients with erectile dysfunction problems. In response to the 250 newsletters we mailed, we received 10 calls from patients asking for the treatment.

The newsletter provides your practice with a mechanism to track the results of your marketing program. The newsletter can contain a reply card or a special telephone number, which is the same method used in conjunction with a Yellow Pages ad. You may want to devise a code or system for distinguishing between new patients attracted to the practice and old patients drawn back. Each time a reply card is mailed in or the special phone number is called, have your staff enter this information into your computer. You can then determine the number of patients that enter your practice as a result of the newsletter. You can also calculate the income derived as a result of the newsletter. (In Chapter 43 I explain how to use the office computer to tabulate results.) The procedure allows you to accurately measure the return on investment of the newsletter.

Finally, a newsletter allows you to target certain groups of people. For example, if you are a pediatrician, you can selectively mail to nursery schools and day-care centers in your area. Such a newsletter might feature articles on preventing the spread of infectious disease as well as contain pertinent immunization information. Because of my interest in male sexual dysfunction, I have targeted audiences who need the information most: diabetics, spinal cord injury patients, cardiac patients, ostomy patients, alcoholics, and senior citizens. To obtain addresses for these people, I simply asked for a mailing list after the presentations I made to these groups. If you want to target white-collar patients with health insurance and incomes greater than $30,000, you can obtain mailing lists for this group. When you target this group, keep in mind what subjects they would most likely be interested in.

Mailing list brokers are listed in the telephone book under "mailing lists." The price is usually between $60 and $80 per 1,000 names. The broker you use should be able to provide you with demographic information in addition to the names of the people who live in a specific zip code. Then you can choose recipients on the basis of income level, ethnic makeup, age, and sex. If you wish to have unlimited access to the list, you will probably pay twice the base cost. Ask to have the list supplied on magnetic tape; a computer can then print the names and addresses directly on the envelopes.

KEEP THE FAITH

No marketing tool or program is without its disadvantages. Unless you subscribe to a newsletter service, you will put considerable time and money into developing your newsletter. The results from a newsletter are not immediate. Do not get discouraged if you get only minimal response after mailing out one or two issues.

Even in this age of high tech, the Internet, and the abundance of health information, patients appreciate and will read targeted information produced in a well-crafted newsletter.

The methodology of a newsletter depends on spaced repetition. Consequently, it may take months or even a year of newsletter delivery to develop the name recognition that is so important in motivating patients to enter your practice. That is why it is important to establish a regular pattern for publishing. Whether the newsletter comes out monthly, bimonthly, quarterly, or semiannually, stick to your publication and mailing dates. Once they become accustomed to regular delivery, your readers will begin to anticipate the newsletter's arrival. It is important to know that the key to effective marketing is that the more your name appears in front of patients or potential patients, the more likely they are to avail themselves of your services and your expertise.

CONSIDER YOUR OPTIONS

One alternative is to subscribe to a newsletter service and add your name and logo to its newsletter. Remember, however, that a generic newsletter will not tell your patients your story, your philosophy, or the details of your practice. But if you are in solo practice, buying from a newsletter service may make more sense. These services charge a set amount for copies. They will print your version of the newsletter, customizing it using your practice logo, your office address, and often a short column written by you. For more information on newsletter services, see "Additional Resources" at the end of the chapter.

Be sure to check out samples of the product before you buy. Make certain you feel comfortable with the writing style and quality of information offered in the service's clippings. Remember, you are using the newsletter to enhance and build upon your image as a caring, informed physician. If you are going to use a newsletter service, make sure the product fits your objectives.

It may be that you are already writing articles for local outlets and are comfortable with the idea of producing your own newsletter. In that case, the next sections will apply to your situation.

PLANNING AND TOPIC SELECTION

You have decided to produce your own office newsletter. You will need to assemble a newsletter "staff" and to devise a timetable (Exhibit 22–1). Schedule some planning meetings for the newsletter. The purpose of a newsletter is to provide advice, entertainment, and education. In your first one or two meetings, you should arrive at a group consensus on the newsletter's concept.

Creating a newsletter consists of four components: writing, designing, printing, and mailing. You may plan to do all the writing yourself. If so, decide whether you want input from the office staff on the selection of newsletter topics. Topics that are popular today are wellness, nutrition, exercise, stress reduction, and cancer prevention. I suggest selecting a single topic for each newsletter. This is my personal preference, since a single-topic issue allows me to cover a subject in more detail. For example, I recently selected urinary incontinence as a topic and discussed all the nonsurgical treatments available to treat this common and often socially devastating medical problem. Of course, the disadvantage of a single-topic issue is that those readers who are not interested or do not fit the topic profile will not read it. You may choose to cover two or three topics so as to reach a broader cross section of patients.

Exhibit 22–1 Sample Timetable for Newsletter Production

Newsletter Production

1. Concept development: two weeks to one month. Staff meetings, brainstorming, meetings with graphic designer. Decisions: name, format, number of pages, frequency (monthly, bimonthly, quarterly, or semiannually), topics to be covered, single- or multiple-topic.
2. Obtain third class bulk rate permit from post office.
3. Write copy: two to four weeks. Research; write first draft; edit; proofread.
4. Typesetting: one and one-half weeks from first galleys to page proofs.
5. Check boards; okay designer's mockup; create a "dummy" of first issue with typesetter.
6. Okay boards and bluelines; newsletter goes to typesetter.
7. Mail and distribute newsletter.

One way to select a topic is to survey your patients or record the most frequently asked questions by your patients and answer them. You might create a regular feature column with a question-and-answer format for this purpose.

You can also select topics by the time of year. For instance, a fall newsletter might address the benefits of flu shots for those at risk and include information on how to obtain shots if you do not offer them. To make the newsletter more personal, include (with your patients' permission) success stories from your practice.

A newsletter needs a catchy and unique title. This requires a little thinking. You may want to hold a staff brainstorming session to suggest titles. The title is important, so spend some time selecting it. It is the one thing that remains a constant and does not change. A play on words, if not too corny, can make a memorable title.

WRITING THE NEWSLETTER COPY

The writing style used in the newsletter is very important. Write the newsletter as if you were talking to your patients. To hold the reader's attention, use short sentences, short words, and short paragraphs. Avoid technical terms unless you define them. Develop an informal, relaxed style. Make it personal and use words such as *you, we,* and *us.* Remember, *you* is the second most pleasant word in the English language (the first is a person's own name).

Your patients undoubtedly want the newest information in your field, they want quick answers, and they want new ways to enhance their physical and mental health. The goal should be to seize the reader's attention quickly and maintain it while he or she reads your newsletter.

Do not say anything that you cannot back up. Avoid overstating or making guarantees and false claims. This should go without saying, especially in the field of medical science. Even in this age of medical advertising, we are seen as the purveyors of honest truths about medical conditions. As salespersons know, it is best to "underpromise and overdeliver." Failure to follow this rule can result in unhappy, disappointed patients—the ones who may end up involving you in litigation.

You can make a newsletter exciting by adding a little spice. The public's perception of physicians is that we are often curt, no-nonsense types. A newsletter is an opportunity to show we have a sense of humor by relating some of the funny things that happen to us in our practices. For example, in one newsletter issue I told the story of a patient who arrived at my office and was asked to provide a urine specimen. The woman asked the nurse, "Why do I have to do that?" The nurse replied, "Dr. Baum always asks new patients for a specimen." The woman responded, "Even to have my teeth cleaned?" After that remark, the nurse figured out that the woman had come to the wrong doctor's office!

You might consider using cartoons if you are willing to spend a little extra for reprint rights. Patients and physicians alike can share a laugh about the foibles of managed care, and these cartoons abound these days.

You can create variety by including recipes. For example, if you have diabetics in your practice, you can provide appropriate low-sugar recipes for various times of the year, like Christmas and Thanksgiving. In February, which is American Heart Month, you can include low-fat recipes available through the American Heart Association (AHA). Just call your local AHA chapter and request its noncopyrighted materials on the subject of low-fat diets, or visit their website at *www.americanheart.org*.

You can also key newsletter issues to national and local health-related events. For example, in April, which is National Cancer Month, you can take the opportunity to remind your older patients to get a sigmoidoscopy (the American Cancer society is a great resource: *www.cancer.org*).

A bulletin column is a great place to mention your participation in a health fair or any talks you are giving to community groups. Include your staff, too. The bulletins can inform patients about your staff and special events that are occurring in their lives, such as courses they are attending and honors they have received.

You will need to create some standard information for your newsletter masthead, which typically appears on the second page or on the last page. The masthead includes a copyright statement, a list of personnel responsible for the newsletter, and a disclaimer such as the following: "The information herein is not intended to be used in place of medical advice. In case of a medical problem, please consult this office or your personal physician."

A position statement is a nice addition. For example, you might have printed, just below the newsletter name, "A bimonthly bulletin written for the health-conscious patient."

After your newsletter is written, have someone review and edit it for content and style. Most hospitals have public relations and marketing departments with staff members willing to do this for you. You should always make an effort to meet everyone who is providing you with assistance. Be sure to return favors and offer compensation when it is appropriate. In addition, most universities and teaching hospitals have public relations departments with staff or freelance writers experienced in medical writing and editing. These writers are also sometimes able to produce newsletter copy for a fee.

DESIGN AND PROMOTION

Once your copy has been written and edited, you are ready for the design and production stage. Most of us have little or no experience in this area. My first newsletters were done "in house" on a typewriter, photocopied, and included with the patients' bills. Desktop publishing has become ubiquitous in office settings in the last decade and is highly touted as accessible to anyone with the right hardware and software package. However, be advised: If you have no design experience, using a desktop publishing system could be very time-consuming. There are simple two-column formats available with most word processing programs, and this might be a good intermediate step.

There is a related caveat about using clip art, often a favorite of "amateur publishers." By subscribing to a clip art service, you can add a personal touch to any document and you are able to use the available catalogued images without applying or paying for reprint rights and royalties. (See "Additional Resources" at the end of this chapter for some clip art suppliers.) However, consulting with a graphics designer is still a good idea because just plunking a picture of a stethoscope into the middle of the page may not be pleasing to the eye of the reader.

After seeing the success of our newsletter, I now use a graphic designer and a professional printer. A designer will give your newsletter a more professional and attractive look. He or she will design the format and layout of your newsletter, specify type styles and sizes, and incorporate your logo, if you have one.

If you work with a designer, he or she will recommend printers. You will make the final decision but, to find the best deal, you may choose to use your designer as a broker. It is good to get three estimates for comparison. The cost of printing your newsletter will depend on the number of pages, the page size, the number of copies, the quality of the paper, and the number of colors of ink (black ink is considered to be one color; black ink with blue ink for the headlines is two colors, etc.). The printer may or may not typeset the newsletter. Again, most designers have type houses they already work with and they will help you with the newsletter production.

For do-it-yourselfers I recommend *Newsletters, Patients and You* by Cheryl Farr.[5] This book covers every aspect of publishing a newsletter, including style, content, graphics, printing, and mailing. It is written with the health care professional in mind. Another excellent resource is *Creating Newsletters, Brochures and Booklets* by Val Adkins.[6] These practical guides are user-friendly, invaluable sources for beginning to intermediate designers, offering step-by-step instructions and lots of illustrations. If you're an electronic do-it-yourselfer, check out this website: *www.ttl.dsu.edu/electronic_seminars/word/newsletter.htm*. A professional newsletter writer leads you step-by-step through the process of creating a newsletter using your word processor.

GETTING THE NEWSLETTER OUT

The majority of newsletters we have printed are mailed. I recommend using third-class mail. It is cost-effective and, in the case of local delivery, the mailing time is usually the same as for first-class mail. Check with your local post office for information on bulk rate, third-class mail.

According to the U.S. Postal Service, the following conditions apply to mail that qualifies for third-class, for-profit bulk mailing rates. These were the current rates as of early 2000, but make sure to check with the post office, as rates change on a regular basis.

1. The mail must be presorted by zip code.
2. The minimum amount is 200 pieces of mail.
3. There is a $100 annual fee.
4. The cost is 23.5 cents apiece to any number of zip codes.
5. For 500 pieces to the *same* zip code, the cost is 20.7 cents apiece.

It is a good idea to include on your mailing list your name and address and those of a few family members to see if the newsletters arrive on time.

The times of year you mail your newsletter will affect its impact and the response you get. Newsletters mailed in January are far more effective than those mailed in December. Other good months for mailing are August and October.[7]

If you have fax numbers for a number of patients, you can consider faxing copies of the newsletter; it could also be sent via e-mail. Another distribution route would be to post the newsletter on your website and then e-mail patients to let them know whenever a new issue has been posted on the site.

OTHER USES FOR NEWSLETTERS

In addition to sending the newsletter to your patients and target audiences, you can also use it for other purposes. Your newsletter might make a nice introduction to your practice. You can include the latest issue with your practice brochure as a "welcome to our practice." The newsletter can also function as a take-home for those who attend talks and presentations. It will give the audience information about you and your practice. A special newsletter can be created for and sent to children in your practice. All children enjoy receiving mail, especially from their doctor. And needless to say, their parents will also be impressed!

The Bottom Line   *A newsletter is an excellent vehicle for promoting your practice. You can write and include articles about the latest treatments and technologies in your field. You can let readers know about the latest conferences you attended. All this lets your patients know that you are keeping current with medical advances, and that increases their confidence in you. A newsletter can be created for very specific audiences whom you want to attract to your practice. It is* *timely and, because of its short length, easily read. It is a great way to get out all the news that is fit to print.*

NOTES

1. Cheryl Farr, *Newsletters, Patients and You* (Phoenix: Semantadonics, 1985), 2; (602) 225-9090, *www.smartpractice.com.*
2. "U.S. Helps Consumers Spot Fraudulent Health Claims," *Washington Post,* July 2, 1999.
3. J. Sybil Biermann et al., "Evaluation of Medical Information on the Internet," *Cancer,* August, 1999.
4. Farr, *Newsletters, Patients and You,* 2.
5. Ibid.
6. Val Adkins, *Creating Newsletters, Brochures and Booklets* (F&W Publications, 1994).
7. Farr, *Newsletters, Patients and You,* 8.

ADDITIONAL RESOURCES

- *Sources of clip art from the Internet*: Galapagos Design Group: *www.galapagos.com* or *clipart.com,* which has several hundred thousand pieces of free clip art.
- *The Physician's Patient Newsletter*
  Newsletter Inc.
  (800) 233-0196
  www.newslettersink.com
- *"Health Exchange,"* the Medical Group Management Association's quarterly patient education/marketing newsletter, is a great way to reach patients, referring physicians, and even the local media. "Health Exchange" provides nutrition, fitness, and safety information in an easy-to-read format. Your practice's logo is prominently displayed on the front and back pages. For a free information packet, contact:
  Medical Group Management Association
  Communications Department
  104 Inverness Terrace East
  Englewood, CO 80112
  (303) 397-7871 or (888) 608-5601, ext. 871
  www.mgma.com

CHAPTER 23

Follow the Yellow Page Road

At this moment, you have a marketing medium available to you 24 hours a day, 365 days a year. And it is already sitting in every home in your community. No, I am not talking about the Internet. It is true that the world wide web is available 24 hours a day, every day, but the Yellow Pages are still the marketing vehicle that the majority of patients in your community will turn to for locating a physician.

The simple fact is, placing a Yellow Pages ad has lots of advantages. It is cost-effective, you can track your referrals, and you are not likely to offend your colleagues. But you have to design your ad carefully. This chapter provides some tips on what has worked for me and how you can get the most out of your Yellow Pages ad.

Physicians are no strangers to the Yellow Pages. For years the Yellow Pages have been an accepted method of advertising. But there is a lot you can do to maximize the marketing potential of your Yellow Pages ad. Let me give you an example. I wanted to create a heading for impotence in the Yellow Pages. I knew that this would bring in more patients. When I called the local telephone company office with my request, the answer was an emphatic no. "There are no impotence headings in any Yellow Pages in the United States," I was told. I asked how headings were created. The representative referred me to the regional office.

When I called the regional office, I was told again "no way." But, I countered, "There are other diseases like obesity and infertility listed in the Yellow Pages. Why not impotence?"

I wish to thank **Roger G. Bonds**, President of the National Institute of Physician Recruitment and Retention in Atlanta, Georgia, who provided material for this chapter. He can be reached at (770) 734-9904, *rbonds@flash.net*, or *www.acmsd.org*.

Source: Adapted courtesy of Yellow Pages Publishers Association, Troy, Michigan.

This time the regional office suggested I show that there was a need for a new heading. I obtained testimonial letters from several patients. These were men who had suffered from impotence for years and had not known where to look for help. When these patients saw my Yellow Pages ad listing treatment of impotence as one of my specialties, their search for medical help was over.

I thought surely that with these letters I would get my heading. Again the phone company refused. Finally I contacted several other urologists in the community. They also agreed that it would be a useful heading. Best of all, they said they would buy Yellow Pages space under that heading if it was available. Now the phone company was ready to listen. We were talking its language.

So the phone company approved the first impotence Yellow Pages heading in the nation. This single project took a mere nine months to accomplish. It confirmed my mother's advice that "you can always get your own way, especially if you have more ways than one." It also demonstrated that when you create a win-win scenario, you are much more likely to succeed.

GETTING STARTED

First, take a look at what your colleagues are doing. How can you distinguish yourself from them? Your goal is to make your ad unique and attractive. Like a highway billboard, your Yellow Pages ad will have about one or two seconds to attract the reader.

That reader will be asking, "Why should I choose this doctor for my medical care?" Your ad will answer that question provided you have designed it properly. Your name, address, and telephone number are the most important elements and should be in large bold type. Also emphasize your areas of interest and expertise.

The ad should list special features of your practice. For instance, you might include a section where you mention whether you do outpatient surgery (for example, office vasectomies), accept Mastercard and Visa payments, offer evening or weekend office hours, or perform new procedures and techniques (for example, shock wave lithotripsy). If your practice has a website or patients can contact you through the Internet, you will want to mention this information in your Yellow Pages ad as well.

WHO SHOULD CREATE THE AD?

There are usually two kinds of Yellow Pages ads: in-column box ads and display ads. An in-column box ad is inserted in the alphabetical list under your specialty heading. The display ad is larger and may not appear on the same page as the in-column listing. (Usually the in-column listing will refer the reader to the display ad.)

An in-column box ad is less expensive than a display ad and will often be seen before the display ad, since the reader will be looking for physicians in a particular specialty. Creating an in-column box ad is pretty straightforward, and the Yellow Pages representative will help you for free. However, using phone company designers can result in an ad that looks very similar to your competitors' ads. You can also obtain more information and examples of effective display ads from the Yellow Pages Publishers Association.[1] They will provide an information kit that contains the membership roster, advertising guidelines, and all the major publishers of Yellow Pages directories.

Remember, you want your ad to stand out. If your competitors also have in-column ads, then consider a display ad. I suggest that you not try to create this in house (which means your wife or any family members or friends who have a "flair for good design"). Use a professional graphic artist.

Choosing a good graphic designer is like choosing any other professional. You will need to do some research. Talk to your colleagues. Find out who produced the display ads you like. A list of graphic designers in your community can be located in the Graphic Designer section of the Yellow Pages. I have also found a number of ideas by looking in the Yellow Pages in other communities when I travel. If you like an ad published elsewhere, call the doctor and ask for the name of the graphic designer. He or she will likely help you, since you aren't competition. Your local library usually has directories from other geographic areas.

ELEMENTS OF A GOOD DISPLAY AD

Your graphic designer will design the layout, specify the typefaces, and provide any artwork. Still, you need to be able to tell your designer what you want. A good display ad presents information and illustrations in an eye-catching way.

There are several points to keep in mind:

1. In the heading of your ad, clearly state your medical specialty and any special features (evening office hours, special outpatient procedures, etc.) that you offer.
2. Clearly identify the name of your practice. You may also have a logo or a practice tagline to be included in the display ad.
3. Use large bold print for your address and telephone number. If appropriate, include a map showing how easy it is to locate your practice.
4. The body copy (the main text of the ad after the headlines) should expand on what you have to offer and should set you apart from the competition. Brief descriptive phrases work best. Use terms that will be understood by the majority of people using the Yellow Pages.

5. Consider providing an illustration to add a special touch. This can be a drawing or a photograph. Do not use a photograph of yourself unless you are famous or want to show your ethnic background.
6. A good display ad contains plenty of blank (or white) space, which gives your ad a much cleaner, eye-catching appearance.
7. Choose a typeface that corresponds to the character of your practice. In other words, do not try to make the ad appear too flowery with an old-fashioned script type. Your graphic designer will be the best source of advice on this. It is best to use a sans-serif typeface (one that has no "curls" on the ends of the letters). Avoid using more than two styles of typeface. If you are an ophthalmologist or treat many elderly patients, be sure to use larger, bolder typefaces. And no matter what your specialty is, your telephone number should be printed exceptionally large and in bold. For an example of this, see my ad (Exhibit 23–1).
8. Usually a Yellow Pages publisher offers only one color besides black, and that is red. This adds to the expense. Use it only if you are the first on the page to use the color. However, the publisher may not be able to guarantee that yours will be the only ad using red on your page.

Exhibit 23–1 In-Column Box Ad for Yellow Pages Directory

IMPOTENCE

MALE INFERTILITY
VASECTOMY REVERSAL
VASECTOMY
UROLOGY

Neil Baum M.D.
3525 Prytania
New Orleans, LA

(504) 891-8454
IF NO ANSWER DIAL (504)836-3627

TRACKING THE RESULTS

Placing a Yellow Pages ad is no different from any other marketing project. It is important to measure the results. You can do this in three ways. The most straightforward way is to record the patients who report on their demographic data sheet that they found out about your practice by looking in the Yellow Pages. To ensure that you do not miss counting these patients, you can use a separate fill-in card that asks specific questions, such as "Why did you choose our practice?" Then list possible choices, including "a friend recommended you," "from the Yellow Pages listing," etc. Adjacent to the Yellow Pages question, list the books you advertise in and ask patients which book they used.

Assign a staff member to list the new patients who checked a directory as their source, separating out which directory patients used. Keeping tabs on these numbers for 6 to 12 months will roughly indicate the effectiveness of the Yellow Pages ad. To evaluate the return on your investment, total the revenues generated from services to those patients. Then divide that total by the annual cost of the Yellow Pages ad. If you obtained 50 patients per year from the Yellow Pages, and the total services to those patients equaled $15,000, and your ad cost $5,000 per year, the return on investment is 300 percent.

The second method uses a dedicated telephone number for your Yellow Pages advertising. Simply install a separate phone line with a number that appears nowhere except in your Yellow Pages ad. Each time the telephone rings, you will know that that call has been generated by your directory advertising. If you have been considering installing an 800 (or currently, 888) number, this would be a good way to use that phone number.

These days, you can automate demographic research with call counts, by listing unique phone numbers in each directory ad. Callers do not know that this number actually rings your main number, but the telephone company can total the calls to each "phantom" number (essentially counting the patients using each directory). Local telephone companies contract with an independent company in Florida that will do a survey to determine when a patient calls your office and receives a busy signal. The initial charge is $26.00, with a monthly fee of $20 per telephone line. Also, caller ID is available for about $10 or so per telephone line per month, but this only counts the number of calls and the names of the callers. The wealth of data you can gather from your telephone costs less than you may think, and, most importantly, it costs far less than running unnecessary or ineffective ads.

The third method involves adding a line in your ad such as "Ask for our office manager" or "Mention this ad and receive 10 percent off your first office visit." Your Yellow Pages representative can advise you as to what wording might be best for your practice.

WHICH DIRECTORY SHOULD YOU ADVERTISE IN?

The standard Yellow Pages published by the local telephone company is the most expensive and has the greatest distribution. Today you can target not only geographic areas such as suburbs but also demographic groupings by buying ad space in subdirectories (for example, the Silver Pages for senior citizens and Spanish language pages for the Hispanic communities in your area). Depending on who your patients are and the desired makeup of your practice, you might want to consider additional Yellow Pages listings.

You must be careful to check out the distribution for the directories competing with the phone company's Yellow Pages. Getting the most out of your Yellow Pages ad requires more than just sending your yearly check to the telephone company. In fact, I was once taken in by a competing directory. When I first started my practice, my office received what looked like an invoice from the Yellow Pages for $150 a year. We never questioned that bill and simply sent the money. But then we inadvertently learned that the "bill" was really an order form made to look like an invoice, and the listing we were paying for from New Orleans was in Niagara Falls, New York. I guess they had me "over a barrel" for a time! Now my tracking is reasonably accurate, and the last time I checked we had not received one patient from Niagara Falls!

MORE YELLOW PAGES TIPS

You will enhance your venture into Yellow Pages advertising by following some advice from Paul Weber of Bernstein-Rein Advertising in Kansas City, Missouri.

Physicians can avoid these common mistakes:

- *Size-ratcheting:* Directories offer initial discounts to entice practices to increase the size of their ads or to buy new features like additional colors and white backgrounds. These discounts may tempt you to buy "more ad than you need," at considerable additional expense.
- *Blanket coverage:* Most markets have multiple directories that take some market share from the area's main book. Critically evaluate whether buying ad space in the extra directories is worthwhile. For any Yellow Pages book, you should spend no greater percentage of your budget than the percentages of the Yellow Page market that the particular directory captures. For example, if a directory draws 12 percent of Yellow Page use, then spend no more than 10 percent of your Yellow Page budget on it.
- *Me too! thinking:* Just because a competitor has placed an expensive ad in a directory does not mean you have to meet or beat that effort.

- *Mediocre artwork/layout:* Demand excellence from the Yellow Page designers. Be sure your finished ad communicates your unique image, which includes your logo, slogan, and special area of interest and expertise.
- *Irrelevant information:* Include information in your ads that will be most important to your target audience. If you serve an area where patients tend to be upscale, sophisticated health care consumers, then by all means include information on your special board certification, fellowship, or membership in a specialty organization. On the other hand, your prospective patients might pay more attention to a listing that noted you have Saturday or evening office hours, with a clearly printed map to your office.
- *Making a "gut" decision:* Base your decision to buy a Yellow Pages ad on facts and sound research. Compare your ad's projected cost to the expected revenue it will produce to calculate your return on the investment.

If directory advertising proves worthwhile, then you will want to reevaluate your program each year with a focus on maximizing your ad's return on investment.

The Bottom Line   *When you decide to place a Yellow Pages ad, follow the four basics:*

- *Do not buy more than you need, but make sure the ad is big enough for the important information.*
- *Include information patients look for and portray a professional image.*
- *Clearly communicate your practice's distinct advantages and benefits.*
- *Track your traffic from the Yellow Pages to be sure you are getting a good return on your investment.*

NOTE

1. Yellow Pages Publishers Association, 820 Kirts Blvd., Suite 100, Troy, MI 48084; (248) 244-6200, *www.yppa.org.*

ADDITIONAL RESOURCES

- Barry Maher, *Getting the Most from Your Yellow Pages Advertising*, 2nd ed., Aegis Publishing Group, Ltd., December 1997. This is a completely updated second edition to the perennial bible on the subject. Find out how to get the most mileage out of your advertising dollars, increasing sales as cost effectively as possible.

CHAPTER 24

Care and Feeding of Your Website: Learning to Love Spiders and Crawlers

For most physicians, the majority of patients they serve come from within their community. A physician's "service area" is usually comprised of no more than three to five zip codes or a 25- to 50-mile radius from his or her address. All of us enjoy seeing a patient who has traveled more than 100 miles to see us for an appointment. Imagine the excitement when a patient from 1,000, 5,000, or even 10,000 miles away contacts your office for an appointment. That is exactly what a website can do for you and your practice.

The world of the web is a place of great excitement and opportunity. Medical practices have wonderful new opportunities to grow and extend their relationships with existing patients and to attract new patients to their practices through the effective use of the Internet.

The process of creating a website has simplified so much over the past few years that anyone comfortable with presentation graphics programs similar to Microsoft's PowerPoint can build a web page. However, the quality of the output will depend upon the skills of the designer. If you are a "techie" with good design skills, then building your own website should be fun and easy. If you are moderately comfortable with application software programs and have reasonable design skills, you can build a site on your own or enlist some help from a professional web designer. If you are just starting out with computers, the process might still be a little daunting.

In this chapter, you will learn the basics of domain names, web hosting, and basic web design. In addition, methods for measuring the success of your website

I would like to thank **Michael J. Burke**, MBA, President of Dialog Medical, Snellville, Georgia, for his contributions to this chapter. Dialog Medical is a software company providing patient education materials (800) 482-7963; *www.dialogmedical.com.*

as a marketing tool are provided. By the end, you will be able to assess whether you are ready to move ahead on your own or need to employ the help of a professional web designer.

WEB HOSTING SERVICES

According to Sean Moloney, president of Urology Channel (a developer of websites for urologists), your first step is to find a service to "host" your website. This service maintains a connection to the Internet and allows users to locate and browse your site. The Internet Service Provider (ISP) you choose to host your website should be selected carefully, for it is the quality of their connection to the Internet that determines the speed at which users can view your website. Be sure to select an ISP with at least a T–1 (high-speed) connection to the Internet, that offers 24 hour, seven-day a week backup service for your website information and has a sound service and support system. You can find a list of web hosting services on a web directory like Yahoo! (Several services are provided in "Additional Resources" at the end of this chapter.) Basic web hosting services usually start at around $19.95 per month.

SELECTING A DOMAIN NAME

A domain name is your practice's address on the Internet. It is a personal, original address that is truly unique—once reserved, no other practice or person can ever hold the same Internet address. It is the description that usually starts with "*www*" and often ends in "*.com*," which you are probably used to seeing in advertisements and on business cards, T-shirts, and just about any other commercial space by now. Your patients will remember this name and use it to find out about your practice today and into the future. It is also referred to as a "URL" (uniform resource locator). It is the protocol, like a zip code, that the Internet uses to locate websites with ease.

When you select your domain name, keep in mind that it will be with you for a long time. You can change your Internet address, but it is not an easy task. It involves changing your registration with interNIC (the agency that regulates domain names) and telling your patients (and potential new patients) of your change of address.

To avoid this hassle, and any regrets about the name you choose, consider these questions:

1. Is the domain name consistent with your practice name?
2. Is the domain name short and easy to remember?
3. Is the domain name considerate of human error?

4. Is the domain name something you can live with for years to come?
5. Does the domain name reflect the breadth and depth of your practice's size and services?
6. Is the domain name already reserved and used by someone else?

When you select a domain name, use all lower case letters and avoid hard to spell titles. Internet users make typing mistakes, which they often do not realize. Most will assume your website is at fault and will give up trying to locate it.

REGISTER YOUR DOMAIN NAME

A few years ago, registering a domain name was as time consuming as waiting in line at the Department of Motor Vehicles. Fortunately, the system has been refined in response to the exploding demand for website addresses. You do not need to know the mechanics behind domain name registration except that addresses are maintained by interNIC. There are several "free" services on the web that will assist you in registering your domain name, including most web hosting services. You can find a variety of domain name registration services by searching a web directory like Yahoo! (*www.yahoo.com*) and search "domain registration." The only charge you should have to pay is interNIC's charge for domain name registration, which is currently $70.00.

A domain registration service will allow you to check the availability of the name you wish to use. You will need to specify a "top-level" domain, which refers to the letters that follow the "dot" in a domain name, like the "*.org*" in *www.aua.org*. Mike Burke, president of Dialog Medical, a patient education software company that provides content for doctors' websites, points out that physicians and others involved in health care can now reserve a domain name that ends in "*.md*." For example, my web address could be *www.neilbaum.md*. What could be easier to remember? The new top-level domain is available as a result of the country of Moldavia (md) "leasing" their top-level domain to appropriate users. It is a little more expensive than a traditional top-level domain like "*.com*." (It costs $299 to register the domain, which includes one free year of web hosting by Domain Name Trust, Inc.) Since the use of the *.md* domain is new to sites outside of Moldavia, many domain name registration services are not equipped to reserve these names. You can use *www.register.com* to reserve a "*.md*" top-level domain. Other common top-level domains used in the United States include "*.com*," "*.org*," and "*.net*," which are short for *commercial, organization,* and *network.*

Anyone may register web addresses in *.com, .net,* and *.org.* According to Moloney, the best way to protect the uniqueness of your on-line identity is to register or reserve web addresses in all of the top-level domains.

To fill out the form online, you should be prepared to furnish the following:

1. Your contact and billing information.
2. The name and address of a technical contact (usually the ISP that hosts your website).
3. The name and address of an administrative contact (usually a main contact at your ISP).
4. The series of numbers that identify the server where your website address will reside (called the IP address). This is the most complex of all information required, so be sure to ask your web hosting service for this information. These numbers make it possible for someone surfing the Internet to find your website.

WEBSITE DEVELOPMENT—DO IT YOURSELF OR HIRE A PROFESSIONAL?

Website development can be accomplished with several easy-to-use graphic tools. However, the quality of a patient's experience when visiting your website is directly related to the skills of the website designer. Find sites you like and evaluate whether your design skills would allow you to create something similar.

If you decide to hire a professional, understand that you can spend as little as $500 or many thousands of dollars in website design. Constructing a state-of-the-art website requires the investment of considerable time and energy. According to Maloney, you should not try to save a few dollars along the way, since the potential return on your investment is considerable. For the most part, an effective website should be a more serious undertaking than a weekend project or one that you turn over to your office manager or your partner's teenager who happens to be a high school computer whiz.

If you decide to brave the Internet construction frontier on your own, be sure to adhere to the KISS Principle: Keep It Short and (at first) Simple. Perhaps the best advice is for someone in your office to spearhead the project and use consultants for larger efforts. This way you get some hands-on experience, and you can learn from the experience of the professional designer. You can always expand your Web presence from the initial do-it-yourself model.

For the do-it-yourselfer, I recommend one of the free web tools that come with the popular browsers, Internet Explorer® from Microsoft and Netscape Navigator® from Netscape. The tools are called Microsoft FrontPage Express and Netscape Composer, respectively. These tools are free and can be downloaded at *www.microsoft.com* and *www.netscape.com.*

These free web tools are great for novices and will also allow you to edit and make changes after a professional website developer has fine-tuned your site. This is one of the advantages of creating an on-line presence. The on-line world is relatively forgiving of mistakes. If you make a typographical error on your web page, it is easier to fix than a printed piece that would have to be discarded if it contained any major errors. Another plus for on-line marketing is that any additions or deletions from your practice (such as a partner, change of address, or new technology that is added to your practice) can be updated in minutes at no expense.

You can spend a lot of time creating a web page and it can be fun and exciting to go from ground zero to a web presence in a few weeks. However, the best advice is to do what you do best (and that is practice medicine) and hire someone else to do the rest!

If you decide to use a professional developer, you will need to find a good one. There are a wide variety of individuals and organizations claiming to be website designers. Some have strong technical skills but poor design skills, or vice versa. Their previous work is the best evidence of their competence, so ask for addresses of sites they have done. The ultimate test is the appearance and user-friendliness of their previous work. When you access these sites, ask yourself: Do they load quickly? Are there links to other websites that are no longer functional? Is the design visually appealing? Does it communicate the desired message?

You can use web directories or even the Yellow Pages to find a web designer. I suggest sampling the web to find sites that are appealing to you. The name of the developer and his or her e-mail address usually appear at the bottom of the website's home page. You can contact designers through their e-mail addresses and ask them about their fees and their willingness to develop your site. Make sure the designer understands the unique messages you need to communicate as a health care provider.

Suggested content to consider for your web page is shown in Exhibit 24–1. I would suggest selecting a few of the topics and then slowly add to your page as you and your practice become more comfortable with this marketing concept.

GETTING YOUR WEB PAGE NOTICED

Once you have designed an attractive site with relevant content, your work is only half done. Getting net users to view and interact with your site represents an altogether different problem that requires a creative, multifaceted solution.

When someone mentions website promotion, often the first topic that springs to mind is search engine placement. The term *search engine* has evolved to describe a variety of services that assist net users in locating sites. These services include true search engines, web directories or indexes, and hybrids. A few you might have heard of include Yahoo!, AltaVista, Lycos, HotBot, and Excite. Search engines play an important part in promoting your website, but they are by no means the only method of getting net users to your site. As a matter of fact, they are

Exhibit 24-1 Suggestions for Website Content

The following items might be useful to prospective patients and should be considered for your practice website:

- Photos of the doctors and the staff
- Curriculum vitae of the doctors
- Evidence of Continuing Medical Education attended by the physicians
- Honors and accomplishments received by the physicians
- Articles written by the doctors, both journal and lay articles
- Articles written about the doctors and the practice
- Information on the areas of interest and expertise of the practice (This is where you make an effort to differentiate your practice from other practices in the community.)
- The office logo
- Interesting articles and useful information about your practice and your specialty (You will need permission to use articles from other resources.)
- A map that will help new patients find your practice
- Names of managed care plans and health care plans that the practice belongs to
- A history of the practice, especially if it enjoys a fifty+-year history
- Ability for other physicians to consult with the practice
- Ability for patients to ask the doctor health care questions
- Links to other useful websites
- Testimonials from satisfied patients that give permission to use their quotes
- E-mail address for feedback
- Date the site was last updated
- A window listing the number of previous visitors to the site
- Ability to make appointments with the practice online
- On-line reporting of tests and studies using codes to ensure security and privacy
- Ability to conduct on-line chats

---

potentially less relevant to physicians and group practices than promoting your website within your existing patient base through brochures and newsletters. Before you label me a heretic, let me explain.

Here is an example to illustrate my point. These are the top 10 results from a search of the term *urology* on Excite's search engine:

- *www.uronews.comUROLOGY—News Online*
- *www.urologytreatment.com—the Urology Treatment Center of Sarasota, Florida*

- *www.a-urology.com—A Urology Opinion*
- *www.urologyhealthcenter.com—Urology Health Center*
- *urologyresearch.com—urology studies, clinical trials, and clinical studies*
- *uroworld.azn.nl—Department of Urology, Nijmegen, The Netherlands*
- *www.cairns-urology.com.au—Cairns Urology, Urological Surgery and Consulting, Queensland, Australia*
- *urology.viagra-access.com—Urology!Viagra On-line!*
- *www.advancedurology.com—the Advanced Urology Information Web Site*
- *www.fetalurology.org—Society for Fetal Urology*

A similar search using HotBot yielded multiple matches, but none of the websites in the top 10 matched the top 10 of the search using Excite. As you probably have already discovered, search engines can be surprisingly inefficient. Imagine how frustrating this can be for a patient who is trying to find your site or pertinent information for his or her medical condition. How many sites will patients scroll through to find what they need before giving up?

If patients are looking for information about their health problems or trying to locate physicians, they may have a difficult time differentiating among these sites. They all sound like they might have pertinent information on urology, but might not help a patient in selecting a local physician. Patients may try one of the commercial "health portals" like Intellihealth (*www.intellihealth.com*), WebMD (*www.webmd.com*), or *www.drkoop.com*, but most patients would prefer for the source of their health information to come from their personal doctor.

If I am a doctor trying to make sure my site comes out at the top of that list, I can attempt to do the things the search engines suggest to get a high ranking. With new websites appearing daily, it is not likely that I will have much success keeping my website's name at the top of each search engine all of the time. So what can you do? You need to address the promotion of your website from several different angles. Search engine ranking plays an important part, which will be discussed later, but it is only part of the equation. You also need to consider direct marketing and links management.

DIRECT MARKETING

The first rule of direct marketing for web pages is: ***put your web address on everything!*** Put it on your business cards, on your practice brochure, on newsletters to patients, on bills, on the sign in front of your office. Put it everywhere. Hopefully you have selected a web address that is easy to remember.

You probably receive a large number of your new patients through word-of-mouth advertising. Your Internet site leverages this word-of-mouth advertising by allowing potential new patients to receive instant information. For example, a satisfied patient informs his friend of what a great doctor you are and forwards a link to your website address in an e-mail to his friend. The friend clicks on the link, sees an attractive, professional site with lots of relevant content, and decides to give you a try. Once your website is completed, you should definitely promote it within your current patient base through direct mail campaigns and office brochures.

Ironically, direct marketing of your "high-tech" website often is most effective when you utilize traditional "low-tech" tools like direct mail, newsletters, radio and television advertising, and good old word-of-mouth.

LINKS MANAGEMENT

Links management is another effective way to drive traffic to your website, and it happens to be free! Links management includes the process of asking for reciprocal links with other webmasters and the use of commercial banner exchange tools like LinkExchange.

The practice of including a "links" page on your site has diminished in popularity. However, many sites weave multiple links to other sites throughout the fabric of their site. You should contact as many webmasters as possible and ask them to include a link to your site whenever relevant. It cannot hurt to ask.

Banner exchange tools are exactly what they sound like. You agree to allow banner advertising on your site in exchange for the ability of your banner ad to appear on other sites in the program. LinkExchange (*www.linkexchange.com*) is one of the most popular of these service types. They make sense for webmasters who choose not to pay the exorbitant fees associated with banner advertising on a premier site like Yahoo! or Excite.

SEARCH ENGINES

Search engines are important, especially if someone is trying to locate your site but they cannot quite remember the exact URL. Let's start with a quick overview of what they are and how they work.

There is a major difference between a search engine and a web directory or index. A search engine uses a "spider" or "crawler" to visit a web page, read it, and follow the links within the site. The spider builds an "index" or "catalog" of everything it finds. Search engines each have their own software that searches through the catalog built by the spider to find the relevant topic. These programs account for the significant differences in search rankings from one search engine to another. Each search engine uses a different algorithm to determine relevance.

A discussion of each major search engine's algorithm, and how to optimize rankings in each major engine, is beyond the scope of this chapter. Entire books and websites are devoted to this subject (see "Additional Resources" at the end of this chapter), and the material changes daily as major search engines change their methods of determining relevance.

You need to do two things to accomplish successful search engine ranking:

* *First,* find a good website designer who understands how to build a website that can obtain a high relevance ranking on major search engines. This will involve the use of metatags and keywords. Metatags are commands that contain your key words and thus help search engines categorize your website so that visitors can easily find your web page. For a complete description of how to insert a metatag into your website, visit the AltaVista site. If this sounds confusing, it is all the more reason to leave it up to a web designer who knows what to do.
* *Second,* after you have built a website designed for relevance with search engines, use a good listing service. A listing service will register your site with many different search engines and web directories for a small fee. If you were to attempt to list your site with each individual search engine, you would never have time to practice medicine. An example of a popular service for listing with various search engines is Submit it! (*www.submit-it.com*). You can view a variety of these services at *http://dir.yahoo.com/Business _and_Economy/Companies/Internet_Services/Web_Services/Marketing/ Promotion/*.

If you really want to know how each search engine determines relevance, I suggest you visit Search Engine Watch (*www.searchenginewatch.com*). This site describes, in great detail, how each search engine determines relevance and how you can take this into consideration in the design of your website.

Here is a brief summary for those of you who are familiar with terms like **metatags** *and* **keywords**:

* Make good use of your document title, particularly the first few words.
* Remember that words near the beginning of a document carry more weight.
* Use metatags, but don't attempt to "trick" search engines by abusing them.
* Keep your home page short and to the point.
* Tricks to fool search engines will be defeated and might prohibit you from getting listed at all.
* Keep in mind that it might take months to get listed on a search engine since they are struggling to keep up with the pace at which new websites are created.

MAJOR SEARCH ENGINES

The popular website Search Engine Watch lists the following search engines and index services among the "major" search engines:[1]

- ***www.aol.com/netfind/.*** AOL NetFind is a branded-version of the Excite search engine in the United States and Canada.
- ***www.altavista.com/.*** AltaVista is consistently one of the largest search engines on the web, in terms of pages indexed. Its comprehensive coverage and wide range of power searching commands make it a particular favorite among researchers. It also offers a number of features designed to appeal to basic users, such as "Ask AltaVista" results, which come from Ask Jeeves (see below), and directory listings from LookSmart. Advertisers can also pay to be listed higher within the service.
- ***www.askjeeves.com/.*** Ask Jeeves is a human-powered search service that aims to direct you to the exact page that answers your question. If it fails to find a match within its own database, then it will provide matching web pages from various search engines.
- ***www.directhit.com/.*** Direct Hit is a company that works with other search engines to refine their results. It does this by monitoring what users click on from the results they see. Sites that get clicked on more than others rise higher in Direct Hit's rankings. Thus, the service dubs itself a "popularity engine." Direct Hit's technology is currently best seen at HotBot. It also refines results at Lycos and is available as an option at LookSmart and MSN Search. The company also crawls the web and refines this database, which can be viewed via the link above.
- ***www.excite.com/.*** Excite is one of the most popular search services on the web. It offers a medium-sized index and integrates nonweb material such as company information and sports scores into its results, when appropriate.
- ***www.yahoo.com/.*** Yahoo! is the web's most popular search service and has a well-deserved reputation for helping people find information easily. The secret to Yahoo's success is human beings. It is the largest human-compiled guide to the web, employing about 150 editors in an effort to categorize the web. Yahoo! has more than 1 million sites listed.

Now that you have taken steps to develop your own web page and to draw patients to it, through direct marketing efforts and search engine links, there is one more step in the "care and feeding" of your website.

MEASURING METHODS

Now that you have devised and implemented effective means to promote your website among your patient base and throughout the web in general, you are going to have to figure out what is working and what is not.

You have probably heard of the term *hits* used in the context of describing the traffic to your website. You may have even heard a slick salesperson mention that his website generated thousands of hits last month. The first thing to keep in mind is that this term is nearly meaningless on its own. Here is an example: the slick website advertising salesperson's site might have 20 individual graphic elements on his home page. A hit refers to the downloading of an item from the server PC to the browser's PC. So when you visit the home page of his site, he registers 20 hits from the download of 20 different graphic images on the page. Kind of misleading, isn't it?

Hits can also be undermeasured. "Caching" refers to the process of storing a recently accessed page so that when you try to view the page again, the cached version is retrieved instead of visiting the original site again. Most browsers cache recently visited sites, and nearly all corporate networks implement caching systems to minimize network traffic. You can probably see how caching would cause a webmaster to miss the recording of many hits to the site.

To get a clearer picture of visits to your site, you might want to measure the amount of time each user spent looking at a particular URL on your site. A listing of the top URLs on the site lets you know exactly what pages your patients are visiting most frequently. You can identify trends and potential issues within your site by analyzing these numbers.

Most website hosting services provide software free of charge to measure and report website statistics. One of the most popular is WebTrends (*www.webtrends .com*). Even if you are not directly involved in the design and maintenance of your site, you can usually access traffic statistics from any browser. There are also commercial services available to track and measure your traffic more precisely. This can be useful if you need to substantiate use to managed care plans or insurance companies. Your webmaster or company hosting your site will have more details.

The most useful information to you would be to identify and track unique visitors. However, these methods are beyond the reach of most physician websites. There is one sure-fire way to measure unique users, and that is to require users to log in to your website at each visit. But this can have a downside. Patients may object to logging on each time, and it can be an even bigger pain having to remember a password.

FEEDBACK

Put a mechanism in place to collect information about your site and your practice. This is an incredibly cost-effective way to conduct market research. Develop an on-line survey and ask your patients to complete it. You will be amazed at the responses you receive. People are often willing to complete an on-line survey when they would not speak to a telemarketer who asks the same questions. Most web hosting services provide a mechanism to submit e-mail forms (ask your webmaster about this). Your patients can complete an on-line questionnaire and press the "submit" button and the form will be automatically e-mailed to you. Do you currently publish a practice newsletter? If so, put it online! In addition to including the content of the newsletter on your website, you should consider an e-mail list. E-mail lists allow users to subscribe to the list and receive messages posted by you or the list members. It is a tremendous opportunity to facilitate communication between and among you and your patients. LinkExchange has a service called ListBot that allows you to create and manage your own e-mail list. You can put a button directly on your website that allows users to subscribe to the list. It is one of the most efficient methods of communication available.

The Bottom Line *Those of us who take the electronic leap and decide to embrace this new opportunity will have a distinct advantage over those who adhere to the traditional methods of building and enhancing their practices. Developing a web presence is a cost-effective method of ethically promoting and marketing your practice.*

NOTE

1. For a more comprehensive listing of major search engines, go to *searchenginewatch.internet.com/links/Major_Search_Engines/The_Major_Search_Engines/index.html.*

ADDITIONAL RESOURCES

Web Hosting Services
- A-1 Hosting Services, *www.a1hosting.com*
- Inter-Link 2000 Web Services, *www.interlink-2000.com*
- Sunshine On-line Services, *www.sunshine.com*

Books
- Daniel S. Janal, *On-line Marketing Handbook* (New York: Wiley, 1998).
- Gregory Sherwin and Emily Avila, *Connecting On-line* (Grants Pass, OR: Oasis Press, 1997).
- Jim Sterne, *World Wide Web Marketing* (New York: Wiley, 1999).

CHAPTER 25

One Small Click for Your Patients, One Giant Leap for Your Practice!

In many communities, patients and doctors have become mutually disenchanted with each other. Over the past 10 years, economic and regulatory pressures have forced doctors to spend less time with each patient and to deliver less quality care to their patients than they would like. For the most part the doctors want to provide good solid health care but just do not have the time. We are seeing doctors who are so frustrated with the current atmosphere in which they are expected to practice that many are leaving medicine at an early age, taking disability leave, looking for alternative methods of earning or supplementing their incomes, and now, for the first time, considering forming labor unions. I have sat at lunch with my colleagues or in the doctors' lounges and listened to doctors complain and say, "Medicine isn't fun or worth it any more."

On the other side of the doctor–patient relationship, patients increasingly complain that they do not have access to their doctors, are paying more for their health care, and that even when they get through to the doctor they feel that their questions are an annoyance.

Today's patients are much more interested in their health and well-being. They want information and patient educational materials, and they would like to be able to communicate with their doctors. Is it any wonder that patients are disappointed and patient satisfaction surveys are reflecting the deep cynicism that patients feel regarding allopathic medicine? As a result, patients are leaving mainstream medicine and flocking to alternative and complementary medicine practitioners. (See Chapter 36, "Generating Referrals from Nontraditional Sources," to learn how you can create networks with these practitioners to maximize your returns.)

Patients by the millions are also turning to the Internet for information. As you probably know from personal experience, much of the information they are downloading is inaccurate and unreliable. The patient is asking the doctor to review the downloaded information, and for the most part the busy physician does not have time to review and critique Internet material.

If your practice sets up a link for patients with your website, the resulting 24-hour-a-day access may be just what the doctor ordered. According to Mike Cataldo, CEO of MediVation in Needham, Massachusetts (*mcataldo@mvation.com*), which is an Internet service to connect doctors and their patients on the web, there is great potential to link physicians' practices and the web.

MediVation has developed the first ePPi (electronic provider-patient interface). By using an ePPi, you can augment your patients' time with the doctor. With the use of this software program doctors can offer reliable and appropriate information from a trusted source. Now patients can receive information related to their medical problem that comes from the doctor. Although this program is not intended to replace the doctor–patient relationship, it does create a more efficient communication mechanism.

For the most part, the average patient retains 20 percent of the information that the doctor explains verbally. After a few weeks, the retention of information is less than 10 percent. You can increase the retention of information by providing a summary that augments the oral discussion.

The MediVation program allows patients to have easier access to practice services. Patients can log onto the doctor's website and then have access to various components of the practice by using a secure identification number. This allows patients to see their own customized web pages from the practice.

These web pages contain their name, date of birth, date of last and next visits, their current diagnoses, their medications with instructions for use, and suggested reading on current topics in health care as well as material related to the specific medical condition. Patients who want to schedule appointments with the practice can access the page 24 hours a day, seven days a week, by entering a secure identification number. The patient can see the schedule and openings that are available and can schedule an appointment at a time that is convenient for the patient and the practice. The patient submits a preferred date and time and indicates the doctor he or she wants to see. The patient then clicks on the send icon and the next day receives an e-mail response confirming the appointment.

Patients can obtain refill prescriptions by clicking on the refill function. They type in their medications, then click on the refill icon. They add their pharmacy name and number, which are added to the database. Patients will never have to enter the name and number again unless they select another pharmacy. The request is reviewed and then authorized by the doctor. The prescription is e-mailed to the pharmacy or the prescription can be manually called to the pharmacy by the practice. The request is followed with an automatic e-mail response to the patient confirming that the prescription has been filled at the pharmacy.

Patients with questions for the doctor or nurse can submit them as "routine," "urgent," or "emergency" and receive a response in a timely fashion. This avoids patients being placed on hold or waiting by the phone for the doctor to call back. The practice can process e-mail requests as they would phone calls. For example, if a young woman wrote her physician, "I am thirty-five and in good health. Do you think I need to obtain a flu shot?" The nurse can check with the physician and respond, "Yes, please make an appointment using our Internet access on our web page. We will have the injection ready for you. This visit should take less than ten minutes."

The Internet is an opportunity to provide patients with previsit forms, such as patient demographics, the medical history, and insurance information that they can complete prior to their first visit.

DISEASE MANAGEMENT

Using this program you can easily communicate with large numbers of patients with a few strokes on the keypad. For example, an infertility clinic can notify its patients daily about injections; primary care physicians can remind their hypertensive patients on a daily basis to take their medication, get regular exercise, and decrease their salt intake; or an endocrinologist can easily send an article on the importance of blood sugar monitoring to all of his or her diabetic patients.

Other uses include the broadcast function. For example, when it is flu season and you want to broadcast to all senior citizens the importance of obtaining a flu vaccine injection, you can put the text into a broadcast generator and send to all patients over 65. The program allows you to select gender, age, diagnosis, and areas of medical interest, procedures, and medications. This function can also be used to immediately reach patients who may be taking medications that have been the subject of a Food and Drug Administration Alert (such as the situation in 1998 with Fen-Phen, short for fenfluramine and phentermine, the popular weight-loss medicine).

SURVEY PATIENTS ONLINE

You can conduct market research online by asking patients to complete brief patient surveys. These can be completed anonymously or can be signed by the patient with an opportunity for the practice to answer all positive and negative comments in a timely fashion.

The program can send a urinary tract obstruction questionnaire to all male patients over the age of 50. Based on responses of patients, those with scores suggestive of lower urinary tract obstruction are contacted by computer to make appointment for a physical examination, PSA test, and consideration for medical management of their disease.

PROGRAM DISADVANTAGES

Doctors were fearful that they would be inundated with questions and giving free advice to patients who would request Internet medicine rather than coming in for a visit. To date the program has not overwhelmed the doctors, nurses, or practices who use it, according to Cataldo. Instead, it serves as a good marketing strategy for the practice. It clearly indicates that the practice is on the cutting edge of technology, provides easy access to the physicians, and is user-friendly. Managed care companies are also impressed with the technology, as their members are assured of easy access to the practice. The program offers opportunities to control costs, enhance patient satisfaction, and control outcomes—all goals that managed care is interested in.

CONCERN OVER DOCUMENTATION

Every request and prescription refill that the practice receives can be printed and placed in the chart. The program does not allow anything to be removed unless documentation has been printed. If your practice has electronic medical records, you can easily move text to the electronic record as a means of documentation.

WHAT DOES IT COST?

Currently, practices that have implemented the MediVation program are offering the service at no charge to their patients. It is a value-added service that develops patient loyalty. Visionary doctors recognize that this is a real differentiator between their practices and the competition. Offering on-line services to patients helps retain them in the practice, improves patient satisfaction, and improves practice efficiency.

There is a one-time $250 per doctor set up charge and an annual $250 maintenance fee for each physician. There is also a $5.75 per year charge for each patient who logs onto his or her own page, regardless of how many times they access the system. Once there are more than 10 percent of the practice's population who have logged onto the program, the annual yearly fee for each patient is slightly reduced. For example, if 30 percent of the patients of the practice have logged on, the cost goes down to $4.00 per patient, which is equivalent to a 30 percent discount.

Physicians can direct their patients to the web page to buy durable medical goods, such as crutches, blood pressure cuffs, glucose monitoring equipment, or even diapers. MediVation brings sponsors to the practice or the practice can bring in the sponsors to MediVation to reduce the costs of the program.

Dr. Jan Wyneck, the medical director at Martins Point Health Center, has implemented the MediVation technology in their physician multispeciality practice in Portland, Maine. She reports that from the physicians' standpoint, the program is no different than a telephone request for information or a prescription refill. The advantage is that the program makes the practice accessible to the patients 24 hours a day, seven days a week. She has received accolades from her patients that the self-research potential is very appreciated and useful. Patients are able to find educational material and even the latest research on their medical problem or their disease from the most trusted resources, such as the American Diabetes Association (*www.diabetes.org*), the American Heart Association, or the American Cancer Society.

Dr. Wyneck also notices that patients who have checked out the drug resource information on the web page have fewer questions regarding their prescriptions. They can check every drug they are taking and find the purpose of the drug, the instructions for using the drug, the side effects, and the potential drug interactions.

She indicated that for the most part the response from the physicians has been positive. The physicians enjoy the structured communication with their patients. She advises any practice interested in implementing the program to have all the doctors learn about the program, approve the concept, and review the material that the patients will be viewing when they log onto the website. She also suggests that the staff be involved from the very beginning and become involved in the process of implementation.

Dr. David Howes, the president and chief medical officer of Martins Point Health Center, feels that the program helps patients maintain control over their health care. The information tools that allow patients access to good health care data help the patients communicate with their providers. He believes that the program signifies the commitment of the health center to enhance their communication and service to their patients.

GETTING STARTED

Amy Weinschenk, director of marketing and communications for Martins Point Healthcare (Amy@martinspoint.org), describes the process of implementing the MediVation program with her clinic. Weinschenk sent a direct mail piece to all of the clinic's existing 16,000 patients to let them know about the new program. Patients could call or come to the clinic, or complete a reply card included with the direct-mail piece to sign up for the program.

One way to create a groundswell of support for the program, suggests Weinschenk, is to find one physician champion who really understands the value of patient communication and the use of the web to enhance existing practice methods. She encourages doctors to talk directly with their patients about the program and to ask them to sign up to obtain their own health page on the web. She also recommends that all the technical aspects of the program and the operation bugs be worked out before bringing the remainder of the physicians on board. Finally, she emphasizes to the doctors and their patients that the program is a means of improving communication between them, but it is not intended to be a replacement of the doctor–patient relationship.

FUTURE OF THIS TECHNOLOGY

According to Cataldo, communicating with patients over the Internet will become as common as ATM machines for banks. The MediVation program is a valuable tool, which is good for the doctor and good for the patients. Cataldo predicts that nearly every practice will have some version of this technology in place within the next 10 years. This technology has the potential to evolve from a simple doctor–patient education tool to a disease-management vehicle and even to case management integration with prescription-benefit management. This technology provides the practice with a handle on patient and doctor compliance. We will soon see this technology reporting on patients who do not refill their medication, and a reminder will be sent to the doctor who can then help the patient return to compliance and better health.

The Bottom Line   *Check out the newest doctor–patient interface and you will be able to leverage the communication channel. You can enhance both your website and your practice image by using an electronic provider–patient interface. You, the doctor, will never be more than a mouse click away!*

CHAPTER 26

Creating Powerful Presentations through Public Speaking

The human brain starts working the moment you are born and never stops until you stand up to speak in public.

Anonymous

Public speaking is one of the best and most inexpensive ways to market your practice. First of all, there are not many physicians out there doing it. Second, with the public's increased enthusiasm for health information, you have a built-in audience. Physicians are currently in demand as public speakers. We are the acknowledged experts in the health care profession. Through public speaking, we have an opportunity to leverage that expertise and attract new patients to our practice.

What you have to say may or may not be new or unique, but if few physicians are speaking about the subject in your community, you might easily find yourself talking to eager audiences filled with people willing to give you and your practice a chance.

In this chapter, I review techniques for getting speaking engagements and preparing and delivering speeches. Public speaking is not for everyone. But if you have the desire to try, you will see that, as with other skills, this one is 99 percent perspiration and 1 percent inspiration. A lot of your butterflies can be calmed by taking the time to prepare your presentation properly.

If you are comfortable talking to one patient, you can probably become comfortable talking to a dozen, a hundred, or even a thousand potential patients.

The best speeches are those that are prepared well in advance. Giving a speech is not a situation in which you can "wing it." You cannot take a carousel of slides you presented to physicians at grand rounds and use the same material for a lay audience. Fellow physicians may tolerate and even expect a talk punctuated by lots of graphs, charts, anatomic drawings, and medical jargon. Lay audiences expect straightforward explanations of complicated subjects, direct information, and suggestions for improving their health and well-being.

GETTING ON THE PROGRAM

First of all, you need an audience. Where do you look? Social, civic, and professional associations frequently combine speakers and presentations for programs that accompany their regular membership meetings. Some of the most common organizations (to which you may already belong) are the local chamber of commerce, the Kiwanis, the League of Women Voters, the local PTA, and church groups. Your local chamber of commerce can furnish you with a more complete list for your community.

It is a good idea to select an organization with members you would like to target for your practice. Obviously, if you are a pediatrician, you will not want to speak to the local chapter of the American Association of Retired Persons. But, the local PTA would probably welcome a talk about children's health.

In contacting most civic, social, and professional organizations, there are correct channels to follow. If you would like to get a speaking engagement at a selected organization, call and find out the name of the program chairperson. Let the organization know that you are available. Many programs are scheduled 6 to 12 months in advance. Take this into consideration when you contact an organization.

Before you contact the organization, decide on several presentation topics. Then send a letter to the program chairperson offering to talk on one of these topics (Exhibit 26–1). In your letter, discuss the potential benefits to the group and why they would be interested in the topics. The letter should also include your curriculum vitae, the names of other organizations for which you have spoken, or any other materials that emphasize your expertise in the subject areas. Make a follow-up phone call two to three weeks after you send your introductory letter.

KNOW YOUR AUDIENCE

The more you know about your audience, the better you can tailor your speech to their needs and the more likely it is that some members of the audience will become your patients. Before preparing your speech, ask the program chairperson for background information about the membership and any expected guests. It is important to know the purpose of the organization, how many people are expected to attend, their age ranges, their educational background, and possible areas of challenge or resistance if your topic is controversial. For example, a talk on male health problems would be prepared differently for women at a Junior League meeting; for a service club, such as Rotary International, the Lions Club, or the Kiwanis Club; or for a senior citizens' organization.

Exhibit 26–1 Example of "Pitch" Letter I Send to a Local Organization Asking To Speak at a Membership Meeting

[Date]

[Meeting Planner] [Organization]
[Address of Organization]

RE: Presentation to [organization] on prostate cancer.

Dear [Meeting Planner],

In 1999 nearly 40,000 men (half the capacity of the Louisiana Superdome) died from cancer of the prostate gland. Many of them could be alive today if they had had an annual prostate examination, because with early detection prostate cancer can be successfully treated.

I am a urologist in private practice at Touro Infirmary. I have prepared an educational talk for men and their partners on cancer of the prostate gland. My talk is a slide presentation twenty to twenty-five minutes long, followed by five to ten minutes of questions and answers. During the presentation I will (1) describe the anatomy and function of the prostate gland, (2) describe the methods of early diagnosis of prostate cancer, and (3) briefly mention the treatments available for management of prostate cancer. I will provide everyone in the audience with a handout that summarizes the presentation.

I am enclosing several articles I have written on prostate cancer, including a recent article from the *Times-Picayune*. I am also including a few letters of recommendation resulting from previous talks I have given in the community.

I will give you a call in two weeks to discuss the possibility of talking with [name of organization].

Sincerely,

Neil Baum, M.D.

PREPARING YOUR SPEECH

"Tell the audience what you are going to tell them, then tell them, and finally tell them what you told them," is the old adage about public speaking. It still holds true. All successful presentations have a circular structure (that is, the end comes back to reinforce the beginning).

I suggest that you focus on what you want the audience to do as a result of listening to your speech. This goal or objective should be stated in the introduction and should also be stated emphatically at the conclusion. If, for example, I am talking to middle-aged men during Prostate Cancer Week, I might have as my objective "that all men over 50 years of age should have an annual rectal examination." I might start my talk with the number of new cases of and the number of deaths from prostate cancer per year, then state that early detection by rectal examination is essential in curing the disease. I might end my presentation by saying, "Some of you here in the audience may be sitting on a curable prostate cancer. Call your physician or your urologist and get a rectal examination so that you can enjoy the rest of your life!"

Once you have the beginning and the conclusion, you can fill in the middle and have a memorable speech that will motivate your audience to positive action. In the middle portion of your speech, present two to three main points using illustrations, examples, stories, case histories, or visual aids, whenever possible. If you support each main point with a variety of materials, make sure every piece of material refers to the main objective or focus of your presentation. If possible, include a personal story about yourself, a friend, or a family member. This adds a personal touch to the presentation.

Another suggestion is to mention any celebrities or historical figures who have suffered from the medical problem you are talking about. For example, when discussing nonsurgical management of urinary stones, I tell the story of Ben Franklin, who had a bladder calculus that caused intermittent urinary retention. Franklin was able to relieve his urinary retention by standing on his head and allowing the bladder calculus to fall away from the bladder opening. "So," I tell my audience, "Ben Franklin was not only one of the founders of our country but also the founder of nonsurgical management of urinary tract obstruction." There are hundreds of such stories about the health problems of historical figures, such as John F. Kennedy and his famous bad back; ex-senator Bob Dole, who became a spokesperson for Viagra; and ex-boxer George Foreman, who did comical ads about the necessity of rectal exams to screen for prostate cancer. One good source of medical anecdotes is *The Illustrated Treasury of Medical Curiosa.*[1]

If your talk centers around a new procedure or test, you might want to present, as part of your talk, a patient who has successfully undergone the procedure or test. This is very effective and adds credibility. For example, if I talk about impotence or incontinence, I ask one of my patients to come and discuss how his or her life improved following treatment of the problem. (For guidelines on preparing patient guest speakers, see Chapter 18, "There's Strength in Numbers When You Start a Support Group.") Patients who have undergone bone scans to screen for osteoporosis, or who have regular mammography to screen for breast cancer, might be good candidates for public health talks on prevention of those two primary diseases in women.

In case the patient is uncomfortable or does not do a presentation well, a similar effect can be achieved by replaying excerpts from one of the TV talk shows that have patients talking about their experiences with various medical problems. You can set up a VCR to play these excerpts during the middle of your presentation.

Finally, focus on the benefits by recommending that those in the audience follow your advice or suggestions. By emphasizing the personal benefits to the members of the audience, you can hold their attention and motivate them to take action. For example, if your talk is about prostate cancer, wrap up the presentation by urging the audience to get an annual rectal examination. If you are an ophthalmologist, and you are speaking about glaucoma, emphasize that this is one of the most common causes of blindness and that no one needs to live in darkness if they get an annual tonometry exam. If you are a family practice physician talking about hypertension, you can emphasize that this "silent killer" can be stopped and that a regular checkup and blood pressure reading are the first steps to preventing stroke or heart attack.

An effective presentation helps the audience listen, remember, and act on what you say. You become an effective speaker when you are the right person presenting the right message to the right audience at the right time in the right manner.

GETTING THE AUDIENCE'S ATTENTION

An excellent talk needs an attention-grabbing title. A narrative or descriptive title seldom generates excitement or enthusiasm for your presentation, but a catchy title creates interest in your presentation before you get up to speak. You can get ideas from best-selling book titles or famous movie titles. One resource I find useful is Dottie and Lilly Walters' *Speak and Grow Rich.*

Here are a few of their suggestions for creating an attention-grabbing title:

- *Avoid long and boring titles.* The shorter, the better. Write out the entire title and take away all of the unnecessary words.
- *Titles should be clever but not too cute.* Use alliteration (the repetition of initial consonant sounds), rhymes, and rhythms, as people will remember these.
- *Use contrasting meanings to create interesting ideas.* For example, "The Rise and Fall...," "The Agony and the Ecstasy," and "Up the Down Staircase" (I used this to create one of my own, "ECNETOPMI"—Impotence Is Reversible").
- *Whenever possible, state the benefits of the presentation in the title.*
- *Finally, combine several of these concepts, as in "Shoulder Surgery Made Simple."*

The following are some examples from my own presentation titles. Instead of "The Evaluation and Treatment of Impotence," I now use the title "Impotence:

The Tragedy of the Bedroom Can Be Conquered." Instead of "Vasectomy: An Alternative for Contraception," I use "Vasectomy: No Way, Baby!" Instead of "Market Your Practice Using Techniques from Industry and Business," I use "If Domino's Can Deliver Pizza, We Can Deliver Quality Health Care."

Keep your audience in mind when writing your titles. I have observed that professional audiences do not seem to enjoy catchy titles as much as the lay public. I once gave a talk on Peyronie's disease to a group of urologic colleagues. My title for the talk was "Peyronie's Disease: How To Straighten the Bent-Nail Syndrome." The comments on the survey returned after my talk were glowing about the presentation, but critical of the title.

A good title need not be created by Madison Avenue to get your audience's attention, but a catchy title will create interest and encourage people to attend a talk. One note on catchy titles: I do not use them for presentations to my medical colleagues unless the setting is informal, such as a luncheon or dinner.

PRACTICE MAKES PERFECT

You now have your speech written and you are on the program. What next? Like any activity that you do not perform regularly, you need to practice until you are comfortable with the presentation. One of the easiest ways to practice is to tape record your practice sessions. You can then replay the recordings to check your delivery and serve as your own coach or critic. You can use the recordings right before the presentation to remind you of the fine points and the details of your material. You might also want to rehearse in front of your spouse and get his or her feedback, as well. I do not use 3-by-5 cards or an outline to remind me of the points in my speech. The slides become my notes, reminding me of the next transition to make. The next chapter outlines the use of slides in your presentations.

Anyone who has given enough speeches knows that eventually a slide projector will fail. So it is important to know your material so well that if you experience a speaking disaster, where the notes get dropped and the slides are backwards, that you will not become flustered or lose your cool. Only through familiarity with your material and diligent practice will you be able to continue your presentation without any props whatsoever.

MAKING PREPARATIONS

Prepare a checklist of everything that must be brought to the speech, including slides, information, handouts, brochures, and calling cards. Hotels, hospitals, and lodge facilities frequently have sophisticated audiovisual equipment. If this is the case, you can request hands-free microphones, remote control slide projectors, double screens, or additional lighting. If you need or would like any additional audiovisual equipment, submit your request in writing to the meeting planner. (There are additional tips for setting up your PowerPoint presentation in Chapter 27, "Make Slides That Sizzle.")

A good speaker, like a good athlete, arrives early to inspect the "playing field." Larry Bird, the basketball great from the Boston Celtics, reportedly dribbled the ball for hours on a basketball court so he could identify the dead spots on the floor and avoid them during the game. You should be familiar with the room, the microphone system, the slide projector, and the audiovisual equipment before you start to speak. Ask the program chairperson whether technical support personnel can show you where everything is located before the speech. Nothing is more distracting at the beginning of a presentation than to test the microphone by saying, "Can you hear me?" or to ask, "Would someone adjust the focus on the slide projector?" These details should be attended to before the presentation begins.

"LET ME INTRODUCE MYSELF"

Do not take chances with your introduction. This is a key element of public speaking that is often overlooked or left in the hands of the meeting planner. Since it sets the stage for your presentation, you should treat it as your responsibility.

Prepare your own introduction. Make it about two to three paragraphs, double-spaced, so it will be easy for whoever is making the introduction to read. Send one copy to the program chairperson and bring an extra copy with you in case the original gets lost or the introducer has changed.

A professional introduction should be short (45 seconds long) and relevant to the audience. Avoid detailed background information, such as a lengthy list of your credentials, where you went to school and did your residency, and your family history and hobbies, unless the information is pertinent to the presentation.

The introduction should include three essentials: (1) something interesting about you and the reason you were selected to speak, (2) the topic and its importance to the audience, and (3) one or two relevant facts about you. Mention the title of the presentation at the end. The final words of the introduction should be your name. (See Exhibits 26–2 and 26–3 for examples of introductions for lay and professional colleague audiences.) A good introduction is like an American Express card: "Don't leave home without it!"

DON'T RUN OUT THE DOOR

You have delivered an informative, well-planned presentation. Do not be in a hurry to pick up your slides and leave after it is over. You should now be ready for the question-and-answer session. One way to get the ball rolling is to "seed" the

Exhibit 26–2 Example of an Introduction to a Pharmaceutical Company Audience

Dr. Neil Baum is a urologist in private practice in New Orleans, Louisiana. He is on the clinical faculty at Tulane and Louisiana State University School of Medicine. He has authored more than 1,000 articles and six books, including a best-selling book, *Marketing Your Clinical Practice—Ethically, Effectively, and Economically.* His area of expertise is medical marketing and practice enhancement. He is a motivational speaker and magician. He focuses on practical techniques to improve communications with physicians. I believe you are in for an informative and entertaining presentation. Let's give a warm welcome to the Wiz of New Orleans, Dr. Neil Baum.

audience with a few questions that you would like to have asked. I usually have one or two prepared questions on 3-by-5 cards that I give to several audience members before I speak. I ask them, "If there are no questions, would you mind asking this one or one of your own?"

It is also a good idea to anticipate some of the frequently asked questions regarding your subject. If you give the presentation often, you will hear certain questions repeated, and you should have answers to these questions readily available. If your topic is controversial, you must be prepared to field questions or comments from audience members with an opposite point of view. This is seldom a problem for most educational or informative medical talks. In the event that you cannot answer a question, say so honestly. Then take the audience member's name and

Exhibit 26–3 Sample Introduction to a Lay Audience

Dr. Neil Baum is a board certified urologist at Memorial Medical Center. He is a clinical assistant professor of urology at Tulane Medical School and Louisiana State University School of Medicine. He has a particular area of interest in the treatment of urinary incontinence and the overactive bladder. He has written numerous articles on this subject that have been published in medical journals throughout the United States. Dr. Baum has written several books and writes for the local *Health and Fitness Magazine.* Dr. Baum is an amateur magician and has developed a program using magic to inform children about the dangers of drug and alcohol abuse. I believe you are in for a very informative and entertaining presentation. Please help me welcome Dr. Neil Baum.

address afterwards and offer to locate the answer. If you entertain questions, have a 30-second windup that again states your purpose or "call to action."

Whenever my talks are part of a seminar for office staff or other personnel, I furnish evaluation forms and invite the audience to fill them out. These evaluation forms are one page long and have room for rating the talk and blanks for additional suggestions. They provide invaluable feedback for you on your presentation skills. Exhibit 26–4 is a sample seminar evaluation form.

After your presentation, audience members may come to the front to congratulate you and offer compliments on your presentation. Many will also come to ask how to get in touch with you. Make sure you have enough handouts for everyone in the audience. The handouts can be sheets prepared by you or members of your staff that briefly review your topic and give audience members information about you and your practice. These can be distributed before or after your presentation. I have been amazed at how long (6 to 12 months) people will hold onto my handouts before calling to make an appointment with my office. If you do not have a prepared handout, you can give those who ask a copy of your office brochure or business card. Exhibit 26–5 is one of the handouts I use at my talks.

The presentation is over and you have left the site. You still are not finished. Send a thank-you letter to the head of the organization that invited you. It is also helpful to ask for a letter of recommendation to use as a testimonial regarding your speaking skills. You can also request a mailing list of the membership to add to your database. For example, I have given talks to women's groups on "It Does Matter If You Have an Overactive Bladder." When I started treating patients with this condition with anticholinergic medication and smooth muscle relaxants, I sent all of the audience members a copy of the newsletter from my office discussing the use of medication to treat this common condition. This generated a number of new patients. Many organizations will ask to audio- or videotape your presentation. I always give permission and I request the first copy, which is usually the best quality. I use it to critique my presentation, and I might send it as an example of my talk to potential meeting planners.

Finally, you have spent many hours working and delivering your presentation. The material is current and informative. Consider stretching the mileage of your presentation by turning the speech into an article for a local magazine or newspaper. This usually requires minimal effort, as most of the material is in the text of your speech and only has to be converted from a conversational to a more formal style. Your hospital public relations and marketing department can be helpful in this area.

For physicians who are interested in improving their speaking skills, I suggest joining the local Toastmasters Association[2] or the National Speakers Association.[3] Do not wait for your hospital speakers' bureau to get you in front of the public. Opportunities are everywhere. All of us make our living as communicators. Try

Exhibit 26–4 Sample Evaluation Form

SEMINAR EVALUATION

Topic: _____

Speaker: _____

Place: _____

Date: _____

Please rate the following on a scale of one (1) to ten (10). Let ten represent excellent and one represent poor or substandard.

Presenter's Knowledge of the Topic _____

Audiovisual Aids _____

Relevance of the Topic _____

Overall Rating of the Seminar _____

Optional

What I learned most from this seminar:

_____

_____

_____

Additional topics that I would like to be presented in seminars:

_____

_____

_____

Suggestions or additional comments:

_____

_____

_____

---

communicating as a public speaker. It is one of the most effective methods of marketing your medical practice. A public speaking checklist is presented in Appendix 26–A.

The Bottom Line   *There is no better way to ethically market and promote your practice than to enter the realm of public speaking. Teach yourself to become*

Exhibit 26–5 Handout Used for Seminars

PROSTATE CANCER
Early Detection
by Neil Baum, M.D.

Cancer of the prostate is now the most common cancer in American men. Last year more than 106,000 new cases were diagnosed and more than 40,000 men died of prostate cancer, making this a major health problem in the over-50 age group.

Unlike many other cancers, which can be prevented by our habits and diet (for example, by avoiding smoking, sun exposure, fatty foods, and the like), there is nothing we know of that we can do to prevent cancer of the prostate. There are factors, however, that make us more likely to get prostate cancer. For example, it is more common in black men and in men with a positive family history, but at least one in ten men will be diagnosed with this disease during his lifetime.

Since we cannot prevent prostate cancer, the critical issue is early detection, that is, finding the condition early when it can still be cured. Up until now we have been able to cure only about 10–12 percent of men diagnosed, and this has really not improved in the past 50 years. Until recently, the detection of prostate cancer could be done with rectal examination alone, but we now have two new tools that show great promise in allowing us to diagnose this condition early: a blood test called PSA and ultrasound examination of the prostate. These are both simple, painless office procedures that can be done in a few minutes.

If the urologist diagnoses prostate cancer, it will be determined if there has been any spread of the tumor beyond the prostate gland itself. If not, many can be cured with either radiation therapy or surgery. If it has spread, there is help available with drugs, radiation, surgery, or combinations of these.

The important things to remember are these:

- Prostate cancer rates are increasing.
- Yearly examinations are a must.
- Prostate ultrasound and PSA blood tests are new and effective tools (but even so, we will still miss some of the cancers in early stages—no test is perfect).
- If found early, cancer of the prostate is frequently curable.
- If found later, there are operations and new drugs that can help.

All men over 50 (or over 40 with a family history) should have yearly rectal examinations. The PSA blood test and ultrasound examination of the prostate are exciting new tools that can help us find these cancers in their early, curable stages. These tests may be akin to yearly breast mammography and Pap tests for women, and they should dramatically improve our ability to cure prostate cancer.

a public speaker and you will reach far beyond your normal circle of influence in attracting new patients.

NOTES

1. Art Newman, *The Illustrated Treasury of Medical Curiosa* (New York: McGraw-Hill, 1988).
2. Toastmasters Association, P.O. Box 9052, Mission Viejo, CA 92690; (949) 858-8255, *www.toastmasters.org.*
3. National Speakers Association, 1500 South Priest Drive, Tempe, AZ 85281; (602) 968-0911, *www.nsaspeaker.org.*

Appendix 26–A

Public Speaking Checklist

_____ Select organizations with memberships likely to be interested in your subject areas.

_____ Contact an organization and ask for the program chairperson's name.

_____ Write a letter to the program chairperson outlining your subject areas, your credentials in medicine and in specialty areas, and why the organization's membership would be interested in your talk. Include your curriculum vitae with the letter.

_____ Follow up with a phone call to the program chairperson two to three weeks after sending the letter.

_____ Mark the speaking engagement on your calendar.

_____ Get background information on your audience from the program chairperson (the number of people expected, the age range, and so forth).

_____ Prepare your speech. Create a circular presentation, with the beginning and ending emphasizing the same points. For the middle of the speech, use case histories, illustrations, slides, and so on, to illustrate your points.

_____ Write your introduction. It should be one or two minutes long.

_____ Practice your speech several times until you are comfortable with your delivery. For feedback, tape it or have someone listen to your presentation. Be sure to time it.

_____ Prepare a list of items you need to take with you to the engagement (handouts, brochures, slides, slide carousel, and the like).

_____ Arrive early. Survey the "playing field." Do audio checks, projector checks, and so on.

_____ Give your speech.

_____ Conduct a question-and-answer period. If necessary, bring questions on 3-by-5 cards to "seed" the audience with questions to get the process started. Think about likely questions and what answers you will give.

_____ At the conclusion of your talk, meet audience members and distribute handouts and brochures.

_____ Write a thank-you letter to the organization. Ask for a copy of its membership mailing list.

_____ Capitalize on the membership mailing list. Send notices to the members when you begin offering a new procedure or service.

_____ Turn your speech into an article for the local newspaper.

CHAPTER 27

Make Slides
That Sizzle

Definition of a medical expert: A physician who is more than 200 miles from home with a carousel of slides.

Have you ever attended a meeting where the speaker used slides with graphs and tables from the *New England Journal of Medicine* and the *Journal of Clinical Investigation*? Odds are that most of you have. And a good percentage of the audiences for those talks were probably bored or confused by the materials. Typically, illustrations from medical journals and texts contain so much information and so many lines and numbers that the audience gives up and fails to follow the rest of the presentation mentally.

When you give a talk—to your colleagues or to a lay audience—you do not want the audience to fall asleep. So you have to employ public speaking techniques to maintain the audience's interest. If your presentation has good content and is delivered with style and enthusiasm, then slides will reinforce, enhance, and support your material. This chapter reviews methods for creating slides to complement your speeches. I think they are a must for any good presentation.

In general, an effective slide is one that can be understood in four seconds or less. Think of your slides as billboards: If you cannot read the message as you pass it at 60 mph, then it is a waste of the advertiser's money. There are four elements to consider when creating effective slides: content, style, color, and space. Whether you create your own slides or pay someone else to do it, you need to recognize the importance of these elements and to use them to maintain interest.

In this chapter I discuss how to create effective slide content, and how to use available software programs to then produce your own slides and interactive presentations.

KEEP THE CONTENT SIMPLE AND DIRECT

Slides should not be inserted haphazardly into your talk. They should act as signposts to your audience, pointing them in the direction you want their attention to go. As you review your presentation, figure out where the best places to insert slides would be (ideally at 30- to 40-second intervals). Your slides should emphasize pertinent points in your speech at logical transitions.

The late Dr. Robert Zollinger, emeritus professor of surgery at Ohio State University in Columbus, Ohio, was considered by his surgical colleagues to be one of the best medical speakers. His talks to colleagues on medical subjects (and to lay audiences on rose gardens) were fascinating, humorous, and, most important, memorable. It was no accident that Dr. Zollinger's slides matched the high quality of his verbal presentations—he made a science and an art out of the well-paced slide show.

In his class on general surgery, which I attended as a medical student, Dr. Zollinger stressed that a good slide "contains only two colors, has fewer than twenty words, and the graphs have no more than two lines." Material reproduced from medical journals, where the reader has unlimited time to study it, is not appropriate for a slide presentation.

Exhibit 27–1 is a table from the *Journal of Urology* that would not be appropriate for a slide. It contains too much information and would leave the audience confused and uninterested. Exhibit 27–2, however, is clear and concise and would be able to hold the audience's attention.

STYLISTIC ELEMENTS

After you have decided where your slide breaks will fall during your speech, you need to write text for them.

The following are a few suggestions on how to make your slides legible and easy to follow:

- Reinforce every major point in your talk with a title or graphic slide.
- Dramatize the most important conclusions in your talk with a title or special effects slide.
- Never use long sentences. Paraphrase the material in the speech, condensing it to a few words. For example, when I discuss the function of the bladder and urethra, I show a photo of a balloon and clothes pin to demonstrate the function of the detrusor and the urethral sphincters.
- Use capital letters for titles. For body copy, capitalize only the initial letter and use lower case letters for the remainder of the text. This style is easier for the eye to follow.

Exhibit 27–1 Example of a Graph and Vertical Labeling Inappropriate for Slide Presentations

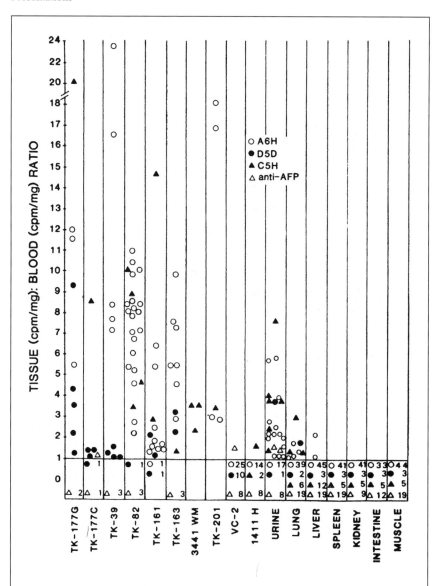

Source: Reprinted from *Journal of Urology* (1989;142[6]:1585), Copyright © 1989, Williams & Wilkins Company.

Exhibit 27–2 An Example of the Kind of Clear, Concise Graphics That Work Best for
Slide Presentations

IMPOTENCE EVALUATION

- History
  —Sexual
  —Medical
- Previous treatments
- Psychological factors
- Partner reaction

- Use asterisks or bullets to emphasize key points. Do not number the points, since this can distract the audience (some of whom may try to remember the sequence).
- Limit the slide to 15 to 20 words. If you have more than 20 words on a slide, make two slides.

CHOOSING COLOR COMBINATIONS

The colors of the background and the type are largely a matter of personal preference. However, graphic artists often suggest a dark background with light-colored lettering (this combination is also used to create easy-to-read traffic signs).

I routinely use a dark blue background with yellow text, and I use red or magenta for emphasis. The best slide presentations use a consistent color combination. Using a wide variety of color combinations and graphic styles tends to confuse the audience rather than grab their attention. By using consistent color combinations, consistent graphic techniques, and a consistent writing style, your slides will continually build one upon the other along with your presentation. Use color combination changes only for a purpose (for example, to differentiate sections within your talk or different subjects within a longer talk).

USING SPACE TO ADVANTAGE

It is possible to create nice graphs with most word processing and desktop publishing programs. The graphs can be photographed directly from the computer monitor, but I suggest using this method only if you need a slide quickly. The resulting slides will not have crisp, sharp edges or good color separation.

Slides should look well balanced, with lots of space between the lines of text. Double spacing between lines is best. If you use fewer than 20 words per slide, this will not be a problem. Make sure you use the whole slide. Do not crowd the text in the center, leaving wide margins and borders. Create horizontal slides whenever possible. Vertical slides frequently do not fit completely on the screen. Do not mix vertical and horizontal slides in the same presentation.

Graphs should be simple and easy to follow, with two lines or a single point on each slide. Always write horizontally when labeling the vertical axis. It is impossible to read vertical characters in only a few seconds. Figure 27–1 provides examples of good horizontal labeling, as compared to Exhibit 27–1, which shows hard-to-read vertical labeling.

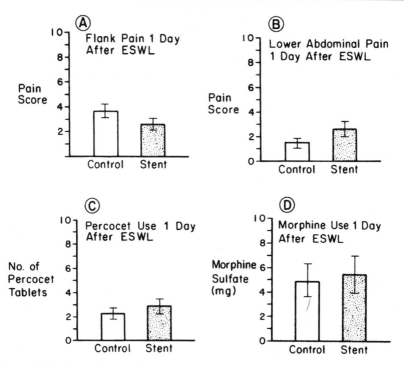

Figure 27–1 Examples of Good Labeling for Graphs on Slides. *Source:* Reprinted from *Journal of Urology* (1990;143[3]:476), Copyright © 1990, Williams & Wilkins Company.

HOW MANY SLIDES?

A well-paced slide talk should have a slide change every 30 to 45 seconds. Longer intervals will bore or lose your audience. If you need to talk without referring to a slide, advance to a blank black slide. Do not leave the space open with a sunburst of light, as this will make it difficult for people to focus on the next slide. Many medical speakers make use of beautiful scenery from their travels, famous paintings, or unrelated cartoons during the lulls in their presentations. In most instances this is distracting. And it is not okay to include pictures of naked women in your presentation, a practice that was more common in the past. Today it is not only politically incorrect and a potential source of embarrassment, it might even trigger litigation.

I once showed a slide from the cover of *The Economist* of two camels in the mating position. My talk was on patient services to a group of office managers. I talked about the importance of providing outstanding patient services and the necessity of "humping to please." The meeting planner was appalled and told me I would never be invited back, even though I had good content and great presentation skills. It was an example where being too cute resulted in being eliminated as a future speaker.

How many times have you heard a speaker at a meeting begin his or her presentation with the statement, "Well, it's time to get started. Let's have the first slide." This is a stuffy and wooden way to begin. By inserting a little finesse, you can make all the difference with your presentation. If you are going to have a slide show, do not use a slide in the first 30 to 60 seconds. Let the audience get to know you first, then begin with the slides.

PRODUCE YOUR OWN SLIDES

The standard medical presentation is made with a carousel of slides, a projector, and a screen in a darkened room. Now, with a personal computer, you can create a presentation that comes alive with color, movement, and even includes sound. It is easy and inexpensive to create a multimedia presentation that will add excitement and sophistication to any presentation.

Just 10 years ago, it was possible to generate designs for your slides on your computer, store the data on a floppy disk, and either mail the floppy disk or transfer the data electronically with a modem to a company that made slides. You could then have the completed slide express mailed to you for a presentation within 24 to 48 hours. This service was usually pretty expensive (sometimes as much as $50 a slide or more). Although you might have utilized this overnight service for an occasional slide, it would not have been practical for most of your presentations. In addition, many hospitals and medical schools had and still have audiovisual departments that make computer-generated slides. The cost is less but usually the lead time is two to four weeks.

For the cost-conscious, the remaining alternative was a do-it-yourself program of creating slides that was quick and inexpensive yet professional and attractive in appearance. In just 10 years we have watched do-it-yourself slide preparation methods go from the rather crude but practical creation of slides using Kroy peel-off lettering and photography to make and develop your own slides, to the ease and sophistication of PowerPoint and other graphics programs.

PUT PUNCH IN YOUR PRESENTATIONS WITH POWERPOINT

There are several graphics programs capable of producing slide presentations, including Microsoft's PowerPoint, Harvard Graphics, and Persuasion. Power-Point is a powerful graphics presentation system designed to take advantage of the Windows operating system developed by Microsoft. The program is easy to use and allows you to incorporate templates that help create slides and special effects that will hold the attention of your audiences. At the same time, PowerPoint creates the supporting materials that you need to make your presentation: an outline, notes that you can pass out, and a description of each slide in your presentation. PowerPoint also allows you to add graphs, diagrams, photographs, logos, and even video segments to your presentation. It is also possible to cut and paste graphics, photos, and text from other programs into your presentation.

Equipment Requirements

To run the PowerPoint program, you will need at least a 386 processor with a clock speed of 66 Mhz, at least 8 megabytes of RAM, and a 100 megabyte hard drive. (Always buy as much memory and speed that your budget will allow.) Nearly every personal desktop computer, laptop, and even some of the palm computers are capable of running PowerPoint.

You can create full-color slides using a color printer or plotter, you can create photographic slides, or you can create black-and-white slides using a conventional dot matrix printer, laser printer, or plotter. The best part about using PowerPoint is that you can create an active presentation using the computer as the delivery system. In the latter case, you will need a projection device to connect to your laptop computer so that you can enlarge your slide onto the screen for the entire audience to see.

For smaller audiences, you can connect your PC or laptop to a television monitor and the presentation can be easily seen by 15 to 20 people.[1] Active computer presentations can incorporate special effects, such as building and fading of text, which elegantly highlights any point you want to make.

Today most hospitals and convention facilities provide projection devices that allow you to cable your computer to the projector. Many facilities will provide the computer and you can e-mail your PowerPoint file or arrive with only your diskette and deliver your presentation using their computer and projector. Always check with the convention facility prior to your presentation to be sure your cable will connect properly to their projector. On the day of your presentation, plan to arrive a few minutes early to iron out any "bugs" in the electronic equipment.

There are remote infrared "mice" that allow you to walk away from the computer and advance the slides from anywhere in the room. This development makes you more mobile and allows you to interact with your audience. I usually place my computer on a small table next to the projector. This allows me to look at the audience and then read my slides on the laptop computer screen, which functions as a "poor man's teleprompter." I do not have to turn my back on the audience to look at the large screen behind me. As a result I can maintain eye contact with my audience. And do not forget the discussions from Chapter 26 on public speaking, in which I emphasized that "practice makes perfect." Be so prepared that if there is an electronic malfunction, you can still deliver a meaningful presentation from your handout material or outline created by PowerPoint.

Learning the Basics

Excellent tutorials are available for learning PowerPoint (see "Additional Resources" at the end of this chapter). The templates included with the program are an excellent launching point for a sophisticated slide presentation. The templates contain a unified pattern and color scheme to help you create a uniform appearance of your slides. Templates are available for creating 35mm slides, black-and-white overheads, color overheads, and even video presentations. I suggest that you begin by selecting a template that shows the overall appearance for your presentation and then create a single slide. Once you select the template, you add the appropriate text and graphics (keeping in mind the principles of good slide content discussed in the beginning of this chapter). The clip art and other visuals, such as video sequences, can be added later.

In addition to templates, the program also provides notes and outlines, a convenient way to organize your slides and review your material during practice. The program also permits you to create handouts for the audience that will allow them to follow your talk and take notes adjacent to the slide material that appears on the screen.

Creating 35mm Slides

Although you can easily print your PowerPoint slides using a black-and-white or color printer, the program is designed to provide output for high-resolution

35mm slides. Because few physicians have the expertise and expensive equipment to perform this function, Microsoft has created a special arrangement with Genigraphics,[2] a company that specializes in developing slides from PowerPoint files. The cost is $4.50 per slide, with a three-day delivery time; and $7.50 per slide for a rush order, with slides delivered the next day by noon. For next day delivery, the order must be requested by 1 PM the preceding day. You can save your PowerPoint file to a floppy disk and mail it to the Genigraphics Service Center or e-mail it directly to the company. The service center then processes the slides and returns them to you. PowerPoint even permits you to create Genigraphic billing information to send with your slide files to speed up the process.

Others may work with another graphics program, but I have found that PowerPoint is not only easy to learn and use but has become virtually ubiquitous in the meeting world.

PRESENTATION TIPS

As mentioned in Chapter 26, *you should always check out the facility and the audiovisual equipment before you speak.* Whether you bring your own slide projector or use one at the facility, make sure you know where the slide advancer is and how to operate the forward and reverse buttons. As your audience arrives, I suggest you already have the slide projector turned on and either have a title slide showing or a blank black slide in the first position. This avoids fumbling to locate the power button in the dark.

Do not totally darken the room, especially after a meal (even the best speakers occasionally find a few members of the audience taking a catnap when the lights are turned on). You want a little light to keep everyone awake and to see your audience.

The Bottom Line   *Bring your slides out of the doldrums. Use color, style, and space effectively, and you will telegraph your message loud and clear.*

NOTES

1. TV Silver monitors are available from Focus—(800) 538-6000, *www.focusinfo.com.*
2. Genigraphics can be reached at (800) 790-4001, *www.genigraphics.com.*

ADDITIONAL RESOURCES

Most of these sources are available at office superstores and computer outlets and are useful in learning PowerPoint:

- Brian J. Dooley, *Learn Microsoft PowerPoint 4.0 for Windows in a Day* (Plano, TX: Woodware Publishing, Inc., 1994).
- Jennifer Fulton, *Easy Microsoft PowerPoint 97* (Indianapolis, IN; Que Corporation, 1997).
- Roger C. Parker, *Microsoft Office for Windows 95 for Dummies* (Foster City, CA: IDG Books Worldwide, Inc., 1996).

CHAPTER 28

Meet the Press: Create Credibility through Celebrity

Appear on local or network television and you will instantly enhance your image. Each year, I obtain about $10,000 worth of television time absolutely free. This chapter will tell you how to effectively meet the press.

Like most physicians, I was initially uncomfortable with the media. That fear does not have to stop you. After all, Barbara Walters would feel a little uneasy in my hospital's operating room. Like any other form of publicity, media appearances require homework and practice. This chapter provides suggestions for booking an interview with the media, preparing for the media event, and handling radio and TV appearances.

If you do not have the time or do not feel comfortable "making a pitch" directly to the radio or TV station, consider using your hospital's public relations department. The staff of this department have the media contacts and are familiar with how things work in your community. They will be familiar with stories covered by the local media and with the sorts of medical "experts" that health and medical editors use.

A small percentage of doctors who seek media exposure may want to take the extra step of developing their own talk show, as I discuss at the end of this chapter.

BOOKING AN INTERVIEW

If you follow your local news, you already have an idea of what is hot in health and medical reporting. A newly developed technology or a new medical procedure is always appealing. A fascinating case with a human interest angle, especially if the patient agrees to be interviewed, will also make you attractive to media decision makers.

Glenn Pomerance, a creative ophthalmologist in Chattanooga, Tennessee, captured the attention of the local media by sending out a van to the underserved rural communities surrounding Memphis to perform free eye examinations. He was able to attract media attention, including coverage by newspapers, radio, and television by this offer to assist people without access to good eye care. He estimated that the media attention was worth thousands of dollars worth of media coverage. And, the idea generated several hundred patients over the year, including several dozen who needed surgical procedures. More important, he received the gratification of restoring eye care to dozens of unfortunate men and women and helping to prevent of blindness in others.

Even if you are not working with the public relations staff, it is good for business and the hospital's image to apprise them of what you are doing. My hospital's public relations (PR) department appreciates my telling them about a local TV or radio appearance I am making.

Every media market is different. Getting booked on national networks in New York or Los Angeles is a tricky business. Of course, you cannot get an interview on the *Today* show by calling Katie Couric or Matt Lauer. Even in the smaller markets, each radio or television station has an assignment editor who is responsible for deciding what stories are covered.

Call the station and ask for either the health and medical reporter or the assignment editor. Do not call right before or right after the program airs, since everyone connected with the program is likely to be tied up during those times. When you do get through, identify yourself and your subject.

The purpose of the call is to identify the decision maker and alert him or her that information will be coming. Keep the call brief. Media staff are extremely busy, and you need to "sink your hook" in the first minute of the call. Then offer to provide additional information, which most producers request.

Now for the pitch. According to Stan Levenson of Levenson Public Relations in Dallas, a firm specializing in public relations and marketing communications, it is best to keep your pitch letter simple and short. Point out the benefit and newsworthiness of your subject to the station's viewers or listeners. Have someone in your office follow up after the letter, or use a PR specialist to do this. The editor should be contacted a few days after you have sent your information packet, which, by the way, should be packaged as professionally as possible. Again, your hospital public relations department may be able to help you in packaging your materials. If the assignment editor has reviewed your material, you will usually get a positive or negative response when you call back.

If you get an affirmative answer, send a letter to the contact person confirming the interview—with the date, the time, and the place (if other than the studio).

PLANNING YOUR PRESENTATION

You are booked. What is next? For television, always think about providing visuals. If you have something for the viewers to see as well as hear, this will increase the impact you have. You cannot bring a 4,000-pound lithotripter to the studio, but you can suggest that a segment of the interview be filmed on site. Or you can bring photographs, slides, a video clip, or simple props to demonstrate your procedure. When I was invited as a talk show guest to discuss urinary incontinence, I used a balloon to illustrate the function of the bladder and a clothespin to demonstrate the function of the urethral sphincter. In another interview on vasectomy, I demonstrated the procedure using a rubber band and allowed the host to apply clips and cut the rubber band. He was delighted to perform his first vasectomy! When I discussed shock wave lithotripsy, I showed a real kidney stone and a vial containing sand-like particles that demonstrated how the technology pulverizes the stone to tiny granules that can then be passed through the urethra.

Let the production staff know that you can provide visuals. They may want to see them before the interview or they may want to shoot some original tape themselves to accompany your interview. Collect a fact sheet that you can send or fax to the interviewer before the program. This consists of a list of questions that you are comfortable answering or that you want the interviewer to ask. (It is also a good idea to bring an extra copy with you.) There is no guarantee that the interviewer will use your questions. But remember, the interviewer wants to look good and wants you to look good, too. If the interviewer knows you are comfortable with the questions on your list, it is likely he or she will use them.

DRESSING THE PART

What should you wear for television appearances? According to Stan Levenson and other media experts, the best color combinations are a gray or navy suit and a powder blue shirt for men or pink blouse for women. White makes you appear anemic, and colors that are too dark will exaggerate your features. Stay away from really narrow pinstripes and busy patterns, like plaids and checks, which tend to create a strobe effect in conjunction with the studio lighting. Men should wear ties that are either plain or have small prints. Do not forget to polish your shoes and wear socks above midleg. If you cross your legs and your pants leg rises, you do not want to have skin showing. For women, it is a good idea to wear something brighter close to your face, such as an accessory scarf.

Both men and women should avoid excessive or heavy jewelry, tie pins included. Empty your pockets before you go on the air. Also, try to sit on your suit jacket so that it will not ride up and make you look like the Hunchback of Notre Dame (this is what the TV anchors do).

PREPARING A CHECKLIST

The night before your interview, prepare a checklist so that nothing is left for the last moment. Include as much detail on your list as possible. Have directions or a map to the station. Know where to park. Take along your visuals, your prepared questions, a short biography of yourself, and a list of the two or three points you want to get across to your audience. Bring along a blank videotape (3/4″) and ask if the station will make a copy of the program for you (the bigger stations will not do this).

If this is your first television appearance, you might want to try something that has worked for me—arrange to visit the set the night before. Usually, if it is after the 10:00 or 11:00 PM nightly news show, the producers will be more than happy to show you around the set (TV stations in bigger markets are exceptions to this).

IT'S SHOWTIME!

Arrive early. First, you will see the makeup person. Then you will usually be shown to a reception area, called the green room, where you and the other guests will wait until it is your turn to appear on the set. This room usually contains a restroom, a mirror, and coffee and soda machines. Avoid caffeinated beverages—you will be naturally wired without them. Most of the other guests, unless they are seasoned veterans of the media, will be more nervous than you. And since you have read this chapter, you will be prepared.

Unfortunately, you rarely have an opportunity to meet with the interviewer or host before the show. You will be given an approximate time that you will go on. A staff person will usher you onto the set, usually during a commercial break. Greet the host and state your name clearly, especially if it is tricky to pronounce.

The set is usually awash with cameras, bright lights, and people. The director (the one with the headphones, moving around quickly) will seat you and attach a microphone to your tie or blouse and do a sound test. You will have a chance to say one or two sentences to the interviewer. Prepare these sentences in advance. It is usual to state the one or two points that you want to get across. A teleprompter will help your interviewer make preliminary remarks about you and your subject. Do not look at the moving camera or the overhead monitors. Look directly at the interviewer. If you are seated in a swivel chair, do not rotate it back and forth. Keeping your back straight, lean slightly forward.

Now it is your turn. Answer the interviewer's questions and tell your story with as much energy and enthusiasm as you can generate. Try to modulate your pitch and speak at an even pace.

Listen carefully to the questions and answer in such a way that you get your story or points across. Avoid jokes or anecdotes unless you are good at telling them. If you do not know the answer to a question, it is okay to say so. You cannot be an expert on everything.

If your host is moving off the topic, find a bridge back to your story. For example, I was once interviewed about a new treatment for impotence. The interviewer asked, "Isn't infertility a common problem you see as a urologist?" Since I did not want to talk about infertility, I answered, "Yes it is, and it is interesting that after treatment of their impotence, many men can have still children."

Wrap up the interview in one or two sentences of positive advice for the audience. At the conclusion, thank the interviewer and exit promptly so the next guest can get ready.

Occasionally you will have an opportunity to be interviewed at your office or your hospital. These interviews are generally easier because you are in familiar surroundings. Usually the interviewer will arrive at your office with his or her camera operator. Be sure to provide plenty of room for the camera equipment. If possible, have visuals available as well as a patient to interview. Avoid tours of the office and chitchat. The interviewer and camera operator are there to shoot your segment and to leave quickly to get their next assignment.

Do not make any "off the record" remarks. Anything you say can be used in the story.

Radio interviews or call-in programs are less intimidating than TV because the listening audience cannot see you. You also can have notes to assist you with your answers. To be effective, however, you have to create word pictures and make your interview exciting and interesting.

Interacting with call-in listeners can be challenging and frustrating. Do not make personal remarks. Sound upbeat whenever possible. It is best to give general information. Avoid diagnostic and therapeutic suggestions. You are always safe if you suggest that the callers contact their own physicians. Remember, prescription without examination is tantamount to malpractice, so be extremely cautious about giving specific medical advice over the airwaves.

After any media presentation, send a thank-you note to the host, the producer, and the director. Courtesy aside, you want to be invited back. Use the tapes of your radio and TV appearances to critique your performance. Do not be too hard on yourself. You will get better. You can also use the TV tapes to show to your patients in your reception room or to your support groups.

If you are nervous about media presentations, that's okay. Everyone is. You may want to consider hiring professionals to help you the first few times. Media trainers are one option in large metropolitan areas. These people are expensive, often charging hundreds of dollars for a half-day of training, but the advantage is that you get on-camera experience, a critique, and suggestions for improvement.

STRUT YOUR STUFF AS A TALK SHOW HOST

In the past, most physicians were content to practice their craft without pursuing high visibility. In fact, until the Supreme Court ruling deregulating advertising, most physicians avoided self-promotion. Now image building through the use of the media is legal, acceptable, and, for the most part, palatable to most of our colleagues.

Doctors gain visibility through many channels: their patients, their hospitals, their publications, their families, and now the Internet. All the marketing techniques in this book are geared to getting higher visibility for your practice. By far the fastest route to local, state, or national visibility is to host a regular radio or television talk show. In this section of the chapter, I will review the advantages and disadvantages of hosting a talk show and the techniques for obtaining your own program.

Dr. David Mobley is a urologist in private practice in Houston, Texas. He hosts a daily talk show, "Health Talk Houston." Dr. Henry Ritter, a San Francisco physician, was the host of a very popular talk show in the Bay Area. Dr. Mobley began with a weekly show early in 1990 and now does a daily radio talk show.

The Advantages

The advantages of hosting a talk show are apparent. You get constant exposure. You will have celebrity status in the eyes of the public. Your name can become a local household word.

You become credible as an expert. In our society, media exposure, in both the electronic and print media, creates an image of credibility and expertise. Although he is a specialist, Dr. Mobley covers nonurologic subjects on his show. This is a common practice. When a regular with the *Today Show,* Dr. Art Ulene made it a point to cover a variety of subjects. Since medical talk show hosts cover all specialties, the public tends to consider them as experts in all areas of medicine. One consequence of this perceived universal expertise is that the public will call to ask for referrals. You will be in a position to reverse refer and help your colleagues. And, you may also receive new patients from the media exposure.

"Tip of the tongue recognition" will be yours, according to Dr. Ritter, who said that while his show was airing, prospective patients often selected his name from the choices provided by the referring physician.

You can help your colleagues promote their practices. Dr. Mobley is sought out by fellow physicians in his medical community who want to appear as guests on his TV program.

You can use the program to keep your specialty's topics in front of the listening and viewing audience. For example, reports Dr. Mobley, when discussing breast cancer and mammography, he used this topic as an opportunity to discuss carcinoma of the prostate and early detection by means of annual rectal examinations. In addition, Dr. Mobley mentions his seminars and support groups on his show whenever he has the opportunity.

You can act as spokesperson for health and safety organizations. Dr. Ritter used his special position in the media to publicize the American Cancer Society's smoke-ending program, the national "smoke out" days, as well as drunk driving issues on behalf of Mothers against Drunk Driving, especially at holiday time. Your shows provide material for spin-offs. For instance, Dr. Ritter saved copies of his programs on audiotape, which he originally used to critique his show. The tapes also served as a legal record of what he said in case a patient or physician questioned his comments. But most important, Dr. Ritter had the tapes transcribed and then edited to produce his best-selling book, *From Man to Man.* Dr. Ritter now is not only a national speaker and media star but a published author as well.

Dr. Mobley has arranged for his hospital to make video and audio copies of his program for himself and for the physicians who appear on the program. These copies can then be distributed to patients or potential patients as a method of demonstrating expertise. Dr. Mobley also shows the tapes before his support groups to educate the patients and reinforce his media status.

The Disadvantages

Now for the reality check. Hosting a talk show takes a lot of time and energy. This drawback was at the top of the list for both Dr. Mobley and Dr. Ritter. Dr. Mobley estimates that a one-hour TV program takes several hours of preparation. Both doctors agree that becoming a media doctor is a big commitment. If you want to be successful and produce a good program, you will need dedication. That means placing it near the top of your priorities. The deadlines can be deadly! And, you can never just casually send in a colleague to cover for you.

You will be recognized constantly. Although this is the reason for becoming a media doctor in the first place, it can also be irksome. Both doctors indicate that the recognition is ego gratifying but note that they can hardly attend a social event without someone asking for nonurologic medical advice ("I have a friend going to Tibet. Does she need malaria prophylaxis?").

Your appointment phone probably will not be ringing off the hook. At least, that was the experience of both Drs. Mobley and Ritter, who caution that if you expect a huge increase in demand for your services, you will be disappointed. Yes, there will be a few new patients, but the increase will not be comparable to the time and energy that you put into the project.

Selecting guests can be a sticky issue. Dr. Mobley notes there is always a certain element of "politicking" to guest selection. On several occasions, a referring physician or a potential referring physician has been upset when not given an opportunity to be on the program. Dr. Mobley solved this problem by telling all those physicians who request an appearance on the show that "the producer is in charge of the selection process."

Your peers may not approve of your media status. Drs. Mobley and Ritter have both experienced jabs and criticisms from their peers. It is difficult to determine whether this disapproval is based on ethical grounds or simple jealousy. Whatever the reason, all those who decide to become media doctors can expect some criticism. Both doctors are aware that they have actually lost referrals because of their participation in media medicine.

Initially, Dr. Ritter received complaints (but not censure) from the local medical societies. The complaints were usually from "anonymous" disgruntled physicians who objected to his remarks or comments on a subject or topic. Dr. Ritter successfully dealt with the problem by referring to tapes of the programs in question. He sent transcriptions of his responses to questions on the show to the local and state medical societies. By defending himself, he developed a high level of credibility and has since become one of the physicians' spokespersons. Therefore, what began as an adversarial relationship with the medical societies has been transformed into a cooperative, even symbiotic relationship. This has been my observation as well. That is, whenever I market my practice through the media, it stimulates referrals and business for my urologic colleagues as well as for me.

You may not be taken seriously as a physician. There is the tendency to consider many broadcast media physicians as entertainers rather than "real doctors." Both Drs. Ritter and Mobley think that some new patients may be afraid that a media doctor will have inadequate time to spend with them as a result of being so involved in his or her media program. (However, this is not an issue for doctors writing articles in local magazines and newspapers.)

HOW TO GET STARTED

Be in the right place at the right time. Suppose you have an opportunity to do what Drs. Ritter and Mobley have done. And, more importantly, you have the necessary time and energy to commit to a talk show. How do you get started? Dr. Ritter entered the media arena when he met a talk show host who invited him to do a segment on vasectomy. It was successful and the host received many positive responses. The station asked Dr. Ritter to do additional programs and eventually gave him his own weekly show. In most cases, however, it is not that easy to get started. Broadcast media is highly competitive and substantial experience is usually required for success.

Start with cable. Dr. Mobley enlisted the assistance of his hospital in contacting the municipal cable station. Such stations provide air time for public service and educational programs. In fact, the cable market is one of the best places to make inroads. This is where a lot of media personalities get their start. The hospital public relations department offered to provide a talk show host, Dr. Mobley, and he and the hospital agreed to produce a weekly medical program.

Prepare yourself. Both doctors suggest that physicians serious about becoming media doctors should get specific training. Both doctors recommend a course by the American Medical Association that is designed to teach physicians how to appear before the media in a relaxed, credible fashion.[1] This three-day course is given each spring. The course teaches physicians how to be television interviewers and interviewees. It also teaches them how to handle a hostile guest or host.

Dr. Ritter's first 12 programs were professionally critiqued by an acting coach, whom he had retained on a consultancy basis. The communications or media department of your local college might be able to recommend an appropriate coach.

Physicians serious about entering the media arena should consider joining the National Association of Physician Broadcasters.[2] This organization provides support for physicians with a special interest in media communication.

KEEPING THE SHOW GOING

Provide your viewers with timely topics. For example, in the fall you can have discussions about the flu vaccine and its indications. In the spring you can address treatment for allergies and hay fever. In the late spring and early summer you can inform parents about camp physicals.

Plan how to handle your guests. For his program, Dr. Mobley selects both the topic and the physicians who will appear as guests. He asks each invited physician to submit 15 to 20 questions that are commonly asked by patients. Because the questions come from the physician's own patients, Dr. Mobley assumes that they will also be of interest to the listening audience. He then arranges the questions in a "flow pattern." He usually starts with some statistics about the condition or ailment: How many procedures are performed each year? How many deaths? How common is the condition? How much of an economic impact does it have? Not only does this type of introduction create interest, it makes the host appear knowledgeable.

Rehearse with your guests. This is especially critical, says Dr. Mobley, for guests who have never appeared on a program. To prepare his guests, Dr. Mobley provides each guest with a videotape of a previous program so he or she can become familiar with the format of the program. Practice sessions are held 10 days before the show. As well as reviewing the show's format, he provides some dos and don'ts.

Here are a few of those dos and don'ts:

- Do use simple, short answers.
- Do talk to the host and to the other guests.
- Do talk as if talking to the lay public.
- Don't give a lecture or get too technical.
- Don't use medical and scientific jargon.

A FEW CAVEATS

Never be judgmental. There will be instances when callers who ask for advice have not received the treatments you would have prescribed. Both Drs. Ritter and Mobley agree that it is important to avoid giving medical advice. Never suggest on the air that a caller get another doctor. However, if someone is clearly doing something irrational or dangerous (for example, using coffee enemas for the treatment of cancer), then you might suggest a second opinion. The station's legal department will probably advise you of the station's guidelines for giving opinions.

Do not plan to use your talk show as the basis of your marketing strategy. Both Drs. Ritter and Mobley enjoyed the feeling of accomplishment in creating their own programs, and they think that the trade-offs in time, commitment, and negative comments from a few colleagues can be well worth it. Although it may be difficult or impossible to track the results of becoming a media doctor, the image you create for you and your practice can be immeasurable.

Dr. Mobley believes that a media doctor who also practices tends to be more in tune with day-to-day medicine than a full-time media doctor. Dealing with patients, coding, reimbursements, increased costs of malpractice, and issues that confront patients on a daily basis puts the practicing media doctor in a unique position. I believe there is going to be more of a demand for practicing physicians to enter the media spotlight.

The Bottom Line   *Like any other area in marketing, the more you are exposed to the media, the more comfortable you will become. "Taking the plunge" to talk to the media brings tenfold the amount of any advertising time you can buy.*

NOTES

1. The AMA Health Reporting Conference (held annually) features workshops on production and on-camera techniques, how to break into cable, and how to be a host of or guest on a TV show. For information, call the AMA at (312) 464-5000.

2. National Association of Physician Broadcasters (NAPB), 1701 River Run, Suite 303, Fort Worth, TX 76107. The NAPB publishes a monthly newsletter, "On the Air."

CHAPTER 29

Become an Instant Expert: Write the Book

Once writing gets into your blood you can't stop...that is, until the editors and critics tell you to!

Neil Baum, MD

"You ought to write a book." Have you ever been given this advice? Have you ever felt that you wanted to commit all your good ideas to print? And that you had so many ideas that just writing articles would not satisfy your need for expression? Join the club! Many physicians write books for the trade market, which is the term for the lay public market. Our aim with this chapter is to give you a realistic overview of the process of getting a book to market.

Many physicians have developed an expertise that places them in rarified air and qualifies them to write a book. There is probably no better way to escalate your standing in the local and even national community than writing a book. Being an author adds to your credibility and acceptance as an expert. When your book hits the shelves, you can expect calls from patients all over the nation.

This undertaking is not for the light of heart. Many a stable marriage has been challenged when one of the partners makes the decision to write a book. That is why so many books are dedicated to the spouse who remained on the back burner while the author worked every free evening and weekend on the tome.

In this chapter, we cover writing a trade nonfiction book from the inception of the idea to one of the best and highest moments in your writing career—the day the first carton of author's copies arrives at your door.

Writing and publishing a book is a long journey, and you will wear many hats as you travel that road. Our approach is to focus on nuts and bolts. As Mies van der Rohe, the famous architect and designer, once said, "God resides in the details." And so it is that the heart of any book project, both content-wise and deal-wise, also resides in the details.

Writing a book is a hard, time-consuming journey. And you probably will not be able to give up your day job seeing patients anytime soon. These details are not presented to depress you or discourage you, but rather to help you realistically evaluate whether you want to embark on such a project.

IN THE BEGINNING IS THE IDEA

A book idea is conceived in many different ways. For both of us, our first full-length book project was the first edition of this book. We were teamed up by a public relations firm and completed the first edition of *Marketing Your Clinical Practice* in just under one year! Other physicians work alone and have their manuscript edited solely by the publisher. And a portion choose to employ a ghostwriter to bring their ideas to fruition. Using a ghostwriter is the most expensive but probably the fastest route to getting your book written and published. The route you choose will depend on your time availability and the willingness to commit extra funds to the project.

We will be drawing on our own experiences as well as other writers to illustrate the process of getting into print.

EVALUATING YOUR IDEA

Many writers have described the excited feeling they got when realizing that they had an idea for a book. As with other steps in this process, after the first rush of inspiration, you will need to step back and evaluate your idea. The number-one question you must ask yourself (because this is what agents and publishers will be asking) is: Is it salable? And to whom? It behooves you to learn as much about the bookselling market as you can. This applies most if you are planning on submitting your proposal to top New York publishing houses, but small presses also tend to be quite specialized.

Are you planning a book on dealing with allergies or are you intent on helping readers deal with their aging parents? The markets will be very different depending on what your subject area is. If you send your proposal to an agent or acquisition editor who does not specialize in your subject area, you most likely will guarantee it will get tossed on a discard pile. Book editors are busy people and they have books in production while they simultaneously consider new acquisitions. For example, in 1995 Random House's imprint Fawcett Columbine received 3,000 book ideas; they published only 120 books that year.

If you are aiming to get your book on the shelf, there must be no ambiguity about its proposed readers and your intended readership. Journalist Mark Thompson, a former staff reporter at the *Los Angeles Daily Journal,* covered organic farming for that paper's business section. He was convinced that an investigation of the organic farming movement would make an interesting book. He traveled throughout California gathering research and submitted a proposal to one editor at a large publishing house. When that did not fly, he sought an agent who dealt with the top book publishers. Two years later, his proposal was in its third draft and he still had not sold the book. One thing Thompson learned throughout this process was that his book could not be all things to all people. He thought the book could be read by business people, environmentalists, gardeners, and even history buffs, because of its varied content that seemed to span all these different disciplines. As a result, however, marketing people did not know how they would place his book. Publishers turned it down because they could not define the book's marketing niche. And oftentimes, it is the marketing potential that determines which books get published. Thompson's advice: "It's really important to produce a very concise pitch" for your book.

RESEARCHING AND WRITING THE PROPOSAL

Most books are sold on the merits of a book proposal. Sure, some books are package deals, where a seasoned writer is teamed with a celebrity for a "tell all" book of the moment. For the most part, a medical book will begin with the submission of a proposal to the publisher. To ensure the timeliness of your book, give some thought to the title. The best titles are short and precise, and give an accurate indication of the content. A good title will enhance the selling power of the finished product. Remember *Chicken Soup for the Soul*? That book sold more than 15 million copies. Not bad for a collection of stories by other people. A catchy title will capture the publisher's attention. The first edition of this book, *Marketing Your Clinical Practice: Ethically, Effectively, Economically,* was intended to provide the benefits of the book in the title. My first book for lay readers, *ECNETOPMI—Impotence, It's Reversible,* suggested the purpose of the book in the title.

The average length of a book proposal is 50 to 100 typewritten, double-spaced pages. A proposal contains a table of contents; an introduction of the book's premise; a discussion of the book's potential markets; a detailed outline of the book, to show that you have thought through the concept; one or two sample chapters; and a page or two about your credentials and why you are uniquely qualified to write this book.

The proposal process is very time consuming, but the good news is that once the proposal is completed, the book will be partially written. The proposal should be written in the style and format in which you intend to write the book itself.

The marketing summary is key to your proposal to convince the publisher to accept your book. Included in this information should be who the potential readers are. For example, coauthor Gretchen Henkel, for her first book on menopause entitled *Making the Estrogen Decision,* cited statistics from the U.S. Census Bureau about the aging of the baby boomer population. Her readers would come, she stated in her proposal, from the 15 million boomer women who would be turning 50 by the year 2000.

AN AGENT OR NOT?

A survey conducted in the mid-1990s by the National Writers Union (NWU) found that it is possible to sell an unagented trade book. A full 51 percent of writers doing nonfiction paperbacks sold their books without agents, as well as 37 percent of those doing hardback nonfiction. In the fiction world it is a different story—only 21 percent of those selling hardcover fiction did so without an agent.

Henkel's two books on menopause were sold without an agent. This was due to several factors: dealing with a small publishing house, her personal relationship with the acquisition editor, and their cooperative development of the ideas.

To deal with the contract, Henkel employed the services of a copyright attorney found through her writer's organization. As a result, Henkel kept a larger portion of the advance, while the attorney's advice ensured her protection under the agreement.

If you decide to go without an agent, here are some steps for approaching the process:

- Pick up the books you like, published by houses you admire, and call or write that company for a catalogue. Write for submission guidelines.
- Go to *The Literary Market Place* (see "Additional Resources" at the end of the chapter) and find the publishing houses that publish books similar to yours.
- Find the name and exact title of the editor in charge of your section.
- Call the publisher to find out whether that same person is still in that position—many editors switch companies frequently.
- Address your query letter and/or proposal to that editor.
- Approach a small press—although you will most likely receive a smaller advance, you are likely to get personal attention and a more direct relationship with your publisher.
- Make sure your proposal has no typos, is nicely printed and perhaps bound, and is sent with a self-addressed, stamped envelope (SASE) for its return to you.
- Go do something else!
- If the editor calls you and says he or she would like to send you a contract, great! Proceed to the section on negotiating the contract.

- If your manuscript is rejected, hope that the editor gives you reasons, not just a form letter. This is material you can learn from. A professional writer takes those detailed rejection letters, thanks the editors for them, and goes on to produce an improved version of the manuscript.

After reading all this, you may prefer to be represented by an agent. *Here are some tips for dealing with agents:*

- To find an agent, consult *The Literary Market Place* for agents who specialize in your subject area, ask a friend for a referral, or read *The Insider's Guide to Book Publishers, Editors and Literary Agents,* by Jeff Herman. Remember that agents are people with their own tastes, and that they reject 99 percent of what they see for all sorts of reasons, including their own personal interests.
- Send a query letter succinctly describing your project and asking whether the agent would like to see a proposal. Consult Chapter 21 on writing that masterpiece for advice on devising a good hook for your introduction.
- If the agent says yes, then send the proposal with an SASE for its return to you.

If the agent indicates interest in your book proposal, here are some questions to ask before signing with that agent (remember, you will be paying this agent; the relationship should be a two-way street):

- What does the agent charge? Standard is now 15 percent, plus you pay for any mailing or phone charges incurred in the marketing of your proposal.
- Does he or she require a written contract to represent you? If so, make sure that the contract only refers to your current project, not any other future "work" you might produce. You want the flexibility to choose agents for each project, if needed.
- Who are some of the agent's clients? What books has he or she sold? Can the agent furnish you with clients to talk with?
- What are his or her thoughts about your proposal? How much does he or she think it is worth? To which publishers does the agent think he or she may send the book? If you've been scouting around, you probably have definite thoughts as well—how open is the agent to your suggestions?
- Will your book be sent in a group with other books or sent singly? Will it receive multiple submissions?
- What about the agent's movie/TV industry connections? Although in the health care book trade this is not a necessity, some authors may be selling a particularly compelling story about patients or autobiographical material that may one day lend itself to production in another medium. You need to know

whether that agent has an affiliate who can handle those negotiations for you, too.

A contract with an agent is usually much shorter than a book contract, but there are important areas that should be covered:

- What is the agent proposing to do for the work? This should be spelled out.
- How much authority will the agent have? The agent must have the right to negotiate on your behalf, but the ultimate power to accept or reject a publisher's offer should be reserved for you.
- What are the financial details? The customary way for money to flow is from the publisher to the agent to you. The agent takes the 15 percent and remits the rest of the money to you. Will the agent be making 15 percent of everything—advances and royalties? This should be stated. There should be a definite time period stated as to when your check will be in the mail.
- How will the agreement be terminated? If the book sells? If it does not sell? This is similar to the listing period with a real estate agent. You do not want this to drag on forever. If you place a deadline on the relationship, the agent may be more motivated to "hustle" for you.
- Are there any assignability clauses, by which an agent could pass you off to another agent either inside or outside the agency without your permission?

In addition, you should stipulate that any modifications to the present agreement have to be made in writing. Inserting a clause about arbitration in case of a dispute is also a good idea.

A CONTRACT IS OFFERED—NOW WHAT?

A marketing vice president once told me, "You get what you negotiate, not what you deserve." There are several elements to the publishing contract, including advance amounts and payout schedules, royalty payout schedules, copyright and subsidiary rights, and stipulations as to manuscript length and deadlines.

You may say, the money is not important, what I am happy about is being published. Even if you are making a good living at something else, you will incur costs producing a book. Research takes time—and also money. Transcription of key interviews costs money. So, if for no other reason than to cover your expenses, you need to negotiate the advance. After all, the publisher is in this to make money. They risk their money; you risk your time. It is a partnership, and you deserve to participate in that partnership.

Again, the statistics: An Author's Guild survey showed 47.4 percent of authors got an advance of less than $20,000, 19 percent between $20,000 to $40,000, and 32 percent more than $40,000. A NWU survey found that the prevalent range of advances was between $10,000–$50,000. The average advance was $20,000 for hardcover nonfiction, $11,000 for paperback nonfiction.

The other important question is: How will the advance be paid out? More than 90 percent of the writers surveyed by NWU found that it was customary to receive half of the advance up front and the remaining half upon acceptance of the manuscript.

For most writers, the advance will be the only money they realize from their book project—less than half of all nonfiction books published earn an amount equal to or exceeding their advances and start collecting royalties.

For physician authors, royalties may be the most important part of the contract. There are two accounting systems used to determine royalties: list or net. Royalties based on the list, or cover, price of the book means that the publisher pays you a percentage of the price charged to the buyer. If a book sells for $15.00, and the royalty is 10 percent, you would get $1.50 per book (paperback rates start lower, because the list price is lower). The basis is net or publisher's receipts. Suppose the publisher sells your book on a 50 percent discount to a large bookstore chain. With a cover price of $15.00, the publisher is only getting $7.50 per book, and your 10 percent calculated on that would yield only $.75 per book. Obviously, royalties paid on list price are a better deal and worth negotiating for. Royalties typically are calculated according to numbers of books sold. For instance:

first 5,000 = 10–15 percent
second 5,000 = 12.5–15 percent

Breaking points may be higher, and we suggest including an incentive clause in the contract. If the book sells better than anticipated, your royalties will go up. If the book should sell more than 20,000 copies, try to get 15–20 percent.

Typically, an author will grant "first North American" rights to the publisher, which means the book can be published one time in the United States. Any rights beyond that should yield an extra benefit to the author. Most copyright attorneys would advise you to retain foreign rights, and as many of the other rights as you can, including foreign sales. Electronic rights are now increasingly an issue, with Internet avenues and webzines (electronically published magazines). Again, the advice from copyright attorneys is to retain electronic rights or, at the very least, limit the format and duration that they can remain posted on a site. Subsidiary rights usually involve selling the license to publish your book in another form (paperback, for instance) to another publisher. A 50-50 split on these rights is boilerplate—go for a better split if you can.

Contracts also should include some language about how your book will be promoted. What does the publisher intend? Who will pay for a book tour and advertising? Other items, such as the cost of indexing, glossaries, photos, illustrations, and permissions, must also be accounted for. Make sure that these expenses will not be deducted from your advance or royalties.

Be sure that the book length and due dates are reasonable. Obtaining legal advice is a must. Do not sign a contract that contains clauses you do not understand. You may decide that it is worth conceding on some issues so that your book will be published. Just make sure you are making an informed decision. As Los Angeles copyright attorney Michael Klein says, "If you go ahead, go in with your eyes open."

GETTING TO WORK!

After all that work to get the book sold and the contract negotiated, were you starting to wonder if you were ever going to get down to business?

It is important to approach writing your book in a systematic way. Ideally, you should have a dedicated office or space at home for the task. You will need ample space to catalogue and to store research, interviews, and backup documentation. You may also want to hire an assistant to help you with the administrative work of putting a book together. This can be a high school or college student who can track down telephone numbers and references, copy and collate the manuscript for shipping, and help with the permissions that your publisher will require before they accept certain materials, such as artwork from other published sources, guest chapters from other contributors, or reprints of tables, charts, and printed matter from books and journals.

Chapter 21 has some ideas on hiring a ghostwriter or editor. In addition, you will need a "team" for the support services: a good researcher, perhaps, if you do not have the time to do all the research yourself; a transcriptionist for the interviews; and a reliable overnight carrier for meeting deadlines.

Only after you have assembled your team is it time to proceed with the writing of your masterpiece. You most likely will have done a fair amount of outlining as you assembled your proposal. When chapters have been outlined and first drafts completed, it is important to get feedback from trusted advisors. If you have established a good working relationship with your editor at the publishing house, ask whether you can send along a few chapters to see whether they meet the publisher's expectations. Better to stop and make changes at this stage than to wait until the entire manuscript is finished and then be asked to do a total rewrite.

THE BOOK IS WRITTEN...YOU'RE NOT FINISHED YET!

Once you have completed your manuscript and proudly shipped it off to your publisher, then the "other work" of book writing begins. It is important to remember, as you grind through rewrites and obtaining permissions, that this is part and parcel of the book writing process. Some novice writers can become discouraged at this stage. After all, they say, I worked hard to meet the deadline and I did my part; let someone else do the editing and proofreading. But other departments will now require additional action steps—and they usually want them yesterday. After waiting for a copyedit of your manuscript to be completed, you may be asked to turn it around quickly. Remember to treat the editors as you would a good referring physician, that is, get back to them promptly and "pretend" that they are doing you the favor. The truth is, they really are; publishing a book is more of a collaborative effort than you might think. Editors are more likely to listen and help you if you are respectful of their time constraints, too.

At times, the "laundry list" of tasks may seem endless: permissions and illustrations must be gathered, queries answered, and galleys proofed. Then the marketing department will contact you and ask for jacket copy, author's biographies, and potential bulk buyers of your book. You will also need to make sure that you have a preface, dedication, introduction, and conclusion for your book. Somehow, the book finally goes to press.

Here is when you start making plans to promote your book. You can use many of the ideas in the public speaking chapter to secure speaking engagements for yourself—and sell signed copies of your book while you're at it. You can promote your book to the press by using the techniques described in Chapter 28. Keep in mind that release dates may "float" a bit, so do not schedule book signings too close to the release date to allow for delays in printing, wrapping, and shipping your book. Remember to work cooperatively with the publisher's marketing department. If you are willing to go the extra mile in promoting your book, they will take you more seriously.

Writing and promoting a book can be one of the most satisfying accomplishments of your professional career. The process, from conception to realization, takes a while. But when the day comes that the first carton of books arrives on your doorstep, it all seems worth it.

Why should a doctor spend several hours a night and months of hard work and deferred gratification to write a book? The reason is simple: the spinoffs, in more patients for your practice, media exposure, requests for speeches, and consulting is worth the effort.

The Bottom Line   *Remember that creating a book is like birthing a baby. Unfortunately, it often takes more than nine months from gestation (the idea) to the delivery room (the bookstore). However, just like having a baby, nothing is more exciting to see and hold the first run of your hard work—the fruits of your labor.*

ADDITIONAL RESOURCES

Books

- *National Writer's Union Guide to Freelance Rates & Standard Practice,* published by the National Writer's Union, distributed by Writer's Digest Books, 1995; $19.95. Written by working writers for writers, this book contains information from a NWU survey of 1,200 writers working in several genres, from magazine to corporate to book writing. Good, sensible advice and very readable.

- *Literary Market Place (LMP), the Directory of the American Book Publishing Industry,* by the R.R. Bowker Database Publishing Group, Reed Reference Publishing Co., 1995; $145.00–$165.00. This reference lists book publishers by subject, geographic, and specialty indexes. Although management titles and names are given, it is best to check on editors in current positions with a phone call. Includes a comprehensive listing of agents, including types of submissions, response times, etc.

- *How To Be Your Own Literary Agent—The Business of Getting Your Book Published,* by Richard Curtis; Houghton Mifflin Co., 1983, 1984; $11.95. Although some of the material may be a little dated, this book, written by an agent, contains thorough information on negotiating the contract. Even if you have an agent or attorney, you will need the information in this book to wind your way through negotiations.

- *Writer's Market—Where and How To Sell What You Write,* Mark Garvey, editor, Writer's Digest Books, 1996; $27.99. Contains listings of publishers, including how many manuscripts each house publishes each year, and lists of agents including their areas of specialty. Although the majority of the book's contents are geared toward other markets, the advice about writing and pitching story ideas is invaluable for proposal writing as well.

- *Kirsch's Handbook of Publishing Law,* by Robert Kirsch, Acrobat Books, 1994; $21.95. Written by the copyright attorney and former book critic of the *Los Angeles Times,* this book includes a section-by-section discussion of typical book contracts. A valuable resource.

- *The Self-Publishing Manual—How To Write, Print and Sell Your Own Book,* by Dan Poynter, Para Publishing, 8th revised edition, 1995; $19.95. This is a very thorough how-to book on the entire process of self-publishing, written in user-friendly language with an interesting layout. It gives the writer a good overview of everything involved in self-publishing. Helpful to read before you make the decision to self-publish.

Associations

- National Writer's Union/UAW Local 1981
  873 Broadway Suite 203
  New York, NY 10211-0079
  (212) 254-0279

- American Society of Journalists and Authors
  1501 Broadway, Suite 302
  New York, NY 10036
  (212) 997-0947

- The Author's Guild
  330 W. 42nd St., 29th Floor
  New York, NY 10036
  (212) 563-5904

Motivating Your Staff

Excellence in customer service is a learned trait, not something genetic, inborn or inherent. Physician and management leadership is crucial.

Dermatology Times, April 1999

The success of any medical practice and any marketing program begins and ends with the staff. A well-motivated, excited, and enthusiastic staff are the key to a successful marketing program.

Your best presentation at a service organization's monthly meeting can stimulate new referrals to your office, but this upturn can quickly become an absolute failure if the receptionist shoves the sign-in sheet at a new patient and then slams the opaque window in his or her face, or if the receptionist is rude to a prospective patient calling for an appointment and then informs him or her that it will be a six-week wait for an appointment. All your best efforts at cultivating referring physicians will be wasted if you have rude staff who take the attitude that they are doing referred patients a favor by giving them appointments in four to six weeks.

There are two different attitudes you can have toward your employees. Consider Attitude Number 1: "My employees don't like to work and avoid it whenever possible. They have no ambition. The only thing they look forward to is a check and the next vacation. I need to supervise them all the time."

Now consider Attitude Number 2: "My employees enjoy their work. It's fun because their accomplishments are recognized and rewarded. My employees are self-starters and need only to be pointed in the right direction to get the work done. My employees not only like having responsibility but they also seek it out when they are given a chance."

Which attitude do you think reaps greater results for the employer? Unfortunately, many businesses, doctors' offices included, are run with Attitude Number

251

1. The employees have narrow job descriptions, are overmanaged or over-supervised, are given little real responsibility, earn only hourly wages, and have little or no incentive to reach above and beyond their job descriptions.

Three decades ago, Abraham Maslow identified the "hierarchy of needs" that you must address when you want to build employee enthusiasm and loyalty.[1]

He theorized that human beings have basic physiologic needs—hunger, thirst, air to breathe, shelter, and sex—that they are driven to satisfy. After these basic needs are met, certain social needs—acceptance, recognition, status, and prestige—become motivating factors for behavior. These tenets of human behavior are universal. By directing your attention as an employer to these social needs, you can create a team of employees who are motivated to do even an ordinary job in an extraordinary fashion.

Why is it important to identify motivators or job satisfiers?

1. The practice of medicine, especially the business side, is becoming more difficult because of the increasing complexity of computer technology, the increasing amount of paperwork, the constant changes in Medicare and third-party payer reimbursement, and the pressures of cost containment in managed care.
2. Job security, a monthly check, and health benefits are just not enough to attract and keep motivated employees.
3. Most employees elect to work in the health care field for reasons other than money. Like physicians, they thrive on the feelings of gratification and recognition that they receive from patients and colleagues.
4. The keys to success in the private practice of medicine in the new millennium will be high-quality medical care, flexibility, superior patient services, and nonmonetary incentives for your staff.
5. Because of time constraints, you cannot rely on close supervision and tight control to keep your staff "in line." The successful practitioner will identify the motivators, delegate responsibility, and empower his or her staff to make nonmedical decisions in the office.

NOTE

1. Abraham Maslow, *Motivation and Personality*, 2d ed. (New York: Harper and Row, 1970).

CHAPTER 30

Go for the Goal: How To Create Team Spirit

If a man does not know to which harbor he is headed, no wind is the right one.

Seneca

You may have a sophisticated and elegant marketing plan. The telephone may be ringing with requests for appointments. But unless your staff is excited, enthusiastic, and knowledgeable when answering the telephone and dealing with patients, your marketing plan will be ineffective and your marketing time and dollars will be wasted.

A motivated staff is one of the key elements in today's successful private and group practices. Your staff are probably your most important and expensive asset. To be successful, you must avoid employee turnover and you must make employee motivation one of your highest priorities.

In this chapter, I review the importance of motivating employees by providing measurable and written goals in the form of a succinct, effective mission statement and policy manual. I also present practical strategies for motivating your employees by sharing the power, the vision, and the rewards.

WORKING TOGETHER TO CREATE GOALS

In our goal-oriented society, we are bombarded by homilies about having goals and sticking to them. Those sayings are popular for a reason: Successful individuals and businesses have specific written measurable goals and specific plans for reaching them.

Your practice goals must answer the questions *what, when, why,* and *how.* For example, you may decide to increase the number of new patients with a specific diagnosis that requires a specific treatment (the what) by 5 percent in the next 12

253

months (the when). The reason for this goal (the why) is that you enjoy treating this problem, you are the local expert on this problem, and it is financially rewarding. You plan to accomplish this goal (the how) by writing articles in local magazines and newspapers and by giving one talk a month to targeted audiences.

A different goal might be to improve the efficiency of your office by decreasing each patient's waiting time (the what) during the next 90 days (the when). This is important because your recent survey showed that patients were upset about excessive delays (the why). You plan to accomplish this by discussing the issue at your regular staff meetings, by conducting a time-and-motion study to identify the cause of the problem, and by examining the scheduling methods of your practice (the how). Note that both of these examples answer the four questions and that the methods for accomplishing the goals can be easily tracked or measured.

You must write out your goals if you want to ensure that you will reach them. Remember that you can't hit a target that you can't see. It is best if you include your staff in preparing the goals. This will ensure that they are attainable. If you arbitrarily decide what the office goals will be, you most likely will not have the commitment of your staff to reach them.

CREATING A MISSION STATEMENT

Nearly every successful practice—indeed, nearly every successful business—has a well-defined mission, goal, or objective. The mission statement should spell out the purpose of the practice and the methods of achieving that purpose. It is really the road map that provides the direction to all the members of the staff, doctors included.

A French hospital in the New Orleans area uses the acronym MERCI, which stands for "medical excellence requires concern for the individual," as its mission statement. Although our staff considered this to be a good mission statement, it really did not fit our practice, which has few French-speaking patients. We developed our own mission statement at our monthly staff meetings over a three-month period. All staff members had input into the final version, which follows:

This practice is committed to:
  Excellence;
  Providing the best urologic health care for our patients; and
  The persistent and consistent attention to the LITTLE details because they make a BIG difference.

CONSTRUCTING A POLICY MANUAL

Every practice needs a manual that contains its rules and regulations. Ideally this manual should also serve as a guide for any new or temporary employee who comes to work in the office. This manual should cover job descriptions, dress codes, hours of operation, the division of office responsibilities, vacation days, sick days, and emergency telephone numbers.

I also believe that an effective policy manual should contain a brief statement describing the behavior expected of all employees. A concise statement created by the doctor and the staff regarding the policy toward the needs and expectations of patients will provide a clear message to the staff about the importance of superior patient services.

When we began the process of developing a policy manual statement nearly 10 years ago, my staff members and I looked to other industries and businesses for examples that could be applicable to our practice. On a visit to a Nordstrom department store in Santa Barbara, California, I noticed that every front-line employee was wearing a "No Problem" pin. That pin said it all (that is, there is no obstacle that a Nordstrom's employee cannot overcome in order to satisfy the customer). I visited Nordstrom's human relations office and asked to see the policy manual. I was given a copy of the manual; it consists of this one paragraph:

> We hired you because of your good judgment. We expect that in dealing with customers you will use your good judgment to benefit the customer and our store. All other policies are null and void.

My staff and I thought that we would not be doing too badly by imitating Nordstrom, which is considered to be the top retail department store in America. We changed the word *customer* to *patient* and tried living with the Nordstrom model for several months. Unfortunately, no one could remember it when asked. Although the Nordstrom policy is a good policy, our staff decided we wanted something shorter that we could commit to memory.

I met a man at a National Speakers Association convention by the name of Stew Leonard. He is the owner of Stew Leonard's Dairy in Norwalk, Connecticut. He is America's number-one grocer, selling more per square foot of retail space than any other grocery store in America.[1] I asked him about his policy manual statement. He told me it was actually carved in stone on a rock in front of the store, where all the customers could see it:

Rule #1: The customer is always right.
Rule #2: If you think the customer is wrong, reread rule #1!

Now this was more like what we were looking for. We wanted something that was short and easy to remember and that focused clearly on the patient.

Our policy manual statement is now a combination of Nordstrom's and Stew Leonard's policy manuals:

Dr. Baum's Policy Manual Statement

Rule #1: The patient is always right.
Rule #2: If you think the patient is wrong, reread rule #1!
ALL OTHER POLICIES ARE NULL AND VOID.

How do we make use of our mission statement and our policy manual statement? We post them in prominent places to remind ourselves and our patients of our dedication to excellent customer service. Our mission statement appears in the reception area and in most of the examination rooms. It is also printed on the first page of our practice brochure. Our policy manual statement is on a large computer-created banner in the employee lounge.

Every employee agrees to accept and abide by the mission statement and policy manual statement. Whenever there is a problem or mistake, the first question we ask each other is, "Did we adhere to the mission statement and the policy manual statement?" Usually we discover that we did not. So we use the mission statement and policy manual statement to refocus on our number-one priority: our patients.

Keep in mind when picking goals that their results should be visible to you and your staff. For instance, if you get a positive response from a patient about being seen promptly, post this remark on the bulletin board in the employee lounge or in the kitchen where it will be easily seen by everyone.

Finally, take action and review your goals frequently. As Yogi Berra eloquently said, "If you don't know where you are going, you'll end up someplace else!"

NO-COST TECHNIQUES TO MOTIVATE STAFF

A well-motivated staff will create an effective team environment. Most enlightened businesses see that team management leads to increased output and productivity.[2]

Give your staff members a reason to be emotionally as well as economically invested in your practice's success and you will see them go the extra mile for you.

The remainder of this chapter is a review of 11 nonmonetary techniques for motivating your staff to participate in the marketing strategy of your practice. These techniques are basically forms of "psychic pay" and are often considered by employees to be just as important as monetary rewards.[3] Remember, employees want to be valued as human beings and individuals, not just as workers. The more you include employees in the process of running the office, the more invested they become in helping to improve it.

1. Perform a fair performance review. I believe employees like to know where they stand and how they can improve performance on the job. Motivated staff members want feedback on their progress—or even lack of progress. That is because uncertainty kills motivation even more than negative criticism. The best way to furnish this important feedback is with periodic performance reviews.

I suggest meeting with your employees on a scheduled basis about every three to four months. At that time you can constructively review their performance. I give each employee a worksheet (Exhibit 30–1) before the scheduled review. They are to use the worksheet to discuss what they like best about their work, what they like least, one or two areas they would like to improve, and what I, as their employer, can do to assist them in their professional growth and development. I then use the employee's completed worksheet during the review. Exhibit 30–2 is a good example of a form for fair employee performance review. I always end the performance review sessions on a positive note. I tell the employees how valued they are and how much of an asset they are to the practice. Of course, these meetings should be documented in the employees' files.

In order to make performance review more effective, I allow a role reversal. Every three months, I allow my staff to review me and my performance. I answer the same worksheet that the employees do, and I have them critique me just as I do them.

During one employee review session, I was told that wearing a scrub suit in the afternoon when I have no intention of returning to the operating room is unprofessional. My staff reminded me that they were asked to wear uniforms, be properly

---

Exhibit 30–1 Worksheet for Employee Performance Review

1. What do you like most about working here? _____
   _____
2. What one or two things would you recommend to improve:
   _____ Working conditions
   _____ Morale
   _____ Team work
3. Where do you want to be professionally:
   _____ Next quarter
   _____ Six months from now
   _____ 1 year from now
4. What can I do to help you reach your goals? _____
   _____
5. What are you going to do to reach your goals? _____
   _____
6. Any other comments or suggestions: _____
   _____

Exhibit 30–2 Performance Management Program Employee Performance Review

---

Employee Name	Emp. #	Date Entered Position

Department Name	Dept. #

Job Title	Class Code

TYPE OF REVIEW:
check one

_____ Annual
_____ Probation
_____ Other _____

Review Period Covered _____ to _____ .

PERFORMANCE DEFINITIONS

6 = Outstanding — Superior performance that is clearly and substantially above acceptable levels; far exceeds the standards for the job, achievable but seldom attained performance.

5 = Commendable — Highly effective performance; exceeds the standards for the job.

4 = Good — Competent performance; meets the standards for the job; the level of performance of most.

3 = Needs Improvement — Performance is below acceptable level; needs improvement to meet the standards for the job.

Employee New to the Job—Performance is below standard due to lack of job knowledge and is expected to improve with experience.

Experienced Employee—Performance is below acceptable level and requires improvement.

2 = Unsatisfactory — Performance is clearly and substantially below acceptable levels in most areas. Needs much improvement to meet the standards for the job.

continues

Exhibit 30–2 continued

GENERAL PERFORMANCE RATING

General Criteria	Rating	Comments Supporting Rating
Customer Service: How well does the employee demonstrate quality care and service to the people who use your department or area (i.e., patients, visitors, physicians, and fellow employees)?		
Work Completion: How well does the employee complete job assignments in terms of quality, quantity, and timeliness?		
Teamwork: How effectively does the employee interact with and assist co-workers/supervisor/manager?		
Adaptability: How well does the employee remain flexible to new situations, changes in routine, workload, and assignments?		
Personal Appearance: How well does the employee maintain appropriate personal appearance, including proper attire and wearing I.D. badge?		
Communication: How well does the employee give, receive, and understand verbal and written information?		

continues

Exhibit 30–2 continued

General Criteria	Rating	Comments Supporting Rating
Dependability: How well can employee be relied upon to adhere to established work hours and to perform and follow through on work without supervisory intervention or assistance?		

| | Subtotal I | + [   ] = [   ]
  # General   Total I
  Criteria   (2 Decimals) |

continues

Exhibit 30–2 continued

JOB-SPECIFIC CRITERIA RATING
(To be used with Job Description attached)

JOB DUTY NO.	Rating	Comments Supporting Rating

$+\ \boxed{}\ =\ \boxed{}$

| Subtotal II | # General Criteria | Total II (2 Decimals) |

TOTAL I _____

\+ TOTAL II _____

= TOTAL III _____ + 2 = $\boxed{}$

FINAL RATING: CHECK APPROPRIATE BOX

☐ Merit Increased Recommended

☐ No Merit Increase (Probationary/Special Evaluation)

☐ No Merit Increase (Performance Probation) Re-evaluate in 90 Days for Unsatisfactory or 180 Days for Needs Improvement

continues

Exhibit 30–2 continued

Supervisor's Comments _____

_____

_____

_____

_____

Employee's Comments _____

_____

_____

_____

_____

Growth and Development Discussion Summary _____

_____

_____

_____

_____

_____

*Employee's Signature _____ Date: _____
Conducted by: _____   _____ _____
                        (Immediate Supervisor)   Date   Title

Reviewed by: _____   _____ _____
                    (Next Level of Management)   Date   Title

continues

Exhibit 30–2 continued

*Employee's signature does not necessarily mean that the employee agrees with this review. Employee's signature indicates that the employee has had an opportunity to self-evaluate, to review the job description, to discuss past performance, and to make development plans with the supervisor.

APPROVAL FOR MERIT INCREASE (IF APPLICABLE)

Administration	Date	Human Resources	Date

Courtesy of Touro Infirmary, New Orleans, LA.

groomed, and to refrain from chewing gum. They felt that my wearing scrubs was not in keeping with the image of our practice.

My staff gave me this criticism in a constructive manner and I could not help but agree with them. As a result, I now make certain that I wear a shirt and tie under my lab coat. I would not have heard this feedback if we had not done a performance review and allowed my staff to contribute to improving my skills as well.

2. Encourage continuing education. Motivating your staff often requires outside assistance and training. Just as physicians need continuing medical education, so do your staff members require continuing motivational experiences. I believe it is a good investment to encourage your employees to participate in various continuing education courses and support their efforts financially. I pay the fees when my staff members take seminars and classes, and I pay them their salaries if they need to take off work to attend. For example, you may want to suggest that an employee enroll in a Dale Carnegie course or in an adult education course on computers or marketing. When the employee completes the course, have the diploma or certificate framed and hung in the office for other employees to see.

Continuing medical education can also be encouraged by creating an office library of tapes and books. There is a large selection of books and tapes available on personal skills, such as proper listening techniques, stress reduction, time management, telephone techniques, coding, and practice enhancement. Employees can read or listen to these materials and then offer to discuss a tape or a book chapter at a staff meeting or employee luncheon. A list of recommended tapes and books can be found at the end of this chapter.

It is also important to send employees to seminars and workshops. There are a number of commercial seminar companies that provide half-day to two-day seminars on subjects ranging from communication techniques to writing effective newsletters. Most physicians are on the mailing lists and receive promotional materials describing courses that are very helpful to medical office employees (see "Additional Resources" at the end of this chapter). I suggest that employees who attend relevant seminars provide, at a staff meeting, a brief review of the information that they have learned.

3. Empower your staff. In the past, most physicians ran their offices by directing their staff. Today, however, office management is very complicated. Few physicians have a thorough understanding of the complexities of the business aspects of a medical practice. Consequently, most physicians have learned to delegate the responsibility of running the office. The most successful have learned to empower their employees to take control and assume responsibility for their decisions and actions.

My philosophy is this: I did not go to medical school to learn how to develop a website, evaluate a software program, or select a remote server. Those are functions more appropriately handled by my competent office staff. In my practice I make every effort to empower my staff to make all nonmedical decisions. If employees come to me with questions or problems, I ask them what ideas or solutions they might have and what the best approach to the problem might be. When employees know that you trust them to make decisions and that office procedures are in their hands, they work harder to accomplish what is expected of them and to reach the practice goals and objectives. Furthermore, empowered employees will be more creative than "do as you're told" employees.

In my office, I empower any employee who has been with us six months to a year to make financial decisions up to $200 without consulting me. For instance, if the office needs a new telephone answering machine, I want my employees to consider which features we need, check off the ones that are applicable, and compare prices at the local electronic outlets or office supply stores to find the best machine.

On larger purchases, such as a fax machine or laser printer, a staff member will be given the responsibility of coming to me with all the research and with his or her recommendations. This policy pays off in terms of efficiency, and it also makes my employees feel important.

So, to empower your employees: (1) pick a cutoff line below which employees can make decisions on their own, (2) make them come to you with their prioritized suggestions and recommendations about new office equipment and investments, and (3) let them live by their decisions. Do not forget to compliment them when they do it right!

There are two main advantages of this method. First, your employees will not feel they are just robots doing mindless work. Second, they will tend to embrace the responsibility you have given them. When you give them the freedom to make responsible decisions, you are letting them know that you care about their working conditions, too.

Today, more than ever before, doctors have to do what they do best—diagnose and treat disease. There are very few physicians out there who are experts on fax machines, and they should not spend their time doing the things that their staff members can do.

4. Promote a positive mental attitude. As Henry David Thoreau once said, "Nothing great was ever achieved without enthusiasm." This is also true in the practice of medicine. When you have a positive mental attitude, you motivate your employees by setting an example.

A positive mental attitude can be promoted by surrounding employees with motivational statements, such as, "It is not your aptitude but your attitude that determines your altitude." Another thing I do is to provide employees with golden attitude pins to be worn on their uniforms. These pins serve as reminders that every employee is expected to enter the office each day with a golden attitude. Figure 30–1 shows an illustration of the golden attitude pin and how it is worn on the lapel.[4]

We use these pins as an additional motivator for employees. When someone does something above and beyond what is expected, he or she is awarded additional pins. For example, a patient had used a piece of diagnostic home-testing equipment that was malfunctioning. One of my staff members got the equipment fixed. Then, instead of calling the patient to have him come in and pick it up, she dropped it off at his house on her way home from work. The patient sent a glowing letter about the staff member, so she got another golden attitude pin. In another instance, a staff member came in on her day off to help us input the names into our computerized tracking program. She got an attitude pin, too.

When a staff member accumulates five golden attitude pins, then I send the member and his or her spouse or significant other out for an elegant dinner or an overnight cruise on one of the Mississippi riverboats. We make a big hoopla out of these pins, which are our equivalent of the extra stars football players get on their helmets. Napoleon said that he could have conquered the world if he had had enough ribbon. We can clearly motivate our staff members to exceed patients' expectations regarding their health care. Never forget that just paying employees a fair salary meets only part of their needs. When you also meet the "psychic payroll," your employees will feel appreciated and will continue to go the extra mile for your patients and the practice.

5. Recognize achievement. Nothing is more motivating for an employee than for the physician to recognize his or her achievements and accomplishments. When you recognize improvement in job performance, tell the person directly. You will be satisfying that employee's need for self-esteem. This improves the

Figure 30–1 The golden attitude pin is worn on the lapel of the uniform.

employee's confidence and also helps him or her fulfill the need for self-esteem from fellow employees.

You can reward achievement by using simple and inexpensive methods. For example, if an employee wins an honor or performs a task above and beyond what is expected, post congratulations on the bulletin board for patients and fellow employees to see.

If your practice has a newsletter, information about your employees' accomplishments, along with congratulations, can be included in it. Your employees will also appreciate being sent a personal thank-you note.

6. Use distinctive uniforms. I think it is important for staff morale for the office uniforms to be different from the customary white ones. Everyone in my office has a uniform that is color coordinated with the wallpaper, the stationery, the rugs, and my uniform. Also, I pay for the uniforms and let my staff pick them out. Make your uniforms distinctive and people will remember you for your signature colors.

7. Show your staff you care. Your employees need to know that you care about them not just as workers but as individuals with their own personal lives. When my employees or their family members are sick, I call them at home to check on them and make sure that they have access to adequate medical care. If someone gets sick in the office, I will make a call to another medical office and get the employee seen immediately.

The husband of one of our employees was stationed overseas in a war zone, so we put a big yellow ribbon on the interior office door, and all of us started wearing yellow ribbons, too. This let her know that we cared.

I try to attend all my employees' functions, like weddings and graduations. My wife attends their baby and wedding showers. If a family member of an employee has some good news or an employee's child achieves some honor, I make sure I offer congratulations by sending them a note or calling in the evening to applaud the achievement. I treat my staff like members of an extended family. As a consequence, I think they treat me like more than just an employer.

8. Catch your staff doing things right. I am a real believer in the idea that praise and compliments are very appreciated. My credo is: "Praise in public, pan in private."

When I catch an employee doing something right, I send a thank-you note to the employee's home address, making sure that it arrives on Saturday. I do not just hand over the note in the office. The note might say, "Thank you so much for going the extra mile for Mrs. Smith." The employee will then show it to family and friends. That is the kind of activity that makes our practice special.

I have two other ways to say "thank you" to employees who go the extra mile and exceed our patients' expectations of our practice. One is the *Extra Mile-O-Gram* (Figure 30-2) and the other is a *Thanks a Million Check* (Figure 30–3).

You will be amazed at how appreciative employees are that you not only recognize their superior service, but that you took the time to put it in writing. I often notice that my employees post these notes at their work stations and share them with other employees. I think this written recognition "raises the bar" for outstanding service from other employees as well.

9. Reward your staff for saving money or reducing expenses. If one of your staff comes up with an idea that saves the practice money, give a bonus. For example, the autoclave we were using for the practice broke down. When I tried to get parts, I was informed that the machine was not being made any more. The nurse in our office took the machine to the hospital's biomedical engineering department, which installed a $30 part that saved me from buying a new $2,000 autoclave. She deserved to be rewarded for that, so I gave her a $50 check right on the spot.

I am trying to motivate my staff not just to earn more money for the practice but to reduce expenses. They are paid for identifying and designing money-saving ideas. For instance, we have an office telephone system we bought from an inde-

EXTRAMILE-O-GRAM

CONGRATULATIONS!
You Did It!

TO:

_____

_____

_____

Go the Extra Mile Every Day!

Figure 30–2 Extra Mile-O-Gram

Exhibit 30–3 Thanks a Million Check

Neil Baum, M.D.
3525 Prytania St., Suite 614
New Orleans, LA 70115
(504)   891-8454

_____ 19____

PAY TO THE
ORDER OF _____ $ __THANKS__

THANKS A MILLION

_____

BAUM'S BANK OF GRATITUDE
WIZ'S BRANCH

_____

pendent company, and we also have a service contract with that company. When the system broke down, it was really expensive to get repairs. One of the employees knew of a man who had formerly worked for the telephone company and had gone into business for himself. She found him, got his references, and arranged for him to provide the service and repairs on our phone system—at one-third the price. I immediately rewarded her with a check, too.

10. Include your staff in the decision-making process. For example, I had planned to have a patient educator come into the office. This was a retired gentleman who would talk with patients about the common urologic conditions and treatments. But my staff unanimously said, "No! Your patients are coming to see you, not an educator. You can't do that!" They agreed that videotapes could be shown in the reception area but that the educator was not a good idea. So I listened to their good judgment, and they appreciated it.

Just make sure that if you ask for your employees' advice, you use it. Your staff members are on the front line, so to speak, and they want the office routine to go well. I think you have to include them in the decision-making process, whether the task is writing a mission statement or policy manual, determining a change in procedures, or meeting new job candidates. Those are the things that make them feel like part of the team.

11. Surprise is the spice of life. Whenever you can provide an unexpected perk for your staff, you can be sure that they will appreciate the gesture. I remember one instance when an employee was on vacation and another employee was ill at home. We all had to work harder to take up the slack for five days. In spite of being shorthanded, we were able to function at the regular speed and capacity without affecting the quality of care that we were providing our patients. Our extra effort was so successful that our patients were not even aware of the shortfall that was taking place in our office! I was so impressed with the extra effort that I arranged for a massage therapist to visit our practice on Friday afternoon at 5 PM and give everyone a 15–20 minute massage as a way of saying thank you.

Whenever your staff members extend themselves and perform at a stellar level in spite of difficult circumstances (such as fewer staff), it is important to recognize their efforts in some way. Otherwise, they most probably will not make the effort the second time such a situation arises.

There is no way to include all aspects of expected behavior in the employee manual. The one for our practice, for instance, does not state that employees need to take equipment to the patient's home or to come in on a day off. But the manual does say that employees are expected to do whatever it takes to make every patient feel special and to exceed his or her experience with our practice, as long as it is ethical and reasonable. When employees are able to do this, we must find ways to acknowledge that extra effort. And remember, properly rewarding employees can be accomplished with minimal expense, energy, and effort.

The Bottom Line   *Encouraging your staff to develop team spirit makes good business sense. When your employees have a personal investment in problem solving and decision making, they will go the extra mile for your patients and the practice.*

NOTES

1. Ronald Zemke and Dick Schaaf, *The Service Edge: 101 Companies That Profit from Customer Care* (New York: New American Library, 1989), 352–355.
2. Elizabeth Kearney, *People Power: Reading People for Results* (Provo, UT: Sterling Press, 1990), 163–182.
3. Abraham Maslow, *Motivation and Personality*, 2d ed. (New York: Harper and Row, 1970).
4. Golden attitude pins can be obtained from Rich Wilkins and Company, (800) 944-7269; *www.mrpos.com*; rich@mrpos.com.

ADDITIONAL RESOURCES

Recommended Tapes

- "How To Win Customers and Keep Them for Life" (Michael LeBoeuf and Associates, P.O. Box 9504, Metairie, LA 70005)
- "In Search of Excellence" (Tom Peters)
- "Think and Grow Rich" (Napoleon Hill)
- "Thriving on Chaos" (Tom Peters)

Other tapes are available from:
Nightingale-Conant Corporation
7300 North Lehigh Avenue
Chicago, IL 60648
(800) 323-5552
www.nightingale.com

Recommended Books

- Leonard L. Berry, *Discovering the Soul of Service* (New York: Free Press, 1999).
- Kenneth Blanchard and Dr. Norman Vincent Peale, *Power of Ethical Management* (New York: William Morris and Co., 1988).
- Kenneth Blanchard and Spencer Johnson, *The One-Minute Manager* (New York: Berkley Books, 1982).
- Richard Carlson, *Don't Sweat the Small Stuff at Work: Simple Ways To Minimize Stress and Conflict While Bringing Out the Best in Yourself and Others* (New York: Hyperion Books, 1998).

- Stephen R. Covey, *The Seven Habits of Highly Effective People: Powerful Lessons in Personal Change* (New York: Simon & Schuster, 1990).
- Harvey Mackay, *Swim with the Sharks without Being Eaten Alive* (New York: Ivy Books, 1988).

Seminars

Among the best seminars for office staff are the **Fred Pryor Seminars** on Effective Communication and Success Skills for Secretaries. These seminars are given frequently in most metropolitan areas on an annual basis. Call (800) 255–6139 for information; *www.pryor.com.*

Conomikes

Conomikes Reports, Inc.
6033 W. Century Blvd., Suite 990
Los Angeles, CA 90045
(800) 421–6512
www.conomikes.com.

CHAPTER 31

Add Sparkle to Your Staff Meetings

*Coming together is a beginning, keeping together is progress . . .
working together is a success.*

There is no better way to bring your staff together than to have creative staff meetings that produce positive changes in behavior that translate to enhanced quality of care for your patients.

One of the best staff meetings we ever had was attending the movie "The Doctor," starring William Hurt. The plot concerns an arrogant cardiac surgeon who develops throat cancer and gets a dose of his own medicine. As a result, he becomes a more sensitive and caring physician and loving husband. I took my staff to see an early showing of the movie. We then went out for dinner and discussed its application to our practice. As a result, I believe that our empathy button for our patients was reset at a higher level. Although few of us can walk in the shoes of our patients, all of us can be much more sensitive to the feelings that patients carry with them through the door of our offices.

Adding sparkle to your staff meetings can really make a difference and bring your staff together, encouraging them to function as a more productive team. This chapter will provide several ideas that can add sparkle and excitement to your staff meetings and make them more meaningful and productive.

Staff meetings provide a priceless opportunity to hear feedback from the people best able to identify problems and suggest workable solutions. Furthermore, staff meetings can be fun. They allow staff members to discuss their work in an open and relaxed atmosphere. During these meetings they can present any grievances or problems they are experiencing as well as any suggestions they have to increase business.

TYPES OF MEETINGS

In my practice we have three types of staff meetings. We have formal or standard meetings, which are held every other week. Less formal meetings are held once a month during lunch. These meetings do not have an agenda. They provide an opportunity to have open discussions about the practice. The staff also holds monthly lunch meetings without me to discuss staff-to-staff interaction. Staff meetings are held more often if there are any problems or new programs being introduced.

When organizing staff meetings, keep the following points in mind:

1. Avoid having meetings on Monday or Friday.
2. Meet in the morning, when everyone is rested.
3. Keep the meeting to between 35 and 40 minutes.
4. Avoid interruptions; have your answering service pick up all calls.
5. Serve refreshments, such as coffee, rolls, or lunch.

STARTING ON A POSITIVE NOTE

I have always been impressed with the wonderful things that happen to most of the staff. At the beginning of our meetings, I ask that everyone relate some positive incident that has happened since our last meeting. Such incidents might include successfully dealing with a difficult patient, getting new lab coats, or receiving an award. The staff meeting is an excellent forum for sharing these positive events with other staff members. Beginning each meeting with these presentations creates a positive atmosphere.

I also ask everyone to contribute one idea that will help improve the practice. I borrowed this concept from Stew Leonard, who is the top retail grocer in America. We record each suggestion. Those whose ideas are implemented are rewarded either verbally or monetarily (if the cost savings are significant).

All aspects of my practice have been improved as a result of using this idea-a-month approach. Do not criticize your staff's suggestions. You will stifle any future creativity if you indicate that some of the ideas are ridiculous or useless.

WORKING TOGETHER

You can use staff meetings to emphasize staff teamwork. I once took my staff on a trip to the moon. The journey was on paper, of course. But when we returned to earth, we found we had learned a lot about how we work together as a team.

The "Lost on the Moon Test," developed by Jay Hall of NASA,[1] is an exercise you might want to try.
Each staff member assumes that he or she is the sole occupant of a rocket ship that has crashed on the surface of the moon. In order to survive, the staff member has to leave the rocket ship and rendezvous with a mother ship 200 miles away. He or she has to choose among 15 items to take on the hike to the mother ship. The task is to rank the following 15 items in order of their importance for survival (1 is the most important and 15 the least):

_____ box of matches
_____ food concentrate
_____ 50 feet of nylon rope
_____ parachute silk
_____ solar-powered portable heating unit
_____ two .45-caliber pistols
_____ one case of dehydrated milk
_____ two 100-pound tanks of oxygen
_____ map of the moon's constellations
_____ self-inflating life raft
_____ magnetic compass
_____ five gallons of water
_____ signal flares
_____ first-aid kit containing injection needles
_____ solar-powered FM receiver-transmitter

NASA provided the following answers:

1. oxygen (most pressing survival need)
2. water (replacement for tremendous liquid loss on lighted side of the moon)
3. map (primary means of navigation)
4. food concentrate (for energy requirements)
5. FM receiver (for communication with mother ship)
6. nylon rope (for climbing mountains)
7. first-aid kit (for medicines, vitamins, treatments; the needles fit a special aperture in NASA suits)
8. parachute silk (protection against sun's rays)
9. raft
10. flares (to signal mother ship when sighted)
11. pistols (possible means of self-protection)
12. dehydrated milk (bulkier duplication of food concentrate)
13. heating unit (not needed unless on dark side)
14. compass (worthless; magnetic field on moon is not polarized)
15. matches (no oxygen on moon; virtually useless)

Each employee takes the test alone and then all the employees take it as a group. It is interesting that my staff's responses were much more accurate when they worked as a team than when each tried to figure out the correct ranking alone. This has also been the finding of Dr. Hall, whose research indicates that any team results will be closer to NASA's than those of any individual. The Lost on the Moon Test can really demonstrate to your staff that they will accomplish more when they work together.

STIMULATING STAFF INVOLVEMENT

Role playing is another enjoyable technique for evaluating problems that occur during office hours. For example, one staff member can assume the role of an irate patient calling to complain about a bill and another can attempt to calm the patient and solve his or her problem. The rest of the staff can critique the dialogue. Role playing is good training for new staff members as well.

You can also alter the staff meeting format by designating a staff member other than yourself or the office manager to run one of the meetings. This person should prepare the agenda and topics for the meeting. Role reversal helps the staff appreciate the work that goes into preparation of the staff meetings. At our office, we rotate the responsibility for leading the meetings.

Finally, staff members can take turns presenting minilectures about some aspect of the practice. For example, if I plan to do a new surgical procedure, I will give a short presentation of the operation, including preoperative preparation, postoperative care, and complications. This way, my staff is better prepared to answer potential questions from patients and their families. As another example, the office manager might give a summary of a recent coding seminar that she attended. This alerts the staff to the importance of proper coding.

Each staff meeting should end with a summary of what has been accomplished and the creation of a "to do" list for the next meeting. This list can be distributed with a copy of the notes from the meeting.

For a staff meeting to be effective, doctors and managers must be good listeners and accept constructive criticism. Listening is probably one of the most difficult things for a doctor to do at a staff meeting—the author included! If good ideas are suggested, implement them. Show your employees that the time spent during staff meetings is well spent.

The Bottom Line *By adding a little sparkle, you can transform staff meetings from the typical moan and groan sessions into energizing experiences that will generate effective results for you and your practice.*

NOTE

1. David Dee, "Teamwork," in *Make Your Team a Winner—Tips and Techniques for Success in Today's Workplace* (Chicago: Dartnell Corporation. 1990), 18–20.

ADDITIONAL RESOURCES

- Thomas A. Kayser, *Building Team Power: How To Unleash the Collaborative Genius of Work Teams* (New York: McGraw-Hill Companies, 1994).
- Linda Moran, ed., *Keeping Teams on Track: What To Do When the Going Gets Rough* (New York: McGraw-Hill Companies, 1996).

CHAPTER 32

Reach Out and Touch Someone: The Telephone Is the Lifeline of Your Practice

At ten o'clock on Monday morning the telephone is ringing off the hook in the doctor's office.

Patient: Hello, is this Dr. Zhivago's office? I'd like to—
Receptionist (harried, abrupt): Can you hold, please? (Muzak comes on.)

How would you like the first (or second, or even one hundredth) call to your practice's office to be handled in this manner? Of course, you would be upset, and rightfully so. Every patient values his or her time as much as you do yours. Abrupt behavior on the telephone, as in the example above, just might prompt a patient to look elsewhere for medical treatment.

The telephone is the lifeline of your practice. Too often, employers delegate the job of answering the telephones to the employee with the least amount of training and the lowest salary.

Consider this: A new patient's initial telephone call is the first interaction between the patient and your practice. During that interaction, you have a golden opportunity to create a positive first impression. If you (or your office ambassador, the receptionist) fail to create a positive impression, the patient may form a negative attitude toward you and your office even before visiting your office. Worse yet, such negative impressions can result in a loss of patients. Remember, bad news seems to spread more quickly than good. And, as I said in Chapter 6 on your reception area, you never get a second chance to make a good first impression.

Nothing is more vital to your practice than using the best telephone techniques and the best telephone etiquette. In this chapter, I provide a five-step technique for enhancing telephone answering in your office. After that, I discuss other ways to use your telephone as a marketing tool.

ANSWERING THE PHONE: A FIVE-STEP TECHNIQUE

1. The most important thing is for your receptionist to answer the telephone with enthusiasm and a smile. Yes, I mean that literally. If you have a smile on your face, this will come through the phone lines. You want your callers to feel the receptionist's warmth and compassion.

How do you put a "smile" in someone's voice? Although this may seem on the surface to be an illusive or intangible concept, a well-trained receptionist should be able to communicate warmth and friendliness by the tone in his or her voice. You can encourage your receptionist to smile when answering the telephone by putting a small mirror near the phone. This provides the receptionist with the necessary visual feedback. One of the drawbacks to this technique is that the receptionist may spend a lot of time checking his or her appearance. The feedback that the mirror provides is always needed, and in our office we do not remove the mirror even after the training period.

2. Have the receptionist identify the time of day and the name of the practice. Examples: "Good morning, this is Dr. Baum's office" or "Good afternoon, this is the New Orleans Urology Clinic."

3. The receptionist should identify him- or herself and, if appropriate, give his or her title. All callers like to know to whom they are speaking. Also, because the receptionist is no longer anonymous, this technique encourages him or her to be polite and courteous. Example: "Good morning, this is Dr. Baum's office. This is Jackie speaking."

4. The receptionist should then ask if he or she can be of any assistance to the caller. Example: "Good morning, this is Dr. Baum's office. This is Jackie speaking. How may I help you?"

5. Finally, the receptionist should make an effort to use the caller's name at least twice during the conversation. The most important word in any language is the sound of the listener's own name. The more you mention a person's name in conversation, the more likely you are to connect with that person. When the receptionist uses the caller's name during the phone conversation, the caller feels special. Repeated use of the caller's name is an excellent method of enhancing that vital first impression.

When first instituting this system or training a new employee, you can provide a fill-in-the-blank form next to the telephone (Exhibit 32–1). With constant repetition and positive reinforcement (for example, compliments), the receptionist will learn the habit of answering the phone in a pleasing, effective manner. Written guidelines on telephone technique should also be included in the policy manual for all new employees. Do not leave such an important task as the telephone to the receptionist's memory or assume that his or her previous training was adequate.

Exhibit 32–1 A Fill-in-the-Blank Sheet Used When Training Receptionists

---

1. Smile, be enthusiastic.
2. "Good morning, this is Dr. _____'s office."
3. "This is _____ speaking."
4. "May I help you?"
5. Use caller's name.

Additional information on telephone technique is listed at the end of this chapter. You can also contact your local telephone company for information about training classes in telephone technique.

SCREENING CALLS

To conserve time and increase office efficiency, use your receptionist as your first line of defense. Most physicians already do this, instructing their receptionists not to put through just any call. To help your receptionist screen your calls effectively, provide a list of all those who must be allowed to speak to you immediately, such as the emergency room or other physicians.

Make sure your receptionist and anyone else who answers the office telephone know how to "qualify" callers. For instance, how do you want calls from drug representatives to be handled? What about representatives selling various office services? Do you want a list of these callers so you can call them back? Do you want certain callers to be discouraged from trying your office again? Make a decision about these calls and then make a plan. If you are involved in giving media interviews, you also need to give special instructions if you expect to receive a call. Often reporters on tight deadlines call for short interviews. Let your receptionist know what to do in such cases.

What about calls from patients? Are there certain emergencies when the receptionist should put the caller through to you, or is your policy never to interrupt an office visit and to call the patient back? All these contingencies should be covered during the training period. And if new situations arise, bring them up at staff meetings so that everyone agrees on how each situation will be handled.

Determine callback times. The standard time in our office is from 11:45 AM to 12:00 PM and after 4:30 PM. Your receptionist can tell patients when you will return their calls. This is helpful in two ways. First, it prevents patients from tying up your telephone lines. Second, it saves the time you might waste trying to locate the patients or making repeated calls if they are not at the number they left. In addition, as pointed out in Chapter 8, this practice is a nice way of indicating to your patients that you are considerate of their time as well.

You should train your receptionist to prepare you for each caller. If a patient calls about test results or prescription refills, the receptionist can find the patient's chart and write a note to you on the callback slip that is attached to the chart. If you use the "vital statistics" format outlined in Chapter 5, your receptionist will have pharmacy telephone numbers and regular prescriptions listed for each patient. Otherwise, have the receptionist ask patients calling for prescription refills to have their pharmacy telephone numbers available. This prevents your staff from having to spend time finding the numbers, and you will not be delayed by patients' attempts to locate the numbers while you are on the phone.

TRAINING AND BACKGROUND

The receptionist needs to be knowledgeable about you and your practice in case a prospective patient calls to ask about your qualifications. Provide your receptionist with a concise biographical update outlining your training (and your partners' training, if applicable), your board certification, and your memberships in societies and professional organizations.

You should also make sure that your receptionist is informed about the specifics of your practice. As your front-line ambassador, your receptionist must be able to tell patients about your services, areas of interest, and expertise if they ask about them. In addition, it is important to make sure that your receptionist knows how to give directions to your office from most areas of the community. If the directions are complicated, mention that a copy will be sent in the "Welcome to the Practice" packet or that directions can be faxed to their home or office. This is another opportunity to mention your website if the caller has access to the Internet.

Rehearsal makes everyone feel more comfortable when faced with the "real thing." One of the best methods of training your receptionist is to role play some of the most common situations. Whoever is responsible for training employees, whether you or your office manager, can do this in a private setting at a slow time of day. The office trainer can play a patient who is calling the office. The receptionist should be asked to respond to such questions as "Can I get an appointment today?" "Can I have my prescription refilled?" "Can I have copies of my medical records?" and "What is the doctor's fee for a certain procedure or operation?" Each of these common questions should be role played before the receptionist is asked to answer the phones by him- or herself.

Another effective technique is to tape-record the receptionist's conversations (with permission) and critique them. Most people would prefer such a critique to be done in private, which is appropriate. However, if all the staff are working on improving their telephone technique, you might schedule a separate workshop session. If your staff feel comfortable with the idea, you could tape practice calls with each of them and then critique the tapes in a constructive group setting. Make sure you and other staff members frame criticisms in a positive way (for example, "Marcy, I think if you added another greeting, the patients would really appreciate it," or "Jackie, you should remember to mention the caller's name during the conversation").

MAKE EVERY "HOLD" SECOND COUNT

The hold button must be handled tactfully and judiciously. Callers should never be cut off and perfunctorily put on hold without their permission. Encourage your receptionist to avoid leaving callers on hold for more than 30 seconds at a time. If the phone lines are extraordinarily busy and callers are kept on hold for an extended period of time, encourage your receptionist to make repeated contact with those callers. If you find that callers are being placed on hold frequently, you may need to hire an additional receptionist. You can ask the telephone company to perform a free survey of your lines to help you identify busy periods. This gives you objective data for determining the number of phone lines and receptionists that you need. (See "Additional Resources" in Chapter 23, "Follow the Yellow Page Road.")

You can also market your practice during the hold period by playing prerecorded messages. This is an excellent method of informing patients about timely topics related to your specialty, new services you are offering, or seminars or public speaking engagements you are participating in. You can have prerecorded messages created for you, or you can tape them yourself.[1] Make sure that you keep the messages brief and encourage callers to ask for more information when they get the receptionist on the line.

OTHER EXTRAS TO INCREASE TELEPHONE POWER

If you have a large number of calls from patients living outside your area code, then consider providing a toll-free 800 (or 888) number. This reduces the cost of long distance calls to your office and thus makes patients more likely to call. Getting an 800 number might be helpful in conjunction with a direct-mail project as a way to track the results of your marketing efforts.

In addition, Chapter 43, "Let Technology Simplify Your Life," offers information on automated phone answering programs.

To stress the importance of the telephone to your staff, I suggest a sign be placed on every telephone stating *TELEPHONE = OPPORTUNITY* (see Figure 32–1). This sign serves as a constant reminder to you and your staff that the telephone provides an opportunity to create a positive impression on your callers.

TELEPHONE = OPPORTUNITY

Figure 32–1 Example of a Sign for the Telephone

There are myriad opportunities to expand the marketing power of your office telephone. Except for face-to-face interactions with patients, telephone contacts are the most critical for your practice. Once you embark on a program of perfecting telephone techniques, you will see the payback in patient satisfaction and positive referrals.

The Bottom Line *In your practice, "please hold" is a phrase that equals a missed opportunity. Make sure callers to your office do not often hear that message.*

NOTE

1. One company that specializes in creating prerecorded messages is ***Marketing on Hold, Inc***, 5311 Kirby Drive, Suite 115, Houston, TX 77005-1315; (713) 522-4333.

ADDITIONAL RESOURCES

- ***Better Telephone Receptionist Techniques***, by Conomikes Reports, Inc., 6033 W. Century Blvd., Suite 990, Los Angeles, California 90045; (800) 421-6512, *www.conomikes.com.*
- "Making, Serving and Keeping Customers: A Practical Guide to Profitable Customer Relations," February 5, 1990, issue of *Conquering Fear of the Telephone*, by Robert R. Morris, Dartnell Corporation, 4660 Ravenswood Avenue, Chicago, IL 60640; (800) 621–5463.
- "Your Telephone Personality," a monthly newsletter on improving telephone techniques (especially how to handle difficult callers), published by the Economics Press, 12 Daniel Road, Fairfield, NJ 07004; (201) 227–1224.

CHAPTER 33

Break Bread and Break the Ice: Start a Lunch-and-Learn Program and Referrals from Colleagues Will Follow

Mr. Jones needed some help. He called his primary care doctor's office and spoke to Susan, the receptionist.

"I'm having some burning when I urinate. Do you know of a good urologist?"

"Do I have the doctor for you," said Susan. Then she proceeded to give Mr. Jones my name and telephone number. "He's the urologist we send all our patients to."

Mr. Jones thanked Susan and immediately called my office.

How did Susan know about my office? Was I one of the recommended specialists on the doctor's list? Yes, but there were other urologists on that list as well. Susan knew about my office because she and her coworkers had just visited us for a catered lunch two months previously. Obviously, she was impressed by what she had learned at that luncheon.

Many patients call their primary physicians and ask the receptionist or the nurse for a referral recommendation. If a physician's staff are familiar with your office, they are more likely to recommend you.

A good way of introducing other physicians' staff to your office is to start a "lunch-and-learn program." Once it gets started, it can largely be run by your staff. Of course, you reap the financial rewards when more referrals come in.

A lunch-and-learn program is a great way to enhance staff-to-staff relations. All that is necessary is for your staff to invite a referring physician's staff to lunch in order to exchange ideas, resources, and friendship.

We host these luncheons on a monthly basis. They are an effective means of solidifying relationships between medical staffs and will often lead to increased referrals. One of my office staff members recently commented that she had been talking with a receptionist in another office for five years before we invited the staff to lunch. "Dr. Baum, I didn't realize it, but I had been riding the elevator with that woman for all those years, not knowing she was the same one I spoke to every week on the phone!"

ORGANIZING THE LUNCHEON

I suggest you begin the lunch-and-learn program by inviting practices that are already referring patients to your practice or other practices in the building to whom you would like to start sending referrals. Later, you can add other practices in the area, managed care and insurance company personnel, hospital marketing and public relations department staff, and anyone else who can increase your referrals and make your practice run better and smoother.

We try to arrange the luncheon for a day when the referring physician is not working or has a light schedule. The luncheon is catered, and we set up the reception area as the dining area. I suggest that you assign the process of organizing the luncheon to one staff member, such as the nurse or office manager. That person can contact his or her counterpart in the other office to extend the invitation. Once it is accepted, then they can set the date together, usually two to three weeks in advance.

The office manager will circulate the menu among the guest staff and take their orders. You may want to check whether any guests have dietary restrictions or preferences and offer to accommodate them. Confirm with the caterer the day before that all the food will be arriving enough ahead of time to allow for preparations. I also suggest that name tags be prepared for all members of your staff and the guest staff as well.

Be sure you check out your caterer thoroughly. One time our office used a new catering service and the food was terrible. I called the caterers back and told them how disappointed we were. They offered to serve us another luncheon, free of charge, if we would try them again. That was good marketing on their part!

THE LUNCHEON PROGRAM

The office manager usually begins the luncheon with a brief welcome. All our office staff then take turns introducing themselves, giving their job descriptions, and providing brief biographical sketches. The office manager then asks the visiting staff to do the same. The visiting staff are then given a brief tour of the office. Our staff hand out brochures and written materials relevant to our practice.

During the lunch several of our staff members give "mini-lectures," two to three minutes in length, about some area of medical interest that our office specializes in, such as impotence, urinary incontinence, urinary tract infections, or infertility. I have found that when I encourage my staff members to give the mini-lectures, they make an effort to become more knowledgeable about the assigned subject or topic. As a result, they can also better explain the procedure or subject to our patients.

Our staff members try to learn about the interests and areas of expertise that are unique to the guest staff and their office. Our staff then encourage an exchange of ideas about issues such as insurance billing, coding, patient scheduling, dealing with HMO approvals, and computer technology.

LEAVE YOUR STAFF ALONE

The whole point of this program is for your staff to get to know their guests. That is best accomplished if you, the doctor, stay out of it. Many staff people are inhibited by the presence of physicians. If they are afraid to speak up, the effectiveness of the get-together will be diminished.

The first time we hosted a luncheon for a referring physician's staff, I made one mistake: I showed up! Afterwards, my office manager said, "Dr. Baum, if our purpose is to get to know the other staff, would you mind not coming next time?" I was not insulted. My staff had a valid point. What they were saying was true. I had been so enthusiastic that I got carried away and did all the talking!

I suggest such luncheons be given once every month or two. My office has tried going "off campus" to a restaurant or hotel, but this has been less effective than having lunch at the office. Besides, leaving the office adds another hour to the luncheon, and many referring physicians will be upset if you take their staff away for two hours.

PROGRAM BENEFITS

The lunch-and-learn program has provided our staff the opportunity to get to know other medical staff in the community in an informal and relaxed atmosphere. Often they know each other through their telephone conversations, but the luncheons give them the chance to become familiar with the "face at the other end of the line."

We have been conducting luncheons monthly for nearly 10 years now. Everyone in our office really likes the program, and we have received glowing letters thanking us for being gracious hosts.

The lunch-and-learn program also gives my staff a nice break from their usual routine. My staff members tell me that this program is fun, not work. The program allows us to educate the referring physicians' personnel about our office and to become educated about what the referring physicians do.

During a recent luncheon, my staff found out that one of the guests from an internist's office was unaware that we saw children with urologic problems. They showed her the examination room created just for children and gave her several articles I had written on pediatric urology. When she gave birth to her twin sons the next month, she brought them to me for circumcision.

Since starting this program, we have noticed that other medical practices in our community are beginning to follow suit. Several have reciprocated and invited our staff for a lunch-and-learn experience. We have also invited the staff from our hospital's business office and admitting office, as well as the scheduling nurse from the operating room. Not only have we generated a few patients by our invitations, but we believe we also have improved our patients' experiences at the hospital.

We have also invited managed care directors and insurance company medical directors to have lunch in our office. Now we have become more than an application or a file in their records. The feedback we have received has been favorable, and I cannot help but think that it helps when reapplication time rolls around every year or two.

The Bottom Line   *Breaking bread is the social grease that can generate referrals, enhance relationships with your colleagues and their medical staffs, and solidify relationships with your hospital and managed care plans.*

CHAPTER 34

A Match Made in Heaven: Hiring the Perfect Employee for Your Practice

For the health of your practice and your marketing program, you must have high-quality staff. Someone not suited to your practice can create a negative impression among your patients and cause the morale of your staff to decline.

It has never been easy to hire the perfect candidate for a job opening at a practice or business. With today's tight health care labor market in the majority of metropolitan communities and competition from large hospitals and other industries that are offering higher salaries and more benefits, the challenge of finding the right person for the job is made even more difficult. Does this mean that you should settle for a less-than-qualified employee? Certainly not!

Despite other opportunities, job seekers still seem to find the idea of working at a medical practice attractive. A position with a private practice offers status as well as the gratification and enjoyment that come from helping others. By offering fair salaries and challenging working conditions, you can build a top-notch staff.

Finding and hiring the right person to fill a staff position requires a great deal of time and attention. In this chapter, I review some of the techniques—ones I rely on in my own practice—for hiring the person who is right for your office. Not all these techniques will work in every practice and local job market. If you compare them with the methods you use now, you may find some new ideas to add to your list or ways to refine techniques you already use.

Hiring staff members is an ongoing process, one which you will probably keep improving as your business becomes more sophisticated. When I was first in practice, I was always in a hurry to fill office vacancies. As a result, I would often hire the first person to walk through the door. After a number of comings and goings, it occurred to me that I needed to invest time in hiring so that I could cut down the rate of turnover.

Studies show that the average cost of turnover, whether you are correcting a hiring mistake or replacing a long-time employee, is two and a half times the salary of the worker you are losing. But turnover also brings hidden costs in addition to salary and benefits. The time it takes to do interviews, the overtime you pay others to pick up the slack, and the loss in institutional knowledge can also cut into your bottom line.

The best way to find your candidates is word of mouth. You might consider taking advantage of job-listing services at local schools, universities, and professional organizations. I have previously run newspaper ads with minimal success.

SCREENING YOUR APPLICANTS

Your office manager should speak to each applicant personally when he or she calls your office the first time. This phone call is too important to be screened only by your receptionist. The office manager should specify the time of day when he or she can receive calls from applicants or set a time to return calls to the applicants. After the office manager has screened applicants and narrowed down the choices, you should interview the finalists.

Talking with an applicant personally allows you to evaluate

• the applicant's telephone manners
• the applicant's curiosity about you and your practice.

You want an active, vibrant individual who exudes enthusiasm. If you do not sense vitality and enthusiasm in a phone conversation with the applicant, your patients will not either.

Ask the applicant to send a handwritten letter along with his or her resume and application. Suggest a topic for the letter. For example, you might suggest that the letter explain why the applicant wants the job, why the applicant is qualified for the job, or how the applicant could enhance your practice. You might also suggest that the letter address a nonmedical topic, such as the applicant's hobbies or last vacation.

This letter will serve several functions:

• It allows you to see how quickly the applicant responds. In most medical practices, a speedy response can often be vital.
• It allows you to analyze the applicant's writing and spelling skills. (Obviously, you do not want to hire someone who cannot spell correctly or whose handwriting is more illegible than yours!)
• Finally, a written letter will frequently reveal something about the applicant that is not available in his or her resume.

THE INTERVIEW PROCESS

Encourage preparation. The interview will be more productive if you allow applicants to prepare. Before an interview, send the applicant a job description and information about you and your practice. If you have a primary care practice, you may want to send information on what you do, what kinds of patients you see, and typical situations that someone who works in your office might encounter. If you are a specialist, send the applicant information on the nature of your specialty or some educational material that you give to patients about the various diseases, illnesses, and conditions you treat. I am impressed when applicants demonstrate that they have read this information and if they ask questions about anything that they have not understood.

If you have them, send a patient brochure, articles written about you and your practice, and any articles you have written. If you have written out a statement of your practice's mission or philosophy—something I believe all practices should have—include it as well. (See Chapter 30 describing the mission statement and practice philosophy.)

Make the most of each interviewing session.

You can do this in several ways:

The first few minutes of the interview can be used to break the ice. For example, you might tell the candidate about yourself, your practice, and the job description.

Next, I provide the candidate at the time of his or her visit with a written list of questions (Exhibit 34–1). I allow the candidate to answer the questions while I listen and take notes. I use a written question list so that I can listen more closely and so I am sure that each candidate is asked the same questions. Using a written list also encourages candidates to do the talking. (Do not forget who is hiring whom. A good rule of thumb is to listen 80 percent of the time and talk 20 percent of the time.)

Interview promising applicants more than once. I have interviewed the top few finalists for a job as many as three times. First impressions are important,

---

Exhibit 34–1 List of Questions To Ask Job Applicants

Name _____
1. What are your strengths?
2. What are your weaknesses?
3. Why are you interested in changing jobs?
4. What was your best job? Your worst?
5. Tell me about your best boss.
6. Tell me about your worst boss.
7. What do you think your references will say when I call to inquire about your past employment?
8. What do you want to be doing one year from now? Five years from now?

certainly, but most couples do not get engaged on their first dates! Many applicants will be eliminated after the phone call or first interview. Those still in the running need a second, third, or even fourth interview before the job offer is made.

Interview applicants in more than one environment, for example, at the hospital as well as at your practice. This provides an opportunity to observe the applicants' behavior in more than one setting.

Ask "curve ball" questions. At least one time during the interview process ask the candidate a difficult-to-answer question. In any medical practice, circumstances will arise that require the staff to think and respond quickly. Failure to react quickly can adversely affect the health of patients and might even lead to litigation. If the candidate has worked in a medical office or has health care experience, I might ask a question such as, "What would you do if a patient called with a medical emergency and the physician couldn't be reached or located immediately?" Exhibit 34–2 contains additional examples of curve ball questions you might consider using.

Give a "homework assignment." In addition to the curve ball questions, which require immediate answers, I also present each applicant with a more involved problem and allow him or her time to work on the answer after the interview is over. For example, I may ask the applicant to propose a solution for a problem at the practice. How quickly the applicant responds to this "homework assignment" tells me a lot about the applicant's creative problem-solving abilities as well as the strength of the applicant's desire to get the job.

Let the applicants ask questions. This allows you to evaluate their level of interest in and curiosity about the job. If an applicant fails to ask any questions, this suggests that the applicant is intimidated by the interview process or is not

---

Exhibit 34–2 List of Curve Ball Questions To Ask Job Applicants

1. If I did a procedure that did not have a CPT code, how would you attempt to obtain insurance coverage from a third-party payer?
2. How would you handle it if a patient began arguing with you in front of other patients about the cost of his visit?
3. If a patient called on the telephone and demanded that he be seen the same day as he called, and you knew that the problem was not an emergency, what would you tell him?
4. What would you say to a patient who requested that his records be sent to another physician?
5. Suppose that you saw a patient in the grocery store and you were with your spouse. How would you introduce them?

Exhibit 34–3 Release-of-Information Letter

Release Form

I am an applicant for employment with <u>Dr. Baum</u>, who is requesting the attached information. I have read all the information in the attached request concerning your experiences with me as an employee. I approve of all the information being sought and I request that you furnish it. I hold you harmless for any information you furnish regardless of this prospective employer's decision regarding my application for employment.

Date   **Signature**

Notary Seal and Date

Courtesy of Don Meyers, PhD, Virginia Commonwealth University, Richmond, Virginia.

---

very curious. If either is the case, you are learning something important. You want to hire people who are both curious and not easily intimidated. For instance, if an applicant's only question is about the salary or vacation pay, that would be a clue to his or her priorities, and I would probably begin to lose interest. If an applicant asked about furthering skills through seminars, night school, and so on, I would start to consider putting this applicant on the short list.

Get good references. However, getting good, honest references, according to Don Meyers, a professor of business in Richmond, Virginia, can often be difficult because of this unwritten rule: Do not give references out, but do not hire without them.

Today many previous employers will give out a name and job title but will not provide the important information because they are fearful of a lawsuit. This situation can be avoided by asking the applicants to sign release-of-information letters (see Exhibit 34–3) and mailing them to their previous employers before you call.

Applicants will not give you names of references unless they expect them to respond favorably. To get around this hurdle, ask applicants for additional references during later interviews. The length of time it takes them to respond will tell you something about the quality of the references.

Have your existing staff members interview each applicant. They will let you know whether or not that person will be a team player. I did this when hiring someone to assist with the marketing and public relations aspect of the practice. One of the candidates was an instructor at the local university. She met with my staff and it was immediately apparent from their response that she was not going to be a good match. Although she was eminently qualified, I was not able to hire her.

However, I referred her to another urologist and a plastic surgeon, who did make use of her services.

Pay attention to follow-up. Did the applicants return your phone calls promptly? Did they send you thank-you notes after their interviews? Remember that the way they handle the business of looking for work now is how they will handle the business of working for you tomorrow. But more important, the courtesies and manners they extend to you will be a barometer of how they will treat your patients.

Get help from the staff of your hospital's human resources or employment office. Ask them to assist you with the interviewing process. They are experts at interviewing and do it several times every day, whereas your expertise is in diagnosis and treatment of disease. For example, I was interviewing potential employees for a job that could involve marketing and public relations. I asked the hospital marketing staff to interview the two finalists. The staff gave the candidates insight into my needs and work style and were able to help me in the selection process.

Finally, ask a friend in another business to interview the applicants. This will often provide you with another perspective. For example, I asked my accountant to interview candidates for office manager. Because the accountant would be working regularly with the office manager, I thought it would be helpful to get his opinion.

Although the hiring process is time-consuming and stressful, it is essential for creating an excellent practice. Its costs are much less than the costs of high employee turnover.

I have four office staff members, and every day they use the most important skills that I was looking for when I hired them—not typing and word processing, but courtesy, assertiveness, and persistent attentiveness to the little details that make a big difference. My office runs efficiently and smoothly because of my staff, and I am glad that I took the time to find the right people.

The Bottom Line   *You may find the hiring process time-consuming and stressful, but that does not come close to comparing with the time and stress it will cost you if the candidate you hire is not a good "fit" with your practice. Follow the suggestions in this chapter and you are much more likely to hire right the first time!*

Communicating with Other Physicians, Other Professionals, and Managed Care Plans

In this section, we turn our attention to the fourth pillar of your marketing plan: communicating with other physicians, other professionals, and managed care plans. Patients, both existing and new, form the core of your practice. And your staff help to keep them coming back. But these three elements will not comprise a complete marketing strategy. It's only when you become an asset to potential referring colleagues that you'll ensure solid market share.

Whether you have a solo private practice, or are a partner of a large multi-specialty practice, marketing to your colleagues should also be at the top of your list. Many physicians may still fear that marketing to one's colleagues will be viewed as crass opportunism. Done the way I've outlined in this next section, nothing could be further from the truth. In many ways, marketing to other physicians, professionals, and managed care plans boils down to the same principles for attracting new patients to your practice.

Communication is key. So is putting yourself in your colleague's shoes, and finding ways to make their professional lives easier when they deal with you and your practice. Finding common ground offers marketing opportunities for both sides, as is the case with making your hospital your ally.

Don't discount or disregard alternative health care practitioners or allied professionals; referrals can come from this sector as well, if you have communicated your message clearly about your practice's specialties. Managed care plans needn't be your adversaries, if you learn how to meet and exceed their expectations.

And finally, if you are part of an academic or large multispecialty practice, you cannot afford to be complacent and leave the marketing to the administrators. As with the other preceding sections, you'll find strategies and tips that are affordable, doable, and that net results for increased referrals to your practice.

293

How To Obtain and Maintain Physician Referrals: It Takes Patience, Persistence, Politeness, and Prompt Reporting

Talks on medical marketing often begin with the three A's of marketing: availability, affability, and affordability. Since all physicians probably think of themselves as available, as likable, and as offering appropriately priced services, how do you differentiate yourself from the competition? Just using fancy stationery, a slick office brochure, or a practice logo will not do the trick. I have been marketing my medical practice for several years, and the last things I did, in terms of marketing, were to get a brochure, stationery, a logo, and a web page.

One of the biggest misconceptions about marketing is that to do it well you must spend lots of money on peripherals. There are many other steps that are far more effective and essential to marketing than polishing your public relations image. The most essential element of your marketing plan is to make your practice user-friendly. Nowhere is this more important than in the area of working with your referring physicians.

The traditional methods of obtaining physician referrals usually involved trial and error. They were seldom discussed and some were almost intangible. Perhaps you went to school with another physician and later he or she referred patients to you. Perhaps you joined a group practice and got the overflow patients. Maybe you went to emergency rooms and made yourself available to treat patients who did not have their own physicians.

One of the cardinal rules, especially for new physicians, was to always be available. If a new physician did an excellent job with every patient, gradually the word-of-mouth method would start working. The word would get back to the referring physician that the new physician was truly competent. The new physician could slowly build a good reputation in this way.

By relying on word of mouth and outstanding service, it could take from two to three years to get a practice up and running. These methods worked in the past because there were enough primary care doctors, enough patients, and enough referrals to go around. Today we are seeing fewer physicians start out by themselves in private practice. Many physicians are opting to join large group practices or are going into salaried positions with health maintenance organizations. That means you have to be a lot more organized about getting those physician referrals.

In this chapter, I take physician referrals out of the realm of "hit or miss"—you will not have to use the scattershot approach to physician referrals. If you follow the steps outlined below, you will have a guaranteed plan for making your name visible and your reputation known within the medical community. By targeting your efforts, your practice, in essence, will become user-friendly—your colleagues will want to refer patients to you and will enjoy doing so.

The main strategy for getting physician referrals is to have your name cross the minds and desks of referring physicians and their staff members frequently and in a positive fashion. If you can do that, physician referrals will come your way. This strategy derives from the tactics of William Wrigley, the chewing gum magnate, who, at the turn of the century, set down this dictum: "Tell 'em quick, and tell 'em often."

All the 25 techniques outlined in this chapter, from prompt reporting to gift giving, are designed with this strategy in mind. There should be good chemistry between you and your referring physicians. If they have good feelings about you, they will want to refer patients to you. You can make yourself more attractive to referring physicians by making it easy to do business or work with you and your staff.

Almost all the techniques require minimal amounts of time and energy and negligible expense. Yet their effectiveness in generating physician referrals is quite significant. Remember, you must have a staff capable of handling patients, and you must ensure follow-up and develop excellent communication with referring physicians.

1. Report to referring physicians promptly. When it comes to writing a book, I have found out that the three most important steps are rewriting, rewriting, and rewriting. When it comes to increasing your attractiveness to referring physicians, you need to communicate, communicate, and communicate. If you are looking for the best way to make yourself accessible to your referring physicians, consider prompt reporting. When primary care physicians were surveyed about why they make referrals, prompt reporting was at the top of the list.[1] You must always keep your referring physicians informed about their patients' progress.

When you see a patient by referral, follow this cardinal rule: Never allow the patient to return to the referring physician's office before your report does. Nothing is more embarrassing to the primary care doctor than to be in the dark about what is going on with the patient. If the patient or the patient's family calls the referring physician before he or she has had a full report from you, it makes you both look bad.

The following story is a prime example of what must never happen. A primary care physician called his patient's relatives at home to tell the family that the grandfather, in the intensive care unit, was not doing too well. The family said, "Yes, we know, he died last night." This was a gross lapse in communication that resulted in embarrassment for a primary care physician. You must avoid communication failures with your referring doctors as well.

When a physician sees a patient referred by a primary care physician, it is often 7 to 10 days before the primary care physician receives the referral letter. The report has to be dictated, transcribed, and mailed. Frequently the patient will beat the referring letter back to the primary care physician.

How user-friendly are you when a patient returns to his or her primary care physician and the referral letter has not arrived? The physician asks the patient what the specialist said or did. The patient responds, "I don't know, but he gave me a large yellow pill and now I have a rash and am itching all over." Now the primary care physician has to ask his nurse to tell the receptionist to call your office, have your receptionist or nurse locate the chart, and then track you down if you are not in the office to discuss your management of the patient. That scenario does not endear you to the referring primary care physician.

My solution for avoiding this scenario is to use what I call the "lazy person's referral letter." This is a referral letter that requires absolutely no dictating. Here's how it works. As soon as you have seen the patient, write down, at the end of your office notes, your impressions, the medications you prescribed, and the plan of treatment. For instance, if I see Mrs. Smith for cystitis, recommend that she take a course of sulfa, and suggest that I see her again in two weeks, I circle these words in the notes. I call these the buzz words.

When my nurse goes through the chart after Mrs. Smith's visit, she sees that I have circled these words. She calls up our boilerplate referral letter on the computer screen, which has blanks for filling in (see Exhibit 35–1). The nurse types in the appropriate physician's name, the diagnosis, the medications, and so on. The letter closes with the statement, "I will keep in touch with you regarding her urologic progress." We then print out the letter and mail it that day or fax it directly to the physician's office.

This letter delivers the essentials to the referring physician. What are primary care physicians looking for? Most will tell you that there are three ingredients of an effective referral letter: the working diagnosis, the medications you have prescribed, and the treatment plan. You can bank money on this one—they are not interested in the depth and detail of your history or the fine nuances you detected on the physical examination. For the most part, they are as busy as you are and do not have the time to read a lengthy two- to-three page report that you dictated and conduct a "hunt for Red October" to find the diagnosis, prescribed medication, and treatment plan. You can create a user-friendly referral letter that meets the

Exhibit 35–1 Boilerplate "Lazy Person's Referral Letter"

Date

Dear [Referring Physician],

[Patient] _____ was seen for a problem of [diagnosis], and he/she is being treated with [medication] _____ . I recommend that he/she have [treatment] _____ .

I will see him/her again after he/she finishes the medication and will keep in touch with you regarding his/her urologic progress.

Sincerely,
Neil Baum, M.D.

---

three necessary criteria and that lands on the primary care physician's desk before the patient returns for an office visit.

Because the letter is sent out immediately, if the patient calls with any questions, the physician can answer them without having to contact me. Furthermore, the letter can usually be generated without any dictating at all. For those who must dictate the two- or three-page traditional referral letter, I suggest you underline or boldface the essential information, including your impressions, the medications, and your recommendations. I have surveyed many of my referring physicians and almost all of them indicate they prefer a timely computerized referral letter over a delayed three-pager. I am frequently asked whether referring physicians are upset when they receive a computerized, impersonal form letter. Surveys of referring physicians indicate they prefer timely information as opposed to a delayed personal letter.

You say you do not have a computer? You can still employ the lazy person's referral letter. Before getting an office computer, I used photocopies of a typed letter with blanks on it. I simply filled in the blanks.

Although 95 percent of visits can be handled in this manner, some of your examinations will uncover a problem that is complicated or has ominous implications. If your examination turns up a significant finding or you need to make a decision regarding the patient's treatment plan, you should contact the referring physician by phone and notify him or her of your findings. Failure to do so can potentially result in embarrassment for both you and the referring physician. If the patient calls the referring physician to discuss your suggestions, and you have not yet informed the physician about your treatment plan, it makes him or her appear uninformed or even uncaring. The referring physician will likely think of you as unprofessional, and will probably stop referring patients to you.

If you operate on a patient, call the referring physician's office immediately afterwards. Notify the physician's nurse that the surgery went well and everything was successful. Also, if the surgery is going to be significantly delayed, let the doctor's office know. The doctor will then be up-to-date on the patient's progress in case he or she runs into the family on the way over to the hospital. However, if a complication develops during surgery or if the patient has changed rooms or has been sent to the intensive care unit, notify the referring physician in person. If there is a significant lab or pathology report, call the referring physician and let him or her know what has been found. In those situations, the patient or the patient's family may contact the physician immediately. If you have not apprised the physician of the situation first, then he or she will not be well informed.

There are other economic considerations involved in using the lazy person's referral letter. Do you know that the typical referral letter can cost you anywhere from $13.50 to $25.00 or more every time you pick up the tape recorder? How can this be, you ask. Let's do the math: Today most physician time is valued at $150 to $200 an hour. The typical referral letter requires three to five minutes of physician time. So, for your time alone the cost would range from $7.50 to $16.65. The charges of a transcriptionist who makes $25,000 to $35,000 a year plus benefits and charges you $2 to $3 a page must be added to the equation. Finally, there are costs for stationery and postage. This works out to $13 to $25 or more per letter. Using the lazy person's referral letter, you reduce your costs to under $1 per letter. Plus, it satisfies the needs and wants of your primary care physicians—the letter arrives before the patient returns.

I have nearly 50 referring physicians in my database. I have surveyed these physicians (see Chapter 1) about the lazy person's referral letter, and 48 of the 50 indicated that they are delighted with the letter and "hoped that my colleagues would learn to use the same technique." However, I send the longer version to the two who did not like the lazy person's letter and preferred the lengthy traditional letter. Remember, one size does not fit all.

2. Make your referring physicians look good. Your objective should be to keep the referring physician involved and functioning as the captain of the health care ship. I am reminded of the story of a patient who went to see an orthopaedic surgeon. During the history and physical, the doctor asked the patient, "What have you done for your problem?" The patient said, "I've been to a chiropractor." The doctor asked, "What did that fool tell you?" The patient responded, "He sent me to you."

Whenever possible, compliment the referring physician. Of course, you do not want to appear unnatural or superficial. When the referring physician's name comes up in conversation with the patient, you can make a comment such as, "He is such a fine doctor and is very knowledgeable about your medical problem," or "She is one of the best doctors in our community."

Sometimes I get complimentary notes from patients referred to me by other physicians. I photocopy each note and send it back to the referring physician with an accompanying note that reads, "Thought you might like to see that your patient had a positive experience at my office." After all, the kind of experience the patient had reflects back on the referring physician.

If a patient tells me, "Boy, I sure am glad that Dr. Jones sent me to you," I have a response. "Do me a favor," I say. "The next time you see Dr. Jones, mention that you had a good experience at my office." The patient is more than happy to oblige, which increases the positive feedback received by the referring physician.

Also remember that how the patient perceives you is partly determined by how the patient perceives the referring physician. If you make the referring physician look good, then you are really enhancing your image as well.

3. Vary your referral patterns. Today, the number of patients referred to specialists is decreasing. One of the reasons for this is that certain specialists (for instance, gynecologists and general surgeons) are doing more primary care and keeping the patients in their practices. When patients go to a multispecialty group practice or preferred provider organization (PPO), they are kept there and do not circulate in the community looking for other health care providers. Also, primary care physicians are treating more medical conditions that were once referred to specialists. In addition, most metropolitan communities are experiencing a surplus of physicians, with a resulting contraction of the number of referrals to specialists.[2] Finally, managed care's emphasis on cost containment means that many primary care physicians now treat adult-onset diabetes, arthritis, benign enlargement of the prostate, urinary incontinence, and even common dermatological conditions.

Often referral patterns are "cut in stone" and specialists refer to only one or a few groups of primary care doctors. One of the benefits of your marketing efforts will be that patients will come directly to you: You will become the primary care doctor and control the referrals. If a patient comes to me with a urologic problem and I have to send her to a gynecologist or a cardiologist, I become the referring physician and direct the referrals.

It is important that specialists make every effort to send new patients to primary care doctors who have frequently referred patients to them. Now more than ever it is important to acknowledge referrals from primary care doctors and other specialists. The best way for you to do this is to take advantage of your marketing and send them new patients. They will appreciate new patients more than a fruit basket at Christmas.

4. Provide courtesies to your referring physicians and do not inconvenience them. One of the best ways to prevent inconveniences for your referring physicians is to assist with the hospital paperwork on patients whom you share. For example, have your office notify the referring physician when you are admitting his or her patient. If you do this, the hospital secretary will not be calling the referring physician late in the evening, which may require the physician to see the patient even later that evening or early in the morning. Likewise, contact the referring physician when you discharge his or her patient. By doing this, you ensure that the referring physician will not make a needless trip to the hospital to see a patient who has been sent home.

One time I received a call from a referring doctor at about nine o'clock at night about a routine admission. I asked him why he was calling me so late. He said, "The hospital secretary just notified me that the patient was admitted to the hospital." Although that was not my fault, I tend to be associated with that oversight. If that happens repeatedly, that referring physician will not think favorably of you. You can avoid this by having your office call the referring doctor's office when you receive notification that the patient has been admitted.

You can fill out the prescriptions that apply to your specialty and leave them in the patient's chart so that the referring physician does not have to write all the prescriptions. Specialists can also help the primary care physician by filling out the hospital records face sheet. Fill in the diagnosis, the operative procedures, and the dates of the procedures. This will facilitate the referring physician's dictation of the discharge summary. These are necessary and time-consuming details that the referring physician undoubtedly will be glad to have out of the way.

If your referring physicians do not receive compensation for furnishing discharge summaries, then it is a nice gesture for you, the specialist, to dictate that summary. Remember, you want your referring physicians to feel that it is easy to work with you and that you will go the extra mile on their behalf.

5. Recognize your referring physicians' accomplishments and those of their children. There is no better way to enhance your relationship with your referring physicians than to acknowledge their accomplishments. It is a friendly gesture to cut out articles from local newspapers that mention your referring physicians or their families. Whenever one of your referring physicians receives an appointment or promotion, acknowledge it with a written note.

When my son was four years old, he rescued a bird from our pool. My family took the bird to the zoo, where it was saved. Our rabbi, on hearing the story, sent my son a letter:

I just heard the story of your wonderful good deed in saving the bird from drowning in the pool. You should be proud of yourself. I am proud of you for doing such a wonderful thing. Whenever you hear the birds chirping to themselves, you can be sure they're singing your praises. Well done, Craig.

Rabbi Cohn

Can you imagine how much Rabbi Cohn's stock has gone up since Craig received that letter? I could not wait to contribute to the synagogue's annual fundraising campaign!

We all like to hear positive comments about our children. Taking the time to find out about their children is a guaranteed way to let your referring physicians know that you are thinking of them. (This is also a nice gesture to do for your patients.) If a referring physician's child just received a scholarship or an athletic award, send a note. Your staff are usually familiar with the names of your referring physicians and they can call them to your attention when reading the newspaper. This is a simple little thing to do, but it is universally appreciated.

6. Send birthday cards. Sometimes it is difficult to find out your colleagues' birthdays. You can try calling their hospitals or the county medical society. Ask for the birthdays, not the birth years, and you should have no problem. You will not be given the years—that is confidential—but frequently you will find out the days. You might want to compile a list and ask for all the birthdays at the same time.

Exhibit 35–2 is an example of the kind of birthday cards I send to my male colleagues. Humorous cards are always appreciated.

7. Don't step on your referring physicians' turf. Today, many physicians are trying to generate additional practice income by performing procedures or diagnostic tests in their offices. You need to be aware of who performs which tests. Avoid performing tests or procedures that your referring physicians are equipped to handle. For example, if you plan to admit the patient of a referring physician to the hospital, ask the patient to have the preadmission blood work, EKG, and chest X-ray done in the referring physician's office rather than at the hospital or a third-party lab. If blood work is all you are requesting, have your office draw the blood, send it by courier to the referring physician's office, and ask for a copy for your records. When you use the referring physician's facility, you are being considerate and allowing the physician to maximize the use of his or her equipment and employees.

8. Show an interest in your referring physicians as people. Make an effort to know about your referring physicians' nonmedical interests and hobbies. Whenever you see or read something that is of interest to one of your referring physicians, take the time to send it or call it to their attention. This is one way of saying that you are interested in your referring physicians even when you are not professionally relating to one another. I remember seeing a book on fly fishing offered in a catalogue I was reading, and knew that one of my referring doctors was an avid fly fisherman. I sent him the book just before he left for a trip to Alaska to go salmon fishing. He told me later that having the book increased his anticipation about the trip, and it also helped him with his casting technique!

9. Invite your referring physicians to support groups or seminars. This increases their exposure in the community and also provides them with an opportu-

Exhibit 35–2 Example of a Birthday Card Sent to Male Colleagues

At birth it is a common custom to
cut the foreskin of the male child.

Fortunately, all subsequent birthdays
are celebrated with cake.

nity to attract more patients. If you try to involve colleagues in your specialty, they will be less likely to try to torpedo your marketing efforts. You will create allies, not adversaries, in the medical community.

10. Do not forget your referring physicians' staff. In addition to building a good relationship with your referring physicians, you must include their staff. In Chapter 33, I discuss one excellent method of relating to the referring staff: asking them to a lunch-and-learn program. Whenever you have contact with them, make it a point to be pleasant, cooperative, and interested in them as people. Learning their names will go a long way toward building a good working relationship.

11. Ensure that you are easy to contact. You can make it easier for your referring physicians and their staff to contact you and your office by supplying each office with a colored Rolodex card. The card can be made more visible by making it slightly higher than the standard Rolodex card. It should contain your telephone number; private line; office hours; answering service number; and the names of your office manager, secretary, nurse, and any other employees who may be requested by the referring physicians or their staff. Rolodex cards can also be provided under the heading of your specialty as well as your last name. (By the way, since I am a urologist, my Rolodex cards are yellow.) I obtained my Rolodex cards from a company in California that provides a letter and a punch-out card.[3] In addition, there is an electronic rolodex system that works very well.[4]

12. Start a journal club network. As every physician knows, it is no trivial pursuit to stay abreast of the medical literature. With the literature doubling or tripling every decade, it is nearly impossible for the busy practitioner to read all the journals in his or her areas of interest and expertise.[5]

By developing a journal club network with your fellow physicians, you maintain an awareness of the literature and help your colleagues at the same time. When I read the early information on ophthalmic side effects of Viagra, I photocopied the articles and sent copies to those of my friends who are ophthalmologists and primary care physicians.

Here is how to start your network. Send a letter to about 10 of your colleagues. Explain what you are doing and what they can gain from participating. Exhibit 35–3 is an example of the letter I sent when I started our current journal club.

The network is best kept informal—you do not want to add work to your colleagues' loads. Enlist the help of your staff for photocopying and mailing the articles you find. Your staff can also be alerted to look for articles in newspapers and lay magazines that relate to your colleagues' specialties. This helps keep your colleagues informed on what their patients are reading.

13. Target your colleagues' reading. As with the journal club network, targeting their reading can facilitate your colleagues' continuing medical education and yours as well. If you send a referral letter that mentions a new diagnosis or treatment modality, attach an article that contains the new information. By doing this,

Exhibit 35–3 Letter for Starting a Journal Club Network

[Date] _____

Dear [Physician] _____,

With the rapid pace of developments in medicine today. it is difficult for most physicians to keep up with the progress. As a way to stay abreast of all the changes, I suggest that you and I establish an informal journal club.

I will be reviewing the urologic literature on a regular basis. If I see articles that are pertinent to [physician's specialty], I will make copies and forward them to you. I hope you will do the same for me.

Perhaps in this way we can extend and increase our coverage of the medical literature.

Sincerely,
Neil Baum, M.D.

---

you increase the likelihood that your colleague will actually read the article. I use a yellow highlighter pen and mark the one or two sentences most pertinent to the patient and the referral letter. For example, the use of thiazide diuretics is associated with the side effect of erectile dysfunction. The use of ACE inhibitors or calcium channel blockers is less likely to produce impotence. Before I recommend that a patient start on one of these antihypertensive drugs and stop the thiazides, I include a copy of the journal article with the referral letter. I underline the one or two sentences describing the efficacy of this medication.

To further direct a colleague's attention, you can apply a note to the front page of the article with a message (for example, "Please see page. . . ."). Although this might seem like you are setting up a treasure hunt, you can be sure your colleague will appreciate being directed to the appropriate information. You have supplied new information and saved your colleague time.

A note on sending out articles: Our office keeps preprinted address labels for physicians in the files. So, if I pull an article and ask a staff member to send it, all he or she has to do is photocopy it, put it in an envelope, and stick on the address label. These labels are computer-generated in our office on the word processor. If the articles are short, they can be faxed with the referral letter. Longer articles are mailed.

14. Identify interests that you share with your referring physicians. Another way to let referring physicians know you care about them is to send them books, tapes, cartoons, and articles that may be of particular interest to them. For example, one of my colleagues graduated from Notre Dame and is a fan of Lou Holtz, who was a longtime coach of the football team. When I received a tape of a Lou Holtz speech, I immediately thought of my friend. So I sent a copy of the tape to him. He was just delighted to listen to his hero on his car stereo while driving to work.

I was stimulated by reading Bernie Siegel's book, *How To Live between Office Visits*. I thought my friends in oncology, the pain unit, and physical medicine would also enjoy it, so I bought several copies and sent them out. Another book that is entertaining, fun, and helps people reduce tension in their lives is Richard Carlson's *Don't Sweat the Small Stuff—and It's All Small Stuff*.

15. Hold on to old friends. When physicians retire, their former patients often continue to call them. They still have a lot of clout in the professional community. And, of course, their patients ask them for referrals to primary care physicians as well as to specialists. Acknowledge a colleague's retirement in some way, by sending a note of appreciation or taking him or her to lunch. Then continue to remember your colleague on the same dates as before. This will help you maintain a referral source even after your colleague's shingle has been taken down.

16. Keep tabs on the movers. When a physician moves to another area of the country, it is important to maintain communication. If you send a "good luck" letter, cards at the holidays, and a Rolodex card, this will encourage the physician to send you patients when someone from the old community asks for a referral.

17. Develop intraspecialty referrals. You can do this by finding niches in the marketplace. Just because you are a urologist does not mean you cannot get referrals from other urologists. You may be doing procedures or diagnostic tests that they are not doing and that may be helpful to them. You may have equipment or training that they do not have, allowing you to develop referrals from colleagues in your specialty.

The key to these referrals is to make sure you get the patients back to your colleagues and that you do not operate on these patients for other urologic problems that the original doctors can handle. Treat the patients only for the problems that the referring physicians requested.

Let your colleagues know that you are willing to see their patients and give their patients back. The easiest way to do this and make your colleagues feel secure is to offer to help at their institutions. See a referred patient in your office but admit the patient to your colleague's hospital and get temporary privileges at that hospital. In that way, the referring physician gets to see the procedure and has the security of knowing that you are not taking the patient away.

Another way to get referrals from specialists in your field is to refer patients who call when you are not available. Sometimes patients call out of the blue with a problem that cannot wait. Rather than have your staff say, "I'm sorry, Dr. Baum is not available," and let that patient go back to the yellow pages, you can have them refer that patient to your colleagues. For instance, if you are out of town, have your staff call the covering doctor's office to get an appointment for the patient. Your colleague appreciates getting a new patient and hopefully will return the favor.

18. Develop cooperative projects with referring physicians. There are times when you will be asked to do a project for a drug company. If you can include your colleagues in this, it is a way of endearing yourself to them. For example, I worked on a project for treating psychogenic impotence with self-injection and I collaborated with a sex therapist and several other local urologists. After the report was written, the therapist presented it at her society meetings and I at mine, and we both got recognition and publicity. It also brought us both new patients.

19. Personally meet every physician who refers a patient to you. Many times, in the doctor's lounge, I have heard the following remark: "You know, I have a referring doctor down in St. Elsewhere. He's sent me two to three patients a month for the past five years, and I've never even met the guy!" When I hear that, I think, if you do not go out of your way to meet that physician and invite him to your office, somebody else will. And that referral source will dry up.

If a physician refers two to three patients a month to you, you need to visit his or her office and meet personally. Offer to give a talk at the physician's hospital. Make an effort to make your paths cross. Otherwise, that golden goose (your referring physician) will cease laying the golden egg (referring patients to you).

20. Meet all new physicians in your area. Every July and August, when physicians announce they are starting their practices, you will get announcement cards in the mail or you will see these announcements in the paper. Most doctors throw those cards away. Some doctors write "congratulations" on the cards and send them back. I think it is best to take this gesture one step further.

Write a welcoming letter to each new physician. Offer to get together for breakfast or lunch. Then offer to share resources. If the new physician is in private practice, make a visit to the office with your office manager. Indicate that you would be more than happy to have your office manager assist the new physician's office manager.

Frequently, new physicians will have lots of questions. For example, when a new physician saw my office's printed materials, he asked me who had done the printing. I put him in touch with the printer and asked the printer to give him an initial price break. The printer was willing to do that because I send him lots of business. That one suggestion endeared me to that physician, who has since referred one or two patients a month to me.

21. Refer patients to physicians new to the area, especially those just starting their practices. Send patients to new physicians as soon as possible. Everyone remembers who his or her first few patients were. And if you are the person who referred those patients, you will be forever appreciated by the primary care doctor. First patients make an indelible impression.

22. Offer marketing advice to new physicians. In addition to sending new patients to new physicians when I can, I refer them to the marketing chapter from Debi Carey's *Private Medical Practice: Getting It Started and Making It Work.* This book provides ideas for new physicians just starting their practices, and the marketing chapter discusses ethical but effective methods of practice promotion. Another good resource is an article I wrote for *Private Practice Magazine* entitled, "Ten Action Steps to Transition from Residency to Private Practice." That entire issue was dedicated to marketing a medical practice, and for the physician just entering practice, it is an invaluable resource.

23. Keep your referring physicians abreast of changes in your specialty. About once or twice a year, after I attend a meeting of urologists, I send out a single-sheet informal newsletter about the latest developments in my practice and in urology in general. These newsletters are often much appreciated by referring physicians. Samples of those newsletters are available on the Internet at: *www.urologychannel.com/neilbaum.*

24. Give your referring physicians useful and unique gifts. Giving gifts to your referring physicians is not the most effective method of generating referrals. However, there are techniques of giving and certain types of gifts that will make you stand out from the others at holiday time. If you send wine or a fruit and cheese basket, it will most likely get lost among the dozens of similar gifts the physician receives.

For something a bit different, consider giving gifts that your colleagues will use or receive all year long. Membership with Harry and David's Fruit of the Month Club is a good choice, since the physicians will receive a box of fresh fruit each month of the year.[6]

If you know your colleagues' reading habits, you can consider giving them subscriptions to their favorite magazines. I know several doctors who give subscriptions to *Architectural Digest, Connoisseur,* or *National Geographic* as gifts.

One year I sent Lucite cubes that could be used either as picture holders or as holders for motivational quotes by such people as Winston Churchill ("Never give in, Never give up, NEVER, NEVER, NEVER"), Vince Lombardi ("If you strive for perfection, you may not always reach it, but you will achieve excellence."), or Abraham Lincoln ("Success may come to those who wait, but they will receive only the things left by those who hustle."). Then each month I sent another motivational message to insert in the cube, as well as a story or comment about the author and how the quote applies to the contemporary practice of medicine. My colleagues really seemed to appreciate that one. Several times that year, when visiting referring physicians, I spotted those Lucite cubes with the motivational quotes on their desks.

You could send a holder for Rolodex cards. These come with a card punch so that any business card can be converted into a Rolodex card. These items are available from most office suppliers. Of course, when you send this gift, make sure you insert your colored and raised Rolodex card in the holder.

One of the best gifts I have sent were sets of personalized luggage tags. The tags were bright red with the colleague's last name in white type, and laminated, with gold stretchy cords attached.[7] The owner of the luggage with these tags has no trouble recognizing it when it comes down the baggage chute.

By varying the time of year when you send your gifts, you can also make them stand out. For instance, consider sending your gifts and holiday wishes at Thanksgiving instead of during December. People are usually not as rushed at this time and chances are that they will remember your gifts.

One very generous and effective gift is to make a donation to a charity or civic organization in the name of one of your referring physicians. Of course, it really helps if you know your colleague well and choose a charity or foundation that he or she has worked for or supported. This will require a little investigation by you and your staff, but if you are creating a "WIN" notebook, you will have that information already (see Chapter 1).

I do not consider gift giving essential to a successful marketing plan or effective physician referral program. But if you decide to give gifts, make them timely, unique, or lasting.

25. Finally, go the extra mile for your referring physicians. Make it a pleasure to use you and your services. Find the little extras that make working with you a convenience instead of a chore. These little extras can make a big difference in your relationships with your referring physicians.

For example, one of my referring physicians once asked about our office's unique uniforms. I had my office manager send a copy of the catalogue from which we purchase them to the doctor and his office manager. Both of them were extremely appreciative of this gesture, and all it took was a little effort from us.

We have a sign in our office that says, "If you're feeling less than a B+, let us know and we'll give you a hug." This is our reminder to patients that we are still a high-touch as well as a high-tech practice. (I do not think anyone can get into trouble if you tactfully hug a patient who asks to be hugged in front of other patients or staff members.) One of my colleagues was interested in that sign, so we had a copy made for him and had it framed for his office. He was very appreciative and told me that he and his staff get regular requests for hugs from their patients.

FACTS OF LIFE

All of us would like, whenever possible, to have a bilateral referral arrangement with our colleagues. Have you ever experienced a situation in which you are sending patients to another physician and getting no reverse referrals? Of course, you can change your referral source, hoping that the other physician will notice that there is a decrease in referrals and will call you to ask what happened. But do not hold your breath. Chances are that that physician is busy enough and will not notice the decrease in patients.

A better alternative is to have a discussion about the facts of life with the physician. During your meeting, recall for the physician the number and names of patients you have sent him or her in the last 6 to 12 months. Ask whether the quality of patients was satisfactory and whether the physician would like to continue receiving your referrals.

If the physician answers yes to both questions, ask how he or she feels about your quality of medical care: "Do I enjoy a good reputation in our community? Have the patients I have sent you, as well as any others we may both be treating, been satisfied with my medical services?"

If the answers are again yes, then it is time to initiate the facts-of-life discussion. At this time you should suggest that you want to see some patients in return if you are to continue referring patients to that physician. If he or she does not agree, it is time to find yourself another referral source.

I had a facts-of-life discussion with a physician when I had been in practice for only three years. I had been receiving calls from an internist in the intensive care unit on a regular basis late at night to insert urethral catheters for patients in urinary retention. I did this for three years, hoping to demonstrate that I was available to provide urologic care for all his patients. However, when this internist had patients with nonemergency urologic problems, he referred them to another urologist. After years of being inconvenienced in this way, I decided to ask for a meeting with this physician. I said, "I am capable of seeing patients not only in the middle of the night but also between 8:00 AM and 5:00 PM as well!" I did not request all his urologic referrals, but I did ask for a few. If that was not acceptable, then he could get someone else to come in the evening hours to insert catheters. "What was the worst that could happen?" I asked myself. That I could get a good night's sleep.

As it happened, this discussion brought about a change in that physician's referral pattern. I was satisfied to notice that I began getting a few daytime referrals as well. I am not recommending this approach for everyone and in every circumstance. But whenever you feel exploited or that referrals are a one-way street, consider having a tactful discussion before abandoning the potential referral source.

If you are worried that marketing is going to leave you all alone, perhaps even generating contempt from your colleagues, remember that effective marketing includes rather than excludes your colleagues. As an example, whenever I do a support group on impotence, I get patients coming to my practice. Sometimes they are already patients of other urologists in my building. The way I handle this situation is to tell each of these patients, "You have an excellent urologist. I'll be happy to work with him. Let me call him and tell him what I have found and work with him on this."

I also have an effective letter that I use when I have to ask a colleague about transferring a patient's records to my office. See Chapter 13 for an example of that letter.

The Bottom Line   *Marketing yourself to your colleagues does not mean that you are trying to take away "market share." When you open up possibilities, you actually increase their business as well as yours. The way in which you do this does not take away, it just adds—to your stature in the professional community, to the respect you get from your peers, and to the bottom line.*

NOTES

1. Greg Korneluk, *Physician Survey for the Practice Enhancement Institute* (New York: McMillan Publishing Co., 1985), 13.

2. Gregg Easterbrook, "The Revolution in Medicine," *Newsweek,* January 26, 1987, 56.

3. Colored Rolodex cards can be ordered from PSI Research/Execards, 720 S. Hillview Dr., Milpitas, CA 95035; (503) 479–9464.

4. *REX* is a credit-card sized electronic Rolodex system that runs for up to six months on two lithium batteries. You can enter organizer data from your personal computer and download the data to REX. REX can be ordered from Franklin Electronic Publishers, 122 Burrs Road, Mount Holly, NJ 08060-4405, *www.franklin.com.*

5. Anne McGee-Cooper, *You Don't Have To Go Home from Work Exhausted* (Dallas: Bowen and Rogers, 1990), 334.

6. Harry and David's can be reached at (800) 547-3033; *www.harryanddavid.com.*

7. These tags are available from *The Envelope Please,* (352) 338–6091 (phone and fax) or by e-mailing kteevens@aol.com.

CHAPTER 36

Generating Referrals from Nontraditional Sources

Traditionally, physicians have looked to other physicians as the primary source of patient referrals. But do not forget that there are other professionals who can serve as excellent sources. Any effective marketing plan will identify the professionals and organizations that have the potential to refer patients. By pinpointing common areas of interest and approaching these other practitioners, you can create a need for your services or expertise. I have found most of these professionals eager to have physicians address their associations and communicate with their members. They are also eager to refer patients to physicians who respect them professionally as peers.

For example, I asked a podiatrist who has sent me a few patients over the years if I could address his professional organization. He told me that a medical doctor had never asked to come to one of their meetings. Since podiatrists see many patients with diabetic foot problems, I suggested a talk on the urologic complications in men with diabetes, which include impotence, incontinence, urinary tract infections, and retrograde ejaculation. Several weeks before the talk, I arranged to meet with my colleague to review my presentation. I wanted to be sure I would be providing useful information for his group. The podiatrist also suggested that I discuss methods to improve communication between physicians and podiatrists.

I began the presentation by emphasizing the basic philosophy that the two specialties have in common: that our fundamental purpose is to ease pain and make patients feel better. I showed slides from both medical and podiatric texts, pointing out the common areas of education.

I would like to thank **Dr. John F. Demartini** for his contributions to this chapter. Dr. Demartini is a doctor of chiropractic who practices in Houston, Texas, and an international speaker, author, and consultant. He can be reached at (713) 850-939, *www.drdemartini.com*.

I discussed the technique of taking a sexual history in both men and women. With the assistance of one of the members of the audience, we role-played the taking of a patient's sexual history.

Finally, I ended the presentation with a discussion of current treatments of urologic problems, including new surgical and nonsurgical treatments. I also provided handouts of recent articles on the subject, patient brochures, and an algorithm for evaluating impotence, incontinence, and infertility. I also reviewed indications for urologic referral.

Following the meeting I sent a letter to all who had attended, thanking them for the opportunity to speak at one of their meetings and invited them to my office if they were ever in the area.

Numerous benefits have occurred as a result of this presentation:

- I now receive two to three referrals a month from podiatrists. That is two to three referrals I would not have received had I not contacted the podiatrists for a presentation. Also, two podiatrists have become patients.
- I was asked to give a talk to the Louisiana State Podiatric Society meeting, increasing my exposure to several hundred podiatrists.
- I have arranged for several of my colleagues to give presentations at the podiatric association's meetings, and one of the podiatrists had the opportunity to reciprocate at a meeting of other specialists.
- I have been asked to write an article in the state podiatric journal.

None of these opportunities would have come about had I not approached the podiatrists about talking at one of their meetings.

I also have an excellent relationship with my community's chiropractors. In addition to the dozens of patients with chronic back pain that each chiropractor has, there are also substantial numbers of their patients with such conditions as impotence and urinary incontinence. Reputable chiropractors do not treat these latter conditions with spinal manipulations or adjustments, so they are happy to send them to a physician who will appreciate the referral and be sure to send the patient back to the chiropractor. The smart physician in the new millennium would be wise to develop contacts with reputable alternative practitioners, since millions of Americans now seek health care from a full range of such practitioners. If you are able to intelligently inform your patients about complementary remedies and their reasonable use, instead of discounting alternative remedies altogether, you are more likely to retain that patient. You become a resource instead of an adversary.

According to John F. Demartini, DC (doctor of chiropractic), who practices in Houston, Texas, "Alternative methods of healing and complementary medicine are on the rise. Differences in the various ideologies as well as methodologies are still causing unnecessary friction among health practitioners. As we enter the twenty-first century, an ever-growing percentage of patients are choosing alternative methods of healing and/or doctors and practitioners of complementary medicine." This reality has not been lost on the mainstream medical community, and many MDs now collaborate with doctors of chiropractic and practitioners of acupuncture, among others. Large cancer centers have established departments of integrative medicine, seeking to take advantage of the large sums of health care dollars being spent on alternative remedies and herbal medicines. An article appearing in the *New England Journal of Medicine*[1] pointed out that in 1990 Americans made an estimated 425 million visits to providers of nonconventional therapy. This number exceeds the number of visits during that year to all U.S. primary care physicians (388 million). Expenditures associated with use of nonconventional therapy in 1990 amounted to approximately $13.7 billion, three-quarters of which ($10.3 billion) was paid out of pocket. This figure is comparable to the $12.8 billion spent out of pocket annually for all hospitalizations in the United States. This is evidence that an increasing number of our patients are seeing nontraditional health care providers. We must make an effort to communicate with these providers in a professional manner.

In this chapter I talk about other hookups between physicians and nontraditional referral sources. In the section entitled "From Alternative to Complementary," Dr. Demartini shares some of the marketing methods he has employed to foster good faith between alternative and allopathic practitioners.

TARGET YOUR MARKET

The following is an example of an orthopedist who took this advice seriously. For years orthopedists have had a symbiotic relationship with the legal profession. Many orthopedists now communicate directly with attorneys to generate referrals. An orthopedic clinic in New Orleans has escalated its outreach efforts to include insurance claims adjusters. More than 10 years ago, Dr. Ken Adatto, of the Louisiana Clinic, a group of orthopedists and other related specialists, identified attorneys and insurance adjusters as important targets for the clinic's marketing because "they are the ones who authorize payment for our services."

Initially the clinic hired a marketing consultant to organize seminars at a hospital to explain the medical aspects of certain legal cases. Local attorneys and insurance adjusters were invited to attend. These seminars became so successful that the clinic decided to hold larger seminars at a local hotel. These all-day conferences include extensive handout materials. They are always well attended and result in more referrals. At a recent seminar, such workshops as "Common Injuries and Their Symptoms," "Determination of Disability," and "Role of Diagnostic Testing" were conducted.

The marketing consultant identified two more important authorizers of payment: risk managers and insurance rehabilitation specialists. The clinic's mailings extend to thousands of attorneys, insurance claims adjusters, rehabilitation counselors, and risk managers all over the southeast United States. The clinic offers continuing medical, legal, and nursing education credits for its seminars.[2] Because these seminars are now rather expensive, Dr. Adatto charges a nominal attendance fee to cover the cost of renting the hotel, producing the brochures, and filing the paperwork for the continuing education credits.

Because of accurate tracking, the clinic has found that marketing has attracted a substantial number of new patients. Dr. Adatto describes the tracking component as "recording the results just like you would the results of a clinical study or the outcome of a new surgical procedure." The marketing consultant for Dr. Adatto's clinic reports that tracking the number of referrals from third-party guarantors (attorneys and insurance adjusters) for the period following inception of the clinic's seminars until a point four years later revealed that referrals had increased to an average of 15 percent over their previous levels.

At the end of the first year referrals had increased by just 2 percent, but at the end of the second year referrals were up a whopping 20 percent. The increase in referrals had leveled off by the end of the third year, to a respectable 10 percent. At that point, the clinic hired two new physicians to handle the overload. By the end of the fourth year of concerted marketing efforts, referrals went up another 16 percent. As you can see, the clinic's efforts have paid off handsomely.

Dr. Adatto also finds other spin-offs or advantages of his marketing program. He has adapted his seminar for audiences of medical professionals and has given similar presentations to his orthopedic colleagues. He has also published his clinical data in local, state, and national medical journals. Because he is an accomplished speaker, he has been invited to speak at the local and state trial lawyers association meetings. He has also been invited to make presentations on medical ethics to the local medical school and the local law school. He also has an excellent newsletter that he continues to send to attorneys, insurance companies, and managed care plans (see Exhibit 36–1 for an example of a recent issue).

Dr. Adatto feels that this targeted marketing effort has made him more organized in his personal and professional life. As a result, he has happier patients, happier third-party payers, happier staff, and he is a happier Dr. Adatto. He feels that "by being organized you become happier professionally and economically."

OTHER REFERRAL SOURCES

Nurses and hospital employees are important sources of referrals. It is common for consumers looking for health care providers to ask nurses for recommen-

Exhibit 36–1 Example of a Newsletter

The Louisiana Clinic NEWS

Chiropractic Gets Results That Last!!

Chiropractors are a cost effective way to treat patients. They are licensed as doctors, authorized to diagnosis and treat conditions concerning the spine, muscle and nervous systems. Chiropractors work to promote optimal health and wellness through positive life-style changes. The Chiropractic approach is to perform a thorough case history and examination. X-rays are commonly taken unless they were done prior and available for review. Based upon the findings, the Chiropractor will establish a treatment program in order to appropriately manage care. This may include the application of ice to reduce swelling or heat and/or therapy. Spinal adjustments form a large and important part of care to return the spine to normal mobility as soon as possible. Often, after an adjustment, significant relief can be experienced. Later exercising is an integral part of care. It makes good sense to keep the spine maintained instead of allowing it to degenerate to the point of extreme pain.

The spine is directly affected by the chemical, physical, and emotional stress of everyday living. Whiplash, no matter the direction of impact can have *devastating* results. Following impact, the head is forced back and forth moving beyond the normal limits of movement. Whiplashes are not all confined to the neck, especially in cars with only lap-type seat belts lower back whiplash is common. The tendons, ligaments and muscles are over stretched and occasionally torn. The pressure generated on the disc may cause bulging, or in extreme cases, rupture (herniation). Spinal joints are subluxed and their motion greatly restricted. The nerve roots and possibly the spinal cord itself are stretched causing serious irritation and pain. The instability that results from the soft tissue damage can cause headaches, dizziness, blurred or "fuzzy" vision, ringing in the ears, pain in the neck, arms and hands and loss of strength and limited movement. *The clinic has established several payment options for the Chiropractic Division as well as payment upon settlement.*

Nicole Cossé, D.C.

Dr. Cossé currently practices in two of The Louisiana Clinic office locations:

4145 Canal Street		3715 Prytania Street, Suite 501
New Orleans, LA 70119	&	New Orleans, LA 70115
(504) 486-0670		(504) 895-2055

For more information contact Joan Golden, Director of Marketing and Development (504) 896-3842.

Courtesy of The Louisiana Clinic, Inc., New Orleans, LA.

What is a Soft Tissue Plan?

In an effort to further diversify the clinics services, The Louisiana Clinic recently adopted a Soft Tissue Payment Plan. The Soft Tissue Plan, currently being marketed to attorney payors, consists of four office visits with any orthopedic physician, x-rays with in those four visits, an MRI plus report. The fixed price for the plan is $1,300.00. The standard deposit of $300.00 and a signed credit agreement are required with payment terms of $100.00 per month for ten months. Election to participate in the plan also includes discounted deposits and payment terms for additional testing and surgery.

For more information regarding Soft Tissue Plans, contact Joan Golden, Director of Marketing & Development at (504) 896-3842.

New Physician in Baton Rouge

The Louisiana Clinic has added a new face in our Baton Rouge location. Dr. Andrew Kucharchuk, Board Certified Orthopaedic Surgeon, will be performing Orthopaedic Consultations and Disability Evaluations in our Baton Rouge location Tuesdays thru Fridays. He graduated from the University of Illinois Medical School in 1972. Upon completion of his Orthopaedic Internship and Residency at the University of Chicago Hospital, Dr. Kucharchuk went on to the University of Oklahoma for a one year Sports Medicine Fellowship. He also spent two years in Puerto Rico as the Chief of Orthopaedic Surgery at the Naval Hospital. Licensed in three states, Louisiana, Oklahoma and Illinois, Dr. Kucharchuk has spent the last twenty years in private practice, primarily in the Denham Springs area.

Please contact Rose Roberts in our Baton Rouge Office for more information (225) 343-7500.

Did you know...

Did you know that many patients with neck or back injuries have urological problems? A recent article written in the Orthopaedic Spine Journal showed that as many as 55% of spinal injury patients developed urology symptoms or problems. The problems can include erectile dysfunction, frequent urination, urgency and incontinence. The force of the trauma causing the neck or back injury (such as a ruptured disc) can affect the spinal cord, especially the pathways of the spinal cord that regulate normal bladder function and normal erectile function. The patient rarely volunteers this information because of embarrassment and misunderstanding as to the etiology. But if you ask the patient they will admit to symptoms such as urinary frequency/day and/or night, urgency and sometimes wetting on themselves. In addition they may notice decreased ability to maintain an erection. The etiology is usually due to the spinal cord trauma sustained in the accident and rarely due to the patients medications or psychosomatic.

Dr. S. McSherry, Board Certified Urologist, works with The Louisiana Clinic and has a background in working with patients having bladder and/or erection problems after an accident. Dr. McSherry treats patients in a cost effective way tailored to each patient's needs. Bladder and/or erectile function is usually treated with medications.

Dr. McSherry is available for appointments in our New Orleans office, Monday to Friday 9am-5pm. Call (504) 895-2055 for an appointment.

The Louisiana Clinic
(504) 895-2055

New Orleans	Hammond
Mid-City	Baton Rouge
Metairie	Lafayette
Kenner	Lake Charles

Announcements...

Orthopaedics

Dr. Alexis Waguespack, Orthopaedic Surgeon joined The Louisiana Clinic in August, 1998. Dr. Waguespack completed a one year Spine Fellowship at the Arthur White, San Francisco Spine Institute. Dr. Waguespack welcomes new patients at both The Louisiana Clinic Uptown and Metairie locations. For a copy of her CV or to obtain more information call (504) 895-2055.

Office Consolidations:

Effective Feb 31, 1999 The Louisiana Clinic office locations in both Slidell and LaPlace have been consolidated. The clinic continues to maintain eight locations throughout the state including Uptown, Metairie, Kenner, Mid City, Hammond, Baton Rouge, Lafayette and Lake Charles.

Dr. Raul Reyes, a Board Certified General Surgeon will continue to perform Orthopaedic Evaluations in our *Uptown, Baton Rouge, Lafayette and Hammond* sites. Please contact Joan Golden, Director of Marketing & Development at (504) 896-3842 for more information.

dations. Doctors who are kind, considerate, and attentive to their patients are frequently the ones who are suggested by nurses.

Several times I have been asked to speak at meetings of the American Operating Room Nurses Association, and I get a number of referrals after each talk. I also always make it a point to give in-service instruction. Whenever I am going to perform a new procedure, I go to the hospital and give a talk about it to the operating room nurses. This accomplishes several goals: It makes the nurses knowledgeable assistants when I do the procedure, reduces the anxiety they usually feel when assisting with a new procedure or operation, and it lets them know that this doctor is on the cutting edge—he does the newest procedures. Whenever I have an opportunity to speak to nurses, I always leave handouts. Just as with my other speaking engagements, I give additional information to anyone who requests it. As a result, I get one to two referrals a month from the nurses.

Pharmacists are another group from whom patients frequently seek advice. Therefore, it is important to become an ally of the pharmacists in your community. For example, before you start prescribing a new medication, call (or have your office call) the local pharmacists and make sure they have the medication available.

You can also head off conflicting advice to your patients if you stay in touch with your pharmacists about nontraditional uses of established medications. For example, in the past I prescribed the antidepressant imipramine for mild stress and urge incontinence. In one case, the pharmacist told one of my patients that the medication was not used for incontinence. That meant I had explaining to do—to both the patient and the pharmacist. I solved this awkward situation by photocopying the journal study showing the efficacy of imipramine for urge incontinence. By sending along the information about the medication with each patient, I educated the pharmacist and avoided several phone calls to explain my rationale for prescribing.

You can also send local pharmacists articles about your areas of interest and expertise. For example, I wrote an article on the use of transdermal scopolamine to treat bladder instability, which was a new use for that antinausea medication. The pharmacists in my community are now knowledgeable about this new use.

Another potential referral source consists of your pharmaceutical representatives. Not only are these men and women able to provide you with educational materials and sample medications, but they are also capable of generating good public relations for your practice. If you have a well-run practice, they will frequently mention it to other physicians and potential patients. If you want to endear yourself to the drug representatives, see them in a timely fashion. That is their "hot" button, and they really appreciate it if you do not ignore them or keep them waiting.

Other possible sources for referrals include: oral surgeons, dentists, and orthodontists. Neurologists interested in treating headache can communicate with dentists who have patients with temporomandibular joint (TMJ) syndrome. *Psychiatrists* can communicate with *psychologists, sex therapists, social workers,* and *the clergy.*

Ophthalmologists can work with *optometrists. Orthopedists* can look for referrals from *chiropractors. Rheumatologists* can connect with *manicurists,* and *dermatologists* can solicit referrals from *barbers* and *beauticians.* Once you open up your thinking about referrals, you can see a wider range of possibilities for your marketing.

IMAGING AND MARKETING

Another excellent example of marketing to nontraditional sources was conducted by Terri Goren, director of marketing at the Washington Imaging Center in Chevy Chase, Maryland. The Washington Imaging Center targeted dentists, podiatrists, and chiropractors through an educational approach.

The center targeted dentists first. It determined that nearly all dentists who had patients with TMJ syndrome had a complicated task in managing these patients. The center's objective was to educate local dentists on the clinical benefit of using magnetic resonance imaging (MRI) to evaluate patients with TMJ syndrome.

The center's goals and objectives were (1) to position itself as an authority on and resource for TMJ syndrome, (2) to build name recognition, and (3) to designate one of its radiologists as an expert on TMJ syndrome in the dental community.

It developed a newsletter-type brochure in which it discussed several TMJ cases that had been successfully managed by using MRI. This brochure was mailed to nearly 1,000 dentists in the Washington, D.C., area. The brochure contained a business reply card that asked the dentists to indicate whether they would be interested in attending an upcoming TMJ seminar and the preferred time of day and week.

The center received a positive response and planned to hold its seminar at the site to include a tour of the facility. The seminar was free and included a catered luncheon buffet. Following the seminar, the dentists were given a tour of the scanner room and a demonstration scan was conducted, using one of the seminar participants as a volunteer "patient."

All attendees of these seminars received a thank-you letter from the center as well as a quarterly newsletter targeted specifically at dentists. Those who had not responded to the initial mailing received a follow-up invitation to another seminar. Repeat seminars are now announced in a local dental journal.

Through this concerted marketing program, the Washington Imaging Center increased referrals from dentists by 40 percent at six months and by 65 percent at one year. One spin-off was that the expert radiologist was asked to address the local dental society and submit articles to the state dental journal.

The center used the same approach with podiatrists. This time, it was so confident of the concept that it omitted the business reply card and simply invited podiatrists to attend a scheduled seminar. On the program was a podiatrist trained in MRI of the foot. The response from the seminars for podiatrists was immediate.

The center now receives from 6 to 10 podiatric referrals a month. These seminars have been so successful that the center is now planning similar marketing programs for chiropractors, pharmacists, optometrists, and attorneys. It also plans to produce a program in cooperation with neurologists in the community. This is an excellent example of attracting nontraditional sources of referrals in a win-win situation for all involved.

FROM ALTERNATIVE TO COMPLEMENTARY

It was not too many years ago that most medical doctors scoffed at the mention of patients visiting chiropractors, acupuncture specialists, or homeopaths. Now that patients are seeking out these practitioners, medical science is taking a second look. As was pointed out in the introduction to this chapter, these approaches are no longer on the fringes. And, if physicians can overcome old notions of what constitutes the healing arts, there may be some fruitful collaborations in store for both types of practicing professionals.

The wise doctor of complementary medicine, points out Dr. Demartini, actively refers patients for second opinions and does not presume to treat all conditions. If professional contacts are fostered, everyone—physician, complementary practitioner, and especially the patient—can benefit. Dr. Demartini recalls one situation when a female patient presented with lower abdominal cramping and heavy aches and pains in the lower abdomen and lower lumbar region. "Upon examination, I palpated a golf-ball sized mass in the lower left pelvic region," he recalls. "Blood tests were found to be within normal ranges. No leukocytosis was noted. The patient had no fever. Radiographs demonstrated a subluxation of the first and fifth lumbar vertebrae and the soft tissue X-ray was inconclusive. I suspected an unruptured ovarian cyst. Since I realized that an invasive neoplasm, endometriosis, malposition of the uterus, or pain of other origins was possible, I sought a second opinion from a gynecologist who I had been cross-referring with and met at a social event the previous year. His diagnosis was the suspected ovarian cyst. The patient was referred back to my office for the adjustments of the first and fifth lumbar vertebrae and within a week the signs and symptoms of her condition improved. It was comforting to have quick access to a competent gynecologist who understood the role that chiropractic played in the care of the patient."

Who's Who in Complementary Medicine?

Dr. Demartini notes that there is often confusion regarding the proper terms to refer to these practitioners. "If the term *doctor* is defined as a 'person licensed to practice medicine,' then the term *doctors of complementary medicine* would be inappropriate for those practitioners who have not been awarded such designations. The term *practitioners of complementary healing* might be considered more appropriate."

However, some still refer to chiropractors, naturopaths, osteopaths, nutritionists, hypnotherapists, and homeopaths as "doctor," because these professionals have undertaken more advanced training and earned the designated degree or title of "doctor."

Practitioners of complementary healing include nutritionists, acupuncturists, reflexologists, acupressure therapists, massage therapists, yoga instructors, Tai Chi instructors, mind/body technique practitioners, biofeedback specialists, meditation instructors, and herbalists. The reason for the distinction is that these practitioners have undertaken less advanced training than doctors in their respective areas of healing. (For an overview of such practitioners and a helpful evaluation of all types of therapies and remedies, see "Additional Resources" at the end of this chapter.)

Interaction with Alternative and Complementary Healers

More and more doctors and practitioners of complementary medicine and healing are enhancing their communication with physicians, according to Dr. Demartini. "This has not only become a fashionable trend but has also become the means of providing the best overall service to the patient. Often patients arrive at the doorstep of one health care provider and actually require the additional services of another." To accomplish successful referral patterns, Demartini believes one must gather a team of interacting health care professionals.

The first way is an "invitation letter" sent by one professional to other selected professionals, one from each field, to a dinner paid for by the inviting doctor. Each person is invited to give a personal introduction and a brief presentation to familiarize the others with his or her practice. This social greeting format helps create a bond between these experts in their respective fields, he says, and opens the doorway for further interaction and visits to individual offices and eventually to referrals.

The second way is a "request letter" where one professional contacts an associated professional's office (see Exhibit 36–2). This can be mailed to many offices at once and can be used in a modified format for each area of expertise.

The results of these letters have been rewarding, says Dr. Demartini. Not only has he been able to develop working relationships with a number of doctors, but he

Exhibit 36–2 "Request Letter" To Stimulate Cross-Referrals

Dear Dr. Jones:

My name is Dr. John F. Demartini. I am a Doctor of Chiropractic in full-time practice. I have been practicing in the city of Houston for approximately seventeen years. I treat a high volume of patients and regularly come upon those who require the additional services of doctors in other fields. I have found it essential at times to seek wise counsel and second opinions in your particular field of expertise and have referred many patients for such services in the past.

I am seeking a physician in your field who is interested in working together with me for the sake of quality patient care. If you are interested in receiving patient referrals and developing a new doctor-doctor and many new doctor-patient relationships, please contact my office.

My office is in Transco Tower at 2800 Post Oak Blvd., Suite 5250, Houston, Texas, 77056. My offices are open five days a week between the hours of 9 A.M. and 6 P.M.

Sincerely yours,
John F. Demartini, D.C.

---

has in turn received numerous referrals that have more than paid for his time and effort.

A third method for increasing cross-referrals is to join the most prestigious or respected business networking club in your city or area. Then, extend a personal invitation to another doctor to join you for a meeting of the organization. This gives you a way to meet the doctor directly and provides a setting in which to develop an ongoing cross-referral relationship.

The fourth way to increase collaborations is to attend the conventions and annual meetings of other health professionals that are held in your area.

Dr. Demartini spends a lot of his time educating other professionals as well as the public about his specialty. He advises other doctors and practitioners of complementary medicine to do the same. Medical doctors may already be feeling the pressure from patients to inform themselves about alternative medicine. See "Additional Resources" for some texts written for doctors to help accomplish this.

AN IDEA THAT DID NOT WORK

Not every idea you have for marketing your practice is going to be a winner. One time I embarked on a plan that was not as successful as some of the others. I began to think about how women share a lot of personal experiences with their hairdressers. And when I go to my barber, he always seems to have a lot of information about people. He asks me a lot of questions about what I do. So I had the idea to give a talk to his organization, because barbers listen to their clients' problems and could be a potential referral source. My barber thought it was a great idea. So I gave the talk. However, it was not very well attended, and I did not get any referrals. So, not every plan you devise will yield the results you want. The key is to evaluate your action steps honestly and make the necessary corrections to your course.

APPROACHING POTENTIAL REFERRAL SOURCES

Some suggestions on approaching nontraditional sources for referrals are as follows:

- Agree to meet "on their turf," at least the first time.
- Find common areas of interest and emphasize them.
- Show respect for the professions of nonmedical colleagues, even if you do not completely agree with their approach. In the past, this was much more of a problem, with physicians discriminating against osteopaths, orthopedists against chiropractors, and ophthalmologists against optometrists. In today's world of shrinking patient bases, we cannot afford to be provincial. It is time to expand our worlds—and expand our practices by doing so.
- Demonstrate the benefit of sharing patients and referrals. Not only will you be increasing your network of potential referral sources, but so will your nonmedical colleagues.
- Provide your referral sources with something new, interesting, and educational. You have an opportunity to increase your awareness and understanding of their professions, and vice versa.
- Promise to provide written documentation on a regular basis.
- Make every effort to refer patients to the specialties or professions of your nonmedical colleagues.
- If all else fails . . . feed them! You can ask pharmaceutical companies to contribute to the cost, as most of them are happy to have a chance to help physicians who use their products.

As you can see, the principles of getting referrals from other professionals are the same as for soliciting referrals from your medical colleagues: Make yourself and your practice attractive and easy to do business with and you will see the payoff.

The Bottom Line   *By moving "outside the box" of traditional referral patterns, you can garner additional patients. All it takes is a little innovation and a little time.*

NOTES

1. David M. Eisenberg et al., "Unconventional Medicine in the United States—Prevalence, Costs, and Patterns of Use," *New England Journal of Medicine,* 328, no. 4 (January 28, 1993).

2. Information regarding the certification and accreditation needed to offer continuing medical education credit can be obtained from the Accreditation Council for Continuing Medical Education, P.O. Box 245, Lake Bluff, IL 60044; (708) 295–1490.

ADDITIONAL RESOURCES

- Barrie R. Cassileth, PhD, *The Alternative Medicine Handbook: The Complete Reference Guide to Alternative and Complementary Therapies* (New York: W.W. Norton & Company, 1998).

- Website for the Department of Complementary Medicine at the University of Exeter, England: *www.ex.ac.uk/FACT.*

- *FACT* (Focus on Alternative and Complementary Therapies) is an online journal containing book reviews, conference reports, extensive lists of complementary and alternative medicine literature, and links to other complementary and alternative medicine-related sites.

CHAPTER 37

Avoid Managed Care Paralysis: Conduct a Practice Analysis

As discussed in Chapter 35, the key to a successful medical practice used to be the three A's: availability, affability, and affordability. Today, in order to make your practice attractive to managed care plans, you have to demonstrate cost-effectiveness and high quality as well.

If managed care is just beginning to penetrate your community, almost any managed care organization will be eager to contract with you. Just completing the application and including a copy of your curriculum vitae, your medical license, and documentation of your malpractice coverage will ensure your inclusion on the panel of providers. However, if managed care has already invaded your area, then it will be much more difficult to join a plan. It will take energy and effort on your part to promote your practice and sell the plan on the advantages of adding you to its panel.

This chapter describes methods to make your practice attractive to managed care plans. It discusses the importance of preparing a practice analysis, the necessary ingredients of a practice analysis, and how to present the material to managed care plans.

The purpose of a practice analysis, in addition to demonstrating your practice's cost-effectiveness and quality, is to showcase the unique characteristics of your practice. The practice analysis should point out to managed care plans the benefits and advantages of your practice in an objective fashion.

DOING YOUR HOMEWORK

One of your first tasks is to prepare a list of all the procedures and services you offer your patients. Provide the *Current Procedural Terminology* (CPT) code for each item on the list and the relative value unit for each procedure (available in

324

California Relative Value Studies).[1] You also need to note your fee for each procedure and the hospital cost for each diagnosis-related group (DRG) and *International Classification of Diseases,* ninth edition code. Now the managed care plan can compare your charges to those of other physicians and practices that are already accepted or are applying to be included on the plan's panel.

You can demonstrate your cost-effectiveness by listing all the procedures that you do in your office or in an ambulatory treatment center. Using these settings is less costly than using the hospital. For example, a cystoscopy performed in the office uses approximately $85 of disposable equipment, compared with a hospital charge to the third-party payer of more than $1,000. Most ambulatory treatment centers can operate 30 to 50 percent more efficiently than a hospital operating room, and many offer discounts for managed care business.

Also mention aspects of your practice philosophy that might result in cost savings to plan members. If you use conservative, nonsurgical treatments or cost-effective testing, be sure to include this information. For example, if you believe that an acute uncomplicated urinary tract infection can be successfully treated with a one-day or a short course of antibiotics instead of the traditional 10 to 14 days of medication, then point that out in your practice analysis.

Next you want to survey your current patients. Your questionnaire should ask patients how easy it was to make an appointment, how long they waited to see the doctor, how friendly the staff was, and whether the doctor answered all their questions. (Exhibit 37–1 is a patient questionnaire I have used to survey patients, and Figures 37–1 and 37–2 graphically show the results for individual questions.) If you get responses from your patients that might make good testimonials about your practice, ask the patients for permission to include them in the practice analysis (see Exhibit 37–2).

If you are a primary care doctor, indicate your referrals per 100 patients seen. Also, it is a good idea to survey physicians you refer to. If you are a primary care physician, query your specialists and ask them if the referrals are appropriate. Are patients worked up prior to the referral? Are reports and documentation sent well in advance of the referral so that the specialist does not spend precious time tracking lab and X-ray reports? If you are a specialist, survey your primary care physicians about the completeness of your evaluations, about your promptness in communicating with them, and whether you obtain proper authorizations before you perform any procedure or test.

The practice analysis should also describe the setting and environment of your practice. Provide the number of full-time staff and the ratio of full-time staff to physicians. Since staff salaries constitute one of the highest components of overhead, this statistic will give plans some idea of your overhead expenses and the efficiency of your practice. Indicate your office hours, especially if you offer early morning, evening, and weekend hours for appointments. Offering extended

Exhibit 37–1 Patient Satisfaction Survey

To provide you with the best possible care, we need your feedback.

1. How did you decide to come to this practice?
   ___ Recommended by another patient
   ___ Recommended by another doctor
   ___ Physician referral service
   ___ Yellow Pages
   ___ Office close to home
   Other: _____

2. When you telephone our office, is your call answered courteously?
   ___ Yes ___ No   Comments: _____

3. Are you able to obtain an appointment easily and timely?
   ___ Yes ___ No   Comments: _____

4. During your last visit to our office, how would you describe your treatment by our staff?
   ___ Warm/friendly
   ___ Professional
   Other: _____

5. How interested do we seem to be in you as a person when you visit the office?
   ___ Genuinely interested and concerned
   ___ Usually interested and concerned
   ___ Sometimes disinterested and unconcerned
   ___ Usually disinterested and unconcerned

6. Do you find our reception area warm and comfortable?
   ___ Yes ___ No   Comments: _____

7. Are the reception area materials to your taste? ___ Yes ___ No
   If "No," your preference: _____

8. When you arrive at our office, how long do you normally have to wait after your scheduled appointment time? _____ minutes. If you wait longer than 30 minutes, are you given an explanation for the delay?
   ___ Yes ___ No

9. How would you rate the overall quality of care you receive?
   ___ Outstanding ___ Good ___ Fair ___ Poor
   Comments: _____

continues

Exhibit 37–1 continued

---

10. How would you rate the doctor on patience, warmth, and interest in your problem?
    ___ Outstanding ___ Good ___ Fair ___ Poor

11. Does the doctor fully explain your illness and treatment to you?
    ___ Yes ___ No   Comments: _____

12. Are you comfortable recommending our services to your family and friends?
    ___ Yes ___ No   Comments: _____

13. What other services could we offer that you would like available for you or your family?
    _____

14. Have the financial policies of this practice been completely explained to you?
    ___ Yes ___ No   Comments: _____

15. During your last visit, were the charges explained to your satisfaction?
    ___ Yes ___ No   Comments: _____

16. Is our superbill helpful in filing with your insurance for reimbursement?
    ___ Yes ___ No   Comments: _____

17. Other: _____
    _____
    _____

Thank you for taking time to complete this information.
We value our patients' comments.

| _____ | _____ |
| Date | Signature (optional) |

---

hours shows that you are really managed care-friendly and willing to see patients when it is convenient for them.

List your hospital affiliations, since the plans may already have contracted with one or more of the hospitals. If you do not have privileges with one of its hospitals, that will make it difficult for the plan to send its members to you.

Analyze your existing patient base. Indicate the percentages of Medicare, fee-for-service, and managed care patients. If you already have a large percentage of managed care patients, that is an indicator that you understand the system.

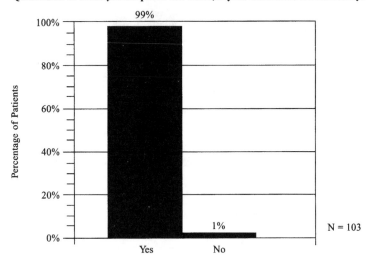

Figure 37–1 Graphic display of responses to Question 2 of the patient satisfaction survey. *Source:* Reprinted from N. Baum, *Take Charge of Your Medical Practice*, p. 275, © 1996, Aspen Publishers, Inc.

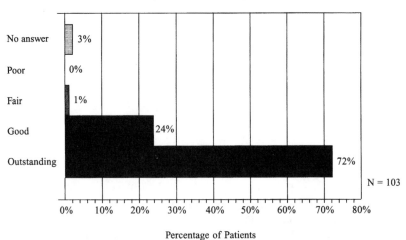

Figure 37–2 Graphic display of responses to Question 9 of the patient satisfaction survey. *Source:* Reprinted from N. Baum, *Take Charge of Your Medical Practice*, p. 275, © 1996, Aspen Publishers, Inc.

Exhibit 37–2 Additional Comments Made by Patients in Response to Question 17 of the Patient Satisfaction Survey

---

- "It would be nice if you and your staff could teach your philosophy of office management to other staffs and doctors. . . ."
- "Dr. Baum and staff are always positive thinking people and relay that attitude to others. Wish all doctors had that attitude."
- "I am extremely pleased with the quality of care I receive from Dr. Baum and the outstanding support of his staff. I have never encountered such a relaxed openness and respect in a doctor–patient relationship as I do with Dr. Baum."
- "Stay as sweet as you are."
- "Dr. Baum's a great guy and runs a terrific business, personable and professional. I'm glad to avail myself of the services the practice offers."
- "I would like to know where I can purchase some of those puzzles in your examining rooms."
- "Would not let anyone else be my urologist."
- "You run a good show!"
- "I, as a senior citizen, feel that we as a group would be very grateful if you would accept assignment of our Medicare claims plus whatever else we might be able to contribute from secondary insurance to reach your gross charges."
- "Keep up the good work. Congratulations on your excellent staff."
- "Thank you for your care. The patient detail your office is committed to is evident even in this questionnaire."
- "Would have liked a little more in-depth discussion of condition and all treatment options."
- "Out of all the different physicians I see, Neil Baum is THE BEST!!"
- "Dr. Baum and the entire staff conduct themselves in a very professional, caring, and warm manner. I am extremely satisfied."
- "Very patient in dealing with insurance claims and delays."
- "Dr. Baum, you have given me the Best."
- "Great motivational literature."
- "It was a pleasure to be a patient at your office. Have a wonderful Christmas and a Happy New Year."
- "Jackie was very kind and especially nice to me."
- "This office is by far the most comfortable doctor's office I have ever gone to."
- "We are very satisfied with the doctor, the service rendered, and their staff. Thank you kindly for caring."
- "Sometimes too rushed/overbooked (not recently)."
- "Superb!"

Nearly every managed care plan is interested in utilization management and quality assurance. Plans will be particularly impressed if you have electronic medical records and provide patients with medical information electronically (see Chapter 43). Plans like to know whether you have an electronic patient recall system. This ensures that patients will not fall through the cracks and will be notified of important follow-up appointments. Plans want to know your system for documenting and charting lab and diagnostic tests. Nearly every one of us has had the experience of having a report filed in a patient's chart without it ever being read by the doctor. Plans want to be sure that this will not happen in your practice—that you have safeguards to prevent it.

Plans also want to know that you are a managed care team player and will adhere to guidelines and protocols. I have given managed care plans a copy of the "Suggestions for Urologic Referral" that I send to primary care doctors. These cost-saving suggestions outline what primary care doctors can do as part of the workup before seeking a urologic consultation. (Exhibit 37–3 is the cover letter I send to primary care physicians, and Exhibit 37–4 presents the actual suggestions.)

For example, if a patient has hematuria, I suggest that a urine culture, an intravenous pyelogram, and a urine cytology be done before the patient is referred to

---

Exhibit 37–3 Cover Letter Concerning Suggestions for Urologic Referral

---

Dear [primary care physician],

In this time of change and health care reform, the relationship between the primary care physician and the specialist is being modified. In order to facilitate the transition, I would like to provide you with some suggestions regarding referrals to a urology practice. Of course, these are only suggestions and are not carved in stone.

It is my purpose to ensure each of your patients is seen in a timely fashion and receives a cost-effective workup and treatment and to improve the communication between your office and mine. Following a patient's visit to my office, I will provide you with an immediate report that contains the diagnosis, the medications that I have recommended, and the treatment plan.

I am including educational materials, appropriate consents, and drug information. If you need additional copies, please give my office a call and we will be happy to fax/mail them to you.

If you have any questions or comments on these suggestions, please let me hear from you.

Sincerely,
Neil Baum, M.D.

Exhibit 37–4 Suggestions for Urologic Referral

General ☐ All required labwork, studies, and radiologic films (NOT REPORTS) must be sent with the patient at time of referral.

I. REFERRAL FOR A MAN OR WOMAN WITH GROSS OR MICROSCOPIC HEMATURIA THAT IS NOT ASSOCIATED WITH A URINARY TRACT INFECTION

Please send patient with:
1) results of urine C & S
2) IVP report
3) urine cytology report

Please give patient:
1) consent for cystoscopy
2) the educational material on hematuria (note there is a different one for men and women)

II. REFERRAL FOR FEMALES WITH RECURRENT UTIs OR COMPLICATED UTI (FEVER, CHILLS, OR FLANK PAIN)

Please send patient to our office with:
1) results of urine C & S
2) results of IVP

Please give patient:
1) consent for cystoscopy and cystogram
2) information on recurrent UTI

III. REFERRAL FOR IMPOTENCE

A suggested evaluation by your office can in most instances differentiate psychogenic from organic erectile dysfunction. I recommend that you:
1) obtain serum testosterone, glucose—if the testosterone is at the lower limit of normal or decreased (<225 ng/dl), then include a prolactin level
2) provide the patient with a Snap Gauge band to determine the presence or absence of nocturnal erections

Please give patient:
1) sexual function questionnaire
2) educational information on impotence
3) results of the Snap Gauge test

continues

Exhibit 37–4 continued

IV. REFERRAL FOR BPH

The Agency for Health Care Policy and Research (AHCPR) has developed guidelines that are based on symptoms and treatment according to patient preference. These are:
1) quality of life symptom score
2) physical examination/digital rectal examination
3) urinalysis
4) PSA
5) serum creatinine

Indications for urologic referral are:
1) moderate to severe symptoms
   unresponsive to pharmacologic management
2) urinary retention
3) possible neurogenic bladder (patients with diabetes, Parkinson's, multiple sclerosis)
4) recurrent UTIs
5) uninfected hematuria
6) PSA > 4 ng/ml, PSA rising more than 20 percent a year
7) abnormal digital rectal exam
8) azotemia

Please give patient:
1) results of PSA test
2) alternative treatments for the enlarged prostate gland
3) if patient has an abnormal rectal exam or elevated PSA test, provide the patient with information on the transrectal ultrasound/biopsy

V. REFERRAL FOR URINARY INCONTINENCE

Suggest that patient keep a voiding diary for 5 days.
Please give patient:
1) incontinence educational material
2) consent for cystoscopy and urodynamic evaluation
3) copy of urine C & S report

VI. PATIENT REFERRED FOR VASECTOMY

Please give patient:
1) educational materials on no-incision vasectomy
2) consent for vasectomy
3) pre- and postvasectomy instructions

Courtesy of Michael Alabaster, MD, and Mark Saslawsky, MD, Southeast Urology Network, Memphis, Tennessee.

the urologist. When a patient calls for an appointment and the receptionist learns that the appointment is for evaluation of hematuria and the studies have been completed, then the patient is scheduled for a flexible cystoscopy on the first visit. The information on the procedure, the consent, and the instructions for the preparation are sent to the patient, who reads and signs the forms before coming to the office. This method, which allows the evaluation to be completed in a single visit, is a cost-effective way of evaluating many medical conditions and is thus very attractive to managed care plans.

If your practice performs weekly or regular random chart reviews to check for documentation and completeness of records, the plan will be impressed. Indicate that all allergies are noted on the front of any chart and that all patient telephone conversations as well as all prescription refills are noted in the chart.

Today, it is necessary to demonstrate that your practice has a compliance plan in place and that you are making every effort to enhance the quality of care that you are providing your patients. If you have a compliance plan, send a copy of the plan to the managed care administrators. If you do not have a plan, then indicate that you are going to implement such a plan in the near future. In Chapter 44, we have provided you with the basics of drawing up a compliance plan and resources for obtaining a plan for your practice.

You can demonstrate your attention to detail by including a copy of your employee manual and your compliance plan. If your practice has regular staff meetings, send the plan a copy of the most recent notes from those staff meetings. You should also indicate whether you conduct periodic performance reviews of the staff and physicians and provide records of the last two years of continuing medical education for them (this shows their medical knowledge is current and up-to-date).

Finally, indicate the distinctive characteristics of your practice. List all its advantages for current patients and potential new ones. If there are any areas of particular medical interest or expertise that distinguish your practice as an innovator or leader in your field, then you want to note them in the practice analysis. For example, you will want to mention if you have written papers in peer-reviewed journals, made presentations at national meetings, conducted seminars, or taught postgraduate courses.

HOW TO USE PRACTICE ANALYSIS MATERIAL

Contact the provider relations representative of the plan you wish to join. Send the representative a letter of introduction saying you wish to join the plan and would like to present your practice analysis material. Request a meeting and mention that you will call to arrange a time.

When you meet the representative, show him or her the practice analysis and focus your presentation on cost-effectiveness and quality issues. If you merely send the analysis to the representative, you do not know if it will be reviewed or even looked at. At least this way you know the representative is aware of the highlights.

Ask about the current panel and inquire whether there are any obstacles to your inclusion on the panel. Conclude by explaining why it would be beneficial for the plan to contract with you. You might present the features and benefits of your practice in a one-page summary you leave with the representative. Indicate that you will follow up with a call in two weeks to learn of the plan's decision.

AFTER YOU ARE ACCEPTED

Once the plan has approved your application and has listed you in its directory, you must let the other plan physicians and the plan members know of your participation and availability. I suggest you write a letter to the physicians that introduces your practice and emphasizes your commitment to cost containment and quality. (Exhibit 37–5 is an example of a letter to the physicians that are already on the plan.)

SUPPOSE THEY SAY NO

Early in the managed care game, it was easy to gain entry into a managed care plan. Once managed care made greater inroads, doctors found that the panels quickly became closed. They would receive requests from patients to have their records transferred to physicians who were on their plans' panels. After a number of such requests, the nonplan doctors would call the plans and ask for admission—only to find the panels closed.

If a panel is closed for your specialty, or the plan has enough physicians in your geographic area, then you have to mount a campaign to make your practice seem attractive to the plan. You have to tune into the plan's Station WIIFM (What's in It for Me?). You have to demonstrate that you have something to offer that will be of benefit to plan members.

Do your homework. Find out what the plan's needs and wants are and if there are any voids in its existing panel. If you have a service that is not being offered by the plan, then it can justify adding you. For example, if you have special training in allergy and immunology and the plan does not offer allergy and immunology services, point this out when making your pitch.

Occasionally you will hear that the plan has all the doctors in your field that it needs. Ask to see the plan's directory; and when an existing member retires, moves, or is dropped from the plan, act quickly and be the first to contact the physician representative with your new application.

Exhibit 37–5 Introductory Letter Sent to Plan Physicians Announcing Participation in the Plan

---

Dear [plan physician],

As a new provider on your health care plan, I would like to take this opportunity to introduce myself and my practice.

I have been practicing urology in this community since 1978 and am on the staff at Touro Infirmary and Southern Baptist Hospitals.

In an era of cost containment I would like to mention my sensitivity to the spiraling cost of health care. I avoid the "mega" workup for common urologic problems such as recurrent urinary tract infections and prostatism. Whenever possible I do my diagnostic studies and even surgical procedures during a one-day stay or in an ambulatory treatment center.

My approach to prostate cancer in older men with disease confined to the prostate is to offer these patients radiation therapy using I^{125} implants. This is a very cost-effective method of treatment compared to radical prostatectomy.

I also offer collagen implants for women with severe stress incontinence due to intrinsic sphincter deficiency. This procedure can be performed on an outpatient basis and even under local anesthesia in the office in selected cases.

One of my areas of interest is the diagnosis and management of impotence. I have recently reported my results with several other colleagues, and my success rate exceeds 95 percent with a two-year follow-up.

I make an effort to provide my patients with educational materials that inform them about measures they can take to prevent diseases and for early detection of urologic cancers. I provide all men with a testicular self-examination card encouraging them to perform self-examination on a regular basis. Patients are given a quarterly newsletter that discusses recent topics in health care. I also send a semiannual newsletter to referring physicians that reviews the latest developments in urology.

One of the most common complaints that patients have with managed care plans is that they can't obtain appointments in a timely fashion with the physician. I would like to emphasize that my practice will not discriminate or differentiate a managed care plan patient from a traditional fee-for-service patient. I reserve 30 minutes every afternoon as "sacred time" that is left open for the emergencies and urgencies that occur every day.

I also provide primary care doctors with a fax referral form that can be used to communicate with my office in an efficient fashion. This form will identify the patient with immediate needs. I can assure you that those patients with emergencies can be seen immediately and patients with urgencies can be seen in 24 to 48 hours.

continues

Exhibit 37–5 continued

I also recognize the importance of timely communications between the primary care doctors and the specialists. I have utilized a method of notifying you in writing within 24 hours of the urologic diagnosis concerning the medications prescribed for your patients and the treatment plan. If you have a fax machine and request a report immediately, it will be electronically sent to your office the same day your patient is seen.

I hope this letter gives you an overview of my practice and my office staff. I look forward to working with you and your physicians on the [name of plan].

Sincerely,
Neil Baum, M.D.

Use your practice analysis to demonstrate your cost-effectiveness as well as your patients' satisfaction with their care. The plan does not want to hear any complaints from its members about their health care providers. If you can show your practice has a high patient satisfaction rate, the plan will not have to worry about the potential problems associated with patient complaints.

CARING ENOUGH TO SEND THE VERY BEST

Next consider organizing a letter-writing campaign. Letters from old patients of yours who are members of the plan and cannot see you because you are not on the panel will have some impact. I often ask patients to write a letter to their plan's patient representative and to their employer. Many of them would like to write a letter but do not have the necessary letter-writing skills. In such cases, I offer them a sample letter (Exhibit 37–6) and ask them to write it on their own stationery.

You can also ask employers to lobby on your behalf. Ask them to send a letter to the plan administrator or physician representative and ask that you be included on the panel. I gave a talk on incontinence and urinary tract infections to a local oil company's female employees. Many of those in the audience wanted to make an appointment but could not because I was not on the plan. I suggested that the health nurse send a letter to the plan requesting that I be included. Shortly thereafter I received a call asking me to join a plan that was previously closed to me.

Finally, ask your physician colleagues who are on the plan to write a letter on your behalf. Have them emphasize that you are already seeing many of the plan's patients and that you enjoy an excellent reputation in the community. (Exhibit 37–7 is a sample letter from a colleague to a plan's administrator.)

Exhibit 37–6 Letter Supporting Physician's Attempt To Be Put on a Physician Panel

Dear [employer],

For the past five years I have been under the urologic care of Dr. Neil Baum. I called to make an appointment with Dr. Baum and learned that he is not on our new insurance plan. Dr. Baum informed me that he has submitted an application to [insurance plan] and has been told that there are too many urologists already on the panel.

I would like for you to consider recommending Dr. Baum to [insurance company]. Unlike the urologists currently on the plan, Dr. Baum takes early morning appointments and will allow me to come to his office after 4:30 PM. If I select one of the urologists on the plan, I will be required to miss several hours of work in order to see a doctor.

I also know that Dr. Baum's office conducts an annual patient survey in order to meet the needs of his patients. He is the only physician that I have been to that asks patients if they have any concerns relating to the doctor and the staff. Dr. Baum also emphasizes preventive care and provides all his male patients with a testicular self-exam card to check for testicle cancer.

I hope you will take all of these reasons into consideration and will recommend that Dr. Baum be included on our plan.

Sincerely,
[name of patient]

Exhibit 37–7 Letter of Recommendation from a Plan Physician

Dear [medical director],

I am writing this letter to recommend a colleague, Dr. Excellent, to be a provider for [specialty] referral to the plan members of [managed care organization]. I have worked with Dr. Excellent for the past [number of years] and have found his performance to be exceptional. He presently is seeing a number of the plan's members, and I know that they are very satisfied with his services. He is a member in good standing with [hospital] and the local and state medical societies.

Dr. Excellent has been instrumental in organizing the physicians in his specialty into an independent physician association. He understands the concepts of managed care, guidelines, and cost-effectiveness.

I believe he will make a fine addition to our panel of providers and I recommend him highly.

Sincerely,
[name of physician]

Exhibit 37–8 Annual Letter to the Medical Director of a Managed Care Plan

Dear [medical director],

As a member of your managed care plan, I would like to tell you about the activities in my practice that have taken place this past year.

I have received 75 hours of continuing medical education. This includes attendance at the American Urologic Association's annual meeting, a seminar in urodynamics, and a postgraduate course that describes a new technique for the treatment of urinary incontinence that will significantly reduce patient discomfort, length of stay, and costs.

I have had five articles in peer-reviewed journals published in the past 18 months. I am including copies for your review.

My practice conducted a patient survey (a copy of the survey is enclosed). This survey demonstrates that 94 percent of patients have found the services provided to be satisfactory and would recommend my practice to others.

I have compared my practice to other practices in our community, and I am including data on the length of stay, complication rate, readmission rate, and hospital costs for the 10 most common urologic procedures that I do in the hospital.

We have conducted a time and motion study on the time patients spend in my practice. We have demonstrated that the majority of patients spend less than 20 minutes in the reception room. Nearly all established patients are seen, processed, and discharged within 40 minutes of their arrival in the office. This means that plan members can be seen in a timely fashion and return promptly to their jobs.

My practice offers early morning hours two days a week and weekend hours once a month. This enables plan members to receive urologic care without losing work time.

My practice has a computerized callback system that notifies patients when they need to call for their next appointment. Consequently patients are contacted months later and reminded when they need to return for their follow-up care.

Our practice is a believer in wellness and prophylactic urologic care. We encourage all men over 50 years of age (or 40 if they have a family history of prostate cancer or are African American) to have an annual digital rectal exam and a prostate-specific antigen test.

All men are given a testicular self-examination card (enclosed) for their shower or closet. This card serves as a reminder for all men to examine their testes on a monthly basis to detect early testis cancer.

I am including a copy of my practice analysis. This handout reviews the above information in greater detail and includes a recent survey of my patients.

continues

Exhibit 37–8 continued

> I know this is an interesting time for all of us in health care. It is my goal to make patients' experiences with my practice positive ones. I hope that my practice can continue to provide that level of service to your plan members.
>
> Sincerely,
> Neil Baum, M.D.

Trying to get on a closed panel is a situation where strong-arm tactics seldom work. However, polite persistence, along with lots of information, testimonials, and letters, will pay off in the long run.

STAYING ON A PANEL

Getting on a panel is only half the challenge in modern health care. The second half is staying on the panel. You have to continually provide objective evidence that you meet the standards of the plan.

I suggest that you provide annual satisfaction surveys of patients, particularly members of the plan and referring physicians. You will want to accumulate outcomes data, and for this you will need a managed care software program. *The goal is to gather and analyze data in a way that allows you to compare the quality of your practice to that of others in your community and throughout the nation.*

Look at your inpatient and outpatient services. Identify your cost per diagnosis-related group (DRG) and submit your average length of stay for each DRG. For your office-based services, provide the charges for the most common diagnoses, the frequency of office encounters for each diagnosis, and the average charge for each office encounter by diagnosis. If you can identify complications, readmissions for each diagnosis, and the results of your clinical decisions, you will have information to give that is very useful—especially if the outcomes are favorable.

I suggest that you write a letter to the plan administrator once a year describing what has taken place in your practice. (Exhibit 37–8 is a sample letter of this type.) Let the administrator know of any continuing education courses taken, any awards received, and any articles published during the past year and what your plans are for the future.

The Bottom Line *The best way to get results from managed care applications is to do your homework and demonstrate to the managed care plan that your practice is well-run, cost-effective, and user-friendly. Enlisting the support of* *some of your loyal patients can also help to convince plan administrators that they would like to send their members to you as well. Finally, if you tune into the plan's station, WIIFM (What's in It for Me?), you will see things from their point of view.*

NOTE

1. *California Relative Value Studies* (San Francisco: California Medical Association, 1974).

CHAPTER 38

Deselection: A Game of Musical Chairs

With so many doctors chasing a limited number of health maintenance organization (HMO) contracts, it is statistically impossible for them all to be selected for inclusion. Managed care contracting is similar to a game of musical chairs in which fewer than two-thirds of all specialists will locate a chair when the bargaining music stops.

And finding a chair is only the start; retaining it is just as important and requires a different set of skills. People working in other industries have become familiar with this "musical chair" game, under the name of downsizing or right-sizing. Doctors contracting with HMOs have come to know this as "deselection" or "delisting." By any name, the result is the same, and if the contract is large, the impact can be devastating.

WHERE ARE YOU IN THE NETWORK CHAIN?

Both economic and quality of care issues are and will continue to be important in securing HMO contracts. HMOs are in competition with each other and a key feature in marketing their physician networks to big business purchasers is being able to assure them that the network not only contains a sufficient number of doctors to "service" their members, but that these doctors will be geographically dispersed and accessible. For this reason, HMOs tend to select more physicians than might be necessary during the initial building phase of a network. Later, when the HMO has accumulated enough statistical data to enable the organization to evaluate the cost and quality of each participating physician, the "extra" doctors are eliminated. These are the physicians who score poorly on patient satisfaction surveys or who continuously order unnecessary tests or whose patients have extensive length of stays in the hospital. HMOs justify this deselection process by maintaining that if it is conducted appropriately, they will achieve a network of higher quality, cost-effective physicians who make that extra effort to satisfy their patients. Ultimately, these physicians are more valuable to the HMO, and they will reap the rewards of their efforts.

TAKE A PROACTIVE APPROACH

Deselection is one of many risks inherent in an HMO contract. Legal experts advise that it is better to take proactive steps to avoid deselection than to seek legal remedies to fight it after the fact. According to Jon Hultman, author of *Reengineering the Medical Practice*, intentional planning by physicians can make the difference between survival and flourishing as the managed care era evolves.

In order to take a proactive approach, it is essential that you understand the criteria HMOs are using to make deselection choices. An HMO attempts to use objective criteria in developing a profile for each physician in its network. This profiling allows the HMO to determine whether a doctor should be retained, rewarded, "re-educated," or released. While there may be variation among HMOs as to which criteria are measured and the relative weight given to each, physicians can expect that their performances will be evaluated by HMOs using objective, measurable standards.

DO NOT DISCOUNT QUALITY OF CARE

Successful business people know that a business exists for two reasons: to meet customers' needs and to make a profit. If it fails at either, it will cease to exist. Some physicians mistakenly believe that "economic profiles" are the only criteria scrutinized by HMOs. While economics are critical, patient satisfaction and quality of care are equally important. Farsighted HMOs understand that prices will all eventually reach parity or the same low level. At that point, price will no longer provide a competitive advantage, and competition will focus on quality. Given that HMOs already attract an adequate supply of well-credentialed doctors, the competition in quality comes to mean "quality of service." With this in mind, it is fair to expect that HMOs preparing for the future will not only be measuring those criteria that help control costs, but also those that encourage patient satisfaction. This will be essential for marketing their product to payers.

WHAT DRIVES PATIENT SATISFACTION?

Quality of medical care is essential, but with a plentiful supply of well-qualified specialists, HMOs have little problem recruiting the best. Quality of care is simply the price of entrance into this game of musical chairs. In reality, few complaints are received involving poor quality of medical care. Instead, most complaints focus on "time problems" that range from "too much time waiting" to the doctor spending too little time with the patient. Time problems lead to patient complaints, and 90 percent of all HMOs claim to use patient complaint information in their recredentialing process. If patient complaint information can result in deselection, then striving to increase patient satisfaction is a critical proactive step that you can take to avoid deselection. Following the actions outlined in the first chapter of this book, "Giving Your Practice a Checkup," which includes how to conduct an effective patient satisfaction survey and Chapter 3, "Don't Be Late for a Very Important Date," will go a long way toward ensuring that you know what will be on your "report card."

PHYSICIAN PROFILING

Paul Bluestein, M.D., the chief medical officer at ConnectiCare Inc., spoke on the topic of profiling at *Podiatry Today*'s "Survival Seminar" held in late 1995. The lecture was reprinted in the February 1996 issue of *Podiatry Today* and is notable for the "insider information" provided that can be invaluable as you strive to position your practice favorably in the HMO market. When profiling physicians, says Bluestein, ConnectiCare gives equal weight to quality of care (the science of medicine), patient satisfaction (the art of medicine), and resource management (the business of medicine). Each of those elements is worth 25 percent on its rating scales. The remaining 25 percent is split between patient access (15 percent) and physician participation in educational programs (10 percent). I view patient access as linked to patient satisfaction. So, if you add patient satisfaction and patient access measures, that means that patient satisfaction actually attains a weight of 40 percent!

While most patient complaints come to HMOs unsolicited, ConnectiCare actively solicits patients' comments by sending out surveys within two months following patients' visits to physicians. Each doctor receives an annual summary of these survey results, which include all practices in the network. This information could be used either to help physicians improve their performance or to eliminate them from the network.

In addition to patient surveys, some HMOs use computers to assist them in physician profiling. Protocare markets a software program that evaluates claims data to produce comparative profiles of physicians in the areas of quality and cost-effective care.[1] This method removes subjectivity and emotionalism from profiling and appears to place more weight on economics. Again, HMOs may apply different relative weights to categories, depending upon their short- and long-term goals.

Regardless of how much weight an HMO applies to each profiling category, all categories are important. It is in both your interest and that of the HMO to control costs and achieve a high level of patient satisfaction.

HOW PATIENTS PERCEIVE VALUE

Patients who resist being switched by their companies from indemnity insurance plans to managed care plans often perceive that managed care plan patients are treated like cattle—kept waiting in holding pens and then herded quickly through the system. Unfortunately, providing low-cost care to an increasingly large number of patients can make even a "good" doctor look "bad."

There is a maxim in business that, in the mind of the buyer, price goes from highest to lowest priority the instant a product is purchased. When a customer purchases a discounted product, however, he or she expects it to perform as well as a more expensive model. For contracting purposes, this statement can be reworded to read, "In the mind of the buyer, price goes from highest to lowest priority the instant the contract is signed."

The amount you are paid under contract is irrelevant to your patients—that is a matter between you and the HMO. Some companies intentionally bid low in order to "buy" market share, but this strategy often backfires if they do not deliver the services promised under the contract.

I recommend that physicians who have underbid their services in order to gain a contract provide the services agreed to under that contract. After all, it is their reputation, not the HMO's, that is on the line. They can renegotiate the contract once they have data to back up their request. This means that you should continually survey your patients about their care and treatment at your practice. That way, there will be no surprises when the HMO also decides to survey your patients. If, however, a significant number of patient complaints accumulate, the doctor will have nothing to negotiate. If this happens, it is likely that the doctor will be deselected and subsequently replaced by another. The new doctor is usually paid at a higher rate based on the data collected from the previous doctor's experience by the HMO.

Make sure you know the criteria by which the HMO plans to evaluate your performance, and the relative weight assigned to each element of care. Remember, after this chaotic and highly competitive phase of HMO growth subsides, those physicians still sitting in the chair when the music stops will find that that chair will increase in value. To proactively prepare for this time, marketing strategies, useful for gaining managed care contracts, must be augmented by operational skills upgrades, such as efficiency and reengineering techniques, to achieve both profitability and patient satisfaction. This strategy will meet any deselection criteria, regardless of how an HMO weights any one factor.

Proactive practices are going to prevent deselection by improving outcomes and decreasing costs for management of chronic illnesses, such as hypertension, diabetes, and heart disease, by facilitating improved patient self-care and medication compliance programs. The proactive practice is also one that implements quality-improvement techniques that identify organizational processes contributing to poor quality and needless use of resources. Finally, the proactive practice makes every effort to eliminate those who do not improve the quality of care that they offer their patients.

The Bottom Line   *Ironically, the "waiting time" problems so intolerable to patients are a symptom of the same inefficiencies that lead to higher costs and lower profits. A physician who focuses on meeting patients' needs will simultaneously avoid the economic problems that lead to deselection.*

NOTE

1. Protocare can be reached at 2400 Broadway, Suite 100, Santa Monica, CA 90404–3077; (310) 315–7400; *www.protocare.com.*

CHAPTER 39

How To Be a Darling of the Managed Care Plans

Because health care costs have been increasing, employers and other purchasers have been searching for ways to cut costs and ensure they receive good value for the money they spend. Major employers have been leaders in the movement to increase the amount of information available on health care.

What does this mean for physicians? We can expect that managed care plans will be interested in gathering all sorts of data on the way we practice. They will use the data to determine which physicians they want to have practicing on their panels. The reason for this is clear: major employers will be using similar data to determine which plans they want serving their employees.

At a recent quarterly staff meeting at my hospital, the medical director, Dr. Stephen Newman, made a presentation on current trends affecting physicians and hospitals. He emphasized the new and increasing emphasis on measuring quality, outcomes, and cost-effectiveness. Like almost all physicians, I believe that I practice high-quality medicine and achieve excellent outcomes, but I could not imagine how quality and outcomes could possibly be quantitated. I made an appointment with the hospital's quality assurance director, Fay Hernandez, and asked to see my profile. I learned very quickly that physician profiling and health plan report cards will play an essential role in the future marketing of health care.

This chapter describes how hospitals, payers, and even patients will use report card information in making their health care decisions. It also looks briefly at some facets of the current emphasis on report cards and member satisfaction surveys. Finally, it presents practical ideas that you can use to make your profile attractive to your patients, your hospitals, and payers.

HAVE YOU LOOKED AT YOUR PROFILE LATELY?

Historically, medical marketing depended on providing excellent health care in a user-friendly fashion. Today, with health care costs rising faster than inflation

346

and millions of Americans lacking access to medical care, cost and quality will be the most significant factors in obtaining and maintaining patients. In the past, it was considered difficult or impossible to measure quality and outcomes. Today, with the assistance of computers and database analysis, measuring outcomes and objectively comparing one physician to another has become a reality. There are still many difficulties in collecting the relevant information, but the pressure to cut costs while maintaining or improving quality is so great that we can expect to see health care data collection increase in the near future.

How is the information obtained and used? To take just one example, the Medi-Qual National Database contains information on 16 million cases from 524 hospitals collected over the past eight years. Each patient you admit to a hospital can be graded or compared according to the admitting diagnosis and the severity of the patient's condition at the time of diagnosis based on objective criteria, such as vital signs and laboratory and X-ray studies. The information is fed into a computer that assigns your patient an admission or numerical severity grade. The progress or the deterioration of the patient will be tracked until the patient is discharged, and your results will be entered into the national database. The outcomes you achieved will then be compared with those achieved by your peers, not only in your community but also nationwide.

For example, suppose I admit a patient who is septic with an obstructing ureteral calculus. The patient has several comorbid conditions, including uncontrolled diabetes and labile hypertension. The patient will be assigned an admission severity grade. How I manage the patient, including the length of stay and total charges, will be compared with how other physicians locally and nationally have managed patients with a similar diagnosis and similar comorbid conditions. Can you imagine the impact on my ability to attract patients and managed care contracts if my outcomes are consistently less favorable than those of my colleagues and if my charges are significantly higher? In those circumstances I will not be very attractive to hospitals or managed care plans and most likely will not be accepted on their provider panels.

As a result of the new methods of gathering and analyzing data on physicians' practice patterns, managed care plans can now make sound objective decisions on behalf of their members. This will almost certainly be the trend of the future and will determine how we receive patients. Physicians who are sensitive to cost and quality will be the ones who have successful practices.

A STANDARD FORMAT FOR HEALTH CARE DATA

During the early 1990s a few health plans began to collect and release information on quality. One problem soon became obvious: in order to make valid comparisons of different plans, everyone needed to use the same definitions and the same measurement criteria. For example, is a plan's mammography rate calculated using statistics for women aged 52 to 64 who have been continuously enrolled during the preceding two years or for just one year? Or does the calculation use some slightly different age range? In order to compare plans, everyone has to agree on the same yardstick. Apples must be compared with apples.

A working group that included representatives of health plans, major employers, and technical experts began meeting under the auspices of the National Committee for Quality Assurance (NCQA), a Washington, D.C.–based accrediting organization for HMOs that has become the leading agency responsible for the accreditation of health plans. The group analyzed which measures were most important and could be gathered relatively easily. In November 1993 they released a standardized data set, including precise definitions, known as the Health Employer Data and Information Set (HEDIS) 2.0. This early version was originally intended as a tool for employers to measure the value of the health care coverage they were purchasing. HEDIS 3.0 includes measurements in four categories: quality of care, member access and satisfaction, membership and utilization, and finance.

Member satisfaction is measured using phone and mail surveys. Access measures include the speed with which the phone is answered and the number of primary care physicians accepting new patients. Membership and utilization measures include enrollment data, inpatient utilization rates, length of stay for well and complex newborns, and readmission rates for chemical dependency and mental illness. Financial performance measures include liquidity, compliance with statutory requirements, and trends in premiums paid by the employer or the employees.

The measures that have generated the greatest interest are the nine quality measures:

Preventive services
1. Childhood immunization
2. Cholesterol screening
3. Mammography
4. Cervical cancer screening

Prenatal care
5. Low birth weight infants
6. Care in first trimester of pregnancy

Acute and chronic illness
7. Asthma inpatient admission rate
8. Diabetics receiving retinal exam

Mental health
9. Ambulatory follow-up after hospitalization for major affective disorders

These nine quality measures indicate how HEDIS will affect practicing physicians. If plans are collecting data on the number of patients who have been screened for high cholesterol levels, the percentage of two-year-olds who have received all their immunizations, or the percentage of women who have received Pap smears and mammograms, then physicians will need to move to a new level of accuracy in reporting data of this sort.

In fact, HEDIS posed a challenge for many health plans. As they began to collect the data, they often found their current information system, while perfectly adequate for internal needs, was not able to collect all the HEDIS data easily. Despite the difficulties, today more than 300 health plans are reporting data using HEDIS, and a substantial and increasing number of purchasers require HEDIS information from all plans they offer to employees. It seems likely that as health care organizations improve their computerized information systems, the amount and quality of data they collect will increase.

MATCH YOUR HEDIS PROFILE TO EMPLOYERS' EXPECTATIONS

HEDIS 3.0 is not perfect. It was produced under severe time constraints, and the people most closely associated with its development seem to think of it as a first step in what will be a years-long process of developing accurate measures of health plan quality. Many of the quality measures in HEDIS 3.0 are straightforward measures of preventive care. It does incorporate two well-known enrollee satisfaction surveys, but plans are simply asked to report members' overall levels of satisfaction. The newer versions will include quality measures related to major chronic and acute illnesses and a version designed specifically for Medicaid beneficiaries.

Meanwhile, employer coalitions in major cities are using HEDIS data, NCQA accreditation status, and consumer satisfaction surveys to evaluate health plans. They are even conducting their own surveys to find out how their employees feel about the health care they receive. *If employers are starting to measure your quality and your patients' satisfaction, you can be proactive by beginning to do the same by improving your profile.*

I asked Fay Hernandez, the quality assurance director at Touro Infirmary in New Orleans, for her advice about what I could do to improve my profile.

These were her suggestions:

1. *Find out how you compare with your colleagues.* Look at length of stay and average charges for each diagnosis-related group (DRG). This information should be available from the hospital quality assurance department. Your data will be compared with those of your colleagues but with their names omitted. Similarly, if a colleague asks to see data, he or she will not know which data come from you or any other specific physician.

If you find that your costs are higher than your colleagues or your average length of stay is longer in a particular DRG, then it is time to reexamine the methods and approach you use in that DRG. For example, a cardiac surgeon looked at his profile and found his patients had a higher-than-average length of stay. By extubating his coronary artery bypass patients sooner than the routine 36 hours that they were on the ventilator, he shortened his length of stay and decreased costs by $10,000 per case.

When Hernandez reviewed my profile, she noted that I always typed and cross-matched my patients who were to have a transurethral resection of the prostate gland. She observed that I rarely gave these patients blood but incurred several hundred dollars of unnecessary expenses. She suggested that I use autotransfusions or else type and hold the blood, which would be considerably less expensive than typing and cross-matching, which is what I was doing.

She also reviewed the prophylactic antibiotics that I used prior to penile prosthesis surgery. I used an expensive aminoglycoside that costs $150 per dose. She suggested an oral medication that the patient could take with a sip of water just before surgery (at a cost of $2 a pill). By looking at your charges carefully, you will almost certainly find hundreds and maybe even thousands of dollars of savings for your patients and their insurance companies.

If your hospital is not collecting physician profile data or they will not share them with you, then you may want to question your affiliation with the hospital. The "economic profile" that is being developed on you and me will be vital to our future. Many of the empowerment-model managed care organizations share this sort of data routinely with their physicians, often on a quarterly basis. Sometimes the average physician receives a brief summary whereas those near the bottom, the lowest 10 to 20 percent, receive more detailed information. In any case, this sort of information is essential for physicians to understand their own practice patterns and be able to search for the most effective and efficient methods of caring for patients. If you take a look at this information with an open mind, then your practice patterns are likely to improve.

2. *Look at physician profile data in an analytical, questioning way.* Ask yourself and others what you can do to improve your profile. Your goal is to improve quality and decrease cost. It is not in your best interest to be defensive and argumentative. If your profile is substandard, consider what you can do to make the next profile more attractive. Remember, yesterday is a canceled check but tomorrow is a promissory note. Do not try to deny past performance data; use them to improve your performance in the coming quarter.

3. *Compare your average length of stay with those of your colleagues and try to identify ways to shorten it.* The reason is that it will certainly reflect total charges and possibly quality of care. One way to shorten your average length of stay is to use same-day surgery whenever possible. Also, prepare your patients

ahead of time by offering preadmission education. It has been my observation that an educated patient does better clinically and goes home sooner. If a patient has a special need for support after the operation, discuss this with social services as soon as possible.

For example, I do same-day surgery for the insertion of the penile prosthesis. During my preoperative discussion with the patient, I explain that he can go home as soon as he is taking fluids and has urinated. A urologic colleague, Dr. Jim Gottesman, from Seattle, does radical prostatectomies and has reduced his length of stay from five to seven days to two to three days. He attributes this significant reduction to his providing educational material describing the hospital and the postoperative course to patients before they are admitted to the hospital. Now the patients are programmed for a short hospital stay even before they enter the hospital.

4. *If you are a primary care physician, look at your consulting habits.* Use only those consultants you and your patient really need. Remember, the more consultants you involve in the care of your patient, the greater the number of tests and the greater the expense. Using consultants will impact your profile as a primary care physician, not their profiles as specialists.

One way to use consultants in a cost-efficient manner is to ask them to call you and discuss their findings before they order tests or schedule procedures. You should decide together what is really needed and indicated. The days of the megaworkup are over. You are the captain of the patient's health care ship and know the patient's requirements best.

For example, when I request a consultation from another physician, I provide him or her with a form that introduces my patient, provides pertinent background information, and indicates the necessary follow-up (see Exhibit 13–10 in Chapter 13, "Leave a Paper Trail"). I merely fill in the blanks and mark the response that I expect from the consultant. After all, I cannot expect consultants to be mind readers and know what action I am requesting. Unnecessary tests and procedures and duplication of tests can be avoided by the use of such a form.

5. *Probably the first place you should look to reduce costs is the prescription of medications, particularly antibiotics.* The latest-generation antibiotics are almost always the most expensive but do not always have special advantages that make them worth the cost. Reducing the prescribing of unnecessarily sophisticated antibiotics is a quick and easy way to cut costs. No one wants physicians to sacrifice quality when prescribing antibiotics. The goal is to select the right drug, prescribe the right dose, and set an appropriate administration schedule.

You must check cultures and sensitivities. Then try to select the least expensive drug that provides the highest blood level and the one that is the most specific for the organ system(s) involved. Inquire about drug costs. If cost information is not available, ask the hospital pharmacy to provide it for you. You can be sure that the payers will soon be collecting prescription data on physicians. You can make your profile attractive by demonstrating that you are cost-sensitive in your prescribing habits. Remember, generic ibuprofen is probably as effective as a third-generation nonsteroidal anti-inflammatory drug and is only a fraction of the cost. And if you really want to demonstrate your cost sensitivity, you will recommend that the patient take aspirin first.

6. *Do not order tests and procedures that are unnecessary for the diagnosis or treatment of your patients.* Whenever possible, complete workups on an outpatient basis.

7. *Talk with peers about cost-saving techniques and quality issues.* Perhaps this type of discussion will be more productive than complaining about politicians, Washington, and health care reform. (One way of pursuing joint discussion of cost and quality issues is to participate as a member of hospital quality assurance and utilization review committees, something that Hernandez suggested I do.)

As physicians, we must recognize that costs do matter. Finding the best possible way to continue to provide high-quality care while taking costs into account is our responsibility. Smokey the Bear says, "Only you can prevent forest fires"; similarly, only you can decrease the spiraling cost of American health care.

Although few of us are ready to calculate HEDIS scores and construct report cards, all of us need to understand that managed care plans will be looking for objective evidence to evaluate our practices. How soon use of evaluative data becomes standard will vary in different parts of the country, but in the next few years all physicians will have to find a method or a system to report back to the plans what they need to know in a form that allows them to compare medical practices.

There is probably very little that any single physician can do to impact decisions made in Congress. But each physician has substantial control over his or her physician profile. The current trend is toward demanding demonstration of superior outcomes and cost-effectiveness. Those who fail to recognize this trend will see not only a reduced number of patients but also an erosion of their income.

The Bottom Line   *If you want to make your practice attractive to managed care plans, you will have to be proactive and check out your profile. If you do not, you may soon find someone asking, "Mirror, mirror on the wall, who has the fairest profile of them all?"*

CHAPTER 40

Make the Hospital Your Marketing Ally, Not Your Adversary

Too often in today's medical climate, physicians are placed in an adversarial relationship with their hospitals. Because of government-mandated diagnosis-related groups (DRGs) and pressure from third-party payers, many hospitals are motivated to decrease lengths of stay, move patients from expensive intensive care units (ICUs) and cardiac care units (CCUs) to skilled nursing facilities (SNFs), and even regulate which drugs physicians can prescribe for their patients. As guardians of their patients' well-being, physicians become the advocates for patients who may be too sick to leave an acute care facility. This is just one of the many examples where physicians might not see eye to eye with their hospitals. Only the physician knows how sick his or her patient is. The physician is in the best position to determine the safety of discharging a patient from an ICU to another unit in the hospital or to that person's home with a visiting nurse or home health care order.

Yet these situations need not turn into adversarial ones for doctors and hospitals. For example, I have consciously worked to remain a loyal referring doctor of my two hospitals, Touro Infirmary and Memorial Medical Center-Baptist Campus, both in New Orleans. In turn, both hospitals have assisted me in the marketing of my practice.

As part of your external marketing efforts, you might want to list yourself with your hospital's speakers bureau. However, be aware that getting referrals from the hospital for speaking engagements is sometimes problematic. I remember getting a call from my hospital's speakers bureau informing me that a senior citizens' organization had requested a speaker. I eagerly went with my wife and a carousel of slides to talk about impotence. As I was setting up the projector in the room, all the members of the audience started arriving in wheelchairs—most of them with nasal oxygen. This audience needed air, not sexual intimacy! I realized that my game plan had to be changed—and fast. Since I dabble in magic, I asked for some newspapers and a deck of cards. I did some paper magic and a few card tricks, then took my slide projector and disappeared.

There were no senior citizens calling my office for an appointment the next day. However, the director of the center sent her child for bed-wetting and two nurses came as patients.

Lessons learned:

1. Marketing is not always easy.
2. You must be flexible and willing to shift gears.
3. If you are given a lemon, squeeze it and make lemonade.

It is important not to have unreasonable expectations about marketing. Just because you give a presentation to a group of lay people does not guarantee that the phone will start ringing and dozens of patients will be calling for appointments to see you. This kind of marketing takes time and the gratification is often deferred. Many factors are at work here. It is not uncommon for someone who hears one of your presentations to wait 6 to 12 months before making the call to come in for an appointment. Have patience and you will have patients!

SHARED INTERESTS

Hospitals today consider physicians their number-one customers. They really are rooting for us and want us to succeed. They know full well that if we have more patients, so will they, and everyone's bottom line will get longer. You must be careful not to abuse your hospital's services. Make sure you are giving services in return.

Keeping our mutual interests in mind, I have used my hospital's services to increase my business, which in turn creates more business for them. Following are a few examples:

1. *My goal in the case of referral letters is to see that the letters arrive before the patients do.* To help achieve this goal, I often use the "lazy person's referral letter," which reduces the typical two- to three-page referral report to a one-page summary (see Chapter 35). In addition, I often ask the hospital courier to deliver a referral letter to the referring physician's office. Not only does this reduce the cost of postage, but the letter is also on the referring physician's desk within 24 hours after I see the patient.
2. *Most hospitals have in-house printing capabilities.* I have asked my hospitals to do the printing for my office at its cost. I have asked the art department at my hospitals to help with the design of my business cards and stationery, and the printing department to print the job. Your hospital might be able to duplicate your office forms, preprinted hospital orders, patient

handouts, and so on. Be realistic in making printing requests. Do not expect a five-color brochure gratis, for example.

3. *Hospitals have collected thousands of computerized files on their patients.* This information can be helpful in tracking your own patients. You may be able to obtain a free computer profile of potential patients. For example, if you conduct a support group for urinary incontinence, you can ask the hospital for names of gynecologic patients over 40 years old. As long as you invite your urologic and gynecologic colleagues to participate in the support group, there should be no problem about getting the list of names.

4. *Ask your hospital to be sure that patients are informed of your services.* For example, my hospital has a diabetic unit. The urologist and ophthalmologist have asked the diabetic unit to provide information on impotence and retinal diseases to all the patients that attend the diabetes teaching classes. These physicians furnish the diabetic unit with their own brochures and handouts for distribution. The labor and delivery units might be encouraged to furnish a list of all the pediatricians on staff at the hospital. If the hospital has a sleep lab, those staff can work with otolaryngologists who perform somnoplasty for sleep apnea.

5. *I asked my hospital's personnel and administration office to interview a secretary for my practice.* I provided the staff with a description of the job, the salary, and the benefits. They reviewed the resumes and interviewed five candidates. They then gave me a list of the three best candidates. I interviewed the candidates and then ranked them and asked the hospital interviewers to do the same. I compared the lists and selected the secretary.

6. *You will be amazed at how hospitals are willing to cooperate with you if your patient does not have insurance and is willing to pay cash for a procedure.* I have arranged a bundled fee for patients who request a penile implant and do not have insurance coverage. The hospital has reduced the fee for the implant, the operating room, the lab, the anesthesia, and the medications if the patient pays the entire fee up front in cash. I usually arrange to do such cases on Saturdays, which reduces the cost of hospitalization to the patients. After all, I am using the hospital when it would not normally be used (or staff must be available whether there are cases scheduled or not), and I am filling beds during slack time.

   In these situations, I have also reduced my fees—the only fair thing to do when asking the hospital and other departments to decrease their fees. When I assured the hospital's chief financial officer that I was reducing my fees for these patients, the hospital and involved departments agreed to reduce their fees by an equal amount.

7. *The hospital marketing and public relations departments are very helpful in getting placement in the electronic and print media.* One suggestion is

to make sure you ask the media to mention your hospital—after all, that is how you got there!

The above is just a partial list of examples showing the good relationship I have with my hospital.

The following is a wish list of possibilities that could make the relationship even better. I have suggested some of the ideas to my hospital. Perhaps you can find some ideas of your own.

- *Hospitals need to have a temporary pool of employees that their physicians could hire on an emergency or urgency basis.* These would include employees from the medical records department or the business office who are trained to answer the phone, make appointments, and schedule surgeries. The physicians would be expected to pay their daily salaries.
- *Hospitals could provide accommodations for families of patients, especially those who come a long distance for their medical care.* Sequoia Valley Hospital, in Redwood City, California, is already doing this. If a hospital does not have the room, it could offer to locate hotel accommodations in the area. The accommodations might be gotten at a discount if the hospital established a referral agreement with certain hotels. The hospital could also arrange transportation from the airport for patients arriving by plane.
- *Hospitals could streamline their admissions procedures.* Their computers can be linked electronically to admitting doctors' offices, and admissions could be handled by modem.
- *Hospitals could help physicians by identifying trends, such as the spread of certain infections, increases in certain types of lawsuits, and so on.* When such trends were identified, the hospitals could then help physicians tactfully by reviewing recordkeeping, documentation, or even surgical technique. (Notice, I say "tactfully.") For example, if a hospital's physician referral service tries to schedule patients for diagnostic tests or procedures and hears repeatedly that the doctor is booked up for two or three weeks, this indicates that the doctor needs an associate or is not running an efficient office.
- *Hospitals could assist physicians by reviewing the physicians' inactive files.* The hospitals could then either create systems for contacting old patients who need checkups or help the physicians' staff perform the same function. This was done at a local ob-gyn practice when one of the physicians with a large patient base retired. To avoid losing his patients from the practice, the hospital collected the charts and contacted the patients by letter or phone and told them about the new associate. As a result, more of the patients remained in the practice than would have been expected.

- *Hospitals could arrange* locum tenums *(substitute physicians) so that their physicians could take vacations without undergoing some of the normal difficulties (including loss of practice income).*
- *Hospitals could offer to buy retiring physicians' practices, locate new associates for the retiring physicians, and thus maintain the patients within their sphere of medical referrals.*
- *Since most hospitals have publications that are sent regularly to patients, board members, and business people in the community, the editors could be encouraged to write articles about the hospital's physicians and their practices.* The physicians could also offer to write articles for the publication.

The Bottom Line   *In this era of regulation and managed care, differing agendas between doctors and hospitals may be the prevailing reality. But if you look for opportunities where your interests intersect with those of the hospital, you can transform an adversarial relationship into a mutually advantageous one.*

CHAPTER 41

Big Can Be Better: Marketing for Large Groups and Multispecialty Group Practices

Are you a physician associated with a large multispecialty group practice? Perhaps you feel that medical marketing is not a necessary part of your agenda. If so, you are not unique. But watch out. There could be danger in a complacent attitude. In this age of competition for the public's health care dollar, even a large group practice is not enough to protect you from the effects of changes in the marketplace.

Dr. Jay P. Goldsmith, chairperson of the Department of Pediatrics at Ochsner Clinic Foundation in New Orleans and professor of pediatrics at Tulane Medical School, notes that many physicians who are members of a multispecialty group practice tend not to realize the necessity of participating in marketing on behalf of the entire practice. Goldstein believes that physicians can be lulled into complacency, as they are protected by the umbrella of the reputation and size of the multispecialty group practice. They may believe that the few superstars of the multispeciality group practice will attract most of the patients and that they can enjoy the spin-offs from the business generated by the superstars. They may also believe that it is the responsibility of the administration and the public relations department to take care of the marketing for the institution.

Dr. Goldsmith strongly objects to that blasé attitude. In interviews with Dr. Goldsmith and other physicians and marketing staff at clinics and academic institutions, I found that marketing is considered an important part of running a group practice. In this chapter, I present some of their ideas for effective marketing to area communities and referring physicians.

Dr. Goldsmith believes it is the responsibility of every department in the multispecialty group practice to have a marketing plan, a marketing budget, and a tracking system to monitor the results of marketing efforts. Furthermore, he believes every department and every physician must identify a niche and develop a level of expertise to attract new patients to the institution. (The only exceptions to this rule, according to Dr. Goldsmith, are physicians in the service departments, such as pathology, radiology, and anesthesia.)

Dr. Goldsmith believes that large multispecialty group practices are not self-sustaining. Once the system is set in motion, he says, it is not in perpetual motion. So what can the individual physician in a multispecialty group practice do that will increase the number of new patients and maintain the loyalty of the patients already within the system?

HOW TO HELP YOUR GROUP

The marketing methods will differ from those used by solo and small-group practitioners, but the principle is still the same: Let others know what you do, then make it easy for them to use your services.

Large multispecialty group practices recognize that large bureaucracies tend not to be user-friendly. Many have established satellite primary care facilities to allow patients who have minor problems or who require follow-up visits to have access to quality health care without the inconvenience of making their way through the bureaucratic maze.

Large multispecialty group practices frequently discourage referrals from physicians within the local community. Local primary care doctors fear losing their patients to the large institution and will not refer patients to local multispecialty groups that do primary care. Multispecialty groups that provide primary care will frequently obtain referrals from 25 to 50 miles away or farther because primary care doctors in rural or smaller communities know that their patients will return to their community for their primary health care. Therefore, multispecialty group practices that provide primary care should be sensitive to the local conditions. They should concentrate their marketing efforts on outlying areas. Large multispecialty groups sometimes make a conscious decision not to enter the primary care market. This strategy encourages local referrals, because the group practices are not then a direct threat to local primary care physicians.

THE IMPORTANCE OF NETWORKING

In trying to increase physician referrals, the multispecialty group practice faces problems similar to those of other kinds of practices. The solutions may be slightly different, though. Dr. Goldsmith has observed that referrals follow education. He recommends that the specialists and subspecialists regularly lecture, eat lunch, and work in referring doctors' hospitals and offices. He believes that continuing medical education talks given by the multispecialty group practice physicians provide an opportunity for them to "break bread" with the referring physicians in the outlying communities.

A large group practice might want to consider sending emissaries out into the surrounding community. As chairperson of the Department of Pediatrics, Dr. Goldsmith sends subspecialists to the smaller communities in the vicinity of the Ochsner Clinic. For example, a pediatric cardiologist might rent office space in a pediatric group practice or at the hospital for the purpose of doing consultations once a week (or as often as the situation demands). In this way, the subspecialist can create a bond with the referring doctors and at the same time feed "the mother system."

Another means of creating a working relationship with referring physicians is to make them "associates" of the institution. The associate status provides them with free continuing education, access to publications, and parking privileges whenever they visit the institution.

The Ochsner Clinic and the Ochsner Foundation Hospital have created a physician network called PRN (Physician Referral Network). This is a 24-hour-a-day hotline that is staffed by a triage nurse. Any referring doctor can call the hotline to request a medical consultation for one of his or her patients. The nurse locates the appropriate consultant in the multispecialty group and arranges a conference call or appointment with the referring physician. The nurse will also track the patient through the system, making sure the referring physician receives a timely consultation letter. With programs like this, it is no mystery that local doctors choose to send their patients to the Ochsner Foundation Hospital for tertiary care.

The best advice Dr. Goldsmith gives to the multispecialty group practices is to "avoid double referrals, they will kill you!" You must always contact primary care doctors regarding additional referrals. Dr. Goldsmith relates a story of a gynecologist who sent a patient to the multispecialty group hematologist for an anemia workup. The hematologist concluded that the anemia was secondary to gynecologic blood loss and referred the patient to the group's gynecologist, who performed a hysterectomy without consulting the referring physician. The next time the referring gynecologist saw his patient, surgery had already been performed. This is an example of the kind of short-term thinking that can have long-term negative consequences.

PROVIDING SERVICES FOR REFERRING PHYSICIANS

Understanding the needs of physicians who practice in small communities or rural areas is the key to developing networks with these physicians and increasing referrals. Often smaller communities do not have access to subspecialists or sophisticated laboratories or imaging facilities.

Dr. Goldsmith points out that the more informed a referring doctor is about a multispecialty group practice's activities, the more likely he or she will continue to refer patients. Dr. Goldsmith has devised a system in the neonatal intensive care unit whereby once-a-week progress notes are written on no-carbon-required paper. A copy of these notes is mailed to the referring pediatrician, serving as a weekly update on the care of his or her patients. It also serves as a running advertisement for the group practice.

A group practice can use electronic communication to establish good relations with referring doctors. For example, in communities with no local pediatric cardiologist, adult cardiologists, pediatricians, and primary care doctors can fax EKGs to the pediatric cardiologist at the group practice and get quick interpretations. Dr. Goldsmith has arranged for the pediatric cardiologists in his department to install fax machines in their homes. This provides 24-hour-a-day service to the referring doctors. A similar system using express mail is used for EEGs and echocardiograms.

The pediatric cardiology group and several other specialties at the Ochsner Clinic have been instrumental in instituting a telemedicine program that has been helpful for marketing the services of their respective divisions of the hospital. Sophisticated video equipment has been placed in several hospitals located some distance from the parent hospital in New Orleans. A video camera placed in a neonatal intensive care unit in a hospital in Alexandria, Louisiana, can be used to transmit real-time clinical information on newborns in distress to pediatric specialists in New Orleans. For example, those caring for a cyanotic baby at the hospital in Alexandria (200 miles from New Orleans) can send a real-time echocardiogram to a pediatric cardiologist in New Orleans who can help manage the baby's care. If the baby needs additional care or surgery, it can be transferred to the New Orleans hospital. Dr. Goldsmith notes that use of this technology has resulted in improved care of sick babies and has connected the outlying neonatalogists to the hospital in New Orleans. Ultimately, the pediatric cardiology group has increased the number of referrals they receive from physicians outside New Orleans.

The telemedicine program has also been used with patients on oil rigs or cruise ships. Primary care physicians stationed on an oil rig or a cruise ship can connect to the Ochsner Clinic and enlist the help of cardiologists to help monitor cardiac problems. This technology also allows the transmission of EKGs and X-rays to be read by a specialist at the clinic in New Orleans and help make the decision regarding transferring the patient to the city, if it is medically necessary.

Dr. Goldsmith emphasizes that large multispecialty practices have access to expensive technology and the funding to connect peripheral areas, such as rural hospitals, offshore ships, or other remote locations without access to many specialists. Other examples of using technology to market the multispecialty practice include mobile cath labs and mobile MRIs, CAT scans, or other high-tech equipment that is not affordable for smaller outlying rural hospitals.

Wellness has been a topic that baby boomers and seniors alike have embraced. Dr. Goldsmith has utilized the concept by marketing wellness to children. He has worked with a local health club promoting wellness and positive lifestyles and habits to children. His slogan for these children is "Ochsner Kids Are OK." He creates name awareness for the clinic by promoting wellness, no smoking, and drug-free kids and associating all these positive behaviors with the Ochsner Clinic's Department of Pediatrics.

Demographics in most urban and suburban communities have demonstrated that 70 percent of families have two working parents. Therefore, the Ochsner Clinic is now offering clinic hours before 8 AM, after 5 PM, and on Saturday mornings. Dr. Goldsmith believes that having extended hours offers a competitive edge that is hard for solo and small two- or three-doctor practices to match.

Another novel marketing idea that the Ochsner Clinic has used is "Ochsner on Call," a program that offers patients the opportunity to speak with a nurse 24 hours a day, seven days a week. This is an expensive program that costs $750,000 to set up protocols and staff the program. Research has shown that the average physician spends less than five minutes on an after-hours call with a patient. However, a nurse spends almost 15 minutes with each patient. At the end of each call the nurse asks the patient, "Have I answered all your questions? Or would you like to speak to the physician?" If the answer is yes to the latter question, the nurse must put the call through to the doctor. The response from patients using Ochsner on Call is very positive. Physicians appreciate the program, as it screens out 80 percent of calls that do not warrant a physician response. Nurses can also help patients schedule appointments for the next day, since they have access to all the physicians' schedules. The nurse also documents each call and a copy is faxed to each patient's physician the next day in case follow-up is necessary.

A large group practice may organize a system that uses delivery vans or express mail to deliver blood samples from referring doctors or their hospitals to the laboratory at the group practice. This allows referring doctors to have access to a large number of laboratory tests, such as drug-level tests, with a 24-hour turnaround time.

Some large group practices are arranging computer links with their best referring doctors. If a group practice institutes this system, the referring doctors can get reports immediately and can also access the group's appointment system directly. For example, a referring physician can make an appointment with a specific physician in the group and can be provided with a printout showing the date, the time, the location within the hospital, and how to get to the hospital without going through a bureaucratic appointment system.

MARKETING A LARGE SINGLE SPECIALTY PRACTICE

Each large group practice must devise a positioning strategy that matches its own style and configuration. Dennis Bolin, an independent marketing consultant, oversees the overall marketing strategy for the Texas Back Institute, located in Plano, Texas, but known worldwide for its stellar research into the causes, treatment, and rehabilitation of back pain.

Although providers from many disciplines comprise the institute, it is really a single specialty private practice group with a research arm, explains Bolin, so that their positioning strategy is a combination of patient care and academics. The marketing strategy requires a two-pronged approach.

Even though patients travel from all over the world for treatment, including royalty from Saudi Arabia, and the surgeons are renowned for their cutting-edge technology (among the first to do on-line surgery with a live feed to a North American Spine Society meeting presentation), most of their patient cases are local or regional. According to Bolin, 90 percent of Texas Back's patients come from Texas, and a full 33 percent come from zip codes within a 10-mile radius of their main location.

This presents a challenge from a marketing point of view, says Bolin. "With managed care, how do you leverage an international reputation like that to work in the American market which is, because of managed care, becoming increasingly local, based on networks that exist?" Texas Back Institute has solved this dilemma by focusing their paid advertising on the local level, where it can be more retail-oriented, and focusing their public relations efforts on all levels: local, regional, and national. Bolin noted that the academic and leadership messages work well on a national level, using public relations tools.

One of the institute's main public relations tools is something called a "Medical Minute©," which goes out weekly to 250 media outlets. Often faxed to assignment editors at television and print outlets, these one-minute nuggets contain practical consumer-oriented information. Three recent topics included: how your back posture affects your golf swing; what to do when your back becomes sore due to long-distance driving (released during the summer months); and how much weight is appropriate for your child's backpack (sent out in early September just before school started).

It took about six months for the "Medical Minutes" to pay off, reports Bolin, for them to "sink into the consciousness" of magazine editors and others who receive them. But the institute now receives two to three media calls a month.

For reaching the local market, the Texas Back Institute also emphasizes community relations. "We do a number of different activities, some of which are practice-wide," says Bolin. "We identify specific events in the community to sponsor, one of which is renting a booth at the Plano Balloon Festival, which, next to the Albuquerque Balloon Festival, is very large." For an investment of $2,000 for a booth and some helium tanks, a few small balloons and magnets, you can get your name out to literally hundreds and often thousands of people who may become your patients. Physicians from the practice also participate by volunteering to become medical director for a local sports tournament. In return, the institute receives permission to hang banners, place a free ad in the tournament program, and present a seminar that ties together all of the marketing and public relations activities.

OTHER IDEAS

There are many promotional techniques that a local multispecialty group can use. For instance, most communities have a welcoming program (sometimes called the "Welcome Wagon") for newcomers to the area. Clinics can participate in these programs by providing newcomers with introductory visit coupons or advertising in the Welcome Wagon's printed materials. Contacting local realtors for information on new home buyers in the area is another source of referrals. Everyone needs to establish relationships with new physicians when they move. Providing an entree for new arrivals is a service to all concerned.

Another multispecialty group for which Bolin consults does community outreach by taking responsibility for the first-aid tent on local fundraisers, such as an AIDS or leukemia walkathon.

The Bottom Line   *Beware of complacent thinking when you are part of a multispecialty group practice. Build on your group's strengths and follow the dictates of smart real estate investing. Instead of "location, location, location," think "communicate, communicate, communicate."*

CHAPTER 42

Birds Do It, Bees Do It, Even Ivory Tower Doctors Do It

I do not think there are any physicians today, including those at academic institutions, who can afford to leave marketing off the list of things they have to do. Not only do academic physicians have to be available for educating students, residents, and fellows, they have the added pressure of obtaining grant money to fund their research projects. Publishing research and attending meetings to present results may add to the bottom line indirectly, but seeing patients continues to be one of the biggest income generators. Now, with the federal government tightening the research stream and with the patient base still shrinking, marketing has become a concern for academic physicians as well.

In this chapter, I feature the views of Dr. Peter Scardino, chairperson of the Department of Urology at Baylor College of Medicine in Houston, Texas. Dr. Scardino has begun a marketing campaign in conjunction with his institution and his department. As you will see, the techniques must match the circumstances to be successful. The academic physician has a particular set of parameters that must be met. And yet there are many parallels with the basic tenets of marketing for the private practice physician: keep patients happy, cultivate referring physicians, and maintain a motivated and informed staff. The external marketing opportunities are perhaps more diverse than for the private physician, and there are some exciting possibilities.

Academic physicians must be attentive to the needs of patients and referring physicians, according to Dr. Scardino. In this respect, they are no different from their counterparts in private practice. The referring physician who sends patients to a teaching hospital has the same need to be informed and involved in the care of his or her patients. Dr. Scardino notes that failure to communicate with referring physicians will dry up referrals, whether they come from the same medical center or from halfway around the world.

Several of Dr. Scardino's role models provided him with examples of prompt reporting to referring physicians:

- Dr. Oscar Salvatero, the well-known transplant surgeon at the University of California at San Francisco, religiously called all referring physicians from the operating room after dictating his operative notes.
- Dr. Elmer Belt of Los Angeles, California, prepared a whole package for each patient to deliver to the referring physician. Given to the patient upon discharge from the hospital, this package usually included a discharge summary, a pathology report, X-rays, an operative note, and a plan of management.
- Dr. Donald Skinner, chairperson of the Department of Urology at the University of Southern California in Los Angeles, includes follow-up notes to all doctors who participate in the care of a patient. These follow-up notes are sent to Dr. Skinner's former interns, residents, and fellows years after they have left the training center as a reminder of Dr. Skinner's success with managing difficult urologic cancer cases.

Dr. Scardino makes use of these and other ideas of his own as he seeks to expand outreach for Baylor College of Medicine in general and the Department of Urology in particular.

Dr. Scardino's department recently held a retreat at which the subject of marketing was given top priority. Participants agreed upon the following mission statement: "To create in the community, the region, the nation, and in Latin America, an image of urologic scholars who provide cutting-edge research, technology, and education for patients, urologists, and referring physicians." To accomplish this mission, Dr. Scardino created a marketing task force to focus on the following three areas: (1) patient education; (2) communication with alumni, local physicians, and other urologists; and (3) marketing in Latin America.

MAKING PATIENTS COMFORTABLE

Teaching hospitals are not immune to problems of patient attrition. Dr. Scardino feels that coming to a medical center is an anxiety-producing event for most patients. According to him, the efforts spent on even the slickest marketing campaign can be wasted if the patient arrives in the medical center, can't locate available parking, can't locate the building for this appointment, can't see the doctor for two hours, and can't understand the doctor's explanation of his or her medical problem.

Often the sheer size of academic medical centers causes confusion and distress among patients. It is no wonder that although many patients receive technically excellent, state-of-the-art medical care, they feel unhappy with their experience on a personal level. They will tell their friends, family members, and referring physicians about their negative impressions and will not want to return. The only way an academic medical center can keep these patients is if it is the sole provider of a particular service, such as PET scans, bone marrow transplants, or other sophisticated diagnostic testing and treatment. Otherwise, patients who have unhappy experiences will look to their own physicians or community specialists for their medical care.

The first objective is to make a patient and his or her family feel as comfortable and secure as possible. Patients referred to a large medical center are removed from their comfort zones. By making them feel at ease and cared for, you reduce their anxiety and insecurity.

I have referred patients to large medical centers throughout the United States and most patients have received superior medical treatment. But few of them have positive stories to tell about their experience with the hospital and clinic staff, or even the physician. Stellar examples are the Baylor College of Medicine; the Mayo Clinic in Rochester, Minnesota; Stanford Medical Center in Palo Alto, California; and the Fred Hutchinson Cancer Research Center in Seattle, Washington.

Teaching hospitals often treat patients who come from great distances. Dr. Scardino and his department are spearheading a plan to improve the experience of patients who come from far away. Under this plan, his department would make arrangements for a patient to stay at a hotel near the medical center. The office staff would coordinate with the referring physician's office before the patient's consultation, making sure that all X-rays and pathology reports had been received. Finally, the communication between the teaching hospital and the referring physician will be refined to expedite all future consultations.

At the University of California, Los Angeles (UCLA) Medical Center, low-cost family housing at the Tiverton House is offered so that patients traveling to UCLA for surgeries do not have to come alone. The housing coordinator always offers cheerful and prompt service to families who call. I suggest that the medical center or the department consider assigning someone to serve as concierge to make hotel arrangements for the patient and family, to provide transportation to and from the airport, offer translators if necessary, and provide the family with information on local tourist attractions for the times when they need diversion or activities for their children.

One of the best examples of patient relations comes from the M.D. Anderson Cancer Center in Houston, Texas, where the hospital has created a "buddy system" for patients and their families who are new to the medical center. The hospital assigns a volunteer to the family to assist them with any nonmedical problems. Usually, the volunteer is a previous patient or a family member of a patient and can often make the encounter with the strange, seemingly impersonal medical center a more comfortable experience.

ESTABLISHING RELATIONSHIPS WITH "OUTSIDE" PHYSICIANS

Raju Thomas, M.D., chairman of the Department of Urology at Tulane Medical School in New Orleans, concedes that marketing in academia can often be a difficult venture. He believes that academic physicians must be sensitive to community physicians, especially if they want to receive referrals from within the community. Dr. Thomas's approach is that academic centers must have a reason why others should send their patients to a university medical center. He has fostered the idea of having a specialized faculty, allowing each faculty member to develop an expertise in a certain medical area. This allows each staff member to become a local and sometimes national expert, attracting the attention of national and sometimes international patients, as is the case with Dr. Thomas' urology department. He also has an open faculty policy, allowing local and regional physicians to have access to any of the new technologies as well as the aid of residents in caring for their patients. Above all, says Dr. Thomas, academic physicians must be sensitive to the issue of patients returning to their community physicians. *There is no quicker way to dry up a referral source than to fail to return a patient to a community physician who has referred that patient to the medical center.*

Dr. Scardino's second marketing goal is to establish or maintain relationships with alumni, local physicians, and area urologists. He observes that the more he communicates with graduating residents and fellows, the more likely his department will see referrals from these physicians in the years ahead. He sends a monthly newsletter, "Uro-Notes," to all former residents, former fellows, and current urologists in the surrounding area. The newsletter contains schedules of the urology conferences, a calendar of events, and a list of recent articles written by the residents and faculty of Baylor's Department of Urology. Dr. Scardino has received positive feedback from recipients of his newsletter. It is a monthly reminder, he says, that the department is a urologic center of excellence. He also makes use of the hundreds of articles written by himself and other members of the department over the years. For example, he sends copies of appropriate articles to referring physicians. This serves to reinforce the image of his department as having expertise and being on the cutting edge of new technology and treatments in many clinical areas.

Dr. Scardino also believes that tertiary health care centers should provide continuing medical education to potential referral sources. For instance, he has used the urology grand rounds at his center as a forum for education not only for Baylor's residents but also for the local urologic community. To make attending grand rounds attractive to local urologists, he contacts them to find a time that is most convenient. He encourages local physicians to present their own interesting and difficult cases and thus avail themselves of expert opinions on the spot. He also provides food and free parking to make it easy and attractive for local urologists to attend.

Dr. Scardino also stages an annual scientific day to honor graduating residents and bring alumni back to the medical center for purposes of education and socializing. The department honors not only an outstanding resident and faculty member but also an outstanding alumnus.

In addition, Dr. Scardino also organizes alumni get-togethers at the annual meeting of the American Urologic Association. These are purely social events, when alumni gather at a hotel, restaurant, or nightclub to share old stories and renew old acquaintances. It is another way of maintaining relationships and rapport with graduates and potential referring urologists.

Another way he showcases his department and encourages referrals is by organizing an annual postgraduate seminar, which is hosted by Baylor College of Medicine and features one or two prestigious faculty members from other departments as drawing cards. Dr. Scardino believes it is important to hold such seminars at the medical center rather than at a hotel or off-campus site. Because he has a marketing outlook, Dr. Scardino uses this opportunity to show other urologists the medical center's resources. Attended by 300 to 500 urologists each year, these seminars focus on state-of-the-art technological developments and techniques. Dr. Scardino wants physicians to use the center for referrals, so the seminars are designed to demonstrate the department's technology, research, and commitment to educational excellence.

This is just a sampling of the ways large academic medical centers can maintain contact with and cultivate additional referring physicians. The medical center at Ohio State University in Columbus sends copies of studies published in recent journals to referring physicians in its database. This keeps the name of the medical center appearing on the desk and in the mind of the referring physician frequently and in a positive fashion. The next time a patient visits a referring physician with a condition warranting state-of-the-art consultation, that referring physician is much more likely to suggest the institution.

INTERNATIONAL MARKETING

Because of its proximity to Mexico and accessibility to other Latin American countries, Baylor is in a unique position to market its services internationally. Dr. Scardino has begun to tap the Latin American market by building on the connections established by his colleague, Dr. Michael DeBakey, in countries south of the Texas border.

Baylor College of Medicine has created a working relationship with various medical centers throughout Latin America. The college is affiliated with the Clinica de Merida in the Yucatan Peninsula, for instance. The medical school sends its professors to Mexico to teach and lecture, and the clinic reciprocates by sending patients and doctors to Houston for medical care and continuing education.

Dr. Scardino observes that international relationships work best when established between individuals at each site. He often invites Latin American urologists to Houston for continuing education. The physicians are given a tour of the medical center and are invited to observe surgical procedures and to attend conferences.

Dr. Scardino cautions that if international marketing is your objective, you must make sure your institution is prepared to accommodate patients from other countries. You must have translators on staff, appropriate signage in the hospital and medical center, and appropriate lodging for patients, family members, and friends. Finally, this type of marketing will only work if direct flights are available that allow potential patients to get to your institution without undue difficulty.

Dr. Thomas's department also has extensive Central American connections. The medical center at Tulane has also organized a support system whereby foreign-speaking patients can stay for a nominal fee with a family from the same country. This helps with the adjustment of the patient's family during their visit to another country.

OUTWARD BOUND

Like other physicians, Dr. Scardino thinks that public speaking is one of the most successful marketing tools available. He spends from 15 to 20 percent of his time speaking to physicians, especially other urologists. However, he says that public speaking can be counterproductive. He suggests that if you are going to go "on the circuit," you should not speak outside your "marketing catch."

Dr. Scardino is confident that academic physicians can market their practices and their institutions. He has gone out of the way to erase the "town and gown" barriers that traditionally have worked against physician referrals. By placing marketing near the top of his practice priorities, he has successfully implemented techniques that have generated loyal patients and referrals from local physicians.

Community doctors who are sending their patients to academic centers would do well to take a few minutes to prepare their patients about what to expect when they travel to a large medical center for care. Often patients are accustomed to a certain amount of hand-holding from their primary care physician, with whom they have built a relationship over the years. This will probably be absent when they enter an academic medical center. Patients told they will be examined by medical students, interns, residents, and fellows are less likely to be surprised when a whole group of physicians arrive to take their history and perform a physical examination. The referring physician can work with patients to communicate that the medical center offers state-of-the-art diagnostic and therapeutic skills, and that this access to technology is often a trade-off for the usual physician–patient warmth and rapport.

According to Robert Kessler, M.D., professor of urology at Stanford Medical School, academic physicians have marketing opportunities that are not available to other physicians in the community. For example, academic physicians can stress what the university medical center can do that is not done by the private physicians. For the most part, academic physicians have access to more technology and the latest in medical equipment, which often comes later to the surrounding community.

Dr. Kessler also emphasizes that academic physicians are in high demand for media appearances. When given a choice, print and television reporters will want to interview a physician with academic credentials for their perspectives on the latest developments in medicine and health care.

Finally, Dr. Kessler has noticed that academic practices can offer financial incentives to patients and insurance companies, especially for noncovered procedures, such as vasectomy reversals, treatment of sexual dysfunction, and cosmetic surgery. Academic institutions can make financial arrangements with the hospital because of the large volume of cases that they can bring to the hospital. Dr. Kessler believes that if academic physicians have a larger number of procedures to do, they become more efficient and require less time in the operating room, which is one of the largest parts of the hospital charges.

In many ways, marketing an academic medical practice resembles marketing for a community practice: looking for needs and ways to fill them, building "name brand" recognition in both the immediate and outlying area, and being attentive to the needs of your referring physicians.

The Bottom Line   *It is now essential for the "gowns" to come down from their ivory towers and enhance their communication with the "towns." Shrinking federal funding means that marketing needs to be at the top of the list for getting and maintaining a strong patient base. Keeping patients happy, cultivating referring physicians, and maintaining a motivated and informed staff will ensure a steady stream of high-quality teaching opportunities—which is the bottom line for every academic institution.*

Technology, Toys, and Tips

Every method, technique, tactic, and strategy I have described up to this point has been tried and shown to work. In order to make this book more complete, I wanted to include additional marketing chapters to help you solidify your own practice goals.

By using suggestions from Pillar V, you will gain various new allies in your marketing journey. If your office computer is not already a marketing ally, you will learn how to maximize its untapped potential, starting with programs designed to generate quality patient education material. For those willing to take the plunge, I also offer an overview of electronic medical records, allowing you to transition to paperless records.

And speaking of allies, do not forget your attorney and accountant. In Chapter 44 health care attorney Karen E. Davidson outlines the basics of instituting a compliance plan, which is a real necessity to avoid an audit and costly penalties from the Health Care Financing Administration regulators and managed care plans alike. You can also forge a valuable alliance with the right marketing consultant, and Chapter 52 shows you how to judiciously manage consultancy resources. Additional chapters in this section supply ideas on taking on a new associate, as well as generating more practice income (through conducting clinical research and becoming an expert witness).

In Chapter 50 Cynthia Fry, MBA, with expertise in medical accounting, explains how to use a practice cost analysis to market your practice. And, for extra measure, I've included scores of tips on how to give your patients a Federal Express experience, and how to put some fun into your medical practice. That and the Cajun "baker's dozen" will ensure a full storehouse of marketing strategies to try.

And the final chapter gives you a road map of all the techniques I have discussed and a checklist for a profitable practice. Use them in good health!

CHAPTER 43

Let Technology Simplify Your Life

The buzz words today for most medical practices are *efficiency, patient satisfaction,* and *improved outcomes.* By implementing some of the programs reviewed in this chapter, you will have the opportunity to accomplish all three of these objectives. Electronic medical records (EMRs), computerized patient education material, voice recognition software, and automated phone answering may require a significant investment of your time initially as you transition to these systems. But the net result will be more of your time free to spend with the patient, instead of scribbling in a chart, explaining basic patient education information, or proofreading transcribed reports. This truly is a new age in medicine, and the technology will transform the way you practice.

ELECTRONIC MEDICAL RECORDS TO THE RESCUE

President John Kennedy declared in 1960 that the United States would put a man on the moon by the end of the decade. I predict that by the year 2005 most medical offices will have electronic medical records and the chart as we know it today will go the way of leeches, ledger cards, and long hospital stays.

In the mid-1980s the Institute of Medicine (IOM) issued a report setting out the goals and objectives of a practical, useful, and efficient electronic medical record. The report envisioned that the future patient record would be a computer-based multimedia record capable of including free text, high-resolution images, sound (for example, auscultations), full motion video, and elaborate coding schemes. An EMR was expected to offer access (availability, convenience, speed, connectivity, and efficiency) and to provide new functions through links to other databases and decision support tools.[1]

Today the IOM's mid-1980s challenge has been met and exceeded. This first section of the chapter will provide you with an overview of the EMR system and how to transition your practice from paper charts to an EMR.

There are dozens of companies offering to harness the computer to your chart racks. At almost every medical meeting, you will find vendors offering to take you "paperless" with the click of a mouse button—and to take $50,000 to $100,000 per physician in the process! However, with some research, a plan of action, and considerable time investment, you can successfully transition from charts to a paperless record with a minimum of pain.

The EMR Advantages

Once you have an EMR system in place, you will never again have to worry about locating a chart. Every time someone in the practice touches a chart, it is costing your practice nearly $3.00 in expenses. The cost for a misplaced chart is even greater.

With the Health Care Financing Administration (HCFA) demanding a compliance plan and imposing heavy fines for noncompliance, you must be much more cognizant about accurate documentation. An EMR system will provide the documentation to ensure compliance and avoid costly fines. Also, it will provide any auditor a legible form without cryptic abbreviations that are only understood by the doctor who handwrites his or her notes in the chart. In that sense, you might consider the EMR as an automatic compliance auditor that prompts doctors when they are overcoding a visit. The new programs will require that certain fields are completed before the doctor can complete an examination, prompting the doctor for additional information if he or she codes for a higher service. Documentation is standardized across the practice so that outside auditors do not have to figure out each practioner's abbreviation system and nomenclature.

Many practices worry that EMRs would allow a nervous physician or staff member to retroactively change records without a trace. This can be prevented by establishing a standard escrow agreement with an attorney. Every six months, the practice provides a complete backup of the system to the attorney. The escrow agreement prevents the attorney from giving those records back to the physician. Therefore, at any time an auditor would be able to match records in the physician's office with those held in escrow by the attorney. Putting this practice into your compliance plan and policy manual demonstrates your strong commitment to compliance and is sure to convince regulators of your seriousness when it comes to strict documentation.[2] Some of the newer EMRs will "lock" the note once it is completed and signed and will only allow the original note or record to be appended or amended.

An EMR will accumulate information to feed disease management systems, which becomes invaluable at the time of managed care contract negotiations. You will be able to negotiate from a position of strength when you have the data to back up your outcomes and quality of care that you provide the plan's members.

Another advantage of an EMR system is improved efficiency for the practice. Modern programs save time for evaluation and management (E&M) as the computer inserts the history, the date of the last visit, the chief complaint, the patient's medications, and the routine examination into the current office visit note. You can insert lengthy dictation of procedures, operative reports, referral letters, and discussions regarding treatment alternatives into the chart notes with just the click of the mouse or a touch of the light-pen on the hand-held screen that is so portable that it can be carried from room to room. The program can be designed to create an entire package of information, notes, and forms. For example, for a patient who has had a vasectomy, just one click can create a chart note, an operative note, prescriptions, a referral letter, and patient instructions.

This kind of record creation eliminates printing, mailing, and faxing costs as the computer can electronically transmit the information to referring physicians, insurance companies, hospitals, laboratories, pharmacies, and soon the patient's personal health record on the Internet.

With the use of the currently available EMRs, your practice can collect outcomes, utilization, and patient processing data. You can collect data on clinical decisions and activities in real time with the results immediately available to the physicians. One of the essential elements to accomplish these functions is a system based on a codified clinical knowledge base. The knowledge base consists of several thousand words for a single specialty and several hundred thousand words for a primary care physician or a multispecialty group practice. These words are organized in a logical fashion that supports the standard history of the present illness, the past medical history (including every drug in the *Physician's Desk Reference* and the thousands of over-the-counter drugs), the review of systems, the physical examination, the diagnosis, and the treatment plan.

Today, most EMR programs are integrated into your practice management software, which includes your billing and scheduling programs. You can eliminate additional data entry time required for *Current Procedural Terminology* (CPT) and *International Classification of Diseases,* ninth edition (ICD–9) codes because all codes can be generated as a byproduct of creating a note, with data going from the scheduling desk, to the exam room, and then immediately sent electronically to the payer.

Doctors can also enjoy the luxury of having the patients' records available to them in their home or thousands of miles away. When a patient calls about a medical problem, you can look at the medical record from any computer with an Internet access and a modem. Any action you take will be entered into the EMR and you will not have to rely on your memory or pull the chart the next time you are in your office to record your actions or decisions in the patient's paper chart.

There are marketing advantages to an EMR. Such systems can provide graphing and analysis of data from different visits to determine the effects of treatment modalities and compare outcomes. EMR is an engaging technology that can act as a teaching tool for your patients. You will be amazed at patients' reactions when they are able to see a graph of their blood pressure readings or their cholesterol levels after they have instituted treatment and lifestyle changes.

Finally, an effective program allows the doctor to spend more time eyeball to eyeball with the patient rather than scribbling in the chart. By creating the record in real time in front of the patient, you do not have to spend additional time dictating at the end of the day or days later when the memory of the patient's visit has faded. As a result, the quality of the time you spend with the patient is increased.

All these advantages come with a price tag, however. To reach the point of improved efficiency, reduced overhead expenses, and improved productivity, you will have to "pay your dues."

Walk Before You Run

Most EMR integrations take a year to implement. Most experts in EMR technology advise running the EMR in conjunction with the paper chart initially, just as you did when transitioning from ledger cards to computerized billing. You must expect that the transition will affect patient wait times, processing, and staff time. Consequently, in the beginning of the transition to an EMR paperless chart, you can expect a dip in revenue. You can also expect frustration and stress on your staff. Many staff members will be concerned that the EMR will eliminate their jobs and may even attempt to sabotage the program. Most experts suggest transitioning the practice slowly—starting with one or two doctors at a time or beginning in one clinic or one location rather than the entire health care system. During early stages, consider temporarily decreasing the patient load for a few days or weeks until the doctors and the staff get comfortable with the new system. This "go slow" strategy allows you to fine-tune the program and work out the bugs that are sure to occur along the way. Often doctors who have initiated the process become the advocates and will create the groundswell to assist the newcomers' entry to the program. They can also serve as the experts or teachers helping the new users to become acclimated.

Do Not Skimp on Support

Maintenance is also the key to the success of the program. Your vendor should agree to several days of training and staff support. The vendor should also commit to training a staff member or physician who can monitor and fix routine issues. Nothing can derail a good program more quickly than to have a crash early on that requires bringing in a technician to resolve a simple problem that could have been resolved by someone on the staff with proper training. Make sure that the program is backed up regularly, so that in case of a crash you do not lose all the data or have to hire an expensive "disk doctor" to retrieve the data from your hard drive. You should also expect a quarterly update of new drug information, as well as additional clinical content.

"Show Me the Money"

Before you implement an EMR system, your practice manager or chief financial officer will want to know what the return on investment (ROI) will be. You will need to convince yourself, if you are in solo practice or a small group practice, or the chief financial officer if you are in a larger practice, of the cost savings of going to an EMR system.

Most practices that have converted to an EMR system have experienced an improvement in efficiency and productivity. Such systems often yield more time to spend with patients and more time slots for additional patients as a result of the time saved. An EMR system can also help with accurate coding and prevent thousands of dollars being left on the table from undercoding. A good program can accurately provide the appropriate code for E&M and can alert the doctor when a code is too high for the service provided or offer suggestions for moving to a higher code if it is appropriate. Not only will this aspect of the EMR add to the practice's coffers, but it also will prevent costly errors if overcoding is discovered at the time of a HCFA audit.

EMRs also reduce the time spent pulling charts and transcribing procedure and operative notes. These two aspects alone can justify the investment in an EMR program. For example, if a practice sees 100 patients a week or 5,000 patients a year at a cost of $3.00 for touching each chart, that is a savings of $15,000 a year just in chart pulling. If 20 percent of the patient visits are new patients and the chart materials cost $2.00 for each new chart, that is another $2,000 in savings. Then consider the cost of a transcriptionist, which is $25,000 to $35,000 a year. You can easily demonstrate to the number crunchers a savings of $42,000 to $52,000 a year and plan to recoup your investment in one or two years.

That ROI does not include the chart space in the office or the cost of storage facilities used off-site to maintain the paper charts. I have talked with several practices that have converted the 100 square feet of office space that was once used for chart racks into exam rooms that will be used to accommodate more patients. That results in a gain in productivity that will return the investment on an EMR almost immediately.

Deep Pockets?

The cost of an EMR system can range from $10,000 to more than $500,000. Prices vary tremendously and you can often negotiate the costs, especially if you have a large number of doctors who will be brought on-line. You may also find it less expensive to pay for each location of the program rather than by each physician.

To some extent your practice size will limit your vendor selection. Some companies such as IDX and Oacis can handle large groups and hospitals.[3] If you are a small practice, make sure you have good technical support.

You will also want to check that the EMR vendor has experience working with your specialty or subspecialty since the clinical content and clinical knowledge are vital to the success of any EMR system. Each specialty has its own vocabulary, and the learning curve can be cumbersome if you are using a voice-activated system and must train the program with the vocabulary that is unique to your specialty.

Also ask your vendor if they have experience interfacing the EMR with your practice management software. Most practices that have gone electronic suggest that you obtain in writing how much it will cost to establish the interface between the EMR and the billing program. This is especially important if you plan to use EMR coding options (ICD-9 and CPT codes) to transfer straight into your billing software or to automatically transfer demographic information from the scheduling program to the patient's EMR. This saves an enormous amount of time and prevents the necessity of double entry of these data into each program.

Other costs to consider are new hardware and equipment interfaces to connect your existing billing program with your EMRs, and service agreements.

Dr. B's Best Bet

I have reviewed dozens of EMRs, and the best program for the small as well as the large practice is the Purkinje Dossier of Clinical Information (DCI) system.[4] This EMR is a powerful, cost-effective clinical documentation tool designed to run on a desktop personal computer (PC); a laptop computer; or a portable, battery-operated, pen-based computer. Developed especially for physicians when they are face to face with patients, the program allows users to easily create comprehensive records, including patient history, physical exams, problems, diagnoses, and treatments.

The Purkinje program contains an interface that promotes true-to-life clinical note writing. The base program contains more than 300 customizable templates covering all major specialties. Therefore, if you have a primary care, specialty, or multispeciality group practice, one program can accommodate your needs.

These dynamic templates function as a filter to the extensive knowledge base that is the foundation of the system. Therefore, from any template you can reach anywhere in the knowledge base. For example, if a man arrives with a headache but later in the history taking reveals to the doctor that he has the symptoms of a sexually transmitted disease (STD), the doctor can easily move through the knowledge base from headaches to STDs. Consequently, both primary care physicians and specialists can easily use this program. Another benefit of the program is that the doctor can chart by exception, which means that everything that is normal is accepted by the program, and only the abnormal findings need to be entered. This makes the program user-friendly and fast, as many patients have normal findings for most of their review of systems and their physical examination.

The program allows the doctor to produce clinical notes by simply tapping with a pen on a lightweight, hand-held screen that connects by radio frequency to your computer, making the doctor and the program very mobile. Handwritten notations or drawings can be added directly into the note at any time. The program also accommodates voice recognition software that will allow spoken notations to be input as well (see the section on voice recognition software later in this chapter). This unique user interface and clinical templates allow physicians to improve the quality and efficiency of patient care.

Purkinje also uses hyperlinks that allow easy connectivity to other medical resources, including on-line access to Merck Manual, the PDR, an extensive drug database, and patient instructions.

The Purkinje program can be easily integrated into your billing and scheduling programs. Data providing practice patterns, outcomes measurement, and patient tracking can be easily extracted. Guideline and expert system interfaces will be available from Purkinje as well as from outside sources.

The Purkinje E&M Expert allows for real-time analysis and comparison to the HCFA guidelines for appropriate evaluation and management coding. The program will actually compute the appropriate E&M code that supports the documentation of your office visit. Now you can avoid upcoding and the risk of costly penalties and fines when you are audited. The system also prevents downcoding and leaving money in the pockets of the payers that rightfully belongs to you.

The cost of the Purkinje program is $3,000 to $5,000 per physician. The cost decreases as the number of physicians increases. This means that the technology can be afforded by small and large practices alike. Like most programs, the vendor offers toll-free telephone support and on-site trouble shooting for more significant problems. The program provides additional clinical content that is available on a quarterly basis. The learning curve is short: two half-day training sessions. After just a few hours of using the hand-held screen, the doctor is ready to use the program.

PROMOTE YOUR PRACTICE WITH COMPUTERIZED PATIENT EDUCATION MATERIAL

How would you like to increase patient satisfaction and compliance, enhance the efficiency of your office, and simultaneously reduce the risk of lawsuits? If any of these sound appealing to you, implementing a computerized patient communication system may be a good idea for your practice.

A Good Idea or a Necessity?

Has this happened to you yet? Your patient shows up clutching an article he downloaded from the Internet wondering why you recommend a transurethral resection of the prostate (TURP) instead of the latest advancement in microwave thermotherapy for treating his benign prostate hyperplasia (BPH). Or maybe you have just been served with a complaint in a lawsuit where the patient charges that the risks of a procedure and alternative treatment choices were not adequately explained.

These are easy problems to avoid with a computerized patient communication system. However, the benefits go far beyond avoidance of problems, and into the proactive realm of increased compliance with instructions, improved outcomes, and higher patient satisfaction. In addition, your malpractice insurer may offer a premium discount for the use of a qualified patient education product.[5]

What Do You Need?

It is not as complicated as it sounds. Many companies offer software products that are easy to install and use, even for the computer novice. Every week, computer systems become more and more affordable. PCs for less than $1,000 have become standard in the computer market, and many patient education software programs are available for less than $500.

The Hardware To Drive It

To get started, you need a PC, software, and a printer. Most patient education software programs state the system requirements you will need in order to run them. My advice is to preview software programs, if you can, and to gear up according to what your selected program will require. You can also check with the several software companies listed in Table 43–1 to make sure what size and speed of PC will be adequate.

Although the definition of "entry level configuration" also changes almost weekly, most systems include at least a 200MHz Pentium processor or equivalent, 32 megabytes of RAM, a 32x CD-ROM drive, and a large hard drive, with 2 gigabytes (GB) or more capacity. When you buy your computer, check to see how much extra it would cost to upgrade your processor, RAM, and hard drive. Often going to a faster speed (up to 350 MHz) and a larger hard drive (4–6 GB) can cost less than $100 and will be worth the expense.

Table 43–1 Patient Education Products

Vendor	Product	Description
Dialog Medical (800) 482-7963 *www.dialogmedical.com*	Urology Discussion™ v.2.2 $399 single user	Used by more than one-third of all urology offices in the United States. Contains patient education, consent forms, patient instructions, drug information, tests/admissions, forms for chart/office, questionnaires, authorizations, and diets. More than 600 urology-specific documents.
Lippincott Williams & Wilkins Mosby-Yearbook W.B. Saunders (800) 401-9962 *www.mdconsult.com*	MDConsult™ $34.95 per month; requires Internet access	Web-based product from three well-known publishers. In addition to library of general patient education, MDConsult provides access to on-line reference books and practice guidelines.
Clinical Reference Systems (303) 664-6485 *www.patienteducation.com*	Adult Health Advisor $395 single user	Generates patient education handouts on adult medical and surgical topics, written in easy-to-read-and-understand language.
Micromedex (800) 525-9083 *www.micromedex.com*	CareNotes™ $1,250 single user	Information on patient condition, including treatment, follow-up care, psychosocial issues, and continuing health concerns, in English and Spanish.
Medifor (800) 366-3710 *www.medifor.com*	Patient Ed® $395 single user	More than 550 primary care topics: patient instructions, access treatment guidelines, medications, and chart documents.
Patient Education Institute (319) 335-4613 *www.patient-education.com*	X-Plain™ $495	Patient-Interactive modules that cover TURP, impotence, vasectomy, PSA.

Note: The author has a financial involvement with Dialog Medical; he uses them for his website, *www.urologychannel.com/neilbaum.*

Laser printers work best for high-volume tasks like printing patient pamphlets because of their superior print speeds and output quality, but some physicians opt for an inkjet printer so that they can incorporate affordable color graphics in their handouts (color laser printers are still very expensive).

Software Solutions

There are a variety of companies that offer patient education solutions. Some are specific to individual specialties; others are more generic. Some products generate handouts for the patients to read and take home, while others are interactive teaching tools that allow the patient to take a "guided tour" while sitting in front of the computer. There is also a lot of information available on the Internet, but the quality varies and its validity is often difficult to verify. Rather than trying to sift through all the available information on the Internet to try to write your own program, it is better to avail yourself of the affordable, quality patient education programs on the market. Table 43–1 provides a brief description of some of the options available.

In most programs you can personalize the handout materials so they appear to come directly from your practice. Many of the programs allow you to customize the material and edit it so that it matches the language style and opinion of the physician providing the material.

Another advantage of the computerized patient education program is that it saves space. You will not need to have large filing cabinets and messy pamphlet holders. Many programs contain more than 500 documents that are available on a few diskettes or CD-ROM.

Some programs offer educational handouts only. Others handle discharge instructions, drug information, consent forms, or other types of communication. *You should decide what types of communication might be valuable to you and evaluate the available options.*

I suggest that you be sure that the program includes periodic updates that provide new patient education material, as it becomes available. For example, a program written in 1997 and early 1998 would not have sildenafil (Viagra®) information. Periodic updates will contain new drug information and patient education material on new products, procedures, and treatments.

Patient education programs are a real plus for your staff. The efficiency of the practice improves when the staff no longer have to search the office for a pamphlet or brochure on a particular condition or disease. Computerized material avoids the necessity for interrupting patient care to make copies of the last form or handout material. And, most important, the patient education material reduces the number of questions from patients as the most frequently asked questions are answered in the handout material.

Finally, freshly printed readable and current patient education materials enhance the quality of your practice. If you hand out a sheet that has been photocopied five times and is barely legible, your patients might begin to wonder about quality in other areas of your practice. The handouts also become a practice marketing tool.

I have been using a computerized communication system in my office since 1992. Since then, patient satisfaction has gone up, phone calls to the office have been reduced, and I feel better protected from a medico-legal standpoint. In 1992 80 percent of the patients surveyed responded that we provided adequate and useful patient education materials. Our 1999 survey revealed that 95 percent were satisfied with the patient information and educational materials we gave them.

Computerized patient education programs serve as practice enhancers and protectors. Your patients receive additional quality medical advice, and you can be assured that all the disclosure bases have been covered. Read on for more ideas on how technology can save you time and boost income and patient satisfaction.

VOICE RECOGNITION SOFTWARE

Voice recognition software translates the spoken word into a word processing document on a personal computer. Voice recognition software is available in a variety of implementations, ranging from vocabularies optimized for the lay public to systems with vocabularies optimized for the type of speech used by professionals (including doctors and lawyers).

Until the development of continuous speech, however, the software had not evolved to the point of being practical for the average physician to use. In July 1998 the development of continuous speech made voice recognition software a viable choice for use by medical professionals. This innovation allows the user to speak at a normal pace and have the speech instantly translated into text. Prior to this breakthrough, the user had to distinctly pause between each word in order for it to be correctly recognized and translated into text. This was not a practical solution for physicians seeing large numbers of patients each day. With continuous speech most physicians are able to complete their clinic dictation in about the same amount of time needed to dictate into microcassette recorders or digital dictation systems.

Many physicians also objected to the headset microphone, which was awkward and needed to be taken on and off. Now a variety of types are available, including microphones built into computer monitors, hand-held microphones, desktop standing microphones, lavalier style microphones, and microphones that track speech as the user speaks from different positions within a room (for example, as the doctor moves from one side of a X-ray view box to another).

The advantages of voice recognition software will depend on whether you use an off-the-shelf voice recognition software package (see "Additional Resources"), a system containing a medical package that allows you to produce only chart notes, or a system that is completely customized for your specialty or your practice to maximize the productivity of you and your office staff.[6] The latter allows you to write prescriptions, fax referral letters, and even connect to a scheduling program.

With the off-the-shelf voice recognition software packages, be sure to select a version that has been customized for medical terminology and vocabulary. Otherwise, you will have to spend a significant amount of your time making corrections and adding new words for the missed medical terminology. If, however, you are using a version with a vocabulary optimized for use by medical professionals, your initial success and accuracy with the system will be much better and your learning curve will be shortened considerably.

The disadvantages of voice recognition software include the initial outlay of funds, the time to train the computer to recognize your voice, the time to add new words or correct persistent misrecognitions, and learning both the speaking style and syntax of the commands to operate the system. Also, physicians new to the world of personal computers will first need to acquire a working knowledge of their computer and its application software, especially the word processor.

It is important to remember that voice recognition software is an augmentation tool. In and of itself voice recognition software is not a total solution to your transcription needs. You will be able to dictate by voice with varying levels of accuracy, depending on the package you have purchased. Like everything else in life, you can plan on getting what you pay for. Cheaper versions require more time to train and have less accuracy.

The off-the-shelf voice recognition software packages are readily available in a variety of retail outlets and through the Internet. The package systems are usually available for order either through the Internet or telephone. Often these vendors will have short demonstrations available for download from the Internet or that can be sent through the mail. The high-end custom applications will sometimes offer either a videotape demonstration containing examples of applications they have developed. For large practices, on-site demonstrations in your office might be available. With the high-end systems, you simply contact the vendor to place an order for their systems.

It is important for you to consider carefully your goals and objectives in considering voice recognition software. If you are simply interested in eliminating your transcription expense and producing chart notes, then a basic program purchased at a computer store may fit the bill. However, if your goal is to make a significant change in both the quality of your documentation and office productivity, and you do not want to spend a lot of time training and correcting voice recognition software, then you would likely be happier with either one of the chart producing packages or one of the high-end customized applications.

The high-end systems (mentioned in the beginning of this chapter in the first section on EMRs) can include vocabularies customized to your medical specialty and even more precisely tailored to your particular speech patterns. This allows extremely accurate recognition within minutes of beginning to use the system. *Also, the high-end systems can include:*

- templates for production of chart notes organized around particular procedures or diagnoses
- automated prescription writing (including faxing capabilities to send your patient's prescription to the pharmacy)
- automated processes for building normal reviews of systems and physical examination elements
- automation to help build the text associated with family, social, and medical history
- automated insertion of ICD-9 codes and their descriptions
- automated insertion of treatment plan codes and descriptions
- capabilities to look up patient names, diagnoses, and treatments
- facilities to automatically load charts for your scheduled patients on any particular day
- an electronic medical record facility to allow you to view all the documentation you have produced or received relative to a particular patient

Properly tailored to meet your requirements, these high-end systems can rather dramatically improve your productivity and the quality of your clinic documentation. The low-end systems do not offer all these benefits, but, if your goal is simply to eliminate your transcription expense and you are willing to invest the time with these systems, then you might be wise to save the money and purchase one of the low-cost, off-the-shelf voice recognition software packages. (See "Additional Resources" for a list of several off-the-shelf voice recognition software programs.)

USING AUTOMATED PHONE ANSWERING SYSTEMS

One of the most frequent complaints patients have about contacting the doctor's office is the frequency of getting a busy signal. It is frustrating to patients, who often complain to staff, who must bear the brunt of this unhappiness. Now that problem can be solved with a well-programmed automated phone system.

Selecting an Automated Telephone System

First consider your patients and the type of practice that you have. For example, younger patients tend to be more receptive to automated technology than elderly ones. It is also best to make patients aware of the system and to explain it in positive terms. You might consider starting your recording by saying, "Thank you for calling Drs. Jeckel and Hyde's office. In order to help our patients, we have installed an automated call routing system." If the patient is placed on hold, consider using the following message: "Thanks for calling; we apologize for the delay." You can then follow with all types of marketing on hold messages (see Chapter 32 for a listing of those companies).

Use Options Sparingly

Most callers will accept only three or four options. By the time callers hear a fourth option, they have usually forgotten the first one offered. In addition, it will help callers if there is an announcement in the beginning that the message will offer four choices. The caller should be given the option of hearing the menu again and reaching a live person immediately in an emergency situation. Most patients are generally accepting of call routing for nonurgent phone calls. When patients are sick or have an emergency, they will want to talk to a compassionate human being, not an automated phone system. Make sure your system allows callers to press zero at any time to reach a live operator.

However, you will still want to reduce the number of people who use the zero option, so list that option last in the menu. That way, if patients initially hear that they can make an appointment or get a referral, they will most likely press those buttons first.

There's another really good telephone service that can save you and your patients a lot of missed calls.

STOP PLAYING PHONE TAG WITH PATIENTS

If you often call your patients with lab results, you know the frustrations of trying to reach and report to each one. Having your patients call in for results is no better. Calls constantly interrupt your nurse or designated responder while he or she is trying to carry out other important office duties. While most lab results are normal, it's better to inform each patient of his or her results and not just call those with abnormal results.

Your typical process for answering and calling back patients' calls carries heavy hidden costs. Interruptions disrupt the work flow, and phone lines are tied up as you receive and call out until you reach each patient. Charts are pulled and returned to the shelves as you attempt to communicate with your patients. Studies have shown that each time someone touches a chart, it costs your practice anywhere from $3 to $8 in hidden staffing costs.

There is a better way. An outside voice messaging service, such as the Patient Results Network (see "Additional Resources"), can improve both office efficiency and patient satisfaction.

How It Works

When they leave the office, patients are told when to call for lab results and given a card with the service's phone number and an individual access code. When lab reports come in, either the physician or a staff member takes 20 to 30 seconds to dictate exactly what they want to say into the telephone, using the appropriate code number for each patient. It takes only a few minutes to dictate a batch of reports.

When patients call the number for their results, they hear the message in the doctor's or staff member's voice. The system saves the messages so that patients can call back and hear them several times; the system also documents precisely when each patient called to hear his or her message. The messaging service reports to your office biweekly with a list of all reports actually completed and—most important—weekly for the patients who did not retrieve their messages. You can archive the retrieval information indefinitely for reference and to keep as documentation that you did, in fact, report the results to the patient, and that the patient received the information.

Patients with abnormal results on lab work should still be called personally. But for those with normal results, this type of system will reduce your costs and serve your patients well.

When Patients Do Not Call

Although the majority of patients seem to appreciate a messaging system, some fail to comply with this method. When your staff members receive the weekly reports of nonretrievals, they can mail out a prepared letter reminding patients to call the system. Or, they may keep trying to reach patients until they are informed.

The cost of this system runs about $125 to $150 a month for a solo or two-physician practice. Charges for additional physicians vary depending upon message volume. The system does not require any investment in hardware, software, or dedicated phone lines. You can be up and running in just 15 minutes with a very short learning curve. The Patient Results Network's own studies show that the messaging system saves the average physician 8.6 hours per month. Even if you save only half that amount of time, outside voice messaging could be well worth your while. *Remember:* tag is for tots, not docs.

The Bottom Line   *Today, we are going to need to place an emphasis on efficiency, improved productivity, and reducing overhead expenses. Transition your practice from paper charts to an electronic medical records system, and you will accomplish all three of those goals. Adding voice recognition software, automated phone answering, and computerized patient education material to the mix can substantially cut office waste and, more important, patient frustration.*

NOTES

1. M. Amatayakul, "The State of the Computer-Based Patient Record," *Journal of AHIMA*, 69, no. 9 (1998): 34–36.
2. M.B. Kaye, "Electronic Medical Records," *Administrative Eyecare* 1 (Winter 1999): 28–33.
3. IDX can be reached at (888) 439–6584, *www.idx.com*; Oacis can be reached at (415) 482-4400, *www.oacis.com*.
4. Purkinje can be reached at (210) 476-0030, *www.purkinje.com*.
5. Check *www.dialogmedical.com/insurers.htm* for a list of known insurance providers that offer premium discounts for the use of patient education software.
6. Examples include Medical Dictation, which can be contacted at (502) 827-8522; *speech@i-ss.com*.

ADDITIONAL RESOURCES

Off-the-Shelf Voice Recognition Software:
Pacific Voice for Medicine Software
Pacific Voice Software
7731 Bagley Ave. N.
Seattle, Washington 98103
(800) 362-5352; *www.pacificvoice.com*

IBM's ViaVoice
Shop IBM
Dept. YES98
P.O. Box 2690
Atlanta, Georgia 30301
(888) 411-1WEB; code YEF98; *www.software.ibm.com*

Dragon Naturally Speaking
Dragon Systems, Inc.
320 Nevada St.
Newton, Massachusetts 02460
(617) 965-5200; *www.dragonsys.com*

Patient Results Network, LLC
29525 Chagrin Blvd., Suite 105
Cleveland, Ohio 44122
(216) 292-0050
(800) 613-9050
(216) 292-2501 fax
E-mail: *patientresults@aol.com*
For a demonstration, call (800) 448-8520, enter 1008 and the # symbol as the provider code, then 123456# as the medical record number.

CHAPTER 44

Compliance: Minimize Risks and Maximize Marketing Potential

Karen E. Davidson

Today, most physicians are acutely aware of the government and other regulatory agencies looking over their shoulders to make sure that they are not fraudulently billing for their services. You should be aware, if you are not already, that the government has enlisted senior citizens as part of its "fraud busting" arsenal. These patients are being bombarded with messages from the government and others to be on the lookout for "bad apple" physicians and to report improper billing or other suspect activities of doctors and other health care providers. Unfortunately, even the "good apples" can be targeted and subjected to fines and penalties and exclusion from Medicare and other programs.

Until now, you have probably reacted to governmental enforcement efforts with a mix of anger and fear, worrying about what might happen to you if some unknown billing errors were discovered or a Medicare patient complained to the government. Well, it is time to stop reacting and to start acting. The compliance commotion does not need to upset you. Take the opportunity to convert the cost and expense of implementing an effective compliance plan into a marketing tool for your practice.

You will not only garner some peace of mind, but you can also use your compliance plan to help you convey to your patients and payers your commitment to

---

Note: The information addressed in this chapter is intended to provide a general overview of the compliance area. In no event should any of this information be construed as legal advice. Persons interested in implementing compliance initiatives should seek the advice of an experienced attorney.

Karen E. Davidson is a partner in the law firm of Mackarey & Davidson, PC, located in the Philadelphia metropolitan area. Ms. Davidson provides legal counsel to health care providers, with an emphasis on transactional matters, regulatory compliance, and reimbursement issues. She can be reached at (610) 889-0756; *kedavidson@hotmail.com.*

properly bill for the services provided. This good-faith commitment can carry a lot of clout with both patients and payers.

In this chapter we discuss the concept of compliance and compliance plans and the sorts of risks that can be minimized by implementing compliance initiatives. We also discuss how you can turn the cost and expense of implementing these initiatives into a marketing tool for your practice. In the next chapter, we discuss the ins and outs of proper coding, which is a key ingredient in implementing your compliance plan.

THE BUZZ ABOUT COMPLIANCE

Why has compliance been topping the list as a topic of discussion by lawyers, practice managers, consultants, and physicians? The principal reason is that the government has been emphasizing compliance programs in recent years as one way to curtail rampant health care fraud. Compliance has always been an issue in health care, but it has become even more of one in light of new laws and enforcement efforts of the government and private payers.

The General Accounting Office, which is responsible for auditing government agencies and examining all matters relating to the receipt and disbursement of public funds, reported that as much as 10 percent of health care expenditures nationwide are lost to fraud and abuse. Ferreting out fraud and abuse in the health care industry has become one of the most pressing priorities of our government. All physicians, along with other health care providers, face the risk of a health care fraud audit. You need not have intentionally schemed to find yourself the target of an audit. In fact, most physicians who undergo audits or investigations do not know they are doing something wrong.

DEFINING FRAUD AND ABUSE

Health care fraud and abuse encompass a wide range of activities, including improper financial relationships and referrals and misrepresenting or overcharging with respect to the delivery of health care items or services. Fraud and abuse result in unnecessary costs to government-funded programs and private payers. A fraud conviction resulting from government action typically requires proof of intent to defraud; abuse typically involves actions that are inconsistent with Medicare and Medicaid billing rules and policies.

In this chapter, the terms *health care fraud, health care fraud and abuse,* and *fraud and abuse* are used interchangeably.

Various laws are used as part of the arsenal to combat fraud and abuse, such as the federal law prohibiting self referrals (the "Stark" law) and other federal laws, including the Anti-Kickback Law, False Claims Act, Civil Monetary Penalties

Law, and Program Fraud Civil Remedies Act. These laws essentially make it unlawful for physicians and other providers to engage in fraudulent billing practices and other activities and can result in both civil and criminal penalties.

In an effort to respond to the problem of health care fraud in both the public and private sectors, Congress passed the Health Insurance Portability and Accountability Act of 1996 (HIPAA) and the Balanced Budget Act of 1997. HIPAA expands the weapons against health care fraud by strengthening the criminal and civil laws already in effect and allocating more resources to establish a national framework to coordinate federal, state, and local law enforcement efforts. HIPAA enhances the conduct of investigations and audits related to the delivery and payment of health care, while facilitating enforcement of the civil and criminal statutes.

Given the increased vulnerability of health care providers to investigation and possible criminal and civil sanctions, it is imperative that physicians have a basic understanding of the fraud and abuse laws and strategies for ensuring compliance with those laws. While there is no way to eliminate random targeting by the government or a third party payer, there are a number of active steps that a practice can take to reduce the risk of an audit or investigation and, in the event it becomes the target of an audit or investigation, to minimize the potential risks or consequences. Implementing a compliance plan can significantly reduce these risks.

WHY PRIVATE PAYERS CARE ABOUT FRAUD AND ABUSE

Private insurance companies are equally concerned about fraud and abuse because they lose millions of dollars each year due to fraudulently submitted claims. Many private payers have their own fraud control programs designed and managed by individuals who previously served in governmental enforcement roles. These former officials help private payers design comprehensive programs that are designed to complement governmental efforts. Usually, a determination by a private payer with respect to fraudulent submission of claims results in notice to federal and state authorities. These authorities also usually notify applicable state medical boards, and this carries the potential of having your medical license revoked. Thus private payers, in essence, foster self-imposed compliance by physicians because they can reduce both direct costs associated with reimbursement losses and indirect costs associated with fraud oversight and enforcement.

CLARIFYING COMPLIANCE PLANS

A compliance plan is a compilation of policies and procedures followed by an organization in carrying out certain responsibilities (such as billing) to facilitate compliance with applicable laws, rules, and regulations. A well thought-out and carefully implemented compliance program can go a long way toward reducing the risk of an audit or investigation. With such a plan in place, you can significantly lessen the probability of making repetitive billing errors that give rise to liability under the fraud and abuse laws. A compliance plan also establishes a framework so that legal and policy changes by payers can be disseminated quickly and in an orderly fashion to all employees. Moreover, the existence and implementation of a compliance plan can have a dramatic impact on penalties imposed in the event a civil or criminal action is brought against a physician.

The accepted framework for a compliance plan originates from the federal sentencing guidelines ("guidelines") for organizations that establish uniformity in sanctions and various parameters for judges to follow with respect to sentencing violators (referred to in this chapter as "sentencing parameters"). Under the sentencing parameters, judges have little or no discretion in setting fines. Rather, sanction penalties are set by formula. Base fines can vary depending upon the particular offense; they are then multiplied by a culpability score. This score can be adjusted up or down depending upon aggravating or mitigating factors. An example of an aggravating factor would be the failure of a physician to cooperate with the government during the course of an audit or investigation. In contrast, the implementation of an effective compliance plan is recognized as a mitigating factor and may help to reduce a fine.

The government has published a substantial amount of compliance guidance for various types of providers based upon the sentencing parameters. The government originally called the information it published on compliance "model plans" but renamed it later under the more nebulous term *guidance,* most likely because the original moniker was misleading. In fact, the information the government publishes is not in the form of a compliance plan at all. It is instead put together in a more general format outlining the types of information compliance plans should contain.

The compliance guidance issued by the government is also based, in part, upon the settlement (also known as "integrity") agreements the government has entered into with audited and investigated providers. The guidance that has been issued addresses compliance matters for clinical laboratories, hospitals, home health agencies, and other types of health care providers, durable medical equipment suppliers, hospices, and medical billing companies.[1]

To date, no specific guidance has been issued by the government for physician practices, although the compliance guidance for medical billing companies does provide a framework for practices that conduct their own billing. The government has, however, recently indicated its willingness to provide specific guidance for medical practices. At the time of printing this book, the government had issued a notice in the *Federal Register* requesting input from the provider community about such guidance, a process that will perhaps result in publication within a year or so.

Most hospitals and other institutional health care providers now maintain some type of compliance plan. This is not the case for most medical practices. Of course, they are no less immune to being the target of an audit or investigation than an institutional provider. In view of this, the American Medical Association published a model compliance plan in September 1997 for use by physician medical practices ("AMA Model Plan"). Neither the guidelines nor the AMA Model Plan provides the detail usually associated with implemented compliance plans, but rather they set forth guiding principles to be followed in plans.

ESSENTIAL ELEMENTS OF A COMPLIANCE PLAN

A compliance plan can be very general or very detailed. It may only be 10 to 20 pages long, but it should be tailored to your practice. Most important, it should be implemented. Having a plan you do not use could be worse than no plan at all. The government takes a dim view of providers who have recognized the importance of compliance, only to abandon it. A compliance plan should contain seven elements, which are described below.

1. A code of conduct. A compliance plan should contain a general statement of conduct that promotes a clear commitment to compliance, ranging from the provision of only medically necessary care to appropriate billing for services provided. The code of conduct should be more than just another corporate document sitting on the shelf. It should be a description of the ethical standards and procedures that every employee and independent contractor associated with the practice is obligated to follow. These standards and procedures enable a practice to reduce the likelihood of wrongdoing and, when they are communicated to patients, can help convey the practice's ethical commitment.

2. A compliance officer or committee. A compliance plan should recognize the importance of compliance through the appointment of a trustworthy compliance officer with a high level of responsibility and/or a compliance committee of individuals with the responsibility for implementing the plan and the ability to enforce it. In a medical practice, the compliance officer could be one of the physician/owners and the compliance committee could consist of a physician/owner, the practice manager, and a person with billing expertise within the practice.

Some providers ask whether their attorney should be included as part of the internal compliance structure. Opinions are split on this issue. One theory holds that having an attorney serve in a compliance capacity helps preserve the attorney–client privilege during internal investigations of the practice and during the initial stages of an audit. Alternatively, some believe having an attorney serve as the compliance officer or on the committee may dissolve the attorney–client privilege since the attorney is now acting in a management (as opposed to a legal) capacity to the practice. For small medical practices it probably makes most sense for the attorneys to be left out of the internal compliance structure. As a result, they should serve in a strictly "legal" capacity. Obviously, they should be consulted about compliance initiatives generally and should provide counsel with regard to any problems that arise.

3. Training and education. Compliance plans should state a commitment to effective training and education programs for all professionals (that means physicians, too) and support personnel. Simply distributing the compliance plan to the practice's employees is not sufficient. The practice must conduct a formal training program to ensure that all employees including the physicians appreciate and understand the importance of adhering to the plan. The practice should conduct periodic training sessions for existing employees; and all new employees should be given compliance training. The type of training will vary based on the classifications of the employees and the responsibilities that the employees have in the practice.

4. Auditing and monitoring. Auditing and monitoring processes should be put in place. The practice should monitor the plan regularly to ensure that it is serving its purpose. Legal counsel for the practice should be consulted about this aspect of plan implementation. Outside consultants can conduct a "baseline audit" to verify the practice's documentation flow routines and billing processes, such as the coding of services rendered, use of "V" codes, and "bundling." These audits can be costly and are usually done at the outset based upon a representative sampling of charts and claims (prior to submission for payment) for each physician. They are, however, a necessary part of the compliance process. These audits often provide useful information and can help a practice identify problem areas.

5. Reporting. Specific and effective lines of communication between the compliance officer and committee and professional and support personnel should be implemented through the compliance plan. This process should include a procedure through which employees may report illegal conduct in a confidential manner and without fear of retaliation. The government has required some investigated providers, typically institutional providers like hospitals and health systems, to set up 24-hour telephone hotlines. Independent companies offer this service to medical practices. Such hotlines are often costly for small medical practices, especially in view of other lower cost options that may be available. Without question, each practice, as part of its compliance initiatives, needs to establish an effective mechanism for reporting. You should evaluate how you would like to address the reporting requirement and determine whether you believe a hotline or some other method is in the best interest of your practice.

6. Disciplinary Process. A compliance plan should address the policies and procedures for the conduct of internal investigations and enforcement through disciplinary guidelines and actions. An effective disciplinary process for violations of the compliance program demonstrates the practice's true commitment to compliance with the law. There should not be significant variations in the way that similarly situated employees are disciplined. In order to ensure fairness, the disciplinary process should be in writing.

Ultimately, a practice needs to put some teeth into the plan by addressing how it will handle employees who do not cooperate or comply. Usually an organization has one or two individuals who do not believe the process applies to them. The plan must address what happens to those individuals. Some practices and institutions have made cooperating with compliance initiatives a mandatory part of employment. That is, employees may lose their jobs if they fail to meet the applicable requirements. Some practices even use an approach that initially invokes fines (usually for physicians) for failure to attend training and education sessions.

7. Corrective action measures. The plan should detail a process to respond to identified offenses and apply corrective action initiatives. A practice must take all reasonable steps to correct a violation once it is detected. Moreover, the practice should reevaluate its compliance plan during this time to determine why a violation occurred and if the violation was the result of a failure in the compliance plan. If so, then the plan should be modified.

MINIMIZING RISKS

An effective compliance plan can help a practice prevent violations and facilitate the gathering and dissemination of information on legal requirements, changes in laws and regulations, and payer rules. In this regard, each practice should put its compliance team in place. That is, each practice should assess its legal, consulting, and billing needs to ensure that all applicable information is being brought to the attention of practice owners, partners, and staff. For example, does your practice have appropriate advisors (legal and consulting) or adequately trained staff to ensure that the practice is aware of changes in laws, regulations, and billing requirements? Does your practice utilize an outside billing company that has implemented its own compliance plan in accordance with governmental requirements?

How will this affect your practice?

1. Attorney–client privilege. A properly implemented compliance plan may help a practice take advantage of the attorney–client privilege as a tool for protecting the practice. For practical reasons, a practice may ultimately choose not to take advantage of the privilege, due to its desire to fully cooperate with the government during the course of an investigation and thus turn over all relevant, requested information. But it is still better for the practice to be in a position to choose to waive the privilege, rather than having no privilege applicable at all.

For example, a practice may want to conduct an audit using a billing consultant as part of its compliance process. If the practice engages the consultant directly, the attorney–client privilege will not apply to the report and records of the consultant, and the consultant could be subpoenaed directly by the government without the knowledge of the practice. However, if the practice proceeds through legal counsel as part of its compliance initiatives, it may be successful in invoking the attorney–client privilege. In such circumstances, the government may be required to subpoena the practice directly, which would put the practice on notice at a much earlier point in time of an investigation. Ultimately, the same records and reports may be turned over to the government, but the potential for application of the attorney–client privilege may force the government to proceed in a different manner.

2. Qui tam (whistle-blower) suits. Implementing compliance initiatives may also help a practice protect itself from whistle-blower suits, also known as *qui tam* suits. These are suits brought by, or with the help of, private individuals who have an incentive to bring suit because they get a percentage of the recovery, if any. Disgruntled employees often initiate qui tam litigation. If, as a result of implementing a compliance plan, a practice routinely and in good faith inquires whether its employees are aware of any improper activity of the practice or its employees or agents, the practice may be in a position at a later time, after an employee brings a *qui tam* action, to argue that the employee indicated that he or she was unaware of any such activity. This could potentially impact adversely on the *qui tam* suit or be considered a mitigating factor under the sentencing parameters. Practices should consider implementing such inquiries on a formal, written basis as part of employee annual evaluations and upon termination of employment as part of an exit interview.

GOOD COMPLIANCE IS GOOD MARKETING

In addition to concerns about governmental enforcement efforts, physicians also find themselves at the mercy of insurance companies. Being included on payer panels, and the extent of reimbursement from payers, can significantly affect the financial well-being of your practice. This is especially the case when exclusion from a particular panel could lead to significantly reduced patient volume or when decreased reimbursement would adversely affect cash flow. Physicians often have little recourse when it comes to payer decisions in these areas. Yet, if you can show payers how your practice differs from others, perhaps you can show them that you, and not your competition, should be included on their panel or how a higher reimbursement rate is appropriate for your practice. Implementing an effective compliance plan can help make your practice attractive to payers and managed care plans.

Insurance companies must answer to their stockholders, and thus they are interested in the bottom line. Your voluntary implementation of a compliance plan reflects your ethical commitment to rendering medically necessary care and to properly billing for services. Having a compliance plan saves payers money in several ways. First, the implementation of compliance initiatives reduces the likelihood that unnecessary medical services will be provided, thereby improving the odds that a payer will realize a profit from your practice. Second, the payer has less cause to be concerned about billing errors associated with your practice since your compliance initiatives evidence a commitment to appropriate billing and, if effectively implemented, will reduce the likelihood of such errors and potential overpayments to your practice. This means that the payer need not monitor your practice as closely as others and may have reduced auditing costs, further enhancing their bottom line. Given these factors, if a payer has a decision to make between including you on their panel or a competitor who has not implemented a compliance plan, whom do you think they will choose?

You should also keep in mind that your patients are ultimately one of your best marketing opportunities. Of course, you want them to continue to return for care as needed. But they can also recommend and promote you and your practice to friends and relatives. Their loyalty stems from their connection to you and your practice, not only because of their improved health and well-being, but also because of your level of communication with them. The insurgence of managed care, the corporate culture of payers, and the accompanying financial and time pressures on physicians have created constraints in today's health care system that place barriers between patients and physicians. If patients' feelings of isolation can be assuaged, they will feel closer to you and more connected with your practice.

This can be done through communication with your patients about the decisions being made by you and your practice that affect them. Let your patients know you have implemented a compliance plan and a code of conduct as part of your compliance initiatives. Taking these steps shows patients that you care about them. They also show your commitment to providing medically necessary care and ensuring that such care is billed in the appropriate manner.

You can inform patients about your code of conduct through a plaque in your reception area, on a separate notice provided on their first visit to the office, through a mailing, or in your office brochure or newsletter. The plaque or notice should inform them about your commitment to medically necessary care and to proper billing. It could include a copy of the code of conduct adopted as part of your compliance plan. There are patients who are aware of the problems of fraud and abuse in the health care industry (especially Medicare patients who are constantly reminded by the government to be on the lookout for fraud). They will be impressed by your commitment to embracing ethical standards and will feel a closer connection to you and your practice as a result of your having communicated with them.

DOES YOUR PRACTICE NEED A COMPLIANCE PLAN?

Physicians often question whether their practice needs a compliance plan. Naturally, they are concerned about the cost and expense associated with implementing a plan, as well as the time commitment. Most small practices believe that such a plan is unnecessary, especially since the physician owners are sure that the billing staff has everything under control. From an enforcement perspective, the answer to this question is something of a "Catch-22." That is, you only need a compliance plan if you are not in compliance; but, you will only know if you are in compliance if you have instituted some sort of initiative similar to a compliance plan.

One question to ask your practice is: How do you actually know if you are in compliance? In a similar vein, how does a payer know you are in compliance? Your staff may believe that they are doing everything right, but you may be surprised. Do you have a certified procedural coder on staff or accessible to you who periodically checks all the billing and compares the bills with the charts? Do your staff regularly attend seminars or receive publications to educate them on the ever-changing billing and reimbursement requirements? Ultimately, it is the practice and its physicians who will be held responsible by the government and payers, not the staff.

COSTS OF IMPLEMENTING AN EFFECTIVE COMPLIANCE PLAN

Physicians are naturally concerned about the cost and expense associated with implementing a compliance plan. In this regard, think about the amount of time, money, and effort you have expended in evaluating and pursuing business options for your practice in recent years. Most physicians have spent an inordinate amount of time and money in exploring their options and business alternatives during the past several years. These include analyzing whether they should merge with other practices, sell their practices to a hospital system, seek an arrangement with a physician practice management company, or join an independent practice association or physician–hospital organization. If physicians invest as much time and energy into compliance as they have with these initiatives over the last several years, they will be in a good position vis-à-vis compliance. Moreover, the cost of implementing compliance initiatives may be offset to some extent by the marketing opportunities that result from such initiatives and the peace of mind you will have as a result.

The cost of compliance initiatives from preparation of a written plan to completion of a baseline audit varies, in part according to the size of the medical practice.

A representative sampling of claims needs to be reviewed by a billing consultant for an audit to provide meaningful information. Thus, at least 20 to 25 claims per physician must be reviewed, usually at a cost of anywhere from $1,000 to $1,800 per physician, exclusive of travel costs and expenses. (Discounts may be possible with large groups.)

The billing consultant will most likely also be asked to conduct training sessions for physicians to review audit findings and educate staff about billing, coding, and documentation requirements (usually at a cost of $800 to $1,600 per session, depending upon the number of attendees). These fees do not include preparation of the compliance plan and revisions the practice may request, or costs for legal oversight of consulting services and review of the consultant's report. Small- to medium-sized medical practices should therefore probably count on spending from $8,000 to $20,000 for all these services (legal and consulting), depending upon the practice's needs. Some of these out-of-pocket costs can be defrayed if practices take the initiative and educate themselves and staff members sufficiently so that they can take on the bulk of the plan preparation and other functions. But, ultimately, the costs come from somewhere, whether direct costs paid out or personnel time and education costs to become conversant with compliance requirements.

GETTING STARTED WITH COMPLIANCE INITIATIVES

The place to start with compliance initiatives is to assess your needs and get your team in place. Determine what your staffing, consulting, and legal needs are and ask yourself questions such as the following:

- *Do you have an attorney who specializes in health care–related matters and understands compliance?* If not, you may need to hire separate legal compliance counsel with experience in this area. This does not mean you need to replace your present attorney, but rather that you require different expertise in the compliance area. Your attorney should give you an honest assessment of his or her ability in compliance matters.
- *Who in your practice has sufficient authority to assume responsibility as the compliance officer and spearhead the compliance process?* Does the person you have in mind truly have sufficient authority and time to properly meet the demands of the job? Would you rather contract-out the role of compliance officer?
- *Have you ever engaged a consultant to do a practice assessment or audit of your billing records?* Is he or she located in your geographic area? Perhaps you have met consultants at society meetings who have impressed you with their expertise or you are aware of other practices that have been pleased with consulting type of services.

Attorneys well versed in compliance can guide you through the process. They can help you find a consultant (preferably in your locale) who has experience in your specialty and help you determine who in your practice could serve as the compliance officer. Then, the process can begin with the consultant being engaged by legal counsel to provide a variety of services. These include conducting a practice assessment, performing a baseline audit, conducting education and training sessions for employees (physicians included), and drafting or helping the practice to draft policies and procedures to be included as part of compliance initiatives. Legal counsel may draft the compliance plan (and certain policies) or guide your practice in doing so on its own, and will help the compliance officer oversee implementation of the plan.

Throughout the process, legal counsel will also supervise consultants in their responsibilities. Consultants essentially serve as the eyes and ears for legal counsel and the work they are doing is on behalf of legal counsel. Consultants are obligated to report their findings to legal counsel and to alert counsel to potential problems, including those associated with the practice assessment or baseline audit.

Finding a qualified attorney is similar to finding a good medical specialist. First, you want to ensure that the attorney is qualified to handle compliance-related matters. Ask them about the types of matters they have handled and for a list of client references. Many attorneys in the health care field may not have prepared compliance plans themselves, so ask if they have done so. The attorney should also be a member of the American Health Lawyers Association (AHLA, *www.healthlawyers.org*), which maintains a directory of attorneys concentrating in health care. This, however, only ensures that they have access to certain types of information and is not necessarily an indication of their experience level, since membership in the AHLA is obtained through annual dues and is not based upon qualifications.

Once all the various tasks have been completed, from implementation of the compliance plan to education of employees and auditing of medical records, the practice should be in a position to stand on its own. In this respect, a practice should follow its compliance plan perhaps through self-auditing, monitoring, and educating employees. The goal of the compliance process should be to put the practice in a self-sufficient position so that it weans itself from the consultants and lawyers, with perhaps only periodic input needed.

CONCLUSION

Managing the business of medicine is not easy. The pressures of the health care marketplace require physicians to constantly be on the lookout for ways to differentiate themselves from their competition. Moreover, physicians need to be aware of, and address, a whole host of legal, regulatory, and reimbursement requirements in order to minimize their risks. *Compliance initiatives are one way for practices to gain a competitive edge while minimizing these sorts of risks and protecting themselves from government enforcement efforts.*

The government has a multitude of laws, and extensive financing, in its arsenal to fight health care fraud and abuse and to pursue integrated enforcement across the various agencies and departments. Private insurance companies also allocate significant funding to further similar goals. Consequently, no provider is immune from the possibility of an audit or investigation, whether from governmental agents or private payers. Because of this, physicians should be proactive and implement a compliance plan for their practices. By doing so they will enjoy a certain degree of comfort that they are, and will continue to be, in compliance to the best of their abilities. They will simultaneously convey to private payers and their patients that they are providing quality care at the appropriate price.

Compliance initiatives can help practices identify problem areas, decrease the likelihood of billing errors and other problems, protect practices from qui tam lawsuits, and mitigate the extent of fines or penalties that could be imposed by the government as part of enforcement efforts. In pursuing these goals, practices need to address a number of important areas identified by the government in its compliance guidance, from establishing policies and standards to educating employees and disciplining those who do not cooperate. In light of governmental efforts in the fraud and abuse area, physicians would be well served to address compliance matters before they are forced to do so. And, if they can use their own compliance initiatives to help market their practices to payers and patients alike, they will be poised to counter market pressures and remain financially viable.

The Bottom Line *When it comes to compliance, it is best to follow the Scout motto: "Be Prepared." Only by being proactive and instituting and following a compliance plan can you ensure that it will rarely (if ever) be needed.*

NOTE

1. Copies of all this guidance can be downloaded from the website for the Office of Inspector General by going to: *www.dhhs.gov/progorg.oig* and clicking on the "OIG Electronic Reading Room" and then on "Compliance Guidance."

CHAPTER 45

The Buck Stops Here: Is Your Coding Up to Par?

Patricia T. Aalseth

You are responsible for the accuracy of the diagnosis and procedure codes that are submitted on claim forms for your patients. Can you answer "yes" to the following questions?

1. Do the diagnosis codes represent the patient's condition and the reason he or she came for treatment?
2. Do the procedure codes reflect services you provided?
3. Are the diagnoses and procedures documented in the patient's medical record?
4. Have you followed the official coding guidelines?

Chances are you will not be sure about your answer to question 4.

If you did not answer yes to all four questions, then you will want to read this chapter on proper coding. Being unsure about official coding guidelines can be dangerous to the health of your practice. Incorrect, incomplete, or improper coding can actually result in legal actions against you. And even if the prosecutors do not pick up on coding gaffs, you may have patients whose claims under Medicare are not paid or only partially reimbursed, causing them needless worry and anxiety. Those are emotions that will reflect on you, resulting in a "negative cash flow" when it comes to business goodwill. This chapter will provide you with suggestions that will result in prompt and proper payment for your services and help you maintain a friendly financial relationship with your patients.

Patricia T. Aalseth, RRA, CCS, CPHQ, is a medical practice specialist and documenting and coding specialist with University Physician Associates, 1650 University, NE Suite 115, Albuquerque, NM 87102; (505) 272–3644; *aalseth@earthlink.net.*

YES, VIRGINIA, THERE ARE RULES

The Federal False Claims Act, under which medical fraud and abuse cases are prosecuted, was revised in 1986 to eliminate the need to prove that providers had the *intent* to defraud.[1] In other words, a pattern of miscoding that results in overpayment to you may be sufficient grounds for prosecution, regardless of your intent. Ignorance of the rules is no longer an excuse. Before you panic, take steps to ensure that your coding will be audit-proof, from this day forward.
Follow these straightforward steps:

1. Review the official diagnosis coding guidelines (see Exhibit 45–1).
2. Obtain a copy of the Correct Coding Initiative for procedure codes.[2]
3. Review and revise your superbills or charge documents.
4. Make sure your office employees know and follow the rules.
5. Put the medical record back into the billing loop—assign a staff member responsibility for verifying that the record contains adequate documentation to support the codes billed, *before* the claim goes out the door.
6. Analyze your denied claims to see if coding errors are costing you money.

DIAGNOSING THE DIAGNOSIS

As a physician, you know that patients come to your office for a variety of reasons, ranging from the need for a physical exam for insurance purposes to a consultation for an undiagnosed condition, to a follow-up of a chronic condition. In order to be paid for your services, you must condense all the patient's conditions, symptoms, problems, and reasons for being there into the four diagnosis code numbers that best describe the circumstances of the encounter and provide the medically necessary justification for the services.
The most common diagnosis coding mistakes to avoid are:

1. *Coding a "rule/out" condition as if it existed.* Code instead the signs, symptoms, abnormal test results, or other reasons that necessitate your ruling out a condition (see Section H in Exhibit 45–1). Example: instead of "R/O pneumonia," use "cough, fever, r/o pneumonia."
2. *Coding a previous condition that no longer exists.* Make sure the primary diagnosis (first-listed) represents the real reason for the visit, to the highest level of specificity known at the time (see Section J in Exhibit 45–1). Example: the patient had shingles last year but had no sequelae when you last saw him three months ago. He is in today for a routine physical for insurance purposes, and there are no positive findings. Do not list shingles as an existing diagnosis.

Exhibit 45–1 Excerpts of Diagnostic Coding and Reporting Guidelines for Outpatient Services (Hospital-Based and Physician Office)

The terms *encounter* and *visit* are often used interchangeably in describing outpatient service contacts and, therefore, appear together in these guidelines without distinguishing one from the other.

Diagnoses often are not established at the time of the initial encounter/visit. It may take two or more visits before the diagnosis is confirmed.

A. The appropriate code or codes from 001.0 through V82.9 must be used to identify diagnoses, symptoms, conditions, problems, complaints, or other reasons for the encounter/visit.

B. For accurate reporting of ICD–9–CM diagnosis codes, the documentation should describe the patient's condition, using terminology which includes specific diagnoses as well as symptoms, problems, or reasons for the encounter. There are ICD–9–CM codes to describe all of these.

C. The selection of codes 001.0 through 999.9 will frequently be used to describe the reason for the encounter. These codes are from the section of ICD–9–CM for the classification of diseases and injuries (e.g., infectious and parasitic diseases; neoplasms; symptoms, signs, and ill-defined conditions, etc.).

D. Codes that describe symptoms and signs, as opposed to diagnoses, are acceptable for reporting purposes when an established diagnosis has not been diagnosed (confirmed) by the physician. Chapter 16 of ICD–9–CM, Symptoms, Signs, and Ill-defined Conditions (codes 780.–799.9) contains many, but not all codes for symptoms.

E. ICD–9–CM provides codes to deal with encounters for circumstances other than a disease or injury. The Supplementary Classification of Factors Influencing Health Status and Contact with Health Services (V01.0–V82.9) is provided to deal with occasions when circumstances other than a disease or injury are recorded as diagnoses or problems.

F. ICD–9–CM is composed of codes with either 3, 4, or 5 digits. Codes with 3 digits are included in ICD–9–CM as the heading of a category of codes that may be further subdivided by the use of fourth and/or fifth digits which provide greater specificity. A three-digit code is to be used only if it is not further subdivided. Where fourth-digit subcategories and/or fifth-digit subclassifications are provided, they must be assigned. A code is invalid if it has not been coded to the full number of digits required for that code.

G. List first the ICD–9–CM code for the diagnosis, condition, problem, or other reason for encounter/visit shown in the medical record to be chiefly responsible for the services provided. List additional codes that describe any coexisting conditions.

H. Do not code diagnoses documented as "probable," "suspected," "ques-

continues

Exhibit 45–1 continued

tionable," "rule out," or working diagnosis. Rather, code the condition(s) to the highest degree of certainty for that encounter/visit, such as symptoms, signs, abnormal test results, or other reason for the visit. Please note: This is contrary to the rules used by hospitals for coding the diagnoses of hospital inpatients.

I. Chronic diseases treated on an ongoing basis may be coded and reported as many times as the patient receives treatment and care for the condition(s).

J. Code all documented conditions that coexist at the time of the encounter/visit, and require or affect patient care treatment or management. Do not code conditions that were previously treated and no longer exist. However, history codes (V10–V19) may be used as secondary codes if the historical condition or family history has an impact on current care or influences treatment.

K. For patients receiving diagnostic services only during an encounter/visit, sequence first the diagnosis, condition, problem, or other reason for encounter/visit shown in the medical record to be chiefly responsible for the outpatient services provided during the encounter/visit. Codes for other diagnoses (e.g., chronic conditions) may be sequenced as additional diagnoses.

L. For patients receiving therapeutic services only during an encounter/visit, sequence first the diagnosis, condition, problem, or other reason for encounter/visit shown in the medical record to be chiefly responsible for the outpatient services provided during the encounter/visit. Codes for other diagnosis (e.g., chronic conditions) may be sequenced as additional diagnoses. The only exception to this rule is that for patients receiving chemotherapy, radiation therapy, or rehabilitation, the appropriate V code for the service is listed first and the diagnosis or problem for which the service is being performed is listed second.
(Note: The official guidelines contain no section M.)

N. For patient receiving pre-operative evaluations only, sequence a code from category V72.8, Other specified examinations, to describe the pre-op consultations. Assign a code for the condition to describe the reason for the surgery as an additional diagnosis. Code also any findings related to the pre-op evaluation.

O. For ambulatory surgery, code the diagnosis for which the surgery was performed. If the postoperative diagnosis is known to be different from the preoperative diagnosis at the time the diagnosis is confirmed, select the postoperative diagnosis for coding, since it is the most definitive.

Source: Diagnosis coding rules are in the public domain and can be found in the National Center for Health Statistics, "Diagnostic Coding and Reporting Guidelines for Outpatient Services (Hospital-Based and Physician Office)," *www.cdc.gov/nchswww/data/icdguide.*
Note: Revised October 1, 1995.

3. *Using a diagnosis "cheat sheet" that contains common conditions, but not codes for the level of specificity documented in the patient's chart.* Example: the patient has PVCs, but the code for this (427.69) is not listed on the office cheat sheet, so the coder puts it under 427.9 "arrhythmia, not otherwise specified." This shortcut may result in claims denial due to lack of medical necessity.

4. *Using outdated code books.* (See "Additional Resources" in Chapter 12 to order.)

ROUTINE VISITS: THE VICIOUS "V" CODES

What if there are no specific complaints when the patient comes to your office? How should you code the visit? A "V" code is probably the most frequent answer to the question: "What diagnosis do I code if the patient has no complaints?" *In an office practice, V codes are used when:*

1. A person with no current illness is being seen for a specific purpose.
2. A patient with a resolving disease or injury or a chronic condition is being seen for after-care or special therapy.
3. The patient has a history, health status, or other problem that may affect his or her care, although it is not in itself a current disease or injury.

Instances in which a V code is appropriate are: routine physicals, monitoring of long-term anticoagulant use, repeat prescription, suture removal, supervision of normal pregnancy, screening exams for neoplasms, chemotherapy, attention to artificial openings, etc.

If you use a diagnosis code indicating a condition the patient no longer has, instead of using a V code for the visit, you are incorrectly representing the diagnosis to the payer. *This is fraud and will expose you to expensive financial penalties* (see Section E in Exhibit 45–1). Admittedly, payers tend to use the presence of a V code as a flag for nonpayment, but this inappropriate practice is waning, particularly in the light of state laws with mandated benefits for routine physicals and screening exams, such as mammograms.

BENDING THE RULES—JUST THIS ONCE

Every practice has at least a few patients who tear at our heartstrings, perhaps due to poverty or other family circumstances. In your efforts to make sure these patients continue to report for needed follow-up care, it is all too tempting to bend the rules and submit a diagnosis for which you know you will be reimbursed, instead of the diagnosis for the actual condition, which might not be reimbursed.

Consider, instead, other possibilities that are ethically appropriate:

- professional courtesy (follow payer rules)
- referral to community support programs for assistance with payment
- referral to a community clinic with a sliding fee scale based on income

Bending the rules, just once, even for the most philanthropic reasons, leaves you and your practice at risk, jeopardizing all your patients.

BILL WHAT YOU SAY, NOT WHAT YOU DO

Current Procedural Terminology (CPT) is published annually by the American Medical Association (AMA) and serves as the basic coding structure for procedures performed by physicians. The Health Care Financing Administration (HCFA) contracts with the AMA to use CPT for federal billing purposes in an expanded version, called HCPCS (HCFA Common Procedure Coding System). HCPCS includes additional alphanumeric codes not found in CPT that are used to bill for supplies, drugs, and durable medical equipment. (See "Additional Resources" in Chapter 12 for ordering information.)

Dictation Tip: *Keep the CPT book nearby and review the wording of the codes as you dictate.* Use language in your dictation that matches that in the book. An example of procedure description to use in dictation could be "extracapsular cataract extraction," which differentiates it from intracapsular, which has a different code.

Make sure you bill only what you say, not what you do. In other words, you can only bill for what is documented in the patient's record, regardless of what you did. This is why it is so important to have someone else compare the record with the charge document, to make sure!

PROCEDURES—DOING THE RIGHT THING

Just because the CPT book contains a code that seems to describe what you did does not mean that a payer will pay you for billing that code. A notable charge in this regard is the code for telephone calls, which is considered a noncovered service by all payers. Although there is a procedure code for phone calls (a copyrighted CPT code), Medicare considers phone calls to be bundled into other services. With other third-party payers, it might be up to you, the provider, to decide whether to charge the patient.

In addition, a focus of current fraud and abuse investigations is unbundling, the use of more than one procedure code to describe procedures that should be covered by the most extensive code. The Correct Coding Initiative is a HCFA claims editing program designed to ferret out unbundled procedure code combinations. It also looks for codes that are mutually exclusive or otherwise incorrectly used. Unfortunately, you will have to pay to get this book or computer program resource. An alternative is to pay attention to your denials due to unbundling and make sure your staff members understand the reasons for denial so they will not repeat the error.

Some types of procedures that should not be billed:

- local anesthesia administered by you if you are performing the procedure
- procedures integral to surgery, such as skin preparation, positioning the patient, surgical approach, irrigation, cultures, insertion and removal of drains, simple closure
- less extensive procedures; only the most complex from a series performed should be billed
- procedures described in the CPT as a "separate procedure" when performed with a more comprehensive procedure

LINKING UP TO REIMBURSEMENT

Each of the six possible procedure codes you use on your claims to charge for services you provided can be linked to one of the four diagnosis codes on the same claim. The object of this linkage is to provide diagnostic medical necessity justification for the procedures. This is particularly important if you provide services during a single encounter for two widely differing conditions. If no linking is done, the diagnosis defaults to the first listed, which might not match the other services in terms of medical necessity.

One general example of linking:

Primary diagnosis (reason for visit) = hematuria
Secondary diagnosis = genital wart
Procedures = destruction of wart

On the claim form, you would want to be sure that the procedure code for destruction of wart is linked to diagnosis number 2, not the primary diagnosis.

WHAT YOU SAY IS WHAT THEY WILL PAY (WE HOPE)

When it comes to coding, one word can make a huge difference. Let's look at diagnosis first. What gets coded and what does not? (See Section H in Exhibit 45–1.) Following this guideline, the underlined words in the example below would be coded, the others not:

abdominal pain, R/O gastritis
abdominal pain due to gastritis

Likewise, with procedures, the omission of a single word can make a difference. The procedure descriptions below are represented in CPT by two different code numbers, with two different reimbursement amounts:

prostatectomy, retropubic, subtotal
prostatectomy, retropubic, radical

Careful description will be rewarded with appropriate reimbursement. Procedure descriptions must include site, technique, and laterality, where appropriate.

THE WHOLE WORLD IS WATCHING

You may have been asking "What does coding have to do with patients?" Aside from the fact that your goal is to run your practice ethically, effectively, and economically, you need to know that patients are increasingly aware of billing and coding practices. They are being recruited to watch for health care fraud and abuse by the government and by voluntary associations interested in how health care dollars are being spent. Retirees, in particular, are waking up to the fact that their tax money is wasted if fraud and abuse are allowed to continue.

The government's Medicare website[3] warns patients to "be suspicious of:

- Physicians who bill Medicare for a routine checkup.
- Physicians who give the wrong diagnosis on the claim form so Medicare will pay.
- Physicians who bill Medicare for telephone calls, conference with the family, or "scheduled but not kept appointments."

Publication and dissemination of patients' bill of rights for health maintenance organization enrollees have also increased awareness of coding and how the coding process affects the ability to obtain approval for needed services.

The Bottom Line   *In these times, payers as well as patients will be scrutinizing your claims and the resulting explanations of benefits to see if you have billed and coded correctly. Attending to issues of proper coding ensures the health and wealth of your practice.*

NOTES

1. False Claims Act, 31 U.S.C. 3729.
2. National Correct Coding Initiative Reference Tools can be obtained from the National Technical Information Service, U.S. Department of Commerce, Springfield, VA 22161, (800) 363–2068.

Available items include printed manual, quarterly subscription SUB-9576INQ; individual chapters, quarterly subscription; or a CD-ROM or diskette, quarterly subscription SUB-5411.

3. Information on Medicare can be found at *www.medicare.gov/fraudabuse*.

CHAPTER 46

When You Are in the Market for a New Associate

Roger G. Bonds

Thousands of physician practices, hospitals, and managed care companies are actively recruiting physicians today. It is no wonder that the recruitment process has become extremely competitive and sometimes frustrating. Even though medical practices spend large amounts of money and time on the recruitment process, many do not find the physicians they need—or want.

Some practices discover too late that the new recruit is an unsatisfactory personal or professional match with the rest of the practice. Unfortunately, the retention and productivity of newly recruited physicians are all too often unacceptable. For example, our research at the National Institute of Physician Career Development shows that a newly practicing physician stays in his or her first job only 2.4 years.

Deciding to take on another associate and potential partner is often the most important decision you will make in your professional lifetime. This chapter outlines the steps of proceeding on the partnership path. Taking a cooperative approach and implementing an organized plan can help practices of all sizes avoid most of the disappointments and pitfalls associated with recruiting today.

Roger G. Bonds, MBA, CMSR, FMSD, is president of the National Institute of Physician Career Development in Atlanta, Georgia (*www.medicalmgnt.org, rbonds@flash.net*, or [770] 734–9904). Among his publications are *Physician Recruitment & Retention, Practical Techniques for Exceptional Results*, and *The Medical Job Search: How To Find the Best Position for Your Financial Independence and Peace of Mind.* He speaks nationally to physician groups on expanding their practices, and to residents, fellows, and practicing physicians on career development.

The suggestions presented here are based on techniques developed at the National Institute of Physician Career Development on how to properly recruit and retain the most productive physicians.

OBJECTIVELY ASSESS NEEDS

Regardless of its size, each practice should first carefully analyze its practice operations before it proceeds with recruitment activities. A large organization of more that 15 physicians should also develop an objective physician manpower assessment.

A small practice in need of more physicians may find it worthwhile to consider employing a physician assistant or nurse practitioner instead. These professionals, depending on the specialty and the state laws, can often generate significant profits for the practice, while maximizing practice potential.

In larger organizations, a physician manpower assessment is the driving force behind all recruiting activities. When completed, this assessment not only shows whether or not a practice should recruit additional physicians, but also how many and in which specialties the practice should recruit in order to stay competitive in the marketplace.

Typically there are two ways to develop a physician manpower assessment:

- Through obvious need (that is, a member of the practice plans to retire or the practice has more patients that it can accommodate).
- Through an in-depth physician manpower study (usually funded by a hospital, university, or managed care company) that shows the community is underserved in a particular area.

The in-depth physician manpower assessment encompasses a variety of quantitative information, including physician-to-population ratios and community demographic trends. Such information is extremely important to helping practices objectively evaluate their need for physicians.

Physician-to-population ratios provide guidelines concerning the "ideal" number of physicians needed to support a population, according to specialty and even subspecialty. The most universally accepted physician-to-population ratios are reported by Graduate Medical Education National Advisory Committee reports and *Medical Economics* magazine.[1] While these reports do not include all subspecialties, and the "ideal" physician-to-population ratios vary between the two sources, they provide a quick means of evaluating the potential of a practice to support another physician within a given community. Establishing a true need for another associate should be based on specific information in your practice area.

Community demographic trends include valuable information concerning a community's population and age trends, incidence of disease rates, and payer mix.

Each of these factors plays an important role in determining a practice's present and future ability to support additional physicians.

GENERATE A GROUP CONSENSUS

Once the need for additional physicians has been fully substantiated, practice members must agree on the type and qualifications of the physician to be recruited. Without initial consensus, group members may have difficulty agreeing on the selection of final candidates.

Whether small or large, practices should carefully consider and openly answer the following questions before starting the recruitment process.

- Will the practice benefit most by recruiting a newly graduated resident or fellow, or a mature, practicing physician with several years' experience?
- Does the practice want an associate (employee) or partner? Will an associate eventually be offered a partnership? When?
- Does the practice want to recruit locally, regionally, or nationally? While it is much less expensive and productive to recruit on a local or regional level, in some instances it may be necessary to recruit on a national level—particularly when seeking subspecialty physicians.
- Will the practice consider foreign-born physicians, in addition to American-born physicians? Today there are many highly qualified international medical graduates who have spent their residencies at American institutions and who speak fluent English.
- Does the group prefer to recruit (or not recruit) from specific medical schools or residency programs?
- What personal and professional qualities are desired?
- What specialty or subspecialty interest, skills, or certification does the practice want the new physician to possess? For example, an obstetrics/gynecology group may agree that their practice would greatly benefit from a new physician who has an interest in perinatology.

Not only should the practice members define the ideal characteristics and qualifications of a new physician, they must also define and agree upon the responsibilities and compensation for the physician. Again, openly discussing and achieving a consensus at the beginning of the process can eliminate further problems. Practices can purchase a compensation study to help guide them in establishing an equitable compensation package.

To ensure that everyone stays on track with what has been discussed and agreed upon, an opportunity description (Exhibit 46–1) should be developed and distributed to all practice members. This description, which can be developed much like a job description, should be limited to one typewritten page that includes details of

Exhibit 46–1 Sample Opportunity Description

The following opportunity description should be written objectively and signed by each physician or physician partner.

Situation: The Northwest Orthopaedic Surgery Group is composed of four certified orthopaedists, two with subspecialties in sports medicine. This practice seeks a fifth M.D. to join them as an employee for a two-year period, after which a partnership opportunity may be available.

The practice is thriving with a strong referral pattern from primary care physicians in the northern part of the county, as well as some referrals from within the city. Facilities are fairly good, with adequate space, but some outdated furnishings do exist.

Requirements: The ideal candidate will be an experienced female* practicing physician with an interest in sports medicine. She would be best suited for the growing number of 25- to 35-year-old female patients the practice is serving. Preferably, the successful candidate will have lived in the state or in a surrounding state at some point, and will prefer to live in an urban or suburban setting.

To fit well with other group members, the physician should be aggressive, articulate, and able to "stand on her own." She will be expected to be involved in the community, giving presentations and working with local sports groups.

Income and Benefits: A base salary of $200,000 plus a significant incentive bonus is agreed upon at this time. A qualified candidate will be able to command more. Standard physician benefits are covered, including continuing medical education (CME) expenses, vacation, health, disability and malpractice insurance, etc. All members of the group have agreed to be available for interviews with one week's notice, except for the weeks of April 21–May 2 and July 4–10.

Ideal Start Date: On or about September 1.

* Under federal employment laws, you can legally recruit for a female, as females are a protected minority in the work force. You cannot recruit strictly for a male, as that would discriminate against females, who are a protected minority. State laws may vary. If you are recruiting a partner or contracted, independent physician (not an employee), the employment laws do not apply. Check with your administrative staff or attorney if you have questions.

---

the situation, a listing of desired qualifications, and an enumeration of the income, benefits, and activities for professional growth. This document is for internal use only and outlines the parameters of the ideal candidate so that recruitment activities can be directed appropriately.

PERFORM AN INTERNAL ASSESSMENT

Before developing recruitment strategies, a practice should perform an internal assessment that objectively evaluates the benefits and drawbacks of an additional physician joining the practice. Honestly performing this assessment improves the likelihood of successfully interviewing and hiring the right candidate.
Here are some examples of questions to be included:

- Will the new physician be working with a well-respected team with a solid foundation?
- Will the new physician enjoy the benefits of an efficiently run office with good nurses, state-of-the-art equipment, and plenty of patients?
- Does the area have good schools, a strong community spirit, and stimulating cultural activities?
- What about relationships with physicians outside the practice?
- Are there sufficient referrals from other specialists?

Do not neglect examining potential drawbacks for your prospective recruits. These might be revealed by asking the following questions:

- Is the practice situated in a less than desirable location?
- Is there an unwillingness to share call duties?
- Is the practice affiliated with a mediocre hospital?
- Does the hospital or the practice suffer from poor management and nursing support?

Perhaps the most important question to consider is: Will the practice be able to financially support and hopefully make an increased profit by adding another physician? Your accountant should work up a proforma (financial forecast) showing the costs and financial benefits of adding the new physician. You can then weigh this in unison with the nonfinancial benefits, such as increased call coverage, ability to obtain or retain managed care contracts, and expanded office hours for evening and weekend coverage.

Important note: *Do not hesitate to show the resulting proforma to physician candidates you are seriously interviewing.* Many expect such an analysis, and if it shows a solid practice (whether adding profits or not), it will be an excellent sales tool to convince the best candidate to join you.

If your internal assessment reveals significant problems, your practice members should emphasize the positives with potential candidates and not dwell on the negatives. It is always best, however, to reveal any limitations at some point during the interview process. The worst thing that can happen is for a potential candidate to hear about the negatives from someone else—or for a new physician to experience them after coming on board.

ADDRESS HIDDEN AGENDAS

Ignoring the hidden agendas and politics that exist within larger practices and their medical communities can undermine even the best recruitment efforts. It is important to realize that a wide discrepancy usually exists among physicians concerning the desired qualifications, personality, responsibilities, or compensation of a new associate. Bringing a new recruit into a group with dissenting or disdainful physicians will guarantee the waste of a practice's recruitment time and dollars because the new physician will most likely opt to leave such an uncomfortable professional situation.

Recognizing the politics among the medical community is also important. In some instances, the recruitment of additional physicians may be perceived as an economic threat by other community physicians, despite the fact that the local demand fully substantiates the need for additional doctors. This is especially a problem if you rely on referrals or strong working relationships to obtain managed care contracts. When this happens, it is not uncommon for a new physician to experience difficulty in being accepted by the disgruntled medical community. To avoid surprises, it is best to apprise potential candidates about the medical community's attitude.

The best way to determine whether or not other members of a medical community will support a practice's intention to add additional physicians is to communicate as openly as possible. If they are supportive, this open communication can contribute greatly to future referrals. If they are not supportive, a practice can develop strategies to address the situation.

Politics within the hospital community should also be considered. Will the community's hospital support a practice's intentions to bring in new physicians or will they perceive this as a threat to existing staff physicians? The same consideration can be given to an area's medical service organizations (MSOs), health maintenance organizations, and other managed care organizations.

ESTABLISH A BUDGET

One of the most common pitfalls of the recruitment effort is the lack of adequate financial resources. Many practices set out to recruit additional physicians without an indication as to the financial investment incurred to properly complete the task. For even a small practice, the average out-of-pocket expense associated with recruiting and starting a new physician in practice is about $25,000. Employing a search firm will add an average of $18,000 to those costs. The normal expenses include all recruiting activities, such as direct mail, advertising the position, and flying candidates in for visits. However, this is only the "sales" or "marketing" portion of the recruitment budget. Additional expenses include moving costs, income guarantees or initial salary (before any revenue is generated), malpractice insurance, and the provision of office space, staff, and equipment. When considering all the costs involved, it is not unusual for larger organizations to spend more than $100,000 to recruit and support the start-up of a new physician. With this kind of price tag, it may take three to four years to recoup the costs of recruiting a new practice member.

However, the real financial analysis should concentrate on the potential benefits. For example, if a small practice spends $25,000 to bring in a new physician, it may seem expensive. But if the two existing physicians are overwhelmed and badly need help, there may be adequate motivation to absorb such a cost. Or perhaps the motivation is to hang on to the managed care business that is currently on the books. Even if revenues are currently decreasing, astute practitioners may elect to bring in another partner knowing that they cannot compete unless they expand. Another simple analysis is to compute the "opportunity cost"—consider the actual dollar cost of not bringing in another associate (that is, losing out on $350,000 in revenue). Viewed in this context, the recruitment and start-up cost may be minimal, especially when amortized over time (usually 36 months).

FINDING CANDIDATES AND KEEPING COSTS DOWN

Unless you do not want your competition to know, using word of mouth to advertise an opening in your practice can be the most efficient means to find qualified candidates. Contact fellow physicians in the local market and ask them to let you know of anyone who might be interested. You can also target potential recruits through residency and fellowship programs. However, be careful in signing a new graduate; as mentioned above, they normally stay in their first positions for less than three years. To ensure that your new recruit stays with your practice long-term, you might want to look for candidates with local ties to the area, who seem to have their feet on the ground, and who are married and own their own home (or will immediately be buying a home). Additionally, if you are considering a young female physician, a certain percentage may negotiate to work only a certain amount of hours, to balance work with their personal life, whether they have children or not.

You can also find candidates by targeting practicing physicians through mailing lists or placing ads in the journals and publications of state, local, and national medical associations, as well as specialty associations. Letters describing practice opportunities can be sent to these physicians asking if they are interested, along with a request to "spread the word" if they are not. Make sure such letters are on the practice letterhead and signed by a physician, not by an administrator or recruiter. National and state medical conferences and meetings provide additional opportunities to reach candidates. Many conferences have career opportunity boards where an opportunity description can be posted (do not forget your hotel phone number in case someone wants to talk to you during the conference). *Sometimes it is appropriate to develop collateral materials, such as a brochure that describes your practice and community.* You can obtain this information on your community from your local Chamber of Commerce. This can be sent as a stand-alone recruitment piece instead of a letter. You may also choose to place ads in such high-profile medical journals as *JAMA* and the *New England Journal of Medicine.* If several physicians are needed, it may be worth creating collateral materials through professional advertising and public relations agencies to enhance the progressive and professional image of a practice and the community that it serves.

Another way to reduce new physician recruitment and practice start-up costs is to share the cost with one or more hospitals. Many hospitals are willing to contribute their time and money to the recruitment efforts and will help acclimate new physicians to the community by assisting them with marketing efforts. Many hospitals and other large health care providers employ one or more full-time in-house physician recruiters and practice management and start-up experts. If a practice finds that one or more hospitals are willing to assist with these efforts, it should ideally obtain such agreements in writing. Also, if hospitals agree to provide significant benefits, such as income guarantees and liability insurance, these agreements should be carefully reviewed by an attorney who is experienced in health care law in order to protect the practice, the new physician, and the hospital against inurement or Medicare fraud and abuse.

Additionally, you can post your opportunity on the Internet. If you have a website, be sure to post there, and you can list your position with numerous generic Internet job listings. At this time there are a few health care and medical Internet job sites, which are evolving rapidly but are currently cost prohibitive for small practices, unless you have multiple open positions. Your hospital may have a contract with one of the medical Internet job sites and may consider listing the position for you under their contract and at no charge to you.

DEVELOP A RECRUITMENT CAMPAIGN PLAN

If the practice is recruiting multiple physicians, consider developing a recruitment campaign plan to ensure your success. This tactical plan coordinates efforts to cut costs substantially and align any recruitment efforts so the task is efficient and highly productive. With as little frustration and cost as possible, the goal is to sign qualified, motivated, new physicians on a timely basis, who stay with you and are highly productive. To generate your plan, outline specific activities that must be completed during a specified period of time to identify and successfully attract physicians for a specific opportunity. These activities include everything from identifying appropriate candidates to screening, interviewing, negotiating the contract, and relocating the physician.

REVIEWING THE CURRICULUM VITAE AND INTERVIEWING

If you promote your open position widely, you will normally receive numerous curriculum vitae (CVs) and letters from interested candidates. For a greater response, add your e-mail address and toll-free number, if you have one, to your promotions. The marketplace will normally draw many physician candidates who do not meet your standards, so it pays to diligently screen out the unacceptable candidates by reviewing their CVs and conducting telephone interviews, even if they are local. The investment of time on this step can save you substantial time and frustration later by eliminating undesirable candidates early in the screening process.

Special note: *You or your staff must respond to any qualified candidates immediately (within 24 hours).* The number-one reason for the loss of the best candidates is the lack of a rapid response. The best candidates are taken quickly.

Look over each CV carefully. Does the candidate have the education and experience that meet your requirements? Are there problems with the CV? Is it well written and properly formatted? Is there a solid cover letter with it? Are there any unexplained discrepancies, such as missing months or years in the work history?

Your next step is to conduct a telephone interview. Resist the temptation to make this too much of a social call. Identify a good time for each of you to talk and set up a telephone appointment. Find a time when you will not be distracted and can give the call your undivided attention. Get past the niceties and ask pointed questions. Ask what sort of practice this physician is looking for and why he or she might want to work with you. If the candidate would be relocating, ask why he or she wants to live in your area. Does the spouse want to live there too, and why? Carefully consider his or her responses. If a candidate says he or she wants to move to your city but has rarely (or never) been through that part of the country, you will need some assurance that this relocation would work. The number-one reason young physicians relocate is to be in a geographical location where they, or their spouses, used to live—or wherever they call "home," especially if they have a growing family.

If the candidate clears the first hurdle of the telephone interview, you should then schedule an in-person interview. Take care to carefully orchestrate the entire visit. If your candidate is from out of town, invite the spouse. The spouse may prefer to have a separate itinerary and may be interested in job interviews of her or his own. Plan to put your best foot forward, as the strongest candidates will have their choice of where to practice. Touring your facility, hospital, and community will be in order. Schedule several physicians to meet with the candidate, possibly in a group setting such as breakfast, lunch, or dinner, but plan also to conduct some individual interviews. Also schedule any key administrative or management staff to interview the candidate as well. It is often a smart business move to have nonphysicians interview the candidate, since many have training in personnel selection. If applicable, you might also schedule outside parties, such as referring physicians or hospital department heads, especially those in human resources, to interview the candidates.

A visit with interviews and some socializing should not exceed two days. If the candidate is local, try to still set up the interviews and any needed tours within half-day or full-day segments. If possible, do not string it out or you and the local candidate can get frustrated and lose momentum and interest. If he or she is from out of town, include a bit of private time for the candidate. It can be overwhelming to have long days and evenings with every hour scheduled to either be interviewed or wined and dined.

After the interviews, carefully obtain the interviewers' feedback, preferably in person or over the phone. Listen just as carefully to your nonphysician interviewers as to your professional colleagues.

BACKGROUND SEARCHES A MUST

Once you identify the physician candidate you would like to sign, it is impera-tive *that you conduct a background search, even if he or she is local.* Such a search will include the normal verification of education and licensure (commonly called credentialing, which your hospital may conduct for you at no charge). It also *must* include a criminal and civil court records check (it is not true that you cannot have a medical license if convicted in either court system—just ask the television producers of *60 Minutes* and *20/20*), driver's license check (may reveal alcohol or drug abuse), credit check (you probably do not need an associate who has financial problems), professional references, and possibly personal references. Obtain the candidate's written permission to check all these. If he or she has a problem with this, then you may already have an indication to move on to another candidate. Note that background checks are the norm, and failure to conduct them may not only result in a poor associate but expose you to major legal and financial risks as you may be held responsible for bringing a "bad" physician to your prac-tice and community without the due process of conducting such a normal and customary action.

CHECKING REFERENCES

Professional references must be thoroughly checked, and you should listen carefully to what is said. If applicable, be sure to check with whomever the candi-date reported to, fellow physicians, referring physicians, hospital staff, and others.

Because giving a negative reference is risky, you often must read between the lines. Listen for key clues, such as hesitations or answering with nebulous information.

The following is the one best reference check technique that I have found over the years. Have your staff find the direct number or extension of the reference, and verify that that person is not currently travelling or on vacation. Call that person at night or perhaps at lunch time so you have to leave a voice mail. State that you are considering Dr. *[candidate]* "and if he/she is an exceptional physician who you highly recommend, could you please call me back at [your phone number]. If not, please disregard this call. Thank you." You may be disappointed at not receiving a return call, but the technique can allow the reference to safely and confidentially communicate a response, provided however that he or she received the message.[2]

EXPECT A BACKGROUND SEARCH ON YOU, TOO!

Today's savvy physician candidates, young and old, are conducting their own background checks on their potential new partners. In our physician career seminars all over the country we stress that each participant should find out the same information about their potential new associates as they are being required to furnish. Many candidates are now routinely asking for financial data in the form of past years' financials and future proformas or budgets. If you are unwilling or unable to provide such data, you will not attract the best candidates. You may desire to amend such a financial report before sharing it, such as remove the individual income of the existing practice partners (however that may be an excellent selling tool). In any case, do not take offense at such requests. Instead, assume such a request is that of a very astute and responsible individual who may become an above-average associate. We have found that candidates who ask good questions and do their homework will typically select a position that is a good fit, stay for years, and be steadfastly productive.

CONTRACT DEVELOPMENT

A contract should always be developed ahead of time that outlines the professional relationship and financial remuneration. These contracts must be written carefully and may be quite lengthy, possibly outlining employment and benefits, or contracted medical services instead. Once you have identified the candidate of choice, you may prefer to write up the contract as a "letter of intent" that is a discussion document only. This will allow you to ascertain if you are both in the ballpark of being able to have a written agreement and discuss any needed changes. Contract samples and physician job descriptions can be obtained from the National Institute of Physician Career Development in Atlanta.

Recruiting additional physicians for a medical practice is not an easy task. It requires planning, patience, and a commitment from all practice members. In fact, in today's competitive environment, it takes an average of six to nine months to recruit a single physician. Physicians and their staff who take a cooperative approach and work together to develop an organized plan for recruitment efforts help ensure that the physicians they recruit are willing to make long-term commitments and contributions that are necessary for future practice growth and financial success.

The Bottom Line   *There is probably no more important marketing decision that you will make for your practice than hiring a new associate. If done improperly, a poor selection often results in a loss of the focus of the practice regarding patient care or may become a nightmare that can result in expensive litigation. If done properly, you will have obtained a partner who may last your professional lifetime. Give this aspect of your practice the time and attention it deserves.*

NOTES

1. Roger G. Bonds, *Physician Recruitment & Retention, Practical Techniques for Exceptional Results,* 4th ed. (Atlanta: Medical Staff Development Press, 1999).
2. Roger G. Bonds, *The Medical Job Search: How To Find the Best Position for Your Financial Independence and Peace of Mind* (Atlanta: Physician Careers Press, 1999).

CHAPTER 47

A New Revenue Resource: Clinical Research

With reimbursements going south and overhead costs skyrocketing, you do not need an MBA or CPA degree to understand that physicians' net incomes are diminishing. Many physicians are on the lookout for new business opportunities. One area that presents tremendous opportunities for the practicing physician is clinical research. Each year more than 4,000 new investigators secure their first research grant. There are now more than 25,000 physicians participating in clinical research and earning nearly $3 billion annually.

In the past most of the grants were awarded to academic institutions, but today nearly half the grants are given to community physicians. As the National Cancer Institute and other institutes at the National Institutes of Health seek to expand clinical trials programs, community physicians represent a resource, because of their access to patients who might be eligible for trials. Not everyone can travel to a university center to participate in a study. In this chapter the benefits of participating in a clinical investigation, as well as the commitment required by the physician and the office staff and suggestions for getting started, are reviewed. Once you have taken the plunge to set up a clinical research program, you may find that you will reap multiple rewards—not just financial, but also increased credibility and visibility among your colleagues and additional loyalty from patients who benefit from access to the newest study drugs.

INCOME AND INTELLECTUAL CHALLENGES

Clinical research does not represent a "free ride," but is a new business venture that will take time and energy. Becoming a coinvestigator for a clinical trial can also become emotionally satisfying, with significant financial reward. Conducting clinical trials provides revenue per patient that is essentially full fee-for-service compensation for services rendered. Since study grants are calculated on a per patient basis and typically pay 100 percent fee-for-service, this is an excellent means of revenue generation through patients who are already in your practice.

According to Dr. Paul Siami, a urologist in private practice in Evansville, Indiana, and director of clinical research for the Welborn Clinic, participation in the clinical research industry allows physicians to remain close to medical science. You can become directly involved with development of new drugs in your specialty. During the investigator's meetings, and as the study drug is being evaluated in clinical trials, you also acquire more knowledge about the target disease and the particular class of drug.

When your patients participate, they also benefit from receiving free medication, medical and laboratory services, and generally a stipend for their time and travel to the major study site for evaluation. Aside from the increased revenue, many physicians also enjoy the intellectual stimulation of testing new medications and contributing to medical research in developing new therapies and diagnostics. With six years of experience in conducting clinical research projects, Dr. Siami believes that his participation has brought his practice a certain prestige of being on the cutting edge of urology in his community.

Many patients regularly search for clinical research sites as an option for evaluation and treatment of their disease. So, if you are the only site in your area to offer an investigation pill for impotence, your office becomes a desirable place for many men suffering from erectile dysfunction. As an investigator for benign prostate hyperplasia (BPH) treatments, you may find that many patients have self-referred themselves and friends to your urology practice.

By participating in a study you will interact with the movers and the shakers in the field and work alongside the biggest names in academia, who often are the lead investigators of a drug study. You will usually be asked to attend an investigators' meeting before commencing the study. Also, once the study has been completed, your data and your name may be added to all the articles that report on the study. There is probably no easier way to have your name in the *New England Journal of Medicine* than to be a clinical investigator for a drug study.

YOU MUST COMMIT

To accommodate conducting clinical trials, you will most probably need some dedicated space in your office. The most significant expenses for a new investigator will be the office space and the study coordinator. Dr. Siami advises approaching the setup in a systematic way.

The study coordinator is and will be viewed by the sponsor as the most important person at your site. He or she is the person who will help you obtain study grants and negotiate the contract, submit the regulatory documents to the Institutional Review Board (IRB), recruit and see patients, fill out the case report forms, and supervise the conduct of the trial. Therefore, it behooves you to select a study coordinator who is meticulous with details, warm, and has stellar people skills, including good telephone skills and the ability to promptly establish rapport with patients. Last but not least, look for a person with the capitalist spirit—a trait that is often overlooked when interviewing monitors for clinical research. This asset will help you solicit grants, develop marketing materials, and devise creative methods for patient enrollment.

GETTING STARTED

Sponsors of clinical research generally look for sites that have qualified and experienced investigators, and they also emphasize the presence of qualified and experienced study coordinators. The ideal medical practice should have a large and stable patient population.

Securing the first project is often the most difficult step. Once you have the initial study procured and successfully conducted, subsequent studies become easier to obtain.

Dr. Siami suggests several ways to break into clinical research:

- Ask the detail people who visit your office for the names, addresses, and phone numbers of their research project directors.
- Use the *Physician's Desk Reference* to locate pharmaceutical companies and introduce yourself to the research directors.
- Write to contract research organizations (CROs). A directory of CROs is published by CenterWatch, the most comprehensive database for clinical research.[1]
- Contract a site management organization. These companies are generally dedicated research sites that at times contract with area physicians to help them with patient enrollment.
- Read *The Physician's Guide to Clinical Research Opportunities,* by Matthew D. Heller, M.D., and James A. Boyle, M.D.[2] This book is useful reading for the novice investigator.

When marketing your practice as a study site, it is appropriate to highlight your patient demographics, the superiority of your practice, facility descriptions, the range of your services, and the experience of your clinical research coordinator. Include your practice brochure and other informational publications, any press coverage of you and your practice, results from patient satisfaction surveys, and the like.

ATTRACTING PATIENTS TO YOUR STUDIES

The ability to enroll patients in your studies will depend on several factors, including the degree of trust that patients have in you and your practice. *Your existing patients are usually the best and easiest to enroll in clinical research.* Patients who are already in your practice are comfortable with you and your staff, and you can easily qualify them for the study as you are familiar with their medical histories and know their inclusion and exclusion criteria.

Still, you may encounter resistance from patients who fear they are being asked to be "guinea pigs" for the pharmaceutical industry. During your discussions with patients, point out that if there are no clinical studies there will be no progress in medicine. It is important to emphasize the safety of the study as most patients will become concerned about side effects when they read the consent form that they are required to sign. It is advisable for you or your nurse to go over the consent form with patients and reassure them that most of the complications and side effects are rare. At the very least, put the risks in the proper perspective and compare the new study drugs to other medications or procedures that they have had in the past.

It is not uncommon to find that patients will enjoy participating in the studies and often will volunteer for additional studies. This may be due to altruistic reasons (they enjoy feeling that they are "contributing" to medical science) or purely selfish ones (they observe that they get more attention from the doctor and office staff when they participate in a drug study).

Another way to attract patients to your study is to communicate with your colleagues. Let them know you are doing a drug study and tell them about its purpose and the potential benefits for their patients. For example, I usually send a letter informing my colleagues of the study (see Exhibit 47–1). I include an article from the medical literature that supports research. At the end of the project, I send them a summary of the study and the experience of their patient in the study.

CREATE A POSITIVE EXPERIENCE FOR THE MONITOR

One of the givens of conducting drug trials is constant scrutiny. The Food and Drug Administration and other regulatory agencies have been known to shut down studies when regulations, especially regarding consent and the proper recording of data, have not been followed scrupulously. If you follow strict protocol and have hired a detail-oriented research coordinator, the periodic reviews by the IRBs and company monitors should not be a problem.

There are extra ways to be certain that monitors have a positive experience every time they come to your practice. A veteran of nearly one hundred clinical studies, Dr. Jim McMurray, a physician from Huntsville, Alabama, and medical

Exhibit 47–1 Letter to Colleague Soliciting Patients for Study

Dear [name of doctor],

I am participating in a drug study on the new oral medication, apomorphine, for the treatment of impotence. Apomorphine has a centrally acting mechanism of action and will be useful for men who cannot take sildenafil (Viagra™) if they are also taking nitroglycerin tablets or using nitroglycerin patches. The drug is taken as a sublingual tablet and has an onset of action in 20 minutes, which is about half the time for onset of action with sildenafil.

The side effects are nausea and hypotension, but at the lower doses, 2 and 3 mg, these side effects are not common.

The study will provide free medication, evaluation, and follow-up for the six-week study. I will also provide you with a summary of the experience of your patient.

If you have any questions about the drug or the study, please give me a call.

I look forward to working with you and your patients.

Sincerely,
Neil Baum, M.D.

---

director of Medical Affiliated Research Center, begins the process even before the monitor arrives by sending a map with directions from the airport to the office. His staff members offer to make hotel reservations for the monitor and provide a list of attractions in the area.

Monitors are given a separate room to work in while they are in the research center's 5,000-square-foot facility, so that they are free from distractions and noise. They are offered amenities like copy machines, faxing capabilities, a modem, coffee, soft drinks, and lunch while they are in the office. Dr. McMurray also limits the areas of the office that the monitor can use. He says that this prevents the monitor from doing "research" on other companies' products.

One way to endear yourself to the monitor is to have the doctor on site whenever the monitor is in the office. If the monitor has a question about a record that cannot be answered by the research coordinator, the doctor is available to answer the question immediately or at the end of the day when the monitor completes his or her on-site review of the records.

Make sure that your staff members understand that their goal is to make every effort to make the monitor comfortable in your office. You want each visit to be as enjoyable as possible, so that the monitor will look forward to returning. When you are able to do this, you can be sure the monitor will write a favorable report about your facility and you will be recommended to the pharmaceutical company for additional studies.

FUTURE OF CLINICAL RESEARCH

It is estimated that there are more than 2,500 pharmaceutical compounds and nearly 1,000 biotechnology compounds in clinical development. Approximately twice as many compounds are in preclinical development. This growth in clinical research will potentially require more investigators and patients across a wide range of specialties and diseases to participate in this industry.

Financial data from industry leaders indicate that pharmaceutical and biotechnology research and development spent nearly $33 billion in 1997, with approximately $16 billion being spent in clinical development.

The Bottom Line   *Stop looking for love (prestige, money, enjoyment, satisfaction) in all the wrong places (real estate, stock market, multilevel marketing, and other get-rich-quick schemes). Consider participating in a clinical research project. You have a great opportunity in your own practice to be of service to your patients and your profession, while increasing your bottom line and your reputation in the community.*

NOTES

1. CenterWatch can be reached at *www.centerwatch.com*, which contains several hundred listings of current research trials. This site will also link you directly to the sites of the medical centers running studies. The site also contains mailing lists that notify you when new clinical trials become available.

2. This book is available from the Practice Management Information Corp., (800) MED–SHOP.

CHAPTER 48

Market Your Expertise As an Expert Witness

At one time or another, most physicians have probably testified on behalf of an injured patient. Given the adversarial relationship between attorneys and physicians, you may not relish the task of testifying in a legal case.

But have you ever thought of turning your medical expertise into another type of marketing tool—that of expert witness? If you are comfortable speaking in public, have honed your public speaking skills so that you can communicate complicated medical terms in direct and simply lay language, and enjoy the arena of a courtroom, this may be an activity that can be both lucrative and enjoyable.

Based on interviews with three attorneys, this chapter gives you an overview of the expert witness process, the expectations, and the pitfalls, and prepares you to choose whether or not to embark on this process.

WHY BECOME AN EXPERT WITNESS?

Why would physicians knowingly subject themselves to a process where they can guarantee that they will be grilled, criticized, and their reputation called to question in public?

According to Jim Saxton, a Lancaster, Pennsylvania, trial attorney, "expert witnesses are a very important part of the trial process. At times you [the physician] may be asked to be an expert in a medical malpractice case or other form of litigation. This happens often enough that it's worthwhile to set forth some guidelines, general rules, and advice about serving as an expert witness."

In Saxton's opinion, it is both professionally and personally rewarding to become an expert witness, and it should be economically beneficial as well. However, a few threshold decisions must be made before embarking on such a task. Knowing what is involved in the process can help your own decision making.

WHAT IS INVOLVED?

First of all, advises Saxton, do not contemplate this job unless you are willing to take it very seriously. The issues are extremely serious to the parties involved, and being an expert takes a great deal of time and energy. A certain level of commitment is crucial for the job to be done right.

According to Wendell Gauthier, president of the Louisiana Trial Lawyers Association, the credibility of the expert witness must meet the Daubert Requirements, which hold that theories must be reviewed by the experts' peers and meet their peer review standards. Before the judge will allow an expert to testify, the expert must prove that his or her opinion and the methodology used to reach it are recognized by peers as acceptable standards. Being published, and therefore subjected to peer review, is one way to meet that requirement.

Generally, an expert will have several roles, according to Saxton. Traditionally, in a malpractice case, you will be asked to provide a comprehensive review of records and various documents to familiarize yourself with the case. This is a weak spot for many experts, notes Saxton. They are usually busy practitioners and although they know medicine extremely well, they do not always take sufficient time to truly understand the nuances of the case. They may feel certain facts are not important to their opinion. However, you must remember it is not just what you feel is important but what will be the perception of the fact-finding jury.

Experts must review all the facts so they have a complete picture of the case. This is a time-consuming process, but as long as the facts are well organized, readable, and necessary points are summarized, it is worthwhile. Of course, this means you may well have to review voluminous medical records, copies of deposition transcripts, and other reports generated by consultants. And, you will want to remember that it is the standard of care and modes of treatment at the time the treatment was rendered that are in question. At the time of trial, many years have often passed since the incident and treatment protocols are continuously evolving. *Once you have a thorough understanding of the facts, you must compare them to the standard of care at the time in question.*

THE DOCUMENT, PLEASE

In many jurisdictions, a report setting forth your opinions and the basis for your opinions will be required. The attorney who has retained you should provide the requirements for the jurisdiction in which you will be testifying. These can vary significantly from state to state, so make sure the attorney supplies you with specifics.

According to attorney Kurt Blankenship, a defense attorney with Blue, Williams LLP in New Orleans, attorneys usually first contact the physicians via telephone and ask if they will review the records. The attorney then will request a phone conference after the physician has reviewed the records. The reason is that the attorney wants to be sure that the opinion is favorable to his or her case. If not, he does not want any written record in his file and will then request a bill for the review of the records.

If your opinion is favorable, then the attorney will most likely want to proceed to the next step, which is to have you produce a written report. The report you generate is an important document, and testimony and cross-examination hinge on its wording. In many courts, you will be limited to what you have stated in your report. Opinions that are not set forth within the four corners of your report are often excluded at the time of trial. This can be very harmful to an individual party's case.

Lawrence Smith, of Lawrence Smith & Associates, chairman of the Association of Trial Lawyers of America Traumatic Brain Injury Litigation Group and president of the Louisiana chapter of the American Board of Trial Advocates, advises physicians to state the diagnosis in a definitive and clear manner. "Many medical reports are ruined and become great liabilities when the physician writes negative statements such as 'unknown etiology,'" he says. "Many physicians throw in such terms because they do not know if the history given was accurate. They will spend hours on the stand regretting they mentioned such terms in their report." For example, if the only explanation of the symptoms is trauma, then clearly state that as the etiology. There is no need to provide an opportunity for mental reservations and verbal gymnastics when the history is clear.

At the appropriate time, your report will be shared with opposing counsel and often with the court and can become an essential piece of evidence upon which even decisions about settlement may be made. An updated curriculum vitae (CV) should also be provided with your report to set forth your expertise and experience. Including your CV lends legitimacy to your report and validates why, in fact, your opinion should be given the appropriate amount of weight.

TIPS ON DIAGNOSIS

You may be asked to examine the plaintiff as well as review his or her medical records. In taking a history always give the patient the benefit of the doubt and ask relevant questions. For instance, says Smith, it is common in closed head injury cases to be faced with an emergency room record with the words "No LOC" (no loss of consciousness). In Smith's experience, this can often be an erroneous or incomplete statement of fact, since often people can be unconscious for several minutes and not know it. In this instance, a physician should ask questions that establish whether or not there is retrograde or antegrade amnesia. If there was no reported amnesia, it is important to determine whether the patient felt dazed or disoriented. According to Smith, it is possible that patients who have only been dazed and not unconscious for minutes or hours can suffer significant axonal injury from concussion that often results in permanent life changes.

OTHER STEPS

In some jurisdictions, even though you have completed a report, you may be deposed by the opposing party for discovery purposes. The attorney who has retained you will want to prepare you carefully for the deposition. The attorneys taking the depositions want to see your demeanor, understand your opinions, and try to draw information from you that they can later use during cross-examination at trial. If your trial testimony veers away from what you gave previously at a deposition, you can count on your credibility being impeached. At all these junctures, consistency—in your report and during deposition and trial testimony—is the name of the game.

In addition to reviewing records, preparing a report, and participating in a deposition, you may be asked by the attorneys to help them understand certain medical facts about the case or even prepare cross-examinations for opposing attorney's experts. This can be an important part of the process so you can play a critical role in this regard.

WALK THE WALK AND TALK THE TALK

Obviously, the most difficult job you will be given as an expert is at the actual trial. Many attorneys will ask you up front at the time you are retained whether or not you will be willing to come to the trial and participate as a live witness. Most attorneys prefer that the expert testifies in person, but with new technology, including large screens that can project this testimony, a videotaped deposition, done correctly, can be very effective. Either way, preparation time will be necessary for you to connect with the attorney who will be asking questions during direct examination and be adequately prepared for cross-examination.

As an expert witness who appears in court, says Larry Smith, your credentials are important, "but not as important as physical appearance, carriage, and delivery. A physician expert is expected to go to court looking like a doctor. If he chooses to wear a suit, the suit must be crisp, freshly cleaned, and not look like he slept in it. If the physician is a surgeon and is testifying in the city where he or she practices medicine, he or she should wear scrubs or a white coat when arriving at court from the hospital." In short, says Smith, "an expert must walk, talk, and act like an expert." He or she must also communicate with the attorney by defining medical terms and describing anatomy and physiology at a level understandable by the lay person. The best way to do this is through the use of analogy. (See Chapters 26 and 28, on public speaking and meeting the press.)

Consider this example: A physician is testifying for the injured plaintiff who had preexisting osteoarthritis, which was asymptomatic but made symptomatic by the injury. Explaining aggravation of preexisting conditions could be accomplished using the following analogy: Preexisting osteoarthritis means that the plaintiff's neck was like an eggshell: It functioned and contained the yolk and egg white just fine. It did not leak. But now, as a result of this trauma, it is cracked and leaking and not functioning properly.

A physician may testify that the plaintiff, as a result of his or her injury, has 10 percent disability. Even this expression about disability needs to be translated into layman's language. The expert could explain that the plaintiff had worked as a longshoreman and now, due to injury, has a 10 percent disabled back and cannot function as a longshoreman and make a living, and that 10 percent disability has caused him to suffer almost total disability. To illustrate this point you compare the longshoreman's injured back to a watch that only is accurate 90 percent of the time. It loses six minutes every hour. It is only 10 percent disabled, but totally worthless as a watch.

In addition to using understandable analogies to describe medical conditions, the expert witness must be attentive to delivery and the use of impact words and phrases. Many medical terms have connotations that reflect unfavorably on the patient. For example, the term *whiplash* was coined by Dr. Crow in 1936. The insurance industry and defense lawyers in the movie *Fortune Cookie* made that term synonymous with malingering. That is a perception that the public often shares. Therefore, always talk about a patient's whiplash injury as a hyperflexion and extension injury resulting in the patient becoming a neck cripple. This is a much more vivid description of the patient who, after a 15 mph rear-end collision, wound up with fibromyalgia and chronic neck pain for the rest of her life.

DO YOUR HOMEWORK

It is essential that the physician make time to meet with the plaintiff's lawyer before he or she gets on the witness stand. At this trial preparation meeting, the lawyer should apprise the expert of his or her medical theory about the case and what other physicians have diagnosed and concluded. Before the conference, the attorney should provide the expert with copies of all pertinent medical records. He or she should let the physician know about the defense theory of the case. The two of them should come to a conclusion ahead of time about where the "holes" are in the defense theory and why the patient's side is medically correct. This information is vital for the expert to understand before taking the witness stand.

Of course, the physician and lawyer should go over the questions that are going to be asked, the order in which they will be asked, and the anticipated answers. They should construct in the examination the use of visual aids and reasons to move the physician off the witness stand into the teaching position addressing the jury. Jurors have learned from childhood that teachers are right and they should believe teachers. If the physician even unconsciously becomes a good teacher in the jury's eyes, he or she is more likely to be believed.

The expert must be prepared to defend his or her opinion from attack. If you have written articles on the subject matter, the opposing lawyer may have read those articles. Nothing is as embarrassing to a physician and destroys credibility as being unfamiliar or unable to defend articles you have published in medical journals. You should also review pertinent medical textbooks and literature that might be used to attack your position.

DO NOT LET CROSS-EXAMINATION CROSS YOU UP

Cross-examination opens you up to a wide array of questions. You can expect questions about your own credentials and experience and even your malpractice history. You can also expect questions about financial arrangements you have made with the attorney and financial arrangements you make generally when doing this type of testifying. You may be asked about prior testimony you have given and count on a thorough background search of your credentials, background, training, and previously recorded testimony. The attorney will always attain the previous testimony of opposing experts to determine whether they have given contradictory testimony in other cases. This information can often be used effectively during cross-examination.

Experts usually feel that cross-examination is one of the most grueling and exhausting parts of the job. The importance of the case weighs heavily on their minds. They want to do a good job, while being fair with the facts and the medicine. It is quite a balancing act and it takes a lot of skill, perseverance, and preparation to do the job right.

Knowing in advance what some of the pitfalls are can help alleviate some of the pretrial jitters and contribute to solid testimony. Smith counsels prospective expert witnesses regarding the use of leading questions to undermine even a medically valid opinion. A good cross-examination can be conducted by using leading questions to obtain a series of yes answers.

For example, suppose that the physician expert witness has testified that when he examined the patient there were no objective signs of injury and only unsubstantiated subjective complaints. His opinion: there is no medical justification for the patient's complaints. Watch how, in the following interchange, a good cross-examiner could easily undermine this valid opinion.

> *Question:* "Doctor, it is true, is it not, that physicians often make a diagnosis based on history alone?"

Answer: "Yes."

Question: "It is true, isn't it, that the only way to know a patient has a headache is that the patient tells you so?"

Answer: "Yes."

Question: "And with the symptom complex that we have in this case, you would expect the symptoms to wax and wane, wouldn't you?"

Answer: "Yes."

Question: "In fact, objective signs of injury such as muscle spasm can fade and come back when the patient is tired or overuses her neck?"

Answer: "Yes."

Question: "So just because you didn't find muscle spasm doesn't mean she didn't have muscle spasm on other occasions?"

Answer: "Yes."

Question: "Just because you found no objective evidence of pain, it doesn't mean that the patient is not hurting?"

Answer: "Yes."

This is an example of a good cross-examination stringing together legitimate medical questions that are susceptible to a simple yes answer.

According to Smith, if you fall into the rhythm of the cross-examination and simply answer yes to this string of questions, the jury will believe that you agree with the opposing side as much as you agree with the lawyer that calls you to the stand.

The way to defeat this trap is to follow the "yes, but" rule. That is, always on the second or third answer say "yes, but" and forcibly reiterate your position. In the above example, you would say, "Yes, but in this case there is no medical justification for the complaints."

FEE ARRANGEMENTS

Throughout all this, the expert should be appropriately compensated for his or her time. In this regard it is important to set an amount that is consistent with what your peers are charging and fairly compensates you for your time. It is almost impossible to give a set amount, but checking with your peers in the geographical area of the trial is usually helpful. If a doctor charges too much, this will come out during cross-examination and he or she will look like a highly paid hired gun. This detracts from the testimony and can hurt the case in which he or she has been retained to help.

On the other hand, being an expert witness is hard work and the fee arrangement is an important consideration when deciding whether to take the case. Fee arrangements should be in writing, completely discussed, and disclosed up front so there are no questions once the matter is completed.

There is no uniform fee, says Blankenship. Experts charge one hourly rate for reviewing the records and consultations, which is usually less than the hourly rate for the deposition. The deposition hourly rate is usually less than the hourly rate for testifying in court. For example, some specialists charge $300–$350 for review of records, $400–$450 for the deposition, and a flat rate for the trial testimony usually quoted in half-day increments. The rates vary according to the specialty and the area of the country; in New York, California, and Florida the fees are much higher.

It is appropriate to have language in the fee agreement that addresses the issue of cancellation. There is some compensation, usually 20–25% of the fee, if the case is canceled within one or two days of the expected appearance. Also the physician needs to be certain that all travel expenses are in addition to the fee for the testimony.

The initial decision you need to make is whether you want to get involved in this process. As mentioned previously, it can be draining and time consuming, but many find it professionally and personally rewarding. Obviously, you can learn a great deal by watching the mistakes of others. Remember, you are going to play a critical role for either the plaintiff or the defendant. You need to make your threshold decision based on whether you are willing to make that type of commitment. The information presented here is meant to help you understand some of those responsibilities. Some of this will depend on the jurisdiction in which you are being asked to testify and the lawyer with whom you will work.

Attorneys have different styles and your responsibilities may differ depending on whether you are testifying for the plaintiff or the defendant and on the standard of care, causation, or damages. It is absolutely necessary to fully understand what either side expects of you, the time frame, and what your role is going to be. Knowing these things is what will help you make a good decision about your level of involvement.

WHERE THE OPPORTUNITIES LIE

Blankenship explains that becoming a successful expert witness often depends on locale. Because many local physicians are reluctant to testify against a colleague within the community, plaintiffs' lawyers often have to look outside of the local area to recruit an expert witness. Thus, the opportunities to be plaintiff's witnesses are more national in scope, while openings for defense expert witnesses are more likely to be local.

What do trial attorneys look for? Academic qualifications, such as being a professor at a medical school or the head of a department at a major hospital, are highly regarded. Secondarily, an attorney would consider how well a doctor can articulate his or her position and how good a witness he or she is likely to be. The essence of any trial is the ability to communicate medical opinions to the jury in clear, simple, and concise fashion.

Several organizations advertise in legal publications providing experts and expert consultations (see "Additional Resources" for one example). Some experts also advertise in these publications. But the best way to build expert witness consultations, says Blankenship, is to do a good job for one attorney and that attorney will recommend you to his or her legal colleagues.

The Bottom Line   *Becoming an expert witness is serious business. It requires commitment, attention to detail, and the ability to communicate in public. Those who choose to follow this route can add to their professional and personal rewards, as well as economic ones.*

ADDITIONAL RESOURCES

- *Technical Advisory Service for Attorneys* (TASA), 1166 DeKalb Pike, Blue Bell, PA 19422–1853; (800) 523–2319; *www.tasanet.com*. TASA is a nationwide organization that accumulates expert information and provides it to attorneys for a fee. Physicians can contact them, fill out forms, supply a CV, and get listed with this organization. When a physician or expert is retained through TASA, the organization gets a fee for the referral.
- *Journal of the Association of Trial Lawyers of America*, 1050 31st St., NW, Washington, DC 20007-4499; (202) 965–3500; *www.atlanet.org*. Advertising in this journal is the best way to reach large numbers of attorneys.

Additional journals in which to advertise:

- *National Law Review*, The New York Law Publishing Co., 105 Madison Ave., New York, NY 10016; (212) 779–9200.
- *American Lawyer*, American Lawyer Media, 600 Third Ave., New York, NY 10016; (212) 973–2800.

CHAPTER 49

Do Niche Marketing As a Super Specialist

Many people are not happy with our current health care environment. Providers as well as patients do not appreciate the limitations imposed by managed care and government regulation. The assertive baby boomers are now middle-aged, politically active, and they understand how to use the system. They have good organizational skills and are capable of going to Congress in large numbers to influence the passing of legislation that protects their health and access to good care. They do not like to be refused a bone marrow transplant; they reject drive-through labor and delivery; and they still are not accustomed to asking permission from a gatekeeper to see a specialist. These patients are now taking steps to see that such mandates do not become the rule.

According to Regina Hertzlinger, Ph.D., a professor at Harvard University and author of the book, *Market Driven Health Care*, managed care will not last, simply because the administrative costs are higher for a managed care organization than for the traditional indemnity method of hospital and provider reimbursement. Eventually, assertive consumers will undercut the health maintenance organization's ability to limit medical care expenses and these organizations will find it difficult to maintain a cost-effective competitive edge. Dr. Hertzlinger predicts that more providers are going to capitate themselves and accept all or most of the risk of providing their services.

In this chapter, I discuss what Dr. Hertzlinger and others predict will be the wave of the future: application of the "focused factory" concept to health care. This is one way for providers to ensure their own health and well-being in the future.

THE FOCUSED FACTORY CONCEPT

The traditional factory is capable of all the functions required to turn out a product, but no single function is emphasized. A focused factory is a company or organization that performs one function in a stellar, world-class fashion. Two examples are Federal Express and McDonald's. You know that if you turn your package over to Fed Ex that 99.6 percent of the time, your package will arrive as promised the next day. You also know that if you go into any of McDonald's 14,000 fast food restaurants, anywhere in the world, you will receive the same crispy french fries in the white, red, and yellow container.

How does this focused factory concept apply to health care? It was Vilfredo Parado (the "Parado curve") who first noted that 80 percent of most events can be attributed to approximately 20 percent of their causes. Applying this principle to health care, we can see that 80 percent of our referrals come from 20 percent of the total number of referring physicians who use our services. Also, 80 percent of our patients come from only 20 percent of the zip codes that comprise the communities in proximity to our practices.

In a March 1996 article in *JAMA* it was revealed that 76 percent of the total expenditures on medical care are due to a small number of chronic diseases, such as diabetes mellitus, cardiac conditions, cancer, and asthma. At the present time, there are only a few focused factories for managing patients with these chronic diseases. Those responsible for integrating care for these patients are often the patients themselves. For example, a patient with diabetes has to find a primary care physician, endocrinologist, podiatrist, ophthalmologist, nephrologist, urologist, nutritionist, and sometimes a peripheral vascular surgeon.

A focused health care organization does just what its title implies: it focuses, like a laser, on only one disease, one procedure, or one diagnostic category. Like manufacturing companies, focused factories in health care consist of a multidisciplinary team of people who work together over a long period of time. They may not actually be located on the same campus, but instead may form a "virtual" organization, linked by telephone lines, faxes, computers, and treatment algorithms. These organizations work together over time, learn from each other, and use feedback and analysis to improve and hone their specialties.

EXAMPLES OF HEALTH CARE FOCUSED FACTORIES

One of the best examples of the focused factory is the practice of eminent cardiovascular surgeon Denton Cooley, M.D., in Houston, Texas. Dr. Cooley has performed more than 60,000 coronary artery bypass grafts. Watching him operate is pure "poetry in motion." His operating team is every bit as agile and united as were Michael Jordon and the Chicago Bulls. Dr. Cooley believes that when you work together a lot at doing one thing well, you get very good. Not only are his results some of the best in the nation, but his prices for procedures are 33 percent lower than the national average. Quality goes up and costs go down.

Another example is the Shouldice Clinic in Toronto, Canada, which does only abdominal hernia repairs. Patients come from all over the United States and Canada for these procedures. The cost of the procedure, the hospital stay, and the airfare combined is less than the repair would be at other centers. A Shouldice hernia repair runs about $2,000; compare this to a range from $2,500 to $15,000 per procedure in an American hospital. In addition, hernia repairs at the Shouldice are 99 percent successful. This can be a substantial savings, as surgeons who operate on a patient whose hernia recurs must reoperate at no charge if their surgery was the cause of the recurrence.

How does Shouldice create patient satisfaction and perform high-quality work (judged by low recurrence rates) at a lower cost? The focused concept explains this success—by performing a large volume of the same type of procedure, the clinic increases quality. The average general surgeon in the community may typically perform fewer than 30 hernia repairs a year. That is only 5 percent of the yearly volume performed by a Shouldice surgeon. Surgical team members continually work together, so their teamwork is fluid, unlike surgical teams in the community who are separately assembled for different procedures. High-volume teams make fewer mistakes. In addition, the clinic emphasizes patient mastery, encouraging early ambulation, so that patients actually perform some of the tasks that support staff might usually do. These all add up to reduced costs for the overall procedure.

We see examples everywhere now of university hospitals, clinics, or practice groups that have chosen to specialize in one type of procedure (total hip replacement, for instance) or one type of treatment for a disease. The Fred Hutchinson Cancer Research Center in Seattle, Washington, and the City of Hope in Duarte, California, have established reputations as centers of excellence for bone marrow transplants. The Texas Back Institute in Plano, Texas, has become known both nationally and internationally for its multidisciplinary approach to back problems and rehabilitation of chronic back disease.

In the future, managed care organizations will serve as brokers for focused health care factories. They will be attracted to multisite or multidisciplinary providers who are clearly focused on one disease, one product, or one of the chronic disabilities, such as arthritis or back pain.

WHY FOCUSED FACTORIES?

One of the most important advantages of focused factories is that they are truly provider run and operated. Focused factories will not be created by insurance companies. According to Dr. Hertzlinger, physicians are the key to making focused factories function better and more cost effectively.[1] As a result, proactive physicians who look down the road and envision a focused factory will be the ones in charge of their fate and their future.

Focused factories will provide higher quality health care. They will embody a concentration of intellectual capital that will pay attractive dividends for patients in the form of better outcomes. These factories will generate clinical outcomes data for both payers and the public. And, they will be the darlings of consumers because they will be able to provide their services at a lower cost by reducing the needless proliferation of technology and hospital capital.

No longer will you see a dozen CT scanners and lithotripters in the same area or region. New technology will be purchased to improve cost effectiveness and not as bait to attract physicians and patients. Focused factories will also benefit the public sector by shrinking the number of inefficient and expensive hospitals. Managed care organizations will select only the most efficient and cost-sensitive hospitals to work with focused factories and their providers.

Another advantage of focused factories is the possibility for patients and payers to compare the prices and quality of different providers. Since clinical outcome data and costs will be quantified and published, payers will be able to easily compare the prices between focused factories. For example, Dr. Cooley offers a package price for coronary artery bypass operations of $27,040; this is considerably less than the national average of $43,370. Of course, someone who requires an emergency bypass will not have the luxury of traveling to Texas for his or her procedure. However, if a blockage is picked up before an adverse event, the patient would have time to travel to Dr. Cooley's site.

Focused factories usually include a full menu of care required by the patient: the hospital, the outpatient facility, the physician's fee, the medications, and even home health services if required. They can take advantage of the economies of scale, best practice analysis, and flexibility. Focused factories are "lean and mean" and can react quickly to any market changes. Payers are attracted because they can pay one all-inclusive price for a procedure rather than reimburse for several separate providers. It is clear that a managed care organization would rather deal with a focused factory than a large number of multipurpose providers.

ANY BAD NEWS?

Another spin-off of focused factories will be the fierce competition that will be generated among providers as they vie for patients. That is the bad news. But this competition will result in financial incentives for creative providers to devise new, better, and more cost-effective methods of delivering the same care and preserving quality for their patients. Any new methods, technologies, or treatments that improve outcomes and patient satisfaction will give that factory a decisive advantage at the negotiating table with the payer at contract time.

Dr. Hertzlinger suggests that focused factories will substantially diminish the unnecessary expenditures presently incurred because of the absence of integrated operating systems for the treatment of those few chronic diseases that are such a strain on our health care budget.

The Bottom Line   *Focused factories have the potential to substantially enhance patients' quality of life at a reasonable price. If you want to thrive in the millennium, take the road less traveled and get focused.*

NOTE

1. Regina Hertzlinger, *Market Driven Health Care* (Reading, MA: Addison-Wesley, 1997).

CHAPTER 50

When Dollars Make Sense: Using a Practice Cost Analysis To Market Your Practice

Cynthia D. Fry

Hiring and dealing with accountants has always been an important aspect of practice management, especially at tax time. Until a few years ago, the accountant's role was typically confined to an annual meeting with the physician, providing a standard profit and loss statement, and tabulating accounts receivables (AR). Physicians did not anticipate having to understand and interpret practice performance indicators or financial statements. Nor did the accountant's role usually include leveraging off the knowledge gained from the financials or key practice indicators to improve practice management, market the practice, or identify new practice growth opportunities.

Well, times have certainly changed. Physicians who are not aware of key performance indicators and who are not using those to fine-tune practice objectives may be jeopardizing the health and wealth of their practices. Fortunately, your certified public accountant has the tools to do so much more for you and your practice. This chapter discusses the key financial indicators that will reveal the financial status of your practice and provide you with the data to help you identify new growth potential and opportunities and even market your practice.

Translating this information into actions to improve business performance has in the past often been left to the physician, who worked with a practice administrator. In this chapter, you will learn to identify key indicators and know which information to request from your certified public accountant. You will then have the tools to take a proactive approach to the business of medicine. Ask yourself, "Does my practice utilize the most appropriate and revealing key indicators to

Cynthia D. Fry, MBA, is Senior Manager and Functional Leader for Physician Business Services with Price Waterhouse Coopers, LLP, in Philadelphia, Pennsylvania. She can be reached at *cynthia.d.fry@us.pwcglobal.com*.

improve my business performance?" If not, stay tuned. If so, you might want to stay tuned anyway, as a refresher.

There are five steps in a practice financial analysis that are the same as those used by any successful industry or business:

1. Establish analysis objectives.
2. Forecast any related economic developments (changes in payer reimbursement, referral patterns, competitive climate, etc.).
3. Determine and evaluate key financial indicators (trend analysis, comparison with industry benchmarks, operating efficiency, and profitability).
4. Summarize findings and reach conclusions relevant to the established objectives.
5. Act upon information; re-evaluate at regular intervals.

ESTABLISH ANALYSIS OBJECTIVES

Like most businesses, your practice must continuously improve operations to stay competitive and maximize earnings potential.

To establish analysis objectives, be prepared to analyze your operations, with the intent of answering the following three questions:

1. How can my practice provide health care services more cost effectively and enhance the access of patients to services efficiently and effectively?
2. How can my practice improve the quality of care and satisfaction of patients?
3. How can I use the information I collect to improve my competitive advantage and increase profitability?

The key to continuous operational improvement is regularly measuring current performance. It is as simple as identifying and quantifying opportunities, implementing changes, and measuring the results (by repeating the analysis). For example, you may discover in your practice analysis that the front desk personnel are only collecting copayments of $5–$10 from patients 44 percent of the time. This means that there is a 56 percent improvement opportunity that equates to a dollar return of $5–$10 times the number of patients who should be making a copayment at the time of their visit. Thousands of dollars may be falling through the cracks because your practice must bill patients for these amounts. Your implementation plan may involve training front desk personnel on how to ask patients for copays, establishing an expectation or goal (for example, collect 95 percent of copayments for office services), and providing staff continuous feedback on their performance. In addition, you may want to link this key indicator to their annual performance reviews and to pay increases. When the analysis is repeated (at a regularly established interval of time), you can measure your results, make any additional changes, and reward performance if the goal is met or exceeded.

FORECAST ANY RELATED ECONOMIC DEVELOPMENTS

The health care environment is dynamic and physician practices do not operate in a vacuum. Therefore, it is necessary to consider an evaluation and forecast of the practice's financial position in the context of its external operating environment. Include in your forecast such factors as the percentage of patients who belong to managed care plans, the degree of capitation penetration in the local market, payer delays, changes in payer reimbursement, referral patterns, and even the competitive climate in your community. This forecast is a blending of hard facts and soft assumptions.

DETERMINE AND EVALUATE KEY FINANCIAL INDICATORS

There are generally three sources of data you can use to identify practice indicators: financial statements, billing and accounts receivable information, and practice operations. In order to answer the three questions previously posed, you will need to identify the key indicators shown in Table 50–1.

As you can see by the number of source documents and information from them, you will have no shortage of data. However, before interpreting results, you must be cognizant of the origins of data, or data integrity. Checks and balances, such as aged trial balance (ATB) information and accounts receivable turnover, can help identify data discrepancies. The following example illustrates how results can differ depending upon the origin of the data.

For example, in the box below, Practice A looks as if it is performing better with a shorter ATB period.

Aged Trial Balance	Practice A	Practice B
0–30 days	50%	20%
31–60 days	30%	20%
61–90 days	10%	10%
91–120 days	5%	30%
Over 120 days	5%	20%
Total accounts receivable	100%	100%

At first glance, Practice A appears to be managing the practice billing and collection operations much better than Practice B. However, the interpretation of data

Table 50–1 Identifying Key Indicators

Source Document	Data	Definition	How It Can Help
Cash flow statement	Cash flow	The change in all of the balance sheet accounts listing them as inflows or outflows of cash. This statement also categorizes by operating, financing, and investing activities.	Presents changes in the balance sheet accounts between periods. Monitors inflow and outflow of cash.
Income statement	Revenue	The detail of sources of revenue, highlighting the mix of revenue streams—fee for service, capitation, and others.	Provides ability to measure profitability of different lines of business, and compare to trends in the external environment. Expressed as a metric per encounter or per physician, provides useful budgeting tools.
Income statement	Overhead	Nonphysician operating expenses.	Compares practice to industry benchmarks to detect excessive operating expenses.
Income statement	Cost of care	The combination of internal costs and the cost of outside purchased services that are required under at-risk contracts.	Assists in negotiating profitable payer contracts.
Income statement	Operating profit	Earnings before interest and taxes.	Measures overall performance of operations (revenue less expenses associated with the operations of the practice).
Billing system	C-PAW	Charges, payments, contractual adjustments, and write-offs (bad debt) monthly summary.	Trending can identify issues and opportunities. Collection ratios can be calculated. Transaction volume monitored.

Category	Indicator	Description	Notes
Billing system	Aged trial balance (ATB) by payer class and overall	Accounts receivable (AR) aging category by payer class.	Compare to industry specialty benchmarks.
Billing system	AR turnover	Ratio that calculates how many months it takes to cycle through the AR.	Another measure of health of the AR by cross-checking to ATB.
Billing system	Productivity by provider	Number of ambulatory, surgical, and hospital visits. Compare to benchmark.	Tracks productivity. Compare to specialty specific benchmarks to track utilization. Changes in volume also help to adjust staffing requirements.
Billing system	Claim rejection statistics by payer by reason	Ratio of claims submitted that are processed with a claim edit or rejection by payer class and rejection reason category (e.g., service not authorized).	Highlights systemic payer reimbursement issues and/or issues within practice operations.
Billing system	Referral base	Summary zip code report and referring physician/other report.	Identifies geographic catchment area and variances in referral patterns.
Billing system	Lag times	Days between date of service, date entered on computer system, date billed, and date paid/resolved.	Tracks critical lag times, which represent the time value of money.
Operations	Full-time equivalents	Actual hours worked using a standard of 40 hours per week for physicians, mid-level providers, clinical staff, and business staff.	Compares to benchmark to ensure practice staff utilization is appropriate.
Operations	Patient satisfaction survey results	The perceptions of patients about selected service and quality of care.	Can be effectively utilized with payers in managed care negotiations.
Operations	Charge capture	Documents process for all locations where services are rendered.	Ensures capture of all billable events.
Operations	Patient care hours	Access and availability. Compare patient care hours to hours of operation (staff time).	Utilize with payers in managed care negotiations. Compare hours of operation to patient care hours. Also may be a contributor to low provider productivity.

would be different if the origin of data was revealed and taken into account. See the box on page 447.

Origin of Data	Practice A	Practice B
Billing system ages balances from:	Date billed	Date of service
Lag time: date-of-service to date billed	94 days	3 days
Does system restart again if another claim form is printed?	Yes	No

Based on the origin of data, Practice A is most likely performing worse than Practice B.

Finding #1: At Practice A, there is a 94-day lag period before the charge is entered and billed and the information system starts aging the data. Practice B ages data from the date of service.

Conclusion: Practice A's aging is not comparable to Practice B. The box below reflects the ATB with Practice A reclassified to conform to date-of-service aging.

Aged Trial Balance	Practice A	Practice B
0–30 days	0%	20%
31–60 days	0%	20%
61–90 days	0%	10%
91–120 days	95%	30%
Over 120 days	5%	20%
Total accounts receivable	100%	100%

Finding #2: Practice A re-ages accounts when a second bill is submitted (to either a secondary payer or as a second submission to a primary payer).

Conclusion: The ATB for Practice A is inaccurate and accounts are even older than demonstrated in Finding #1.

Take home message: Practice data are not comparable unless the origin of data is first assessed. Not knowing the origin of the data can inappropriately influence interpretation. The initial installation of your billing software program can dramatically influence key indicators. For instance, decisions about how accounts will be aged and where the account balance resides (in the original billed payer class or the current payer or financial class) are made during the installation of new billing and accounts receivable systems. How does your billing and accounts receivable information system age your accounts receivable? From date of service? From date billed? Does your system restart the aging process if a subsequent claim form is generated? When reviewing your payer mix, is the system capturing and maintaining payer mix data in the "first insurance" (original position) or in the current position?

You can select the key indicators for your practice analysis by systematically matching your analysis objectives to the information required to measure performance objectives. From our previous example, one analysis objective was to answer the following question:

How can my practice provide health care services more cost effectively and enhance the access of patients to services efficiently and effectively?

The process to determine what data are needed to perform the analysis could be deduced by progressively populating each column:

Objective	What I Need To Measure	Key Indicators	Data Source
Cost effectiveness	Cost of operations/care	Overhead, cost of care, operating profit, operating profit margin, full-time equivalents (FTEs)	Income statement Operations
Efficiency	Effectiveness of staff in patient care and billing/ collections	ATB, AR turnover, rejection statistics, lag times, cash flows	Statement of cash flows Billing system
Enhance patient access	Patient care hours, patient satisfaction, referral patterns	Catchment area, referring provider statistics, patient survey results	Billing system Patient survey results Operations

Once the key indicators have been identified, you are ready to gather the data, determine the origins of the data, compare the data to local and national indicators, anticipate any external economic changes, interpret results, set goals for improvement, implement recommended improvements, and repeat the analysis to measure incremental changes.

SUMMARIZE FINDINGS AND REACH CONCLUSIONS

Like anything else, selecting, digesting, and acting upon the wealth of information compiled require repetition and attention to details.

Practice expense information is typically captured and categorized by the book-keeper or person responsible for accounts payable using a "chart of accounts" and eventually expressed in an expense category on the income statement. There are industry surveys that capture data on practice costs. These surveys enable you to compare your practice to industry standards. The Medical Group Management Association (MGMA) publishes a number of surveys that permit practices to compare themselves to other practices, by geographic area or specialty, practice costs, compensation levels, production, revenue, etc.[1]

The health of the accounts receivable is a major indicator of practice billing and collection effectiveness. Several indicators can be used in conjunction with industry standards to piece together the practice business operations. The following is an example of how key indicators can be used and interpreted:[2]

Current Key Indicators with Comparison to Past Performance and Industry Benchmarks for Practice X

Net collection percentage reflects what is collected as a percentage to the total that could be collected (charges minus contractual disallowances). Last year, the practice's net collection percentage of 99.46 percent was in line with the national median of 99.98 percent. However, the net collection percentage this year has decreased to 86.93 percent. The difference would seem to reflect uncollected revenue sitting in the accounts receivable.

Last year, annual cash collections per physician (net fee-for-service [FFS] revenue) was $651,971. This was substantially higher than the national median of $515,433. However, annualizing the current year-to-date data indicates a decrease in annual cash collections per physician to $444,917. Slippage in this figure could be derived from an increase in physician full-time equivalents without a correlating increase in production and/or a decrease in collections.

Accounts receivable turnover (number of months it takes to cycle the accounts receivables) is 2.59 compared to a national average of 1.95. This indicates that the turnover (collection) of the AR is not in line with (exceeds) national averages and implies delays in collecting the AR.

Total gross charges as a percentage of total collections for the practice are 154 percent. This means that for every dollar collected there was $1.54 in charges. This was higher than the national median of 118.28 percent. A decrease in reimbursement, or a decrease in collecting the AR, could contribute to the difference.

Another common practice key indicator is production data. In the example that follows, Practice X had a senior physician retire and added two new physicians in January 1999.

Date Range	# FTE Physicians
Previous Year	four
Current Year (senior physician retires plus two new FTE physicians)	five

Production per full time equivalent (FTE) physician was compared to industry benchmarks and the production/revenue impact of the change in physicians documented.

Annual Encounters	Previous Year Average per Physician	Current Year Average per Physician	Industry Median	75th Percentile	90th Percentile
Ambulatory encounters:	4,154	2,402	3,275	4,046	5,003
Hospital encounters:	1,104	590	620	1,019	1,509
Surgical cases:	350	200	120	305	870
Total	5,608	3,192	4,015	5,370	7,382

Physician encounters for the previous year exceeded the national median. However, the current year physician production numbers totaled 3,192 physician–patient encounters, substantially short of their current production numbers per FTE physician and below the national medians. This is due to the addition of the new FTE physicians in the current year. The required action from interpreting these key indicator production data is that this practice must place emphasis on increasing patient access and production for the two new physicians. The reduction in revenue (43 percent) with the added cost/overhead of the two new physicians could drain financial resources if proactive measures are not implemented. The strategy to market and promote this practice might include increasing public awareness through targeted media exposure and increasing patient access. The tactics might entail placing welcoming ads to the new physicians in publications targeting desired patient markets, or adding weekend and evening patient care hours. Of course, the physicians will have to make sure that they regularly monitor their marketing efforts.

Summarizing findings from a practice analysis should include using a standardized "report card" that is easy to read and interpret. A simple monthly spreadsheet (Exhibit 50–1) that contains key indicator trending data (and perhaps quarterly summarized graphs of a subset of the key indicators) can be effective.

ACT UPON INFORMATION; REEVALUATE AT REGULAR INTERVALS

By now, you have identified the key indicators that you need to satisfy your analysis objectives. You have obtained the data and questioned their integrity. You can use the information you have collected to forecast revenue, invest in practice improvements, market your practice, and negotiate favorable terms with payers.

In our scenario, our original objectives (three questions) and associated outcomes (results shown in this chapter) are as follows:

Objective	Analysis Indicated That We Need to…	Action
How can my practice provide health care services more cost effectively and enhance the access of patients to services efficiently and effectively?	1. Improve collection of copayments. 2. Target follow-up collections to reduce accounts receivable. 3. Increase patient market share (excess capacity).	• Train staff and provide feedback on outcomes. • Review follow-up collections process. Implement/monitor accounts worked per day standards. • Expand patient care hours for new physicians to include evenings and Saturday.
How can my practice improve the quality of care and satisfaction of patients?	Not assessed.	None
How can I use the information I collect to improve my competitive advantage and increase profitability?	1. Increase production of new physicians. 2. Position and market new physicians with referring physicians and payers.	• Establish productivity goals for new physicians. • Market expanded hours to managed care payers. • Coach scheduling personnel to route new patients to new physicians.

Exhibit 50–1 Example of a Monthly Spreadsheet Containing Key Indicator Trending Data

	January	February	March	April	May	June	Total
Charges							
Payments							
Contractuals							
Bad Debt							
Total AR $							
0–30							
31–60							
61–90							
91–120							
Over 120 days							
AR turnover							
Ambulatory encounters							
Surgical cases							

FINAL THOUGHTS

Raw numbers alone seldom reveal anything about your practice. Comparison and trending will fine-tune your practice's financial picture. You need to review a few indicators on a regular basis and determine which ones are important for the objectives of your practice. Then you must act upon the findings and repeat the analysis to determine your progress.

The Bottom Line   *You now know the key indicators of a successful practice. Obtaining this information about your practice is easily accomplished by asking your accountant to provide it. Once you have the information, you must translate it into action in order to fine-tune and market your practice. In the words of the Nike commercial: "Just do it!"*

NOTES

1. The Medical Group Management Association is located at 164 Inverness, Englewood, CO 80112; (303) 799–1111; *www.mgma.com.*

2. The benchmarks utilized are for illustrative purposes only and do not reflect actual industry standards.

CHAPTER 51

Giving Our Patients a Federal Express Experience

Wouldn't it be wonderful if we could have two million interactions with our patients and have a patient satisfaction record of 99.6 percent? That's exactly what Federal Express does on a daily basis. Since I started actively marketing my medical practice nearly 14 years ago, I have learned how good customer service in other sectors presents opportunities for translation to the providing of health care. In this chapter, I review some of the techniques that Federal Express has used to motivate its employees to deliver nearly 100 percent successful service and how these techniques can be implemented into nearly any medical practice.

HOW DOES THE FEDEX PHILOSOPHY WORK?

According to Kay Carter, senior manager of employee benefits at FedEx, the company approaches employee relations from the standpoint that a happy employee is one who delivers good service. If Federal Express takes care of its people, they will deliver outstanding service. The mission statement of Federal Express clearly communicates its commitment to people, service, and profit. From the chief executive, Fred Smith, down to supervisors at local offices, management believes that taking care of employees is the key to having a completely satisfied customer at the end of each transaction. If they do that, then the profits will take care of themselves.

FEDEX AND HEALTH CARE PROVIDERS

As you might expect, the company also carries the same philosophy into the process of selecting health care providers for its employees. According to Carter, quality service is the number-one thing that the company demands from health care providers for its employees. Although cost is a factor, it is not as important as

457

the quality of service. Federal Express strives to have happy, healthy, and satisfied employees. Otherwise they cannot deliver America's packages and articles with nearly 100 percent accuracy. Although most managed care plans focus on cost containment, Federal Express believes the higher the quality of the product you deliver, the more cost-effective it will be. Numerous studies have documented that high-quality practices, which produce the best outcomes, are the ones that are most cost-effective.

Federal Express does regular surveys of its employees that have used contracted health care providers. They ask the employees: How easy was it to get an appointment with the doctor? How courteous was the staff? How long did you have to wait in the reception area before you saw the doctor? Did the doctor answer all of your questions? When you called the doctor for a report or a lab test, how long did it take him or her to call you back?

The company also monitors how long it takes the contracted physician to complete the reports and paperwork. They are looking at his or her prescribing habits. They are interested in physicians who do not prescribe expensive antibiotics and nonsteroidal anti-inflammatory drugs when less expensive medications may be just as effective. And, of course, they are looking at outcomes and appropriate use of referrals. Just as many other corporate purchasers do, FedEx issues physician report cards. When negotiating contracts with providers, the company wants only "A" students to take care of its employees! (In Chapter 39, "How to Be a Darling of the Managed Care Plans," I provided examples of how to improve your profile with managed care organizations and insurance companies.)

PARALLELS BETWEEN FEDEX AND PHYSICIANS

Carter points out the many similarities between Federal Express and the health care profession. Both have a customer or patient at the end of the line. *It is our common goal and objective to make customers happy and delighted that they have done business with us or that they have selected us.* We need to make an effort to exceed the patient or customer's expectation. If we fail to do that, we will be out of business with no packages to deliver and no patients to treat.

INVITE AND HEED THE TRUTH

In the past every physician was able to state that he or she had a quality practice. Today we are not able to just say it; we have to prove it. We will have to ask our patients what they think of the service we are providing. All of us will hear some responses that will not be complimentary. But those negative responses will give us an opportunity to get better.We need to embrace complaints, not ignore them. Only when we hear from those who have problems can we learn to improve the quality of our service.

In the first section of this book, I offered multiple examples of how to keep your existing patients. One sure way to do this is to find out exactly what they think of you and your practice. I routinely invite patients to participate in "rap" sessions to voice their complaints and to offer suggestions on how to improve our service. I encourage the participation of our toughest patients or the chronic complainers. I believe that if we can satisfy the tough ones or the most difficult patients, then the average patient will also have a positive experience. Chapter 9 gives tips on how to deal with demanding patients.

Carter believes this is easy. *Find out what the customer wants and give him or her more of it and find out what he or she does not want and avoid it.* We know that patients want to be seen in a timely fashion, by a competent, friendly physician, and with a friendly helpful staff. They do not want delays in getting appointments; long waits to see a doctor who appears to always be in a hurry; and a staff that is rude, unfriendly, and not helpful. Providing a quality practice is not rocket science. It is about asking our patients, referring doctors, managed care plans, hospitals, and payers how can we provide them with excellent service and make their experience with us a satisfactory one. If all of us would ask that vital question and then, most important, do something about it, we will not have to worry about changes in legislation or health care reform. We will not have to worry about the "grades" on our scorecard, because we will be gathering the results ourselves. *The best way to deal with regulatory and marketplace pressures is to survey ourselves proactively, track our outcomes, and be able to present contracting organizations with the quantifiable results they are asking for.*

The Bottom Line   *Perhaps we should all take a lesson from Federal Express. If our surveys indicated that nearly 100 percent of our patients were satisfied with their visits to our practices and our hospitals, we would all be equally proud. I think that if we adopt the personal attention, service, and profits strategy that has made Federal Express the giant of overnight delivery, then all of us in health care can approach that desirable goal.*

CHAPTER 52

Hiring a
Marketing Consultant

Do you feel like a fish out of water when it comes to marketing your practice? Perhaps you are thinking, "I need to hire a marketing or public relations firm." I have never hired an agency to handle my media appearances or public speaking engagements, but I have talked with a lot of marketing professionals and taken away some good counsel.

One of those professionals is Stanley R. Levenson, CEO of Levenson Public Relations in Dallas. According to Levenson and other public relations (PR) specialists, a marketing or public relations consultant can be useful no matter what the marketing challenge.

Even though you may feel perfectly capable of handling your own PR, there are still a number of reasons for hiring someone else to do the legwork for you and provide professional representation. Among those reasons:

1. *Sparing yourself the feelings of rejection when people will not tell you the reason why they have turned down a story idea or project in which you have been involved.* A magazine editor most likely will not have the time to work with you on rewrites for your magazine piece and will not be open to your submitting a reworked version if the first one was way off base. If you enlist the assistance of a publicist who can pitch the story for you and help shape and write it, you save yourself the rejection and reduce the risk of losing contact with the magazine.

2. *Letting someone else toot your horn, so you do not have to do it yourself.* If you are trying to get booked on *Oprah,* it is hard for you to say that you are the best spokesperson in the country on issues of male infertility. But your public relations consultant will have no trouble positioning you and saying that on your behalf.

3. *Saving yourself embarrassment.* A media producer will often need to ask personal questions when deciding whether to book you on a television show. For instance, the producer might need to ask what you look like. You might have trouble discussing your looks that candidly. In fact, a media producer might feel uncomfortable asking you such pointed questions and might decide to drop your appearance altogether.

But, you say, you are not planning any radio or television appearances and there are no newspaper articles on your horizon. You just want to place an effective Yellow Pages ad and clean up your brochure. You may still want to consider taking some money out of your advertising budget and hiring a public relations or marketing consultant on an hourly basis to extend your reach and help build credibility. Ask this consultant to charge you for five hours of looking over your materials and reviewing your strategy. Remember, visibility in the community, including free publicity from writing an article or giving a talk, will often net more new patients than a professionally produced Yellow Pages ad.

Working with a consultant on an hourly basis has another advantage. As a kind of "trial marriage," it allows both partners to see whether they enjoy working together to achieve desired results.

BE READY FOR YOUR CONSULTANT

If you are going to hire a public relations or marketing consultant, you will want to have your marketing strategy worked out, so that you can maximize your consultant's time. Levenson recommends doing a so-called SWOT (strengths, weaknesses, opportunities, and threats) analysis of your practice. Performing this analysis enables you to formulate focused marketing objectives and goals. Sample SWOT items are given in Exhibit 52–1.

By systematically listing all SWOT factors, you have constructed the foundation of your marketing plan. You are basing your plans on research and analysis, not on speculative ideas and gut feelings. Shooting from the hip will not work in the year 2000 or beyond. You have to get the data and devise a systematic, informed research plan.

OBJECTIVES

You need to think in terms of different types of objectives—marketing and communications objectives, as well as personal goals. It is not enough to set general goals. Do not just say, "I want to build up my practice." You need to set specific goals that include numerical values and usually a deadline.

Exhibit 52–1 Sample SWOT Analysis

Strengths

- We have 40 percent managed care patients compared with the community's average of only 25 percent.
- We are an obstetric practice delivering patients in a major tertiary hospital, with all the benefits of high technology and capable of caring for high-risk pregnancies.

Weaknesses

- We are a family practice with only three providers, so we are at capacity and already have waiting lists, particularly because we act as gatekeepers in so many managed care plans.
- Our obstetric patients are increasingly moving out to the suburbs and say they would prefer to see a physician closer to home, even though they like the idea of delivering at a large downtown hospital.

Opportunities

- Recruit additional physicians, nurse practitioners, or physicians' assistants to handle the growing patient load.
- Open satellite offices in the suburbs in which the highest percentage of our patients live (as revealed by a zip code analysis).

Threats

- Younger, upscale families are moving into our community and insist on using a pediatrician instead of a family practice physician because their perception is that a family physician is not as well trained to handle children.
- More and more patients are seeking both obstetricians and hospitals closer to home.

A typical marketing objective might be something like this: "We want to increase revenues by 15 percent and new patients by 10 percent within the next 12 months." Or you might say, "By the end of next year we'd like our clientele to be 40 percent managed care, 30 percent Medicare, and 30 percent fee for service." A primary care practice might set a goal of increasing pediatric patients by 10 percent, since pediatric patients are likely to stay with a practice for a long time.

In any case, you need to think carefully about your goals and objectives and write them down in clear, specific language, because they provide the targets against which you measure your success. ***Remember, you cannot hit a target you cannot see.***

HOW TO FIND A CONSULTANT

Most physicians do not need to hire a public relations agency or marketing firm. Indeed, physicians often require a lot of one-on-one attention, which large agencies are not likely to provide. The best solution is to look for a freelance public relations specialist in your community by contacting the Public Relations Society of America (see "Additional Resource" for contact information). More and more professionals are working from their home. This allows them to charge less per hour than an agency would. The advantage for you is one-on-one personalized attention.

HOW MUCH WILL IT COST?

I am reminded of a story. There once was a 40-year-old marketing consultant who died and went to heaven. The consultant arrived at the pearly gates and asked St. Peter if there were possibly a mistake, since he was only 40—too young to die and go to heaven. St. Peter looked in his book and said, "Sir, based on your billable hours, you're nearly 92."

If you go to a big agency, you can expect the hourly fee of a marketing consultant to range anywhere from $100 to $200 per hour. Your costs for a consultant will most probably be lower if you use an independent contractor. Remember that freelance consultants are still professionals, so expect to pay a fair price.

As an alternative to a straight hourly fee, you might consider discussing the possibility of paying the consultant an initial minimum fee and then additional amounts based on a percentage of additional income generated from the PR or marketing consultant's efforts. Be sure to spell out your agreement in writing. Incentives based on performance, if quantifiable, also could be of interest.

OTHER SOURCES OF ADVICE

Sometimes you can get the best advice from the staff of your hospital's marketing or public relations department. Many of these employees previously worked for consulting agencies that specialize in health care marketing. Be sure to get references and ask to see examples of their work in the health care field.

Before hiring a consultant, ask what you can expect in the way of value. It is important that you have reasonable expectations. Marketing cannot make you a better actor, provide your patients with better health care, or make a prince from a frog. Do not consider hiring any consultant who guarantees he or she can get you on *Good Morning America* or *Oprah*.

Some PR specialists do get bookings for clients on other lesser-known talk shows. Unless you are prepared to "take the gloves off," I suggest you avoid taking on Jerry Springer, Geraldo, or Sally Jessie Raphael during your first forays into television marketing!

Make sure any consultant you hire understands our profession, ethics, and philosophy regarding marketing and public relations. Marketing consultants are usually expert in the areas of media and creative and direct mail, whereas public relations professionals most frequently arrange media interviews and appearances and deal with editorial content.

MEASURING RESULTS

Marketing, unlike computers or mathematics, is not an exact science. No amount of marketing strategy can precisely predict what a marketing program will produce. The best that can be hoped for is a range of responses and building an identity.

With your consultant, you need to set goals that are realistic, put together a timetable, and then work at it. Then, by altering a certain factor, you can modify your marketing program and measure your results. This fine-tuning is what successful marketing is all about. And a savvy consultant, used in the right way, can help you do that.

Every marketing project, from a Yellow Pages ad to conducting a support group, must be documented. For instance, it is necessary to record the people who attend each of your support groups and measure how many have become patients. With the help of separate telephone numbers, you can track how many new patients have been generated by a Yellow Pages ad, a feature story, or a direct-mail campaign. The number of new patients is only one measuring stick. You must also know how much income was derived from these new patients. Adding to the bottom line should be your goal when planning promotions. Unless you want to strengthen your image, for instance, media events are costly.

If you want to see a change in your practice in a positive direction, you will have to accept some risk. The risk will be minimal if you follow the guidelines and tested suggestions that I advocate in this book. And if you choose the right public relations consultant, you will have someone working on your behalf. He or she will keep current with newsworthy medical topics and help you generate new PR or promotional techniques to tie in with those topics.

The Bottom Line   *Tooting your horn is easier if you find an ethical, savvy marketing consultant to do the work. First make sure you know your own marketing goals, by performing a SWOT analysis, among other things, and then methodi-*

cally plan, execute, and fine-tune your strategy as you go. Keep your eye on the bigger picture, and you can expect to see worthwhile results.

ADDITIONAL RESOURCE

The Public Relations Society of America publishes a register that lists independent publicists by area of specialty. It might also be worthwhile to contact the PRSA chapter in your area. For information contact Public Relations Society of America, 33 Irving Place, 3rd Floor, New York, NY 10003, (212) 460–1459, (212) 995–5024 fax; *www.prsa.org.*

CHAPTER 53

Medicine, Marketing, and Mirth: Having Fun with Your Medical Practice

A merry heart doeth good like a medicine.

Proverbs 17:22

A patient called the urologist's office and said, "Is this Dr. Baum's office?"

The receptionist said, "Yes, can you hold?"

The caller said, "That's my problem. How did you know?"

You do not need to see statistics to be convinced that medicine is a high-stress occupation. Not only do we deal with life-and-death situations every day, but many of us are running what amount to small corporations. We have had to learn financial management and deal with often hostile regulatory and managed care environments. All these factors have put most of us outside our comfort zones.

Is it any wonder that many physicians are suffering from burnout and are anxious and upset? The danger is that we can pass this anxiety to our staff and ultimately to our patients. There is no better way to relieve the tension and pressure of our work than to inject a small dose of humor.

Norman Cousins and other researchers have demonstrated that humor has a therapeutic value and a positive impact on patients' health and recovery from illness. Steve Allen Jr., M.D., an assistant dean for student affairs at the State University of New York Health Science Center, Syracuse, has long understood that humor can be a valuable asset to the health care provider and can improve the rapport between physician and patient. ***Consider this chapter your prescription for humor, warmth, and fun.***

HUMOR AND MEDICINE GO BACK A LONG WAY

Dr. Allen, a primary care physician, has observed first-hand a connection between humor and health that has existed for at least 1,000 years. Each year Dr. Allen provides medical care to the Zuni Indians in New Mexico. In that Native American culture, there are three groups of healers: the medicine men and women, the bone pressers, and the clowns.

The clowns use body and face paint, wear funny costumes, and have a social license to do funny and silly activities in public. Zunis who are ill can call for a clown to visit the home and have them perform funny acts and tell funny stories. According to Dr. Allen, this "treatment" is therapeutic in many ways and more often than not works to cure the patient.

In the Buddhist canon there is a recitation that says, "We vow to bring joy to one person in the morning, and to ease the pain of one person in the afternoon. We know that the happiness of others is our own happiness, and we vow to practice joy on the path of service."

What if everyone in your organization took as their personal mission statement "to practice joy on the path of service"? What if all your staff members made it a part of their daily duties to encourage a smile from one of their coworkers and to listen with an open heart to the concerns of the patients? By these simple acts you can create the foundation for some truly astonishing team building and a healthy and healing environment.

HUMOR STARTS WITH THE TOP BANANA

If the doctor and office manager are stiff and sullen, then you cannot expect levity and gaiety in the workplace. When the doctors loosen up, so will the employees. According to Matt Weinstein, the founder of Playfair, a company dedicated to teaching other companies and organizations about the benefits of humor, the three best ways to lead are by example, by example, and lastly by example!

There are many innovative ways to bring fun into your medical practice without losing the focus of providing outstanding medical care. The intentional use of fun in a health care practice can be a positive team building force, increase patient satisfaction, boost employee morale, and increase patient loyalty to the practice. But just as significant is its impact on reducing stress in the doctors and the employees.

WHY DOES HUMOR WORK?

There is nothing magical or funny about it—if your employees are enjoying their jobs and if they are passionate about their work, it shows. Conversely, if your employees do not like what they are doing or for whom they are working, that shows, too, and will be reflected by an attrition of patients in your practice. Weinstein believes your practice will have a competitive advantage if your employees are excited about coming to work, if they are happy to be there, and if they enjoy what they do.

One way to create that kind of enthusiastic work environment is to use fun and play to enhance communication. When two people are able to genuinely have a laugh, they are saying, "You and I have something in common and we share the same values." Humor and laughter can often set off a chain reaction. A humorous interaction in the workplace can inspire the employees to repeat the process. It is possible for the ripple effect from a single laugh to last and endure. For example, a patient knew that we enjoyed riddles and puzzles. One day she brought a puzzle in to us (see Figure 53–1). It challenged a person to connect three rows of three dots each with four straight lines without lifting the pencil off the paper. First my nurse tried for a minute to solve it and then gave pencil and paper to the patients in the reception area. Now the patients in the reception area were working on the puzzle, too.

Several weeks later another patient returned and provided several other solutions to the same problem. We also used the puzzle at a staff meeting to demonstrate how to become more creative problem-solvers and to "think out of the box."

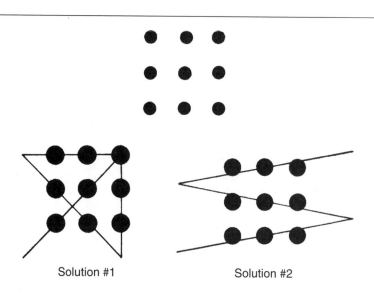

Solution #1   Solution #2

Figure 53–1 Dot Puzzle. Solution #1 is the standard solution; solution #2 is the novel one.

Here are 21 examples of ways to promote fun and levity in your work environment. Most cost next to nothing. Try some of them and encourage your staff to think of others.

1. *Ask your employees to bring baby pictures of themselves to the office.* One employee posts the photos on the bulletin board and everyone tries to guess which picture is which employee. This is a lot of fun and even patients will enjoy participating. The underlying statement of this contest is: "We have a hierarchy here but the truth is that we all started out the same . . . as babies."

2. *Start out your staff meeting by requesting everyone to tell a joke.* People who do not tell jokes can bring in a funny cartoon or toy.

3. *Use cartoons or add humor to your fax sheets.* (See "Additional Resources.")

4. *Conduct a staff meeting at Toys R Us—at the meeting, give each employee a gift certificate to buy a toy that can be used at the office or placed at their work station.*

5. *Provide an inflatable punching bag for instant stress relief.* Pharmaceutical companies and medical manufacturing companies give out stress relief balls filled with sand or small stones that are serviceable, but the punching bag works better. There is no better way to get a short aerobic workout, increase the oxygen to your brain, and release endorphins than a 30- to 60-second round with the punching bag. Let's not forget that we need the healing power of laughter and play just as much in times of stress and pressure—perhaps even more.

6. *Use head boppers.* Head boppers are skinny headbands with two eight-inch springs to which are attached different objects, such as hearts, shamrocks, basketballs, eyeballs, and nearly everything else you can think of and wear them on special holidays like Halloween, Thanksgiving, April Fools, and Mardi Gras (if you live in Louisiana, Mississippi, and Alabama). I have never seen a patient look at the receptionist with a straight face when she moves her head and the head boppers start oscillating.

7. *Stage costume contests for Thanksgiving, Christmas, Halloween, April Fools, or July 4.* In our office, every employee puts $2.00 into a pool and the winner is able to make a donation to his or her favorite charity.

8. *Provide impromptu humor.* According to Weinstein, doing something spontaneous and unexpected will most definitely snap your employees out of their everyday habitual behaviors. By acting spontaneously, you remind people that life is not static but fluid and exciting and even a little mysterious and fun. For example, I brought a balloon bouquet and left it on an employee's desk, telling her to keep the bouquet for a half hour and then

pass it on as a gift from herself to someone else and then give them the same instructions. By the end of the day, everyone had had access to the balloon bouquet, which we gave to a patient who was recovering from cancer surgery. Our office that day was full of levity and excitement. The patient came back the following week telling us how much she appreciated the balloons and how it changed her attitude about her situation.

9. *Stage a "crazy hair" day.* Have a contest for the wackiest hairdo. Employees can get really creative with spray-on colors, hair spray, and gel, and have a lot of fun in the bargain. And your patients will love seeing the normally well-groomed office staff looking a little "far out."

10. *Have an ugly tie and ugly shoe contest.* Each employee brings in a tie or shoe that they actually own—no new purchases allowed—to enter the contest. We then ask the patients and some office staff and referring physicians to vote on the "winner" or loser. The winner receives a gift certificate to a local restaurant. I know this one worked because several of my colleagues conducted a similar contest for their offices a short time later.

11. *Have a float decorating contest.* This works for us because we are located in New Orleans, where each year Mardi Gras is celebrated on the day before Ash Wednesday. It is a time of gaiety and celebration. How do you think we got the moniker "the city that care forgot"? One of my colleagues has an annual float decorating contest. Each employee or group of employees in various areas of the office decorates a shoe box as a Mardi Gras float. The floats are displayed in the reception area and patients vote on the best one. This contest has generated such enthusiasm that patients from other offices will hear about the floats and come to my friend's office just to see their clever creations. You can participate in this Mardi Gras tradition by doing the same. It is also a good way to lighten up those end-of-winter doldrums.

12. *Place mobiles to make merriment.* Each of my exam rooms contains a different mobile. It is common for me to enter a room and see patients blowing on them or gently pushing them to create movement.

13. *Provide funny fortune cookies to make for frolic.* Weinstein describes a fun project of writing personalized fortunes containing specific information or action about staff members who will be opening the cookies. Examples might be: tell Dr. Baum about Sandra's experience in the rest room with Mrs. Hifalootin Gilsbar; have Jackie use charades to tell where she gets her clever earrings; ask Chrissy to parody Dr. Baum on the phone with his mother; or ask Mary to demonstrate her submission to *America's Funniest Home Videos.* This project is a great way to begin a staff meeting. The cost is negligible. The challenge is to remove the real preprinted fortune and insert the customized fortune without breaking or fracturing the cookie.

Advice: use a hemostat to remove the original paper and insert customized paper with a pickups or tweezers. That challenge alone will bring peals of laughter to those assigned to the project.

14. *Celebrate the end of the week. Now this one is for hard core "funatics."* Every Friday afternoon we gather the whole office staff, doctors too, and get on the floor and squeal with laughter that the week is over. This brief Thank Goodness It's Friday dance gets everyone in the mood for the weekend and emphasizes how much fun we have at work. On a few occasions a patient will return to the office, the lab pick-up courier will come in, or even a colleague with his or her staff will come in while the "dance" is being performed and it is the rule, not the exception, that they will get on the floor and celebrate with us.

15. *Play "Ring on the Horseshoes"* (see Figure 53–2). Each of the exam rooms in my office contains mechanical puzzles that range in difficulty from Rubik's cubes to kinetic art that requires just turning the frame or box 90 or 180 degrees, providing a nice optical illusion or moving artwork. One of the puzzles that patients seem to enjoy is the two horseshoes that contain a metal ring trapped between the horseshoes. I will never forget giving the horseshoes to a patient and telling him that if he got the ring off he did not have to pay the bill. The man took the challenge and remained in the office for three hours until he finally extricated the ring from the horseshoes. (I had to ask him to move from the exam room to the reception area as I needed the exam room to see additional patients.) I made good on my offer and did not charge him for the visit, but needless to say I never made that offer again!

Figure 53–2 Ring on the Horseshoe Puzzle.

16. *Play "Flush Your Change."* At the checkout counter we have a toy toilet that says: "Give your spare change a flush." Patients ask about the toilet and are told to put a coin or two into the bowl and flush the toilet. The toilet makes a rather loud flushing sound and the coin disappears into the bottom of the bowl. Nearly every patient that has tried the flushing toilet wants to do it again and again. When the bowl is full we give the money to charity.

17. *Play humor videos in reception area.* In addition to the Access Health videos, we will often play a humor video such as Three Stooges, Abbott and Costello, or Laurel and Hardy. These classic comedians seem to have the timeless ability to make anyone from boomers to senior citizens relax and take a humor break. These videos are available for purchase at most video stores and through the Internet.

18. *Supply "Beanie Babies" to boost smiles.* Nothing has taken the nation by greater storm than the Beanie Baby boom. It is a marketing miracle that soft, tiny dolls stuffed with little stones are so attractive to toddlers and adults alike. I have provided a few Beanie Babies to employees and I have found them placed in such strategic locations as on top of the computer monitor, the phone, the rest room, and even on the X-ray view box. I cannot think of anything that has promoted more smiles than staff and patients cuddling those little dolls.

19. *Provide jokes and tricks, such as "Let me out of here!" We have a box with a "press here button" at the checkout desk.* When patients push on the button, the box starts to shake and vibrate and says, "Let me out of here, please let me out of here!" The reaction of the patients is nothing short of astounding (see "Additional Resources" for addresses and sources of these fun items).

20. *Decorate with "Proverbidioms."* Each of my exam rooms contains a print by the popular artist T.E. Breitenbach. His Proverbidioms contain well-known proverbs and idioms expressed by means of the characters or background of the painting (Figure 53–3). The patient tries to guess the appropriate proverb or idiom. These prints keep patients occupied for long periods of time, and occasionally I have to ask the patient to take a photocopy of the poster (which we provide) and "do their homework" before their next visit!

21. *Be prepared when you hear, "Can I borrow a pencil?"* Often a patient will ask for a pen or pencil to make a note or to write a check. The receptionist reaches under her desk and removes a fake four-foot pencil and offers it to the patient.[1] This produces a peal of laughter and patients in the reception area and exam rooms will open the door to watch the fun.

If you want your practice to provide stellar patient services, you must provide that same kind of attention and appreciation to your employees. You cannot

Figure 53–3 A Proverbidiom by T.E. Breitenbach. In each Proverbidiom, a proverb or idiom is expressed pictorially and the viewer's task is to guess it. Can you find "People in glass houses shouldn't throw stones" and "Too many cooks spoil the broth"? *Source:* T.E. Breitenbach & Company, P.O. Box 538, Altamont, NY 12009, 518-861-6054.

expect your employees to provide "service with a smile" if you do not give them something to smile about. If you create and foster a practice where employees are rewarded, recognized, and given an opportunity to celebrate their successes, an attitude of pride in the organization is passed directly along to the patient.

Another benefit of injecting humor into the workplace is that you can enjoy a remarkably low turnover rate of employees. A company that plays together stays together.

HUMOR AND THE PATIENT

Dr. Allen believes that the patient and the physician are equal contributors to the success of the healing process. Humor is a method of saying to the patient, "I know more about the science of medicine, but you know more about you. Help me to understand you, and I will help you to understand the science behind your medical problem." According to Dr. Allen, humor is helpful in generating trust, and in demonstrating that the physician is also human.

For humor to have a beneficial response, it must be tasteful and tactful. Inappropriate humor can debilitate, humiliate, and cut deeper than a scalpel. Dr. Allen describes a situation where a patient, immediately after a mastectomy, tells her doctor, "My husband won't look at me and won't touch me." The doctor responded, "You tell him that you are as beautiful as the *Playboy* centerfold, and you have the staples to prove it!" Tasteless and tactless humor at the expense of the patient not only can result in loss of rapport, but can prevent the patient from ever risking an emotional exchange of feelings with the doctor again.

Health care is a serious business, but we also must recognize that humor has a role in the healing arts. Those who make the decision to apply a dose of humor and fun in their practices will have more enjoyment, personal satisfaction, happier employees, and, most important, happier and more loyal patients.

One busy morning, it took me a long time to see all my patients. The last patient was an older man and I apologized for the delay. "I don't mind the waiting so much," he said, "but I thought you would prefer to treat my ailment in its early stages!"

The Bottom Line   *Incorporating humor into your practice will let patients know that "humor is tolerated here." Your patients and staff do not need a written prescription to laugh and have a little fun. You do not have to be a stand-up comic or a Patch Adams to inject a little mirth into your medical practice.*

NOTE

1. This oversized pencil is available from the Spilsbury Puzzle Co., (800) 772–1760; *www.spilsbury.com.*

ADDITIONAL RESOURCES

Catalogues of jokes and trick items available from:

- *The Lighter Side*, P.O. Box 25600, Bradenton, FL 34206
  (800) 232–0963
- **Gamepuzzles—For the Joy of Thinking**
  Kadon Enterprises, Inc.
  1227 Lorene Drive, Suite 16
  Pasadena, MD 21122
  (301) 441–1019
  www.gamepuzzles.com

CHAPTER 54

Lagniappe
(Something Extra)

Here in New Orleans we are accustomed to hearing the word *lagniappe* (pronounced LIN-yap), which is French-Creole for "a baker's dozen" or just a little extra. The marketing tips in this chapter are based on the idea of providing something extra.

SOMETHING EXTRA FOR PATIENTS

When you perform an office procedure such as a vasectomy or cystoscopy, provide patients with an audiocassette player and offer them a selection of tapes to listen to while you are performing the procedure.

Provide patients, particularly elderly patients, with written information regarding their diagnoses, treatments, and medication instructions (see Exhibit 7–1). And especially for elderly patients, consider having these instructions typeset or photocopied in larger type (14 or 16 point) to make them easier to read. This take-home information will improve patient compliance significantly. You might also consider photocopying these pages and including them with the notes you send to referring physicians.

When a patient needs more time with you, consider doing the following:

- Ask the patient if he or she would like to get a cup of coffee nearby and then come back at the end of your office hours for additional consultation.
- Offer to call the patient at home on the same day.
- Allow the patient to schedule another appointment at no charge.

When I see that a patient has more questions or needs more time than I have allowed, I offer one of these three suggestions. The patient usually gladly accepts.

Surprise your patients with the good news. Too many know the ominous implication of the physician calling them personally when they need to discuss abnormalities on lab tests. ***Why not return good news to patients as quickly as possible?*** In my practice, if someone has a normal laboratory report, we send a handwritten note that says, "Congratulations! You passed your test" (Exhibit 54–1). It is a way of letting the patient know you care.

WANT SUCCESS? REMEMBER ROLODEX

Your Rolodex cards can be colored (mine are yellow, of course), and you can include lots of additional information on them, such as the names of your office manager, appointment secretary, and nurse; your office hours; who covers your practice when you are away; and your private telephone line.

Distribute your Rolodex and business cards with a magnet attached to the back. The MagnaCard allows you to peel off the front and attach your Rolodex or business card to the magnetic back that will attach to anything metallic (these are available at Office Max and other office superstores).

Exhibit 54–1 Notification of Good Lab Results

Neil Baum, M.D.
UROLOGY

Mr. Cooper,

Your laboratory report is perfect.

Congratulations.

Please call my office for an appointment in 6 months.

Dr. Baum

3525 Prytania Street, Suite 614
New Orleans, Louisiana 70115
504-891-8454
504-891-8505 (fax)

CREATE AN IDEA FUND

Put aside $100 for rewarding on the spot any good ideas with $5 to $25, depending on the usefulness of the idea. This will motivate your staff to think about cost savings and about how to make your business run more smoothly.

CULTURAL REWARDS

Buy tickets to the theater, the opera, symphony concerts, and local civic events. Then give these tickets to deserving employees, along with $100 for a dinner for two. This is a plus for your staff and supports your community at the same time. It is also tax deductible.

REMEMBER YOUR ANSWERING SERVICE

Just as your office telephone and reception area provide opportunities to create a good first impression, so does your answering service. Make sure the answering service operators get positive, constructive feedback on how they handle your patients, your hospital, and your referring physicians.

Either go personally or have someone from your office go to the answering service office and get acquainted with the supervisors and operators. This will increase the probability that you will get personalized service. Send complimentary notes when they do something well, such as handling an emergency or locating you when your beeper was not working. Finally, remember the answering service personnel at holiday time. Do not just send a card; send a gift. As with any other aspect of your practice, if you show them your appreciation, they will take good care of you and your practice.

AVOID HIDE AND SEEK IN THE OFFICE

Does your staff have trouble finding you when you are in the office? It is best if they do not knock on every exam room door or use the intercom while you are with a patient. Instead, have your secretary give you messages on your beeper. Of course, the messages can be coded if you do not want everyone to know who is calling you. For example, "Dr. Green" can be your accountant and "Dr. Honeywell" your wife!

ONE WAY OF GETTING A REPORT TO AN ATTORNEY

It is often difficult to have letters transcribed as quickly as attorneys would like. When an attorney wants a report "yesterday," I dictate the letter and ask the attorney's office to pick up the tape and some of my stationery. The attorney's office can type the letter on my letterhead and fax it to my office for any corrections or changes. The final letter can then be brought back to my office for my signature.

That way, the attorney gets the letter report sooner and my staff is free to work on other things.

THE ALL-PURPOSE PRESCRIPTION PAD

How many of your drawers contain dozens of preprinted prescription pads? *You can easily reduce the number of pads to two or three by having all of a single class of medications that you frequently use (for example, antibiotics) placed on a single pad* (Exhibit 54–2). To use the pad, circle the medication that

---

Exhibit 54–2 A Sample Page from an All-Purpose Prescription Pad

DEA # AB6305444

NEIL H. BAUM, M.D.
SUITE 614
3525 PRYTANIA
NEW ORLEANS, LA 70115
504-891-8454

NAME _____

ADDRESS _____ DATE _____

℞ DITROPAN 5 mg   Disp:

DUVOID 25/50 mg   Sig: T

EPHEDRINE 25/50 mg   Q.D.

MINIPRESS 1 mg   B.I.D.

ORNADE   T.I.D.

PREMARIN   Q.I.D.
  cream
  tabs 0.125 mg   P.R.N.

TOFRANIL 25/50 mg

URISPAS

☐ Label

Refill _____ times   PRN   NR

_____ M.D.   _____ M.D.
  Product Selection Permitted   Dispense As Written
12/05/90   0701-K10432065

you want to prescribe, write in the number of tablets or pills, and circle the dosing instructions. Ask one of your pharmaceutical companies to print these for you. It most probably will, especially if you list its product at the top.

This simple idea saves you 15 to 30 seconds every time you write a prescription. If you see 25 patients a day, and each patient receives two prescriptions, that is 50 prescriptions, with a savings of up to 25 minutes a day or more than 90 minutes a week. If a doctor works 50 weeks a year, that savings could total 4,500 minutes or 75 hours. If a doctor's time is valued at $150 an hour, that might add to more than $11,000 a year in savings! This simple, inexpensive idea allows you to see two more patients a day without any extra energy or expense on you or your staff.

PURGE OFFICE READING MATERIAL

I have discovered a good way to avoid the following comment: "My doctor's magazines are so old, they have advertisements for the Edsel!" I often walk into an examination room and catch a patient reading a magazine. If the magazine is more than a month old, I suggest that the patient keep the magazine and finish reading the article at home. Of course, I do make an exception for the timeless magazines, such as *National Geographic* and *Smithsonian*. Giving magazines away is a nice gesture, a way of purging your office reading material and doing some marketing at the same time.

PICK UP THE PHONE

According to a survey from Accountemps, a temporary personnel service based in Menlo Park, California, nearly half of all business people dislike talking to someone calling on a speakerphone.[1] The complaints range from poor voice quality to lack of privacy. If you still want to talk and free up your hands to sign letters, sort files, or even doodle, get a phone with a headset.[2] Headsets do not distort the speaker's voice, and you will never hear the complaint that you sound like you are speaking from a well. In addition, your staff will appreciate headsets that allow them to answer the phone and maintain correct posture. It is better for your neck and back to avoid holding the telephone handset between your shoulder and your ear.

SOMETHING EXTRA FOR STAFF

The "one-minute motivator" is a technique described to me by an orthodontist who used it to provide daily motivation to his staff. He meets with his entire staff at the end of the work day for one minute (tops two minutes). He recaps the day's events in 30 seconds and outlines the plan for the next day in another 30 seconds.

I asked the orthodontist and his staff to tape a few of these sessions for me. After listening, I decided to incorporate this motivational program into my practice.

Here is how it works:

First, we provide verbal rewards and recognition if any of the staff are doing something helpful for a patient or a fellow employee. We call this "psychic pay." Everyone enjoys hearing that he or she is doing a good job and likes to get credit or appreciation. This fits with my practice of praising in public and criticizing in private. Psychologists point out that the sooner the reward or recognition occurs after the event, the more likely it will be repeated.

My friend Dr. Michael LeBoeuf says in his book, *How To Win Customers and Keep Them for Life,* that you get what you reward. To illustrate this point, he tells the following story (see Figure 54–1).

Once upon a time, a farmer wanted to breed his three female pigs. He loaded the sows into the back of his pickup truck and took them to visit several boars at a nearby farm. While the pigs were getting acquainted, the first farmer asked the second, "How will I know if my pigs are pregnant?"

"That's easy," said the second farmer. "They wallow in the grass when it takes and they wallow in the mud when it doesn't take."

The next morning the farmer awoke, looked out the window and found his pigs wallowing in the mud. So he loaded them into the truck and took them back to the boars. But the following morning the pigs were still wallowing in the mud. Undaunted, the farmer once again loaded the pigs into the truck and took them back to the boars for a third time, hoping for some positive results.

The following morning the farmer was away from the farm, so he anxiously phoned his wife and asked, "Are they wallowing in the grass or the mud?"

"Neither," replied the farmer's wife. "Two of them are in the back of the pickup and the third one's up front blowing the horn!"

The one-minute motivator meeting provides all employees with nearly instant rewards of recognition. It also gets everyone moving in the same direction. Previously, one or two employees "cut out" at 5:01 PM, leaving the follow-up patient calls, clean-up, and chart preparation for the next day to the employees who remained every evening until the job was done. Now that everyone stays for the one-minute motivator, everyone makes an effort to help each other. There has also been job description crossover. Now the nurse is pulling charts and the secretary

Figure 54–1 The Three Pigs. *Source:* Copyright © Michael LeBoeuf.

sometimes cleans the vasectomy trays. This system has resulted in an improvement in morale within the office.

The one-minute meeting can also quickly identify any problems that occurred during the day. Usually, these problems are not solved on the spot, but we are alerted to their existence. They might be discussed at a later date at a staff meeting, but often just identifying these problems at the end of the day will yield solutions the next morning. Staff members think about the problems on the way home. It is similar to the technique for programming the subconscious at night by reviewing a problem before going to sleep.

The one-minute meeting also alerts the staff to potential problems that might arise the next day. For example, if we know that Ms. Smith, who is 82 years old and has peripheral vascular disease, is always cold in the examination room, we will arrange to put a heater in the room and have a blanket ready for her. If we have a busy surgery schedule, we may suggest calling the patients early the next morning and informing them of a possible delay.

I can imagine some of you thinking, "That's a lot of discussion for one minute." Remember, this is at the end of the day. Employees are in a hurry to leave. The one-minute motivator meeting proceeds quickly and accomplishes a great deal in a very short time. This is one suggestion that you have to try before you believe it. Try it—it takes only one minute of your time. It may be the best minute you spend with your staff, and it can result in stellar services for your patients.

Well, I said I would be giving you a baker's dozen, and it is actually 14 additional ideas instead of 13. But who's counting?

The Bottom Line   *As you institute policies designed to exceed your patients' expectations, you will find it easy to add your own ideas to these. Once you are in a marketing frame of mind, you will find that the ideas just keep coming.*

NOTES

1. "FYI," *Entrepreneur* 19, no. 2 (February 1991): 18.
2. I recommend *Plantronics*, the brand used by AT&T operators. The PLX 400-headset and phone are available from Plantronics, (800) 882–7779; SKC, 8320 Hedge Lane Terrace, Shawnee, Kansas 62227, *www.plantronics.com*; and can be obtained in Radio Shack and Staples stores nationwide.

CHAPTER 55

Getting Started: The Secrets of Marketing Success

Do not think that to market your practice you have to write articles and get on TV. Do not think of marketing as hiring a publicist or getting into print or on national TV. Those things should not necessarily be your goals or objectives.

I assume that like most physicians today you are practicing good medicine. I assume that you are delivering the best possible diagnosis and treatment to your patients. But you must also consider how your patients are being treated in your reception area while waiting to see you. You must consider how are they being dealt with on the telephone when they call your office. These are the basics of good patient service that marketing is designed to address.

The following are 10 dos and don'ts on how to begin your marketing voyage and, if you have already launched your ship, how to correct your course and bring your ship safely into the harbor.

1. *Do not begin with external marketing.* Do not start by producing a practice brochure, designing a logo, publishing a newsletter, or developing a web page.
2. *Do have some written goals and objectives.* Make these as realistic as possible so that you do not reach too far and become discouraged early in the marketing process. Start with something small and work your way up the marketing ladder. You do not want to climb the ladder of success only to find that when you reach the top your ladder is facing the wrong wall! You may reach financial success without the accompanying enjoyment and satisfaction.
3. *Do pick one marketing objective that will allow you to measure your results.* For example, you might find it worthwhile to do a time-and-motion study or a patient survey. Survey your patients now, find out what the prob-

lems are in your practice, address those problems, and survey again. Whichever objective you pick, the process of achieving it should be enjoyable—as should the consequences of achieving it. Do not target headache patients or those with premenstrual syndrome if those are not the patients you want to see.

4. *Do work with your staff.* Make sure that your staff buy into your marketing program. Make sure they are motivated. Are your meetings fun? Are you providing monetary as well as nonmonetary rewards for going the extra mile for your patients?

5. *Do devise a marketing budget.* How much money will you invest? How much time? Think about obtaining assistance from your hospital, from pharmaceutical companies, and from medical manufacturing companies.

6. *Do make your practice user-friendly.* Continue to bond with the patients already in your practice. Keeping those patients is one of the most important goals of effective marketing.

7. *Do create a positive image for your practice.* Through marketing you can literally sculpt the kind of practice that you want to have. Pick an area in which you have had training and become an expert in it. Do you want to be seen as a physician who deals with the elderly? As a physician who deals with adolescents? As a physician who makes house calls? There are ways of marketing your practice that create an image of who you are. For a while, I was known as the doctor who called his patients at home and who saw his patients on time. I have worked hard to be certain that the same image still holds true today.

8. *Do take direct aim.* Use your marketing tools like you would a rifle, not a shotgun. If you take a scattershot approach, you will get a riddled response. Have a clear picture of your goals and objectives. When you have a stationary target, marketing will allow you to score a bull's eye.

9. *Do go the extra mile for your patients, your referring physicians, your hospital, and your managed care plans.* Find out what patients want and give them more of it. Identify the "hot buttons" for your managed care plans and push those buttons by providing their members with extraordinary service. If you strive to give those with whom you deal more service than you are paid for, you will find that patients, colleagues, managed care plans, and other professionals will be knocking on your door for your services and your expertise.

10. *Do track and measure your results.* How much did you invest in your marketing program? What was the return on your investment? Did your investment add to the bottom line? Did it decrease costs? Did it increase your positive image in the community?

The Checklist for a Profitable Practice (Exhibit 55–1) can be used when you begin your marketing efforts and also later as a way of finding out how your practice is doing.

DOES MARKETING WORK?

This book would not be complete without some mention of the results I have achieved by using these techniques in my practice. All the techniques included here are within the guidelines of the American Medical Association and have been approved by my local, parish, and state medical societies.

In 1978, I moved to New Orleans from Houston. I went into solo practice in a very competitive medical community. I had no patients on the day I opened my doors. There would often be days and even sometimes weeks between patients. I lived in doctors' lounges to meet physicians, and I visited emergency rooms to be available for unreferred patients.

Though the practice was slow in the beginning, in three years it was moving nicely. I was seeing between 25 and 30 new patients a month. In 1986 I started doing the things discussed in the first three parts of this book. I started calling my patients at home, I tried to make sure that my name crossed the mind and desk of the referring physicians as often as possible, I identified the niches in the medical community, and I made an effort to motivate my staff to assist me in marketing my practice. By doing these things in a consistent and persistent fashion, I have nearly doubled the number of new patients I see every month.

One of the comments that I frequently hear following one of my presentations on marketing is, "Neil, you seem to be sending lots of notes, making plenty of phone calls, and writing a bunch of articles. Do you need to do all of these things to market your practice?"

My answer to that is, "Marketing is like shaving—unless you do it every day, you're a bum."

The truth is that using any one of these marketing techniques will not significantly change your practice. I cannot tell you that giving a talk to the Rotary Club will fill your appointment book with new patients. I cannot tell you that holding monthly staff meetings will motivate your staff to market your practice, or that providing your referring physicians with colored Rolodex cards will change their referral patterns.

But I can tell you that if you develop a marketing mindset, use marketing techniques on a regular basis, and go the extra mile for your patients, your referring physicians, and your staff, you will see a significant change in your practice.

In the next millennium, success will not belong to physicians who merely have the newest widgets with the latest whistles and bells or to physicians who simply

Exhibit 55–1 Checklist for a Profitable Practice

_____ Do you regularly survey those who use your services, including active and inactive patients, as well as your referring physicians?

_____ Do you make use of effective time management techniques, both for seeing patients and for using office hours?

_____ Do you look for ways to better serve your patients, and then implement new ideas?

_____ Do your office reception areas and examination rooms make a positive statement about you and your staff?

_____ Do you maximize each and every contact with patients for its marketing potential: telephone contact, first visit impressions, use of bill stuffers with monthly statements, effective transfer of records?

_____ Do you make your practice user-friendly to referring physicians?

_____ Do you market your services to nontraditional referral sources?

_____ Have you used patients to network with others considering similar procedures or treatments?

_____ If appropriate, have you considered starting a support group?

_____ If appropriate, can you use outside media for marketing your services? (This includes writing for newspapers or magazines, appearing on radio or television programs, and making public speaking engagements.)

_____ Do you facilitate good communications between you and your staff?

_____ Are staff members encouraged to take an active interest in office decision making?

_____ Do staff members handle the telephone graciously and punctually?

_____ Are staff members familiar with your credentials and training and any special areas of expertise?

_____ Do reception area and telephone staff understand and communicate billing and collection procedures courteously to all patients?

_____ Do you have the necessary skills for interviewing and hiring topnotch job candidates?

_____ Do you maximize the potential of your office computer system?

_____ Do you look for ways to make your hospital your ally?

_____ Most importantly, do you and your staff enjoy coming to work each day?

purchase the largest ads in the Yellow Pages. ***Success will belong to those physicians who practice good quality medicine and who also put a premium on giving the best service that they possibly can.*** Marketing is not a one-day, one-week, or one-year commitment; it is a lifelong one. To have the successful practice you want, you will always be marketing and promoting your services. You should always be searching for ways to satisfy your patients, staff, colleagues, and payers. Make an effort to exceed their expectations about their experience with you and your practice. Try incremental improvements, pay attention to the details, as they really do make a big difference, and continually reevaluate to see what works and what does not—for you and for those who come in contact with your practice.

CONCLUSION

There you have it. I have spent 24 years in private practice and the last 10 of those I have been focused on actively marketing my practice. I hope that the ideas you have read about here will help you incorporate marketing techniques into your practice.

I would like to conclude this book with a story

An anatomy professor stood in front of the classroom and asked, "Class, can you tell me what organ in the human body, under certain conditions, increases in size three times?"

The professor looked at a young woman in the front row and asked, "Mary, can you tell me the answer?"

Mary covered her face with her hands and responded, "Professor, I'm much too embarrassed to answer that question."

The professor looked around the room for someone to answer the question. A young man in the back of the classroom answered accurately—the organ was the iris of the eye, which increases in response to a decrease in light.

The professor slowly walked up to Mary's chair and, pointing his finger, said, "Mary, I've got three things to tell you: First of all, Mary, you're not prepared for your lessons. Second of all, Mary, you've got a filthy mind. And finally, I hope you won't be too disappointed in life!"

I do not believe any of you will be disappointed if you take just a few of the ideas presented in this book and incorporate them into your practices.

I am reminded of my late arrival one night at a hotel in Dallas. A young bellman, probably a college student, took my bags up to my room and placed them at the foot of the bed. I wanted to give him a tip but I found that I only had $.32 in change. I reached into my back pocket, and the only bill that I had was a $20 bill and he could not make change for that. I told him I had an idea. I opened my suitcase and offered him my new best-selling book, *ECNETOPMI—Impotence, It's Reversible,* and I would be happy to autograph it for him. The young man looked at the book, saw who the author was, and looked back at me and said, "Dr. Baum, if it's all right with you, could I just have the $.32?"

Well, I hope you got a little more than $.32 worth of useful and practical information that you can use to successfully market your practice. I know many of my colleagues across the country are already engaged in marketing programs. I would like to hear from you. I look forward to sharing ideas and concepts with my colleagues. Happy marketing!

Index

A

Abuse
  defining, 392–393
  private payers concerns, 393
Academic physician
  establishing relationships with outside
    physicians, 368–369
  making patients comfortable, 366–367
  marketing, 365–371
  public speaking, 370–371
  reporting in physician referral, 366
AccentHealth programming, 50
Access, baby boomer, 159
Acupressure therapist, referral, 320
Acupuncturist, referral, 320
Alternative healer, referral, 319–321
Answering service, 477
Antibiotics, 351–352
Apology, 71
  apology for delay letter, 96
  for delay, 28, 29
Appointment card, 74
Appointment scheduling, 28
  time management, 30
Appointment survey, 24
Appreciation letter, acknowledgment of,
  98
Article authorship
  for lay press, 166–172

  editorial pitch, 168–170
  marketing, 171
  rejection, 171–172
  topic, 167–168
  writing, 170–171
  reception area display, 54
Asian patient, 149–150
Attention span, 161
Attorney, compliance plan, 401
Attorney-client privilege, compliance plan,
  397–398
Audiotape, time management, 31
Authorization, 99–101
  fax authorization for office visit, 97
  obtaining, 35
Automated phone answering system,
  387–389

B

Baby boomer
  access, 159
  defined, 156
  delay, 158
  educational material, 158–159
  exceeding their expectations, 159–160
  key patient, 159
  meeting needs of, 157–160
  one-stop shopping, 159

About the Authors

Neil Baum, M.D., is a urologist in private practice and a clinical associate professor of urology at the Louisiana State University Medical School and the Tulane Medical School, both in New Orleans. He has served on the editorial boards of *Postgraduate Medicine, Uro-Care, Medical Office Biller, Cost & Quality, Physician's Payment Update,* and *Physician's Marketing & Management* and has been a monthly contributor to *American Medical News* and *Health and Fitness.* Dr. Baum is the author of several books—including *Ecnetopmi—Impotence: It's Reversible, Take Charge of Your Medical Practice: Practical Practice Management for the Managed Care Market, Urology Office Manual, Effective Letters for the Health Care Profession,* and *Impotence: It's Curable.*

Gretchen Henkel is an award-winning professional writer whose work has appeared in the *L.A. Times, Los Angeles Daily News, UCLA Health Insights, Family Therapy Today, Oncology Times, Anesthesiology,* and *Better Health.* She is the author of *Making the Estrogen Decision* and *The Menopause Sourcebook,* and contributing writer for *The AIDS Textbook,* The American Cancer Society's *Informed Decisions* and Dr. Art Ulene's *How to Outsmart Your Allergies.* Ms. Henkel won the 1997 Frances Larsen Memorial Award for excellence in medical writing and the 1994 Rose Kushner Award for writing achievement in the field of breast cancer.